Marketing For All the Marbles Every day

2017 Edition

People and events shaping the continuing evolution of marketing practice

Here

Then

Now

There

Charles L. Martin

Wichita State University

Charles.Martin@wichita.edu

CIBER Publications: Derby, KS USA

www.MarketingMarbles.com

Library of Congress Cataloging-in-Publication Data

Martin, Charles L.

Marketing For All the Marbles Every Day / Charles L. Martin – 2017 edition

p. cm.

Includes index.

ISBN: 978-0-9981227-0-0 (hardback)

ISBN: 978-0-9981227-1-7 (softback)

To… My early marketing profs at West Texas State University (now West Texas A&M University) in Canyon. They were all stars to me. In addition to teaching me, they inspired me, encouraged me, tolerated my antics and instilled in me a love for all the marketing marbles:

- Ronnie M. Birdsong
- John R. "Rusty" Brooks, Jr.
- William E. Semmelbeck
- James Wilkins

Thank you!

Contents

Here

Then

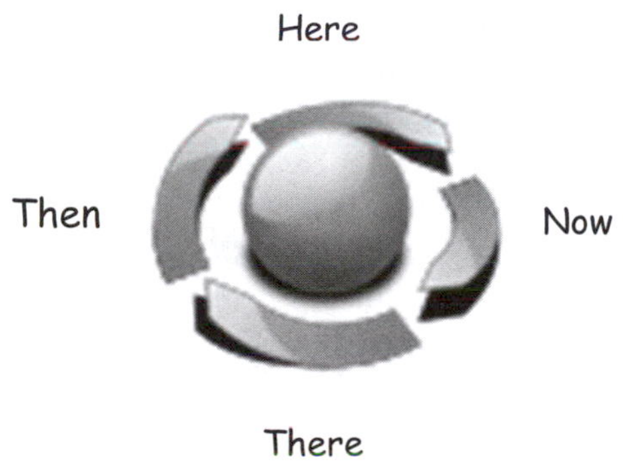

Now

There

Welcome Readers!

Welcome to the 2017 edition of the annual book series, ***Marketing For All the Marbles Every day*** – or *Marketing FAME,* for short. This is a different kind of business book that utilizes a unique format and unorthodox presentation style to create a reading experience like no other – one that challenges you to think about business, marketing and your career in fresh, new ways. Gratefully, *Marketing FAME* resonates with the overwhelming majority of college students who read it. If you're like them, you'll find the reading experience informative, interesting, occasionally humorous, and definitely worthwhile.

Because of the book's unique format and style, this "Welcome" section describes some of the ways *Marketing FAME* differs from traditional business textbooks and makes a few suggestions to help you extract the most value from it.

But you don't have to take the author's and publisher's word for it. Read the accompanying boxes of comments offered by college students who already have enjoyed a marbleous experience reading *Marketing FAME.*

> "This was by far my favorite text to read because of the ability to create additional thought in almost every section. I really liked [*Marketing FAME*] because of the nature of the text. It didn't seem like a textbook and included many real-world examples, which is the type of content that I prefer to read." –Jacob, senior sports management student

> "*Marketing FAME...* was without a doubt the most interesting 'textbook' that I have had in college." – Marie B., senior business student

> "I really enjoyed reading the *FAME* book and I did learn a lot from it. I was able to see marketing in a different light and for that I am thankful!" – Marina, senior marketing major

732 short, concise, stand-alone stories

To begin, *Marketing FAME* consists of 732 short, concisely-written sections or entries we'll call "stories" – ranging in length from 21 to 393 words. Because the stories are short and to the point, *Marketing FAME* can be read quickly in small daily doses and the key take-away points are readily apparent.

Marketing FAME
2017 Edition

Contains **732** stories, including…

- **720** individuals
- **683** organizations & brands
- **100+** holidays, events, occasions
- **48** U.S. states
- **59** countries
- **1.2** gazillion topics (estimate)

Each story stands on its own, so to speak, so you don't have to read the stories in the same order they appear in *Marketing FAME.* You can read them in any order you or your instructors prefer. However, if possible, it's best to read many of the stories as they correspond with the dates on the calendar. For example, on or about January 2, read the story about New Year's resolutions that appears on the January 2 page. By doing so, you'll be more likely to notice and learn from the marketing efforts that pop up in your community and in your favorite media at this time of year – timely marketing efforts such as advertisements and promotions that tap into consumers' interests in setting personal goals in early January. Similarly, by reading about Valentine's Day (February 14) a few weeks later, you'll have a heightened sense of awareness of the many ways that marketers adjust and time their efforts to coincide with that occasion.

> "I liked the non-continuity of [*Marketing FAME*]. Textbooks are topic 1 is pages 1-30, etc. *FAME* was unpredictable and exciting to read." – Andrew, MBA student

> *Marketing FAME* "gives ideas of the different methods of marketing that students can use. It's interesting to see not only businesspeople, but non-businesspeople perform marketing in different ways and all be successful. Seeing the different industries' approaches to marketing gives a well-rounded perspective of how students can use and consider using marketing in their careers. Overall, *Marketing FAME* is very insightful." – Jessica B., MBA student

Throughout the pages of the 2017 edition, *Marketing FAME* discusses more than 100 specific holidays, occasions, events or "seasons" that represent potential marketing opportunities. Even if you first read the stories out of sequence, using the appointment block (to the left of each day's stories) to manage your own day-to-day affairs will serve as a daily reminder to revisit the stories and note the possible marketing opportunities that exist at that time of year.

> "Very unique and interesting to read. It was a nice change from your standard textbook." – Kara, senior marketing major

> "I liked the humor and entertaining stories to illustrate concepts." – Nathan, MBA student

Invitation to think critically

> "I think the quotations were awesome. I even wrote some of them and shared them with my friends while I was reading it." – Lena, MBA student

The 732 stories are about people and events that have contributed to the evolution of business and marketing practice. Many include thought-provoking direct quotes that represent the featured person's perspective, but not necessarily the only perspective or the most commonly-shared perspective; other opinions may be found elsewhere in *Marketing FAME* (Hint: Use the detailed index in the back of the book to find them).

> "[I like the] thought-provoking questions. I also like how there are many subjective questions that gives the reader something to think about." – Stuart R., MBA student

Multiple points of view from businesspeople as well as non-businesspeople are included to show variability in thought about important issues and how "conventional" wisdom is not always universally embraced. Accompanying many of the more debatable perspectives are explicit invitations for you to "Agree or Disagree?" For example, the story on January 28 asks you to agree or disagree with Robert Bartels who maintained that marketing is a science. Be prepared, as your instructors may wish to discuss these issues in class.

"It is interesting to read such a variety of topics and ideas in one book. I was unfamiliar with many of the names and their stories – some inspirational and some cautionary." – Jennifer P., MBA student

Marketing FAME "provides numerous challenges and intellectual questions urging the reader to consider multiple points of view." – Shawn, MBA student

"Interesting reading with a lot of useful information that was presented in a concise, thought-provoking manner." – Ragadeesh, MBA student

Marketing and more

As you read, and hopefully savor and digest *Marketing FAME*, you'll notice the inclusion of a wide variety of issues pertaining to topics you'd expect to find in a "marketing" book. Examples include branding, pricing, promotion, advertising, distribution, customer service, marketing research, buyer behavior, personal selling, publicity, retailing, international trade, and so on. Again, explore the detailed index in the back of the book to see what other marketing topics are included.

"The information available in *Marketing FAME* can definitely be utilized in our marketing jobs." – Akhilesh, MBA student

But *Marketing FAME*'s content is not restricted solely to mainstream marketing topics. Also included are stories and perspectives that address more general career-boosting topics such as leadership, decision-making, technology, human relations, innovation, ethics, teamwork and quality, to name a few. Regardless of where your career path leads – marketing or otherwise – you should find these topics to be highly-relevant.

Emotional distinction

Marketing FAME's story format is not only unique, but advantageous in that it facilitates communication to *both* your head and your heart. That is, dozens of stories nudge you to read beyond the key descriptive details of "information" to consider the emotional context of the stories as well. How do consumers *feel* about various holidays and occasions? What do entrepreneurs *feel* when they encounter setbacks or risk all of their savings to start or grow their companies? Don't be surprised if you feel inspired or motivated by some stories, angered by some and saddened by others.

"I liked the humanization of marketing." – John E., MBA student

For all of us !

Emotions evoked, thought provoked

"Personally I did not like the mention of Charles Manson's birthday [see November 12]. I realize it has a significant marketing story, but the idea of reading about him on his birthday bothered me." – Cari Anne, undergraduate management major

As a future marketing professional, it may be difficult for you to *truly* understand what many holidays and occasions mean to your customers and prospective customers if you don't make an effort to experience these important days emotionally. And as a future business decision-maker, it's okay -- even desirable -- if you find yourself empathizing with people featured in the stories or vicariously experiencing emotions of hopeful anticipation or anxiety, elation or disappointment, compassion or callousness, that challenge them and add to the complexity of business decisions. Go ahead and laugh, cry, or pound your fist as you see fit. The emotions will broaden your understanding of the stories and the story-makers, etch them in your memory, and help prepare you for the range of emotions you'll surely encounter throughout your career.

> "To see something whether it be a story, quote or just a small reminder every day like the ones in the book would be [to] put a positive start to your day… Not many book/calendars are like this one, with inspirational quotes and stories." – Anonymous undergraduate student in an introductory marketing course

Now and then

Many of the 732 stories are about present-day people and events that sculpt the practice of marketing. Many others represent contributions of yesteryear that shaped the direction of marketing's evolution and, more often than not, continue to resonate with today's marketing professionals. In other words, *Marketing FAME* includes a mix of both past and present – a blend that's essential to understanding marketing today, how the field has evolved throughout history, and how its future may unfold.

> "Enjoyed the historical stories. Best way to avoid future failure is by studying the past." – William, MBA student

> "*Marketing FAME* did a great job helping me realize how marketing is an ever-changing field. I'll never be bored in this field." – Anastasia, MBA student

Of course, *Marketing FAME*'s inclusion of many topics' historical backgrounds enables you to learn from the experience and wisdom of past generations – lessons that continue to be relevant today. Further, understanding the history behind an occasion, event, idea or practice offers three other benefits you may not have considered. First, your effectiveness as a marketer developing tie-in promotions to celebrate or otherwise observe occasions and historical events or people will, of course, be limited if you know little about the occasions, events or people. Stanley Marcus, former President and CEO of Neiman-Marcus, the Texas-based department store chain, once observed how employees with liberal arts backgrounds grounded in history tended to be more effective than business school graduates in terms of creating in-store displays to commemorate holidays and events. All too often, Marcus lamented, employees from business schools simply did not understand the occasions as well.

> *Marketing FAME* "did a great job at combining current events and marketing related perspectives." – Courtney, senior marketing major

> "Historical and present-day quotes are inspiring, and it's interesting to know how the marketing terms were developed… It is more interesting to read [*Marketing FAME*] compared to a traditional marketing textbook because it includes actual stories, variety of data, and events." – Eri, undergraduate marketing major

Second, the historical perspectives challenge you to understand the dynamic and ever-changing nature of the business world. To be successful in most careers, you must embrace and participate in the evolution. More specifically, several stories show how common business practices that we may take for granted today did not exist until someone dreamed, developed and implemented them. For example, it is commonplace today for retail stores to use coat-hangers to display clothing items and save labor, but that wasn't the case before the coathanger was invented and adopted by retailers. Previously, retail clerks spent a large portion of their day folding, unfolding and refolding clothes. Accordingly, this aspect of *Marketing FAME* is intended to help you exercise your innovation muscles by implicitly prompting you to contemplate questions such as: "What's next?" and "What practices can ***I*** pioneer that may be commonplace in the future?"

> "*Marketing FAME* certainly did put things in a down-to-earth context by reasoning that all things have not been done the same way forever, and important people had to lead others into thinking differently about marketing. Textbooks often show only what perspectives are in the current times, not how to look past the current marketing structures." – Layton, MBA student

Third, familiarizing yourself with the past equips you with valuable conversation fodder to help you build rapport and otherwise interact with clients, coworkers and acquaintances. Rather than getting the conversation marble rolling by asking others well-worn questions about how they like the weather these days, for example, try "Guess what happened ____ years ago today?" or "Do you know what Edwin Land, inventor of the Polaroid instant camera, did to stir his creative juices?" (Hint: discover Land's creativity practice by reading the story for May 7).

> "In business you are going to have to talk to people that you have never met before, and to know interesting things like this will help in breaking the ice and make the conversations interesting." – Reginald, senior marketing major

Further, if you're a traditional-age college student who is conversant about the past, you're well-positioned to interact with older generations of businesspeople and consumers whose firsthand experiences with episodes of history may have a profound impact on their present-day perspectives and preferences. Being familiar with at least a couple of generations of history will help you to connect and empathize with others, and it can help you to avoid the stigma of being poorly educated, insensitive or inexperienced – perhaps unfair evaluations of those of us who are not familiar with history, but criticisms that exist nonetheless.

> *Marketing FAME* "gives students recent relevant marketing events as well as examples throughout history. These ideas are not always pointed out to us as business students but are definitely important to see and understand." – Tyson, senior marketing major

Here and there

Marketing FAME is geographically inclusive as well. You may find some featured people and events familiar because they are geographically close to home. They may represent brands that you use or stores where you shop. When you read about marketing practices at McDonald's or Wal-Mart, for example, it may be easy and interesting for you to visit these companies' local stores after class to verify the practices firsthand.

> "The marketing info from around the world is very relevant and helps see how marketing works on an international scale." – Sommer, MBA student

Other stories reach out to you from faraway places. As advances in technology, communications and logistics link the world, marketers must be prepared to look beyond their backyards and broaden their national and international perspectives. Accordingly, stories for this year's edition come from 48 U.S. states and 59 countries. To illustrate, take a look at the stories for March 19 and December 22. The first story shows that 42 percent of surveyed students from American universities participating in the Calendar Literacy Survey were not able to correctly calculate the time of day across U.S. time zones. Noted in the December 22 story, about 37 percent of the respondents were not aware that seasons are reversed in the Southern Hemisphere. As the stories explain, the failure to understand time differences across time zones and seasonal variations across hemispheres, which are only two of many examples, could have undesirable consequences for cross-country and global marketers.

> **Tip for American college students**
> As you read *Marketing FAME*, you may find it helpful to periodically remind yourself that less than five percent of the world's population lives in the United States.

Calendar-led marketing and buyer behavior

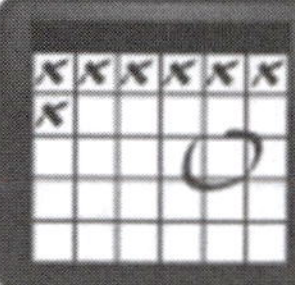

Quite likely you've already thumbed through enough pages of *Marketing FAME* to see that its content is organized like no other book you've been assigned to read in college. It's calendrically organized, featuring one or more people or events that sometimes coincidentally and sometimes not-so-coincidentally correspond to the day of the year they are discussed. This type of organization is intended to sensitize you to the importance of calendrical timing in the marketplace.

> "I really enjoyed reading the *FAME* [stories]. They were fun and educational... [and] were very relevant to marketing students to open up possible marketing opportunities that we didn't realize were there." – Kameron, undergraduate marketing minor

"What's the marketing relevance of calendrical timing?" you might ask. In part, it's attributed to the predictably periodic calendrical timing of seasonal changes, most holidays, and periods when buyers have the need, money and time to shop. These and other considerations mean that buyers' behaviors and marketers' actions are frequently calendar-led, i.e., they are greatly influenced by the date on the calendar. Thus, many marketing initiatives are more appropriate or likely to be more effective during some times of the year than during others. As an example, consider that American retailers who shelve chocolate Santas and heavy winter outerwear in November and December may benefit from their timing decisions by tallying high sales numbers during these two months, whereas those who shelve the same merchandise six months later may suffer the fate of poor calendrical timing and sell few of these items during that period. Therefore, *Marketing FAME*'s calendrical form of organization is a useful way to remind budding marketing professionals, such as yourself, to think about what calendrical periods mean to buyers and organizations, and thus when to do what, or what to do when.

> "I liked that [*Marketing FAME*'s] organization was based on the calendar year, as marketing can change at different times of year." – Logan, MBA student

> "The calendar format is nice and more interesting than themed chapters. The number of stories and the length of stories is just right." – Debra, MBA student

> **Read more to learn more**
>
> Beyond *Marketing FAME*, read the following articles by Charles L. Martin to learn more about calendar-led marketing, calendar-led buyer behavior and calendars as marketing tools. They can be found on the resource website, www.MarketingMarbles.com
>
> - "Calendars: Influential and widely used marketing planning tools," *Journal of Brand Strategy*, 5(2), 2016, pp. 1-14.
> - "How nature, culture and legal calendars influence the calendrical timing of consumer behavior," *Journal of Customer Behavior*, forthcoming, circa 2017.
> - "Calendar-led marketing: Strategic synchronization of timing," *The Marketing Review*, 17 (1) Spring, forthcoming, 2017.

Even when there's no obvious calendrical significance of an individual's birthday or an event's anniversary, each daily dose of information implies a marketing opportunity to celebrate or otherwise commemorate the date and occasion nonetheless. As an example, February 7 is the birthday of John Deere, the founder of the farm equipment maker, Deere & Company (the company that makes the familiar-looking green tractors and riding mowers). Accordingly, recognition of Mr. Deere's birthday could be part of a celebration of agriculture or Rural America & Small Town Day. Or, the date might be used to celebrate the spirit of innovation, in general, or advances in farming-related technology, in particular, or the success of Deere & Company, most specifically.

Although not every day represents the same mix of potential marketing opportunities for every organization, every day does represent one or more opportunities for some organizations whose marketers are willing to seize them. So, as you read *Marketing FAME*, think about how each day is unique and how each day's stories might possibly link with your organization, or with its values, brands or customers. An endless number of opportunities are waiting for *you* to discover them.

"Excellent, well done – it helps students taking marketing courses to relate classroom knowledge with real life marketing happenings/events. A more panoramic view." – Ajaiyeoba, MBA student

"I feel I got to know a lot of important quotes and practical marketing rules from the book, which we normally don't read in [traditional textbooks]." -- Nandita, senior non-business major

More than 15 minutes

The American pop artist Andy Warhol once implied what reality television is confirming, i.e., we're all destined for 15 minutes of fame. Of course, it's doubtful that Warhol was thinking specifically about marketing, because you'll need much more than 15 minutes to fully benefit from *Marketing FAME.*

"The information… actually stayed around in my head, and I have had conversations about what I have learned in those pages of *Marketing FAME* with others. In other words, I was able to comment in conversations that I previously would not have been able to speak to." – Sonya, MBA student

Still, 15 minutes may be ample time to achieve fame-status communication. That is, after reading *Marketing FAME*, please share your evaluation with the marbleous team. In a 15-minute email, let us know what you enjoyed or didn't enjoy about *Marketing FAME*, how future editions can be improved, and what your most and least favorite stories are. If you have an idea for a great story that should be included in future editions, let us know that too. Contact us through the contact page at www.MarketingMarbles.com, or contact me directly at WSU, Charles.Martin@wichita.edu

Thank you and happy reading!

P.S. If you find *Marketing FAME* interesting, informative, and otherwise marbleous be sure to tell your instructors. And, don't forget to read the 2018 edition too – new stories, new facts, and new quotes… Coming next year!

Marbles masquerading as nuts?

"[I liked] the shortness of the stories; I have the attention span of a squirrel so short bursts of interesting info are good." – Michael R., MBA student

January 1, 2017
Sunday

Objectives & reminders

____

____

Appointments

Early morning

8 a.m.

9 a.m.

10 a.m.

11 a.m.

Noon

1 p.m.

2 p.m.

3 p.m.

4 p.m.

5 p.m.

6 p.m.

Later evening

New Year's Day

In the U.S., New Year's Day is a holiday for federal workers. As such, most government offices are closed, including post offices; mail is not delivered. Like most of the dozen or so days designated as federal holidays, state and local governments, banks, and many businesses follow the fed's lead and also are closed on January 1.

Worldwide marketing opportunity?
New Year's Day and/or New Year's Eve (last night) is the most celebrated holiday on the planet – celebrated by about three-fourths of the world's population.

A new beginning -- today!

"Every man should be born again on the first day of January. Start with a fresh page. Take up one hole more in the buckle if necessary, or let down one, according to circumstances; but on the first of January let every man gird himself once more, with his face to the front, and take no interest in the things that were and are past." -- Henry Ward Beecher, 19th century American clergyman and abolitionist

____

"Huddled Masses Yearning to Breathe Free"

On January 1, 1892, Annie Moore, a 15-year-old girl from Ireland became the first immigrant to pass through Ellis Island's Immigration Station in New York Harbor. During the 62 years that followed, millions of immigrants to America followed Moore -- one million a year at the peak. Knowing that Ellis Island and the adjacent Statue of Liberty were the first two American landmarks that these immigrants experienced, today we recognize these landmarks as symbols of American diversity, freedom and hope.

Speaking of hope...
After fleeing France in 1799, Pierre Du Pont and 17 other members of the Du Pont family arrived in America on January 1, 1800. The Du Ponts went on to become one of the wealthiest families in the nation.

January 2, 2017
Monday
Goal Season

Objectives & reminders

____

____

____

Appointments

Early morning

8 a.m.

9 a.m.

10 a.m.

11 a.m.

Noon

1 p.m.

2 p.m.

3 p.m.

4 p.m.

5 p.m.

6 p.m.

Later evening

Marketing & New Year's resolutions

U.S. consumers make an average of 1.8 resolutions each new year. New Year's resolutions most frequently pertain to health and fitness (22%), career (18%), personal growth and interests (15%), personal finance (11%), time management (11%), family and relationships (8%), education (6%), home improvement and real estate (5%), or recreation and leisure (3%). Women are slightly more likely than men to make New Year's resolutions. Not surprisingly, around the first of the year while consumers are thinking about resolutions, marketers are likely to find receptive audiences for advertisements and other marketing communications that tie-in with consumers' desire to achieve or change.

Resolution affiliations

Notice this month's ads for these companies and brands, and how the ads relate to New Year's resolutions.

- Nicorette (stop smoking)
- H&R Block (improve/control finances)
- Weight Watchers (lose weight)
- Bally Total Fitness (exercise more)
- Monster.com (find a better job)

But, as the New Year's celebrations fade away, New Year's resolutions are likely to fade away as well if consumers lack the commitment to follow-through and make their resolutions a reality. One *USA Today* survey suggested that about 23 percent of New Year's resolutions don't survive the first week of January and 45 percent don't survive the month. Fortunately, marketers can play an important role in strengthening consumers' resolution resolve.

Some consumers may have not yet considered New Year's resolutions at all, or none particularly relevant to the marketer's product category. In these instances, consumers may be quite receptive to relevant resolutions businesses might suggest. For example, Prudential Investments recommends three "financial resolutions" to their customers: (1) "Review and rebalance your portfolio," (2) "Keep your education savings plan on track," and (3) "Rely on professional financial guidance." Prudential's newsletter, *Advised Choices* offers specific guidelines and suggestions to help customers pursue those resolutions.

January 3, 2017
Tuesday

Objectives & reminders

____

____

Appointments

Early morning

8 a.m.

9 a.m.

10 a.m.

11 a.m.

Noon

1 p.m.

2 p.m.

3 p.m.

4 p.m.

5 p.m.

6 p.m.

Later evening

National marketing effort helps win World War II

January 3, 1946, marked the effective end of the U.S. Department of Treasury's Defense Savings Program that had raised $185.7 billion to help fund World War II through the sale of war bonds.

The fundraiser had started almost five years earlier and utilized a series of print and radio ad, as well as posters and mailings. A sales force of 500,000 volunteers coaxed Americans to buy bonds to support the war effort. The media donated more than $250,000-worth of space and time to the campaign, free of charge. Leading advertising agencies such as Young & Rubicam also contributed their talent to the fundraiser, as well as artists such as Norman Rockwell and Thomas Hart Benton, and celebrities such as Kate Smith and Betty Grable. Government agencies played an important role too; for example, the Internal Revenue Service supplied mailing lists and income information. Individual businesses participated as well; many included regular reminders in their ads urging customers to buy bonds.

More than marketing bonds
The Secretary of the Treasury during the war bond campaign was Henry Morgenthau. Although he recognized other ways to raise money to pay for the war, he wanted "to use bonds to sell the war, rather than vice versa." When consumers bought war bonds, in other words, Morgenthau believed they would feel more invested in and therefore more committed to the war effort.

Happy birthday: Apple Computer

Founded by Steve Jobs, Steve Wozniak, and Ron Wayne, Apple Computer was incorporated on January 3, 1977. According to one account of the company's history, a group discussion intended to determine a name for the company was headed nowhere, so in frustration Jobs proclaimed that if the group didn't think of a suitable name within five more minutes he would name the company after the apple he was eating at the time. The group didn't, so he did.

January 4, 2017
Wednesday

Objectives & reminders

___

___

Appointments

Early morning

8 a.m.

9 a.m.

10 a.m.

11 a.m.

Noon

1 p.m.

2 p.m.

3 p.m.

4 p.m.

5 p.m.

6 p.m.

Later evening

Motivational pioneer

Frenchman Emile Coue arrived in New York City on January 4, 1923, to spread his self-help recipe for a better life. As the founder of "Coueism," Coue believed in the power of positive thinking reinforced by auto-suggestion. For example, he urged people to chant, "Day by day, in every way, I'm getting better and better."

Fordism

Industrialist Henry Ford, founder of the Ford Motor Company, also believed that people could help themselves by thinking more positively. He reminded workers that whether they believed they *could* or could *not* accomplish a task, they were probably right.

Although chanting may not be common today, it is common for motivational consultants and self-help experts to warn people to guard against negative self-talk: "As you think, so you become." When you find yourself being self-critical, ask yourself if you would talk to others that way. If you wouldn't be harsh of others, why brutalize yourself?

___

Foote in the door

Advertising guru Albert Lasker turned over his advertising agency -- Lord & Thomas (L&T) -- to the three men who had run L&T offices in New York (Emerson Foote), Chicago (Fairfax Cone), and Los Angeles (Don Belding). The trio promptly renamed the company, "Foote, Cone & Belding" (FCB), and opened for business on January 4, 1943.

Over the years, FCB has orchestrated advertising campaigns for several major clients, including Ford Motor Company, Nabisco, S.C. Johnson & Son, and Zenith, to name a few. Two of the most memorable slogans the agency inked include, "When you care enough to send the very best" (Hallmark Cards), and "Does she or doesn't she? Only her hair dresser knows for sure" (Clairol hair coloring).

January 5, 2017
Thursday

Objectives & reminders

____

____

Appointments

Early morning

8 a.m.

9 a.m.

10 a.m.

11 a.m.

Noon

1 p.m.

2 p.m.

3 p.m.

4 p.m.

5 p.m.

6 p.m.

Later evening

Happy birthday: Aaron "Bunny" Lapin

Born on January 5, 1914, Lapin was an inventor best known for whipping-up the 1948 dessert topping in a can, *Reddi-Wip*. First distributed by milkmen in St. Louis, Reddi-Wip soon became popular across America -- earning Lapin the nickname of Whipped Cream King. In 1998, *Time* magazine dubbed Reddi-Wip as one of the century's 100 greatest consumer innovations.

Happy birthday: Kemmons Wilson

Born in Osceola, Arkansas on January 5, 1913, Charles Kemmons Wilson was raised by his mother after his father died when Wilson was only nine months old. At age 14, Wilson dropped out of school to become a drug store's delivery boy to help support the family. From deliveries his career led him into numerous jobs and small businesses, including popcorn machine operator, builder, pinball machine business, and a movie theater.

In 1951, while on a trip with his family, Wilson encountered a number of overpriced, uncomfortable and otherwise unappealing hotel accommodations. So, the next year he built his own motel in Memphis, Tennessee, which he called Holiday Inn. Twenty years later, more than 1,600 Holiday Inns had been built, making Holiday Inn the largest hotel-motel company on the planet.

Work hard
"Work only a half a day; it makes no difference which half -- it can be either the first 12 hours or the last 12 hours."
-- Kemmons Wilson

Build a team; learn to delegate
"No job is too hard as long as you are smart enough to find someone else to do it for you."
-- Kemmons Wilson

Holiday Inn: Presidential appeal
U.S. Senator (1964-1976) and Vice-President (1977-1981) Walter Mondale, also was born on January 5 (1928). In the mid-1970s Mondale ran for the presidency, but eventually withdrew from the race. He explained, "I don't want to spend the next two years in Holiday Inns." Perhaps he was not a member of Holiday Inn's target market.

January 6, 2017
Friday

Objectives & reminders

____

____

____

Appointments

Early morning

8 a.m.

9 a.m.

10 a.m.

11 a.m.

Noon

1 p.m.

2 p.m.

3 p.m.

4 p.m.

5 p.m.

6 p.m.

Later evening

Epiphany

The twelfth day after Christmas, January 6, is known as the Epiphany (meaning appearance). Also known as Three Kings Day, Epiphany is celebrated in commemoration of the day the Magi visited baby Jesus shortly after his birth – presenting him with gifts of gold, frankincense, and myrrh. Recognized as a festive occasion as early as 567, Russian and Greek Orthodox churches, among others, observe Christmas on this day.

Entering someone's house during the 12 days between Christmas and the Epiphany was considered bad luck, hence the tradition of gift-giving emerged. Accordingly, during about the 13th century the Christmas season gift-giving carol regarding *The Twelve Days of Christmas* was first recited, although the timeless classic did not appear in print until about 1780 – in a London-published children's book entitled, *Mirth Without Mischief*.

What to give your "true love" who already has everything else

"12 lords a leaping,
11 ladies dancing,
10 pipers piping,
9 drummers drumming,
8 maids a milking,
7 swans a swimming,
6 geese a laying,
5 golden rings,
4 colly birds,
3 French hens,
2 turtle-doves,
And a partridge in a pear tree."

Packaging innovation

On January 6, 1929, Sheffield Farms of New York began replacing glass milk bottles with paper cartons for home delivery. The paper cartons were lighter, less-dangerous if dropped and broken, and were more convenient in that they did not require recycling. Although other milk producers followed Sheffield Farms' lead in subsequent years, glass bottles continued to be used for milk deliveries by some companies well into the 1960s.

January 7, 2017
Saturday

Objectives & reminders

______

______

______

Appointments

Early morning

8 a.m.

9 a.m.

10 a.m.

11 a.m.

Noon

1 p.m.

2 p.m.

3 p.m.

4 p.m.

5 p.m.

6 p.m.

Later evening

Advertising 100 years ago today

Page 10 of the January 7, 1917, edition of *The New York Times* was devoted exclusively to advertising. A total of 42 ads on that page alone clamored for readers' attention. Some ads were probably more effective than others. Consider these observations:

1. Eight ads prominently mentioned price, but only four of these suggested or implied that the price was a special or sale price.

2. All 42 ads included a product-related picture or drawing. For tangible goods, these typically included the product itself. For services, pictures or drawings attempted to show the results of the service (e.g., an apparent customer receiving "The Nestle Permanent Hair Wave").

3. In six ads the picture occupied half or more of the ad. Only five ads included any noticeable white space (blank areas). Most of the ads were copy-intensive; apparently advertisers tried to cram as many words into the ads as possible.

4. Eight ads included what appeared to be a recognizable company logo or brand trademark image. However, several others used what may have been a unique type font.

5. Thirty-nine ads included a headline with type larger than the copy. Twenty-one of these headlines included only the name of the product, brand and/or company. Examples: "Scotch Wool Socks," "English Sofa," "Freeman's Face Powder," "Parker's... Hair Treatment," and "Trout Jewelry Shop."

6. Another nine headlines seemed to try to capture readers' attention with a reader-relevant benefit or distinguishing product feature/claim. Examples: "Take the Jar Off Your Spine" (cushioned shoe heels), "Improve Your Appearance" (wigs/toupees), "Reduce Your Flesh" ("rubber garments"), "Your Guests Will Admire" (lamps), "Conspicuous Nose Pores: How to reduce them" (facial soap), and "High Quality..." (seeds, plants).

January 8, 2017
Sunday

Objectives & reminders

____

____

Appointments

Early morning

8 a.m.

9 a.m.

10 a.m.

11 a.m.

Noon

1 p.m.

2 p.m.

3 p.m.

4 p.m.

5 p.m.

6 p.m.

Later evening

Buyers notice design before other attributes

"Great design will not sell an inferior product, but it will enable a great product to achieve its maximum potential." – Thomas J. Watson, Jr., former chairman and CEO of IBM, born on January 8, 1914

Education as a journey, not a destiny
"The only person who is educated is the one who has learned how to learn -- and change." -- Carl R. Rogers

Happy birthday: Carl R. Rogers

Born in Oak Park, Illinois on January 8, 1902, Rogers was the psychologist who pioneered client-centered therapy, encounter group techniques, and experiential learning. He believed that clients should play an active role in their interaction with therapists, i.e., they should not be passive recipients of therapeutic prescriptions. When clients are active, Rogers maintained, they are more likely to learn and grow at a faster pace and are more likely to be confident in and committed to the insights *they* discover and the decisions *they* make.

In much the same way, today's effective salespeople realize that solutions can not be dictated to buyers. Buyers do not want someone else to "sell" them; rather, they want to reach their own conclusions as to which product alternatives to purchase. When buyers actively and genuinely interact with salespeople -- rather than passively listen to a sales "pitch" -- their chances of convincing themselves increase. It follows that buyers, like psychologists' patients, are more likely to be committed to the decisions that *they* make than to those forced upon them by high-pressure salespeople.

Creativity defies evaluation
"The very essence of the creative is its novelty, and hence we have no standard by which to judge it."
-- Carl R. Rogers

January 9, 2017
Monday

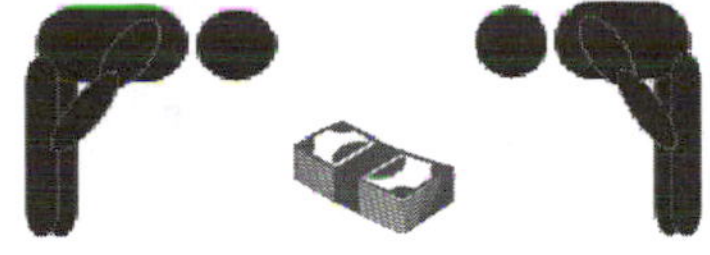

Objectives & reminders

Appointments

Early morning

8 a.m.

9 a.m.

10 a.m.

11 a.m.

Noon

1 p.m.

2 p.m.

3 p.m.

4 p.m.

5 p.m.

6 p.m.

Later evening

Early advice to employees regarding a customer service attitude

"If you feel ashamed at bowing to the clerk or errand boy of a client firm, you will be angry and feel offended, but if you are aware that you are bowing to money, you will have patience."
– Iwasaki Yataro, Japanese industrialist who founded Mitsubishi (one of the world's first big business organizations), born on January 9, 1835

Japanese invade California

The automobile brand names of Toyota and Datsun (now Nissan) appeared in Los Angeles for the Imported Motor Car Show on January 9, 1958. Prior to that date, these Japanese autos were sold in the United States as American brands through joint ventures with Ford Motor Co. and General Motors.

At the time, Japan's brand-building challenge was a formidable one. Many American consumers cited "patriotic reasons" to explain their refusal to buy Japanese-made vehicles. Some American mechanics who also were World War II veterans refused to service or repair Japanese-made automobiles.

Happy birthday: Alvah Curtis Roebuck

Born in Lafayette, Indiana, on January 9, 1864, Roebuck's interest in watch-making and repair led him to team up with Richard Sears in 1887. Their association soon led to a retailing partnership and the incorporation of Sears, Roebuck & Company in 1893. Roebuck played several roles in Sears, Roebuck & Co. (including writing the company's history) as well as in other companies (e.g., Emerson Typewriter Co.) until his death in 1948.

Quest for success
"It was our constant desire to maintain our margin of superiority by means of improvements and new inventions."
-- Alvah C. Roebuck

January 10, 2017
Tuesday

Objectives & reminders

____

____

____

Appointments

Early morning

8 a.m.

9 a.m.

10 a.m.

11 a.m.

Noon

1 p.m.

2 p.m.

3 p.m.

4 p.m.

5 p.m.

6 p.m.

Later evening

"Where's the beef?"

One of the most memorable and most effective TV ad campaigns in history was launched by Wendy's International (hamburgers) on January 10, 1984. On that day, an elderly lady in a Wendy's ad, Clara Peller, examined the contents of a competitor's burger and asked, "Where's the beef?" Before Clara first uttered these famous words, consumer surveys found that 37 percent of U.S. consumers had either seen or heard of advertising for Wendy's. Follow-up research in April showed that consumer awareness had climbed to 60 percent.

Political beef
Given Wendy's success with the line, U.S. presidential candidate Walter Mondale challenged his competitors in his 1984 bid for the Democratic presidential nomination when he too asked, "Where's the beef?" Four years later, while also running for the presidency, candidate Jesse Jackson used the line again. Unfortunately for them, neither Mondale nor Jackson enjoyed as much success with the slogan as Clara did. Neither became president.

19th century birthdays on January 10

1835 Fukuzawa Yukichi. Born in Osaka, Japan, Yukichi was an economist and educator whose highly influential writings in the late 1860s introduced many Japanese business leaders and policy-makers to Western business practices. In 1858 he founded what is now one of the leading universities in Japan -- Keio Gijuku University. Business historian Morgen Witzel studied Yukichi's work and its impact and concluded that, "[m]odern Japanese business owes much of its character and culture to [Yukichi's] work."

1847 Jacob Henry Schiff. Born in Frankfort, Germany, Schiff moved to the U.S. in 1865 and began a career in banking – focusing on railroad finance and becoming head of Kuhn, Loeb & Co. (banking firm) at the age of 38. Schiff was known for his high integrity and strong sense of values – characteristics that were apparent in his business relationships.

January 11, 2017
Wednesday

Marbles are all right !

Objectives & reminders

____

____

____

Appointments

Early morning

8 a.m.

9 a.m.

10 a.m.

11 a.m.

Noon

1 p.m.

2 p.m.

3 p.m.

4 p.m.

5 p.m.

6 p.m.

Later evening

Happy birthday: Harry Gordon Selfridge

Born in Ripon, Wisconsin on January 11, 1858, Selfridge enjoyed a successful career working for Marshall Field's department store in Chicago. In 1909 he moved to England and soon opened a department store of his own.

At Field's store, Selfridge was instrumental in cultivating the price-sensitive consumer market with his 1886 innovation of the "bargain basement" concept -- an idea that was adopted by other department stores and used well into the 1960s.

Loyalty marketing
"Get the confidence of the public and you will have no difficulty in getting their patronage... Remember always that the recollection of quality remains long after the price is forgotten." -- Harry Gordon Selfridge

Selfridge also shaped the philosophy of retailing when he asserted, "The customer is always right." And he developed a technique to help put Christmas shoppers in the mood to buy when he began reminding them, "There are only ____ shopping days left until Christmas."

Today, "Selfridge's" department stores continue to operate in England -- in London, Manchester, and Birmingham.

What is the customer?
What did H. Gordon Selfridge mean when he proclaimed "The customer is always right"? Was Selfridge right? If not "always right," is the customer always something else?

But, when the customer isn't right…

"Whenever you're in conflict with someone, there is one factor that can make the difference between damaging your relationship and deepening it. That factor is attitude." -- William James, pioneering American psychologist, born in New York City on January 11, 1842

January 12, 2017
Thursday

Objectives & reminders

____

____

Appointments

Early morning

8 a.m.

9 a.m.

10 a.m.

11 a.m.

Noon

1 p.m.

2 p.m.

3 p.m.

4 p.m.

5 p.m.

6 p.m.

Later evening

January 12 birthdays

1884 Mary Louise Cecilia Guinan. Originally an actress, Guinan was a night club greeter and hostess in New York in the mid-1920s. She found that customers would spend more money if they were welcomed, joked with, and otherwise recognized.

1905 Oather Dorris "O.D." McKee -- "America's snack king" -- founder of several bakeries including the McKee Bakery Company in 1957 (now McKee Foods). In 1960, his granddaughter, Debbie McKee, had her picture taken for inclusion on the packages of a new line of "Little Debbie" snack cakes. As an adult, Debbie McKee managed of one of McKee Foods' plants in Gentry, Arkansas.

1916 Ruth Rogan Benerito, chemist who pioneered wash-and-wear fabrics (among other accomplishments) to enable producers of cotton clothing to differentiate their products. Her innovations made clothing more convenient ("drip-dry"), more comfortable, and crease- and stain-resistant.

1930 Tim Horton, pro hockey player for 24 seasons (primarily for the Toronto Maple Leafs). Horton entered the coffee and donut retail business in the 1960s. Today, there are more than 2,600 Tim Hortons coffee and donut shops across Canada and more than 300 locations in the U.S.

1947 Edward J. Zander, former president of Sun Microsystems, and chairman and CEO of Motorola (2004-2008). To encourage debate and frank discussions, Zander explains that he "sometimes take[s] a contrarian view just to play it out and see whether there is original thought there, and whether they're willing to... defend their position."

1964 Jeff P. Bezos, founder of Amazon.com, online books and other merchandise. Regarding innovation in a high-tech world, Bezos points out that "[u]nless you [can] create something with a huge value proposition for the customer, it would be easier for them to do it the old way."

January 13, 2017
Friday

Objectives & reminders

____

____

____

Appointments

Early morning

8 a.m.

9 a.m.

10 a.m.

11 a.m.

Noon

1 p.m.

2 p.m.

3 p.m.

4 p.m.

5 p.m.

6 p.m.

Later evening

Flying ideas

Great ideas are not always formulated in laboratories or designed by committees. Often they're unintentionally discovered by those who pay attention to the world around them. That's what happened in the mid-1950s when someone from the Wham-O toy company noticed truck drivers in Connecticut showing a group of college students how to fly pie pans through the air.

The truck drivers worked for the Frisbee Pie Company and may have been trying to create a competitive advantage for the company by demonstrating alternative uses of pie pans (or they could have been goofing off). Regardless of the truck drivers' motives, the Wham-O employee apparently knew the idea would fly so he followed up and on January 13, 1957, the company introduced what would become one of the most popular toys of the 20th century, the "Pluto Platter," which later become known as the Frisbee.

Now well beyond "national" in scope

The National Geographic Society was formed on January 13, 1888, by a diverse group of 33 individuals. The organization soon began publishing *The National Geographic Magazine* that has continued to serve as a rich source of information and insights about countries and cultures around the world. In 2015, the magazine was published in 40 languages with a global monthly circulation of 6.8 million copies (3.5 million in the U.S.).

Fries & Schuele follows trend

Founded in 1868 in Cleveland, Ohio, Fries, Klein & Co. (later Fries & Schuele) dry goods store grew into a department store and one of the country's biggest carpet-selling outlets. One hundred years after its founding -- in 1968 -- the downtown Cleveland store employed 150 people. In the 1970s, however, as more and more customers moved to the suburbs and discount stores grew in popularity, Fries & Schuele found it increasingly difficult to compete. Finally, the store closed on January 13, 1979.

January 14, 2017
Saturday

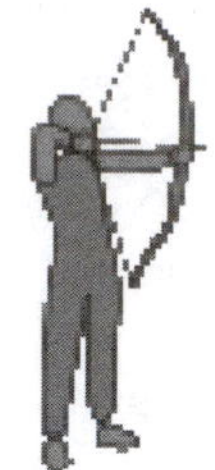

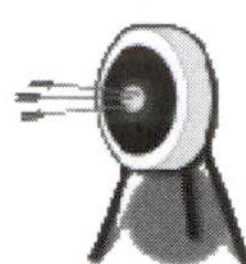

Objectives & reminders

____

____

Appointments

Early morning

8 a.m.

9 a.m.

10 a.m.

11 a.m.

Noon

1 p.m.

2 p.m.

3 p.m.

4 p.m.

5 p.m.

6 p.m.

Later evening

Why contracts should be read carefully

"Nothing in fine print is ever good news." – Andy Rooney, American journalist and keen observer of human behavior, born on January 14, 1919

Float this publicity idea

In San Francisco, on January 14, 1988, Gary Sussman transformed a 6,000-pound bar of Ivory soap into a statue as part of a celebration of the area's 1849 gold rush. Because soap-carving is not an everyday occurrence, the statue successfully generated publicity for both the Forty-Niner event as well as for the Ivory brand. The size of the statue also contributed to its novelty and therefore its publicity potency.

Courage to seize opportunities

"I've never thought I could do everything, but I've always thought that one should be prepared to take risks, and not be confined in some totally predictable way. There are extraordinary opportunities out there, ...look for them, and try to take them! You're going to fail sometimes." – Carol Bellamy, former president and CEO of World Learning, former Executive Director of UNICEF, and former Director of the Peace Corps, born in Scotch Plains, New Jersey on January 14, 1942

Evaporation leadership

"Constant kindness can accomplish much. As the sun makes the ice melt, kindness causes misunderstandings, mistrust and hostility to evaporate." – Albert Schweitzer, German theologian, physician, musician, moralist, and winner of the Nobel Peace prize (1952). Schweitzer was born on January 14, 1875.

Aim high, expect high

"The minute you settle for less than you deserve, you get even less than you settled for." -- Maureen Dowd, *New York Times* columnist and best-selling author, born on January 14, 1952

January 15, 2017
Sunday

Objectives & reminders

____

____

Appointments

Early morning

8 a.m.

9 a.m.

10 a.m.

11 a.m.

Noon

1 p.m.

2 p.m.

3 p.m.

4 p.m.

5 p.m.

6 p.m.

Later evening

Roosevelt wins!

No, not Theodore or Franklin, but 73-year-old Eleanor Roosevelt (widow of U.S. President Franklin D. Roosevelt). On January 15, 1958, she finished in the top spot as the most admired woman in the United States, according to a survey conducted by the Gallup Organization. Among her many accomplishments, Ms. Roosevelt promoted the work of the United Nations and was active in the fight for human rights around the world.

Withholding consent
"No one can make you feel inferior without your consent." -- Eleanor Roosevelt

Slam dunk synchromarketing idea

Seasonal changes in the weather can place constraints on the production and influence the demand of many goods and services. Ski resorts have a tough time attracting skiers in mid-summer, and "ice cold" drinks are more difficult to sell in mid-winter. To offset these seasonal peaks and valleys, often product lines are diversified. Ski resorts become campgrounds in the summer and beverage-makers tout hot drinks during the winter.

Such is the marketing rationale behind the invention of basketball -- introduced on January 15, 1892 by Dr. James A. Naismith, an instructor at the YMCA's International Training School in Springfield, Massachusetts. That's the day the official rules for the new game were first published, in Springfield's *Triangle Magazine*.

Naismith's goal was to improve YMCA attendance during cold weather and he believed he needed a new game to do that. To avoid the winter weather, he concluded that the game should be played indoors. The design of the product (i.e., the rules of the game) would have to accommodate an indoor environment. Thus, running with the ball or kicking it was not allowed (space too limited), and tackling or violent contact with other players was prohibited (playing surface too hard).

Dr. Naismith's innovation caught on and today is not only a winter-time participant activity, but a popular spectator sport as well.

January 16, 2017
Monday

Martin Luther King, Jr. Holiday

Objectives & reminders

____

____

Appointments

Early morning

8 a.m.

9 a.m.

10 a.m.

11 a.m.

Noon

1 p.m.

2 p.m.

3 p.m.

4 p.m.

5 p.m.

6 p.m.

Later evening

Happy birthday: Martin Luther King, Jr.

Born in Atlanta, Georgia on January 15, 1929, Reverend and Dr. King was a prominent civil rights leader who advocated nonviolent protests to achieve equal rights. Tragically, he was assassinated in 1968. In 1986, his birthday was recognized as a Federal holiday in the United States, now celebrated annually on the third Monday in January -- today.

King on compatibility
"We must learn to live together as brothers or perish together as fools."

King on leadership
"There comes a time when one must take a position that is neither safe, popular, nor political; but because it is right."

King on service
"Life's most persistent and urgent question is, '*What are you doing for others?*'"

Good day to salute Desert Storm veterans

At midnight on January 16, 1991, Iraqi troops failed to meet the United Nations' deadline to leave Kuwait, so at 4:30 a.m. EST, U.S. aircraft were launched and soon began bombing targets in Iraq as part of operation "Desert Storm." The Persian Gulf War had begun and included an international coalition of forces from 32 nations against Iraq. The War continued for about six weeks, and although Iraq surrendered, Saddam Hussein remained in power and remained a threat. Twelve years later, another war against Iraq was launched to remove Saddam Hussein from power.

Did you know?
There are more than 2.7 million U.S. veterans of the 1991 Persian Gulf War.

January 17, 2017
Tuesday

Objectives & reminders

____

____

Appointments

Early morning

8 a.m.

9 a.m.

10 a.m.

11 a.m.

Noon

1 p.m.

2 p.m.

3 p.m.

4 p.m.

5 p.m.

6 p.m.

Later evening

Save this week?

During the first World War, the U.S. Treasury Department established Thrift Week to promote saving and discourage waste, and thus aid the war effort. The agency timed the week to coincide with founding father Benjamin Franklin's birthday (born January 17, 1706) who was an advocate of thrift. Thrift Week proved to be so effective and popular during the war that the week of Franklin's birthday continued to be set aside as Thrift Week for several years after the war.

Ben Franklin on thrift

1¢ "A penny saved is a penny earned."

$2 "If you would like to know the value of money, go and try to borrow some."

3¢ "Beware of little expenses. A small leak will sink a great ship."

Franklin became a vegetarian in 1722 – to save money for the purchase of books.

Today, most organizations could benefit from an annual Thrift Week. As expenses tend to attach themselves to organizations much like barnacles cling to the hulls of ships, it's a good idea to occasionally lift the organization out of the water, so to speak, and scrape away some of the expenses. Large amounts of money can be saved by finding alternative methods to accomplish job tasks without sacrificing excellence. Examples: A bank found that they saved $23,000 annually by replacing the paper envelopes previously used in their drive-through windows with reusable plastic containers. A construction company saved $5,000 annually when it canceled the lease of a radio channel and used cell phones instead.

Don't overdo it

Although the efficiency of most organizations can be improved, avoid being overly preoccupied with trying to "slash" the company's budget. Some short-term savings (such as ignoring employee training and equipment maintenance) can be costly in the long-run. Moreover, a business can not "save" its way to prosperity. At some point it must invest money to earn money.

January 18, 2017
Wednesday

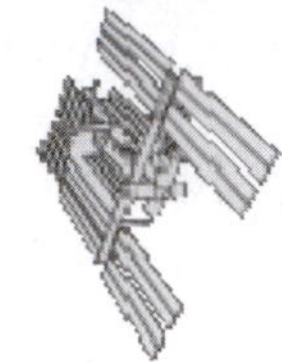

Objectives & reminders

____

____

____

Appointments

Early morning

8 a.m.

9 a.m.

MORE VIDEOS

10 a.m.

11 a.m.

Noon

1 p.m.

2 p.m.

3 p.m.

4 p.m.

5 p.m.

6 p.m.

Later evening

It's official:
Biggest marketing communication

The world's record for the largest communicated message was confirmed by officials at Guinness World Records on January 18, 2015. The message was a short but potent one from a 13-year-old girl named Stephanie to her father who was an astronaut circling the earth at the time on the International Space Station:

"Steph♡s you!"

Etched in the Nevada desert by a team of 11 Genesis brand automobiles, the message was more than 5.5 kilometers tall and could be read from 300 kilometers in space.

Hyundai Motor Company, the maker of the Genesis, seized the publicity opportunity accompanying the record-breaking achievement by pointing out that only vehicles with excellent driving stability and other qualities could create such an elaborate message on such a rough surface. Further, the company suggested to consumers that the message itself reflects the firm's caring vision.

See it for yourself on YouTube
www.youtube.com/watch?v=3EOAXrTrsOE

The feat was included as part of an advertising campaign for Genesis and was preserved on a four-minute YouTube video that has been viewed more than 70 million times. Had the company purchased advertising to generate the same amount of exposure that the publicity generated, it would have cost an estimated $50 million.

Anatomy of a successful publicity effort

1. Amazing, record-breaking event that captured public and media attention.
2. Facilitated by the brand (thus drawing attention to the brand).
3. Tugged at heartstrings (i.e., daughter's love for her far-away father).
4. Preserved and shared on YouTube.

January 19, 2017
Thursday

Objectives & reminders

______

______

______

Appointments

Early morning

8 a.m.

9 a.m.

10 a.m.

11 a.m.

Noon

1 p.m.

2 p.m.

3 p.m.

4 p.m.

5 p.m.

6 p.m.

Later evening

Happy birthday: Auguste Comte

Born in Montpellier, France on January 19, 1798, Comte was a social philosopher who believed that social forces influence individual behavior. He coined the term "sociology" to describe the objective study of these forces.

Today, marketers recognize the important roles that others play in shaping buyers' perceptions, purchases and consumption behavior. Members of the immediate family tend to exert the strongest social influence on consumers. Products that are publicly visible during consumption are more likely to be the targets of social influence than more privately consumed products (e.g., shirts and slacks rather than undergarments).

Indeed, what other people say and do matters, and marketers realize this. That's why marketing communications often imply that prospective buyers' friends also prefer a particular brand. For example, soft drink ads often include groups of people sharing the brand together. Other ads suggest that buyers should consider the effect that purchase decisions have on other people. For example, some automobile tire ads suggest that the family's safety depends on a wise choice of tires.

A third approach is to appeal to *influencers*, i.e., people who are likely to influence others' consumption or purchase decisions. That's why some ads instruct children to "ask your parents..." and why "friends don't let friends drive drunk."

Not you?
If you don't think your consumer behavior is influenced by other people consider these questions:

1. After buying a new piece of clothing, do you ask your friends if they like it? Do you hope they will say "yes"?
2. When shopping for food and beverage items, do you tend to buy less expensive house brands for personal consumption, but well-known "leading" brands when entertaining guests?
3. Before making a major (or not-so-major) purchase, do you first solicit the opinions of family and friends?

January 20, 2017
Friday

Objectives & reminders

____

____

____

Appointments

Early morning

8 a.m.

9 a.m.

10 a.m.

11 a.m.

Noon

1 p.m.

2 p.m.

3 p.m.

4 p.m.

5 p.m.

6 p.m.

Later evening

Inauguration Day

Since 1937 Inauguration Day has occurred in the U.S. every four years on January 20 following a presidential election the preceding November (presidential elections are held every other even-numbered year, i.e., 2012, 2016, 2020, etc.). It's the day when a new four-year presidential term begins, and is always accompanied by an inauguration speech by the new or re-elected president – a speech that typically reinforces American values and looks to the future with a spirit of optimism, teamwork, and patriotism.

To help celebrate the new presidential term, Inauguration Day is a holiday for U.S. federal workers and for workers in many other organizations that follow the federal government's holiday calendar.

Your turn
"And so, my fellow Americans: ask not what your country can do for you -- ask what you can do for your country. My fellow citizens of the world: ask not what America will do for you, but what together we can do for the freedom of man."
-- President John F. Kennedy, 35th President of the U.S. (1961-1963), inaugural address, January 20, 1961

Nixon's twist
Twelve years later, Richard M. Nixon was sworn in for his second term as the 37th President – on January 20, 1973. Nixon put his own twist on Kennedy's famous patriotic plea when Nixon exhorted, "Ask not just what will the government do for me, but what can I do for myself?"

Happy birthday: Donald V. Fites

Born in Tippecanoe, Indiana on January 20, 1934, Fites worked for the $21 billion maker of earth-moving equipment -- Caterpillar -- since the age of 22. Working his way up the corporate ladder, he was named chairman and CEO in 1990. He was a strong believer in empowering employees: "[M]y philosophy is to push decision making as far down as you can, to really make people feel accountable and responsible for their decisions, and then reward them when they do well."

January 21, 2017
Saturday

Objectives & reminders

____

____

Appointments

Early morning

8 a.m.

9 a.m.

10 a.m.

11 a.m.

Noon

1 p.m.

2 p.m.

3 p.m.

4 p.m.

5 p.m.

6 p.m.

Later evening

National Hugging Day

Kevin Zaborney of Port Huron, Michigan sponsors National Hugging Day on January 21. The premise of the special day is that most people could benefit from a few more hugs and that many of us need to be reminded to increase the number of hugs we share -- which traditional non-huggers may find difficult to do.

Because it's not a good idea to cross the hugging line, so to speak, Debra Benton of Benton Management Resources offers a few tips for proper hugging in a business setting. She advises:

1. "Expect acceptance, but if in doubt, the first time you hug, say something along the lines of 'You've been so supportive, I'd like to give you a hug.'"
2. "Grasp right hands and place your left hand around the person's shoulder, then lean your upper body toward him."
3. "Turn your head so that your lips don't brush against the other person's cheek, collar, or lapel."
4. "Hold the embrace a second or two longer than a typical handshake."
5. "Don't touch pelvises."
6. "Release the person from your embrace, look the person in the eye, smile, and step back."

Not a hugger?

If you're not an effective hugger, try a more symbolic approach to hugging -- especially for your customers. For example, in his 2003 book, *Hug Your Customers*, Jack Mitchell advocates thank-you letters:

> "One of the best hugs of all is a letter of thanks, and it's a big hug if it's handwritten and a very big hug if you write an additional handwritten note on the side of a typed letter. This especially matters with someone we've just met. The first-time customer is extremely important, because first impressions are so powerful."

January 22, 2017
Sunday

Objectives & reminders

____

____

____

Appointments

Early morning

8 a.m.

9 a.m.

10 a.m.

11 a.m.

Noon

1 p.m.

2 p.m.

3 p.m.

4 p.m.

5 p.m.

6 p.m.

Later evening

Happy birthday: Harold S. Geneen

Born in Bournemouth, England on the 22nd of January in 1910, Geneen moved to the U.S. as an infant where he later served as the president and CEO of International Telephone and Telegraph Corporation (ITT) from 1959 to 1972. During his reign he transformed the medium-sized ITT into one of the largest multinational conglomerates in the world. Through a flurry of 350 acquisitions worldwide, ITT's sales jumped from $760 million to $17 billion in less than a decade (more than a 22-fold increase). After Geneen left the company, however, ITT proved too diversified for his successors to manage effectively; profitability eroded and numerous subsidiaries were sold.

Is theory important?
Geneen wasn't a big believer in management theory or textbookish models to guide decision-making. For example, he once said, "you can't run a business or anything else on theory." Instead, he seemed to use an intuitive approach to managing ITT and apparently followed few codified rules-of-thumb to guide his decisions. In other words, Geneen tended to make decisions on a case-by-case basis. Could this managerial style have had anything to do with ITT's lackluster performance after Geneen's resignation?

Evaluation of managerial effectiveness: Agree or disagree?
Business leaders' effectiveness is not determined solely by the current success of the companies they *presently* manage, but by the current success of the companies they *previously* managed.

Wishful time management

"There cannot be a crisis next week. My schedule is already full." -- Henry Kissinger, then U.S. Secretary of State, quoted in an interview on January 22, 1977

January 23, 2017
Monday

Objectives & reminders

____

____

Appointments

Early morning

8 a.m.

9 a.m.

10 a.m.

11 a.m.

Noon

1 p.m.

2 p.m.

3 p.m.

4 p.m.

5 p.m.

6 p.m.

Later evening

MORE VIDEOS

Apple begins new tradition

The final and climatic American football game of the season, Super Bowl XVIII, was played on January 23, 1984. For the marketing team at Apple Computer, the game represented an ideal opportunity to reach a huge audience (today 130-140 million people watch at least a portion of the big game) to announce the introduction of its Macintosh computer.

Apple seized the opportunity by having Chiat/Day, Inc. ad agency produce an ad for $1.5 million to be shown during the game. Dubbed "1984" after the same-named futuristic novel written by George Orwell several years earlier, the commercial featured a large screen showing an enthused orator speaking to a captive audience, presumably prisoners. Spliced through the commercial were cuts of a female runner carrying a large hammer as she ran toward the screen. As the orator reached the climatic assertion of his speech, "We shall prevail," the runner hurled the hammer and shattered the screen – showering the audience with a burst of white light. At that point, the voice-over narrator explained: "On January 24, Apple Computer will introduce Macintosh. And you'll see why 1984 [the year] won't be like *1984* [the book]."

Apple ad dubbed one of the best
As the 20th century came to a close, *Advertising Age* magazine identified what it considered to be the top ads of the century. Apple's "1984" ad was 12th on the list.

By so dramatically communicating that consumers were no longer captive to competing computers, the commercial helped Apple's revolutionary Macintosh get off to a strong start.

The effectiveness of the ad was noticed by other firms who in subsequent years began showcasing their new products and promotional campaigns with extravagant commercials first aired during the Super Bowl. Today, the Super Bowl is one of the few television broadcasts that attracts an audience segment that is interested in watching the ads.

View the ad on YouTube
https://www.youtube.com//watch?v=2zfqw8nhUwA

January 24, 2017
Tuesday

Objectives & reminders

____

____

Appointments

Early morning

8 a.m.

9 a.m.

10 a.m.

11 a.m.

Noon

1 p.m.

2 p.m.

3 p.m.

4 p.m.

5 p.m.

6 p.m.

Later evening

Speedy online marketing insight

"[A] company's time to market is quicker on the Net. Products a company can bring online today, it tries out today; if customers don't show an interest, the company just calls it market research and tries out another one." – Jim Barksdale, former president and CEO of Netscape, born in Jackson, Mississippi on January 24, 1943

Happy birthday: Hermann Ebbinghaus

Born in Prussia on January 24, 1850, Ebbinghaus was a German psychologist who studied learning and memory processes. His classic book on the topic, *Memory: A Contribution to Experimental Psychology*, was published in 1885.

Many of Ebbinghaus's discoveries have significant business and marketing implications today. For example, he learned that nonsense syllables (i.e., largely randomly arranged letters) were more difficult for people to remember than those that formed a concrete word, because nonsense syllables are not likely to evoke any relevant mental images which facilitate memory. That's why marketers today avoid choosing randomly selected website domain names and often opt for telephone numbers that spell a memorable word or phrase (e.g., PLUMERS is more memorable than 758-6377).

Ebbinghaus also discovered that most (up to 90%) of what people might learn in a classroom setting tends to be forgotten within a month. That's why it is so important for managers to continually work with employees. By following-up classroom training sessions with periodic review, coaching, and additional training, managers reinforce the original training lessons and increase the percentage of training that trainees remember.

Social responsibility challenge

"Corporations must become actively involved in solving the social problems of America and develop practical means of giving human needs the same status as profit." – Walter A. Haas, Jr., CEO (1958-1976) and chairman (1970-1981) of Levi Strauss & Co., born on January 24, 1916

January 25, 2017
Wednesday

Objectives & reminders

Appointments

Early morning

8 a.m.

9 a.m.

10 a.m.

11 a.m.

Noon

1 p.m.

2 p.m.

3 p.m.

4 p.m.

5 p.m.

6 p.m.

Later evening

Relationship marketing

On January 25, 1964, *Cash Box* magazine and dozens of radio stations noted the #1 hit song was the Beatles' single, "I Want to Hold Your Hand." Today, the same objective is embraced by marketers interested in building business relationships with customers.

New customers often require some extra hand-holding -- to feel welcome, and because they are likely to have limited knowledge of the business and its offerings. They may need products, services or company policies demonstrated or explained. Or, they may need help finding their way around the firm's premises. For example, when guests at Chicago's Parker House hotel ask housekeepers where ice machines are located, they're personally escorted to the nearest one.

Hand-holding often helps nurture relationships with *existing customers* too -- to make these customers feel appreciated and special, and to smooth over occasional mishaps. Promptly and personally following-up customer complaints is a hand-holding technique to reassure customers that the business is taking action to address the issue.

Happy birthday: Charles Digby Harrod

Charles Digby Harrod was the son of Charles Henry Harrod who founded the British store that shares the family name (Harrods Ltd.). The younger Harrod was born on January 25, 1841.

At the age of 16, Digby began his retailing career as a commercial clerk for a grocer. Within four years he bought his father's grocery shop which he successfully repositioned to appeal to an upscale clientele. Over the next couple of decades, the business evolved beyond groceries to include a variety of household items. Today, the Harrod's is the biggest department store in Europe and its 330 departments occupy five acres and more than one million square feet of selling space.

Success tactic: "Cash and carry"
Unlike many competitors, Harrod insisted on cash payment at the time of purchase. This reduced his bad debt and accounting/collection expenses, and freed cash to reinvest in the business.

January 26, 2017
Thursday

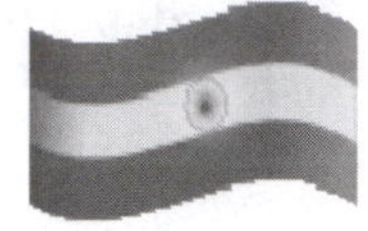

Objectives & reminders

____

____

____

Appointments

Early morning

8 a.m.

9 a.m.

10 a.m.

11 a.m.

Noon

1 p.m.

2 p.m.

3 p.m.

4 p.m.

5 p.m.

6 p.m.

Later evening

Happy birthday: Republic of India

India became the most populous democracy in the world when its constitution went into effect on January 26, 1950. India's new self-rule involved periodic elections and a parliamentary system modeled after the British system. Today, India's population of more than 1.28 billion means that about 17.5% of the world's consumers live in India – second only to China (1.36 billion consumers).

Did you know?
In 2013, the U.S. imported $41.8 billion of goods from India. About 22 percent of India's exports are destined for the U.S. No other country receives even one-third the amount of India's exports.

Time to clean out your sock drawer?

Human nature is such that when it is time to do something unpleasant, we often look for other things we can justify (rationalize ?) doing instead. For example, few consumers look forward to going to the dentist. Unlike going out to eat or to the theater, dental work is an *avoidance service* -- one consumers are quick to postpone or avoid altogether. Needless to say, marketers of avoidance services face a difficult challenge.

One way to counter the avoidance phenomenon is to attack the reason(s) why the service is avoided -- pain, in the case of dental work. On January 26, 1875, a positive step was taken in this regard when the first electric dental drill was patented by George F. Green of Kalamazoo, Michigan. The high-speed drill was less painful than those it replaced. Subsequent improvements in drills have continued to make dental experiences less painful.

Scheduling far in advance of the service is another approach marketers of avoidance services use to counter the avoidance phenomenon. The discomfort and accompanying anxiety seem more tolerable when the impending appointment is several months away. And, like scheduling anything months in advance, there are likely to be fewer other scheduled activities to compete for the customer's time. Once an appointment is made, the customer is more likely to feel committed to honor it.

January 27, 2017
Friday

Objectives & reminders

____

____

Appointments

Early morning

8 a.m.

9 a.m.

10 a.m.

11 a.m.

Noon

1 p.m.

2 p.m.

3 p.m.

4 p.m.

5 p.m.

6 p.m.

Later evening

Goodbye Vietnam

A cease-fire agreement was reached between the U.S., North Vietnam and South Vietnam on January 27, 1973. Finally, the end to the longest foreign war in U.S. history was in sight -- after almost 60,000 American lives were lost. Unfortunately, the cease-fire soon collapsed and the fighting continued.

Today, 7.7 million U.S. veterans of the war still remember their service in the 1960s and 1970s. January 27 is a great day for the rest of us to remember them.

Happy birthday: Lewis Carroll

Alice In Wonderland's author, Lewis Carroll, was born on January 27, 1832. His career management wisdom is timeless: "If you limit your actions in life to things that nobody can possibly find fault with, you will not do much."

Movie ratings re-rated

On January 27, 1970, the Motion Pictures Association of America announced revisions in it system of rating movies. "Parental guidance" was suggested for movies rated PG. Movies designated with an R rating were not recommended for moviegoers under the age of 17 unless accompanied by an adult. Additional revisions/categories were introduced in 1984 (PG-13) and 1990 (NC-17).

The concept of a third-party rating system is generally good for consumers, because ratings provide additional information with which to make purchase decisions. But ratings can be *particularly* useful for service experiences -- such as movie-viewing. Why? Because services tend to be produced and consumed simultaneously, and because of this, prospective buyers can not fully evaluate services prior to purchase.

If consumers can not evaluate services firsthand prior to purchase, they are more likely to pay close attention to the ratings. For the same reason, word-of-mouth publicity tends to play a larger role in the marketing of services than for goods. Before purchasing services, prospective buyers seek out and listen to the opinions of other people who have already purchased the services.

January 28, 2017
Saturday

Objectives & reminders

Appointments

Early morning

8 a.m.

9 a.m.

10 a.m.

11 a.m.

Noon

1 p.m.

2 p.m.

3 p.m.

4 p.m.

5 p.m.

6 p.m.

Later evening

Happy birthday: Robert Bartels

Born in Wheeling, West Virginia on January 28, 1913, Robert D.W. Bartels was a marketing scholar who spent most of his career at The Ohio State University. His marketing contributions began in 1941 with his doctoral dissertation, *Marketing Literature: Development and Appraisal.*

Marketing is a science: Agree or disagree?
"[I]nstead of being merely a secret formula employed for private gain, marketing is a science... While marketing, because it is a social science, may never be regarded as 'exact', it has nevertheless evolved in a scientific fashion." -- Robert Bartels

Throughout his career, Bartels believed that the study and practice of marketing should be guided by conceptual frameworks and, ideally, by theory. Accordingly, many of his contributions to marketing thought dealt with the identification and articulation of the building blocks of marketing theory, such as concepts and principles. In his first major article, "Marketing Principles" (*Journal of Marketing*, October 1944), Bartels' review of the marketing literature enabled him to identify and articulate several marketing principles that remain relevant today. Here are two examples:

P3 "As peoples and nations advance in civilization, trade increases and the structure of marketing institutions becomes more complex."

P4 "So long as exchange is obstructed by a given condition, it will be a function of marketing to overcome that obstruction or difficulty."

Principles defense: Concentrated marketing
If marketing majors read the textbooks and other materials assigned, they will have read about three million words by the time they graduate (not counting another few million words for their non-marketing courses). When condensed into a series of marketing principles, however, the reading can be concentrated into less than 100,000 words. Unfortunately, few marketing textbooks clearly articulate marketing principles -- even textbooks with "principles" in their title.

January 29, 2017
Sunday

Objectives & reminders

____

____

____

Appointments

Early morning

8 a.m.

9 a.m.

10 a.m.

11 a.m.

Noon

1 p.m.

2 p.m.

3 p.m.

4 p.m.

5 p.m.

6 p.m.

Later evening

Not creative enough?

January 29, 1920, was a big day for an aspiring artist named Walt Disney who started his first job for the Kansas City Slide Company. His starting weekly salary was $40. Unfortunately, Disney lost that job because he wasn't considered creative enough. Disney went on to find some Mickey Mouse work later in the decade.

Curiosity drives creativity
"We keep moving forward, opening new doors, and doing new things, because we're curious and curiosity keeps leading us down new paths. We're always exploring and experimenting." – Walt Disney, founder of the entertainment conglomerate that bears his name

Ethics insight

"Real integrity is doing the right thing, knowing that nobody's going to know whether you did it or not." – Oprah Winfrey, television talk-show hostess and head of the company that produces it, Harpo Productions. Winfrey was born in Kosciusko, Mississippi on January 29, 1954.

The first motorcar

A German mechanical engineer by the name of Karl Benz founded Benz & Company in Mannheim, Germany in 1883 to manufacture industrial engines.

Soon Benz began tinkering with the concept of a "motor carriage" which led to the first patent for a gasoline-fueled automobile -- granted to him on January 29, 1886. This early model was a three-wheeler. By 1900, Benz & Company was producing more automobiles than any other manufacturer in the world. In 1926, the company merged with a competing firm run by Gottlieb Daimler to become Daimler-Benz AG.

Today, automobiles represent an enormous product market, but their use also has been tremendous in shaping consumers' lifestyles and shopping behavior. The marketplace probably would look quite different today without automobiles.

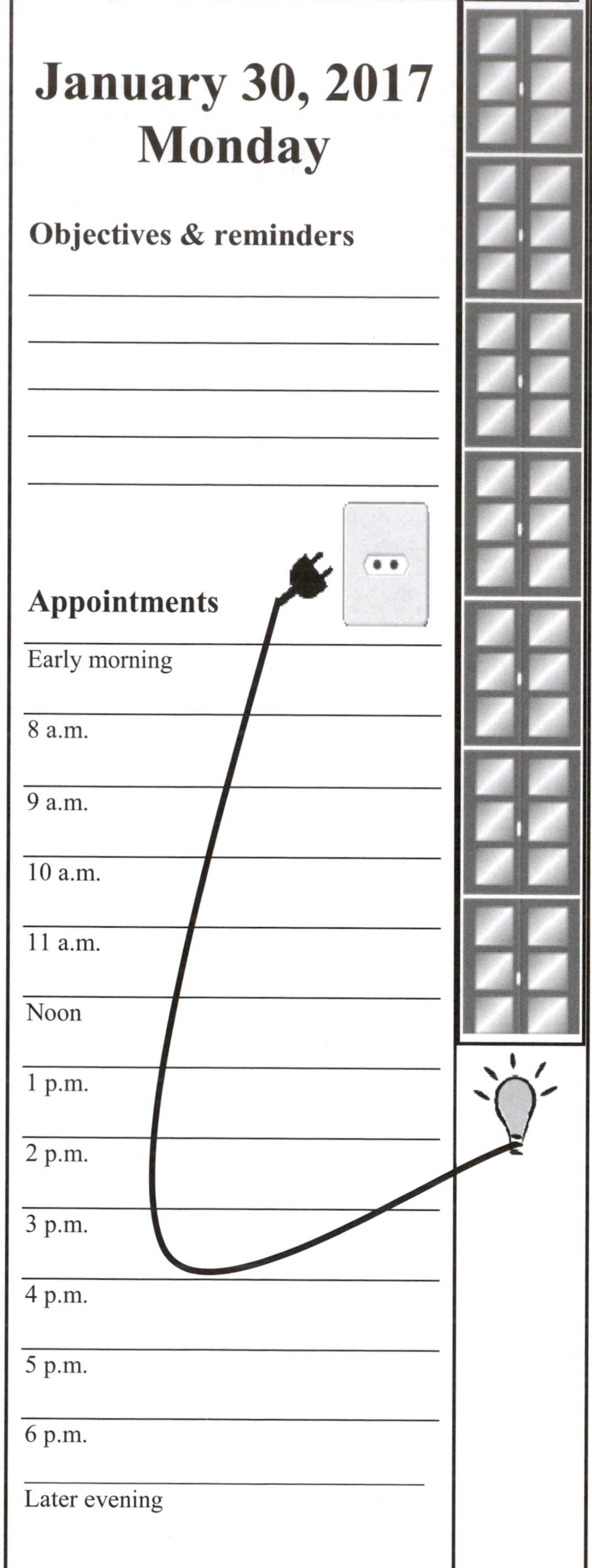

January 30, 2017 Monday

Objectives & reminders

Appointments

Early morning

8 a.m.

9 a.m.

10 a.m.

11 a.m.

Noon

1 p.m.

2 p.m.

3 p.m.

4 p.m.

5 p.m.

6 p.m.

Later evening

The solution: GE window fans?

"Market windows open and shut faster than ever. Product life cycles that were once measured in years now typically last for months -- even weeks." -- Jack Welch, then chairman and CEO of General Electric, January 30, 1997

Opportunities

"*Market windows*" (or *strategic windows*) have to do with the timing of business opportunities. The window metaphor is used to suggest that there are only limited time periods during which opportunities can be seized effectively. Firms must be "open" to jumping through open windows, but move on or wait when facing closed windows.

50 million customers, more than 50 million windows!

On January 30, 1954, the 50 millionth customer was connected to electrical lines in the U.S. At that time, an estimated 98 percent of U.S. households had electricity.

Today, companies marketing a variety of electrical appliances and gadgets in the U.S. assume prospective customers have electrical outlets for the appliances. Outside of the U.S. and other industrialized countries, however, that's a bad assumption. In developing countries around the world, only about 32 percent of consumers have electricity in their homes.

For global firms, this reality raises some interesting and important questions. For example, can "electrical" appliances be re-engineered (or retro-engineered) to operate manually without electricity? Products believed to be obsolete in industrialized countries may be in demand in developing markets around the world.

When electricity first reaches a developing community, what electrical devices are likely to generate the greatest initial demand? After most consumers in the community have those devices, which electrical devices will be in demand next? And so on. So, when should a manufacturer of electric pencil sharpeners, for example, enter the market, versus a firm that makes portable electric fans, radios, or hot plates?

January 31, 2017
Tuesday

Objectives & reminders

____

____

Appointments

Early morning

8 a.m.

9 a.m.

10 a.m.

11 a.m.

Noon

1 p.m.

2 p.m.

3 p.m.

4 p.m.

5 p.m.

6 p.m.

Later evening

Words matter, competition matters

The words people use to express their ideas on the job affect not only communication, but word choice can affect the way workers think and feel too. For example, after an antitrust suit was filed against IBM on January 31, 1969, IBM managers were asked not to use competition-related words such as *market, marketplace, market share, competitor, competition, dominant, lead, win,* and *beat* in either written materials or in internal meetings.

Louis V. Gerstner, who later became chairman and CEO of IBM, claimed that the ban on such words contributed to the firm's erosion of competitiveness in the years that followed. According to Gerstner, "Imagine the dampening effect on a workforce that can't even talk about selecting a market or taking share from a competitor. After a while, it goes beyond what is said to what is thought." Eventually the suit was dropped.

Did you know this about January 31?

1750 The first university magazine was published, by John Newbery. The publication was aptly named *Student* – for students at England's Oxford University. Today, most institutions of higher learning have one or more publications that specifically target students.

1940 The first Social Security check was issued – to 65-year-old retiree Ida May Fuller of Ludlow, Vermont. Check number 00-000-001 was for $22.54. Ms. Fuller lived another 35 years and received almost $23,000 in Social Security benefits before her death in 1975. In 2015, 42 million Americans received monthly Social Security retirement benefits averaging $1,328 for individuals and $2,176 for couples. These benefits ease the financial burden of retirement and help make the seniors market a potentially profitable one for organizations that serve them.

1956 The twist-off bottle cap was invented. Prior to twist-off caps, some soft-drink sales were lost when bottle-openers were nowhere to be found.

Never take a marble for granite! Visit Marketing FAME's official resource support website: www.MarketingMarbles.com

I love the extra resources and materials posted frequently.

The article about calendars as marketing planning tools is my favorite. It's marbleous.

- Test your comprehension by working the sample exercises and taking the practice quizzes posted periodically.
- Read more about the roles that calendars play in marketing and buyer behavior. For example, learn how nature's calendar, different cultures' calendars, and legal calendars affect marketing practices and buyer behavior.
- Learn more about what it means to be "calendar-led." Determine if you are calendar-led.
- Discover how you could contribute to future editions of *Marketing FAME*.
- Find out about the *Marketing FAME* contests that you could enter.
- Communicate with the author and publishing team through the website's "Contact" page.
- Stay tuned for news and updates.

Visit the website regularly, as the content changes often.

February 1, 2017
Wednesday

Objectives & reminders

____

____

____

Appointments

Early morning

8 a.m.

9 a.m.

10 a.m.

11 a.m.

Noon

1 p.m.

2 p.m.

3 p.m.

4 p.m.

5 p.m.

6 p.m.

Later evening

Not what Mr. Woolworth intended?

Frank W. Woolworth opened his first Woolworth's discount variety store in 1879. Almost 81 years later, on February 1, 1960, four college freshmen -- all African-Americans -- ordered hamburgers and Coca-Colas at a "whites only" Woolworth's lunch counter in Greensboro, North Carolina. The waitress refused to serve them.

In response to the disservice, the college students remained seated at the lunch counter for the remainder of the day. They returned the next day with 23 of their classmates and continued the sit-in. Soon after, sit-in demonstrations spread to 71 other cities and caught the attention of businesspeople, public policy makers, consumer advocates, and the general public.

Although such blatant forms of discrimination are illegal today, some businesses and some customer-contact personnel are still accused of systematically treating some customers poorly. Intentionally or not, an estimated 12 percent or more of customer-contact employees vary their service levels based on customers' race, ethnicity, age, gender, attire, grooming, height, weight, attractiveness, language or accent, or other personal factors.

Indeed, *every* consumer may be mistreated from time to time, and few businesses can afford to alienate customers. It makes no marketing sense to discriminate against customers on bases that have nothing to do with their needs, purchase requirements, or ability to buy.

●●●●●●●●●●

Happy birthday: Richard Whately

Born in London on February 1, 1787, Whately became a theological writer and the archbishop of Dublin, Ireland. He died almost 100 years before the Woolworth's lunch counter incident, so we can not know precisely what his reaction to it would have been. However, Whately had a reputation for a keen wit and "blunt outspokenness," so he probably would have said something had he witnessed the Woolworth's sit-in on his birthday in 1960. Some of his comments about the need for timely change could have provided insights for Woolworth's at that time and still can provide guidance today to prevent many types of business crises from exploding.

February 2, 2017
Thursday

Objectives & reminders

____

____

____

Appointments

Early morning

8 a.m.

9 a.m.

10 a.m.

11 a.m.

Noon

1 p.m.

2 p.m.

3 p.m.

4 p.m.

5 p.m.

6 p.m.

Later evening

Groundhog Day

In business and in other spheres of life, some beliefs and practices are driven more by tradition and custom than can be defensibly justified on their own merits. For example, one traditional forecasting belief maintains that if a groundhog can see his shadow on February 2, another six weeks of winter is inevitable. Like most approaches to forecasting, however, the groundhog test is most accurate in the short-term, i.e., if the groundhog can see his shadow today, the sun is probably shining *today*.

First day of Nielsen sweeps

Today begins the first "sweeps" month for 2017, ending on March 1. During this four-week period, ACNielsen Company collects an extensive amount of audience data to determine television program ratings. The ratings, in turn, are used by networks and local stations for a variety of purposes, including the determination of advertising rates across programs, and across calendrical periods, e.g., time-of-day, day-of-week, day/period of year.

Typically, larger audiences translate into higher ratings, which mean higher-priced advertising slots. So, to increase their potential advertising revenues, broadcasters try to boost their ratings during sweep periods by attracting larger audiences. They do this by scheduling programs with extra-appealing content and frequently hyping their programming decisions.

In addition to the helpful audience information and ad pricing implications of sweeps periods, another implication is that the stronger lure of television during sweeps may represent a heightened level of competition for alternative consumer activities – such as shopping at the mall, dining out, and going to the movie theater, as a few examples. Accordingly, mall, restaurant and theater marketers may have to work a bit harder or a bit smarter to attract customers during sweeps periods.

Other sweeps months
"May," "July" and "November" sweeps months scheduled in 2017 begin on April 27, June 29 and October 26, respectively. Each begins on Thursday and ends after four weeks, on Wednesday. For more information, visit www.nielsen.com

February 3, 2017
Friday

Objectives & reminders

____

____

____

Appointments

Early morning

8 a.m.

9 a.m.

10 a.m.

11 a.m.

Noon

1 p.m.

2 p.m.

3 p.m.

4 p.m.

5 p.m.

6 p.m.

Later evening

Paper: The 5th "p"?

February 3 marks the anniversary of the first official use of *paper money* in the western hemisphere when the Massachusetts Bay Colony authorized paper money to be paid to soldiers in 1690.

Prior to the introduction of paper money, coins were the primary method of payment in the North American colonies. Gold and silver coins were welcome, but rare, so unofficial coins (including "decrepit coppers") were minted and circulated.

Today, U.S. marketers tend to rely on multiple methods of payment to facilitate purchase transactions: paper money, coins, personal checks and money orders, credit and debit cards, and so on. As a general rule, the more methods of payment a business accepts, the greater the likelihood and volume of purchase. However, some marketers of discretionary or impulse items prefer cash payments; in addition to the credit-related expenses they prefer to avoid, they note that with cash payments customers receive no monthly bank statements to remind them (and spouses) how much money they spend (waste?) in the category.

P P P P P P P P P P P

Power: Another "p"?

Another marketing-relevant, money-related event also occurred on February 3 -- in 1913 -- when Delaware voted positively to ratify the 16th Amendment to the U.S. Constitution. The amendment granted Congress the *power* to levy taxes on income. Legislation that quickly followed formalized a graduated income tax.

For marketers, income taxes represent both challenges and opportunities. On one hand, income taxes reduce the amount of money consumers and business customers have available to spend, so marketers typically have to work harder to sway purchasers toward their products. But, on the other hand, income taxes are used by the government and their agencies to buy enormous quantities of a large variety of things. Tapping into government markets can be quite lucrative for marketers patient enough to familiarize themselves with the somewhat bureaucratic government purchasing processes.

February 4, 2017
Saturday

Objectives & reminders

Appointments

Early morning

8 a.m.

9 a.m.

10 a.m.

11 a.m.

Noon

1 p.m.

2 p.m.

3 p.m.

4 p.m.

5 p.m.

6 p.m.

Later evening

Happy birthday: Charles Augustus Lindbergh

Born in Detroit, Michigan on February 4, 1902, Lindbergh's love of flight prompted him to buy his own plane and become an airmail pilot at the age of 23.

Soon after he began flying, Lindbergh responded to the lure of a $25,000 prize offered to anyone who could first fly from New York to Paris non-stop. On May 20-21, 1927, he accomplished the feat in less than 34 hours in a monoplane he named "The Spirit of St. Louis." The distinction of being both courageous and "first" made "Lucky Lindy" Lindbergh a national hero.

> **Need publicity?**
> Stage a contest. Name it. Promote it. Offer a prize. Associate with the winner.

But, the first flight from New York to Paris propelled more than Lindbergh's reputation and career. It, and the huge amount of publicity that accompanied the event, served a vital purpose for the aviation industry as well. Up until Lindbergh's famous flight, the general public did not view aviation as a serious means of transportation. With Lindbergh, public perceptions changed and the skies were cleared for the rapid take-off of commercial aviation which followed.

Interstate Commerce Act (1887)

The first federal regulatory commission in the U.S. was created by Congress on February 4, 1887, when it passed the Interstate Commerce Act (ICA). The ICA established the Interstate Commerce Commission (ICC) – a five-member board expected to oversee common carriers (railroads at that time) involved in the transportation of freight across state borders. The commission was charged with the responsibility of licensing the common carriers and ensuring that their freight rates were "just and reasonable." That is, the ICA prohibited discriminatory pricing practices. In the years that followed, additional legislation sought to shore-up some of the weaknesses of the ICA (e.g., Elkins Act of 1903) and broaden the authority of the ICC (e.g., Hepburn Act of 1906).

February 5, 2017
Sunday

Objectives & reminders

____

____

____

Appointments

Early morning

8 a.m.

9 a.m.

10 a.m.

11 a.m.

Noon

1 p.m.

2 p.m.

3 p.m.

4 p.m.

5 p.m.

6 p.m.

Later evening

Super Bowl 51

The final football game of the postseason -- the Super Bowl -- and the festivities that surround it have made the first Sunday in February a *de facto* national holiday in the United States. The annual championship game began in 1967, but has evolved into more than simply a football game. Today, Super Bowl Sunday (SBS) also means food, parties, half-time entertainment, and the launch of dazzling new advertising campaigns.

For television advertisers, the Super Bowl provides the opportunity to reach an estimated 80 to 90 million Americans (130-140 million watch at least a portion of the game). Almost half of the viewers are women. Given the large audience, a 30-second ad spot during the Super Bowl can cost a few million dollars.

Since 1984 when Apple Computer successfully used the Super Bowl to introduce its Macintosh computer, dozens of firms have used extravagant commercials during the Super Bowl to introduce new products or new campaigns. Interestingly, the Super Bowl is one of the very few television programs that attracts an audience specifically interested in watching the commercials.

Rolling the dice: Agree or disagree? Over the years, some dot.coms and other firms have chosen to spend all or almost all of their annual advertising budgets on a single Super Bowl advertisement. Good idea?

Food and parties are closely associated with the Super Bowl. Except for Thanksgiving Day, more food is consumed in the U.S. on SBS than on any other day of the year. SBS is Domino's (pizza) busiest day of the year; they deliver about 1.2 million pizzas on SBS (about twice as many as an average Sunday). The Snack Food Association estimates that more than 30 million pounds of snacks are eaten on SBS. And, according to The Beer Institute and other estimates, almost 3.5 percent of annual beer sales are tallied during the week leading up to SBS -- an incremental increase of 900,000 cases.

February 6, 2017
Monday

Objectives & reminders

____

____

____

Appointments

Early morning

8 a.m.

9 a.m.

10 a.m.

11 a.m.

Noon

1 p.m.

2 p.m.

3 p.m.

4 p.m.

5 p.m.

6 p.m.

Later evening

Shared success trait: George Herman Ruth and Ronald Reagan

What does home-run-hitting baseball great George Herman "Babe" Ruth have in common with the 40th President of the United States, Ronald Reagan? First, they were both born on February 6 (Ruth in 1895; Reagan in 1911).

Second, neither Ruth nor Reagan were afraid of taking risks. Ruth swung the bat hard in an effort to hit home runs, knowing that he might -- and did, quite often -- strike out. Depending on one's political perspective, Reagan never struck out, but he did take a risk when he traded his established career as an actor for one in politics -- serving as governor of California (1967-1975) and two-term President of the United States (1981-1989).

Business decisions frequently involve risks too, and while reckless risk-taking is not advised, accepting the inevitable necessity to face risk and make decisions is essential to an effective career in business.

Baseball
"I swing as hard as I can, and I try to swing right through the ball... I swing big, with everything I've got. I hit big or I miss big. I like to live as big as I can." -- Babe Ruth

Business
"Free enterprise is a rough and competitive game. It is a hell of a lot better than a government monopoly."
-- Ronald Reagan

Waitangi Day (also known as New Zealand Day)

February 6 is a national holiday in New Zealand to commemorate the anniversary of the Treaty of Waitangi signed on February 6, 1840. The treaty between the British and the Maori established New Zealand as a British colony, although the anniversary of the treaty did not become an official national public holiday until 1974. Although some Maori people have staged protests regarding the treaty, more typically the holiday is characterized by celebrations involving parades, church services, and other events.

February 7, 2017
Tuesday

Objectives & reminders

Appointments

Early morning

8 a.m.

9 a.m.

10 a.m.

11 a.m.

Noon

1 p.m.

2 p.m.

3 p.m.

4 p.m.

5 p.m.

6 p.m.

Later evening

Rural America & Small Town (RAST) Day

Collectively, RAST markets are simply too big for marketers to ignore. About 24 percent of Americans live in small towns or rural areas (although historically the percentages have been much greater: e.g., 94% in 1800, 85% in 1850, 60% in 1900, and 36% in 1950).

RAST Day is unofficial, but appropriate, because the evolution of rural America and small towns probably would have followed a different path had it not been for some innovators and businesspeople like John Deere.

Happy birthday: John Deere

John Deere was born in Rutland, Vermont on February 7, 1804. The company he founded, Deere & Company, still thrives today. Mr. Deere developed the first American cast steel plow and invented or improved other farming-related implements. Such innovations contributed to the well being of farmers, and by doing so, helped to "cultivate" the broader RAST market. But Deere was more than an inventor; he was a successful businessman too. By the mid-1850s he was selling 13,000 plows annually.

On John Deere's 80th birthday, Deere's son-in-law and the company's treasurer, Stephen H. Velie, attributed much of Mr. Deere's success to his ability to focus:

> "[H]e owes his success to hard work, integrity of purpose, and a natural faculty of concentrating all his powers on 'one thing at a time.' Whenever he set about doing anything it seemed to be decided in his mind that that was the right thing to do and now was the time to do it."

Today, many businesses strive to adhere to the principle of focus or concentration en route to pursuing a competitive advantage in the marketplace. They ask basic self-assessment questions such as: "What business are we in?" "What do we do best?" "What are the most profitable parts of our business?" "Which parts of our business are essential?" These questions lead them to debate which business functions can be eliminated or outsourced.

February 8, 2017
Wednesday

Objectives & reminders

____

____

____

Appointments

Early morning

8 a.m.

9 a.m.

10 a.m.

11 a.m.

Noon

1 p.m.

2 p.m.

3 p.m.

4 p.m.

5 p.m.

6 p.m.

Later evening

Happy birthday: Boy Scouts of America

Chicago publisher William D. Boyce found himself lost in the fog while in London in 1909. Fortunately for Boyce, a "Scout" assisted him but refused to accept a tip for doing a "Good Turn." Boyce was so impressed that he met with the founder of the British Boy Scouts, Sir Robert Baden-Powell, to learn more about the organization. This meeting eventually led to Boyce forming the Boy Scouts of America (BSA) on February 8, 1910.

As of 2013, there were more than 2.6 million Boy Scouts and 105,000 adult volunteers who belonged to more than 105,000 troops, packs, or teams scattered across all 50 states.

Value-able organization
"Because of Scouting principles, I know I was a better athlete, I was a better naval officer, I was a better Congressman, and I was a better prepared President." – Gerald Ford, Boy Scout & 38th U.S. President

There are dozens of ways businesses and business leaders can recognize and support local Boy Scouts. Here are a few possibilities:

1. Partnering with Scouts to tackle community service projects (e.g., offer to provide equipment, supplies and pizza for Scouts to join with company employees in cleaning up vacant lots in the community).
2. Assisting Scouts with their fundraising efforts. Who says only *Girl* Scouts can sell cookies?
3. Sponsoring field trips for Scouts interested in touring the business and learning about the company's products and processes.
4. Volunteering as merit badge counselors for merit badge topics particularly related to the business.
5. Offering the company's facilities as a meeting place for local Scouts.
6. Staging special "Scouts only" sales events, contests, or other promotions (e.g., offer rewards to Scouts when they're promoted).

February 9, 2017
Thursday

Objectives & reminders

____

____

____

Appointments

Early morning

8 a.m.

9 a.m.

10 a.m.

11 a.m.

Noon

1 p.m.

2 p.m.

3 p.m.

4 p.m.

5 p.m.

6 p.m.

Later evening

History repeating itself

The business history of industrialized countries provides numerous insights in terms of how to best tap emerging markets around the world. That's because the patterns of market development in emerging markets often resemble those that occurred previously in more developed markets.

For example, in the late 1920s and 1930s General Motors (GM) gobbled-up market share in the U.S. partly because they were willing to vary their product line and target specific income segments with specific models (e.g., Chevrolets for lower-income families; Cadillacs for higher-income families; Pontiacs, Oldsmobiles, and Buicks for those in between). As American prosperity grew over the decades, buyers found themselves trading-up from one GM product to another.

Amazing statistic

Twenty times more Chinese consumers owned driving licenses in 2014 than in 2001.

Today, GM is committing several billion dollars to build plants in China and is following a similar strategy with Chevrolets, Buicks, and Cadillacs. Although not all Chinese will be able to afford quality automobiles right away, GM plans to establish a strong presence in China to capitalize on the Chinese consumers' interest in automobiles as their prosperity grows.

Straight from the CEO

"[P]eople [in China] who can only buy [cheap products now in segments we don't want to compete in] with cash up front will be able to use that money as a down payment and get retail financing to buy a bigger, better car. It… will clearly happen over time... It is pretty much the way we created GM in the U.S. market. This is 75 years later, the closest thing we've seen to that, in China. The idea is market segmentation and the use of the brands." -- Rick Wagoner, Jr., then chairman & CEO of General Motors, born in Wilmington, Delaware on February 9, 1953

February 10, 2017
Friday

Objectives & reminders

____

____

Appointments

Early morning

8 a.m.

9 a.m.

10 a.m.

11 a.m.

Noon

1 p.m.

2 p.m.

3 p.m.

4 p.m.

5 p.m.

6 p.m.

Later evening

Good news, bad news

Slogans can be powerful messages that signal to customers, employees and other constituencies the organization's values, purpose, and position. Slogans let the world know what the company stands for, what the company believes to be important, or why their brands are distinctive. Ideally, slogans should be engaging, memorable, meaningful, enduring, used regularly, and associated with the company or brand.

Today marks the anniversary of one of the oldest slogans still in use. That is, on February 10, 1897, *The New York Times* first claimed to report "All the news that's fit to print." In today's edition of the newspaper, the slogan may be found on the front page, near the upper left-hand corner.

Decades after the slogan was first used, the newspaper staged a contest to challenge readers to formulate a better slogan (which is a great way to generate feedback, get customers involved and garner some publicity too), but management decided that none of the entries improved upon the original slogan (it is not clear whether any of the entries were fit to print).

Speaking sloganese

Recognize these slogans?

1. "When you care enough to send the very best."
2. "Quality is Job 1."
3. "You're in good hands with ________."
4. "You can't eat just one."
5. "Nobody doesn't like _________."

●●●●●●●●●●

Enjoy the journey

"Often the search proves more profitable than the goal." -- E.L. Konigsburg, American author, born on February 10, 1930

A matter of perspective

"Don't call the world dirty because you forgot to clean your glasses." -- Aaron Hill, British writer, born on February 10, 1685

February 11, 2017
Saturday

Objectives & reminders

____

____

____

Appointments

Early morning

8 a.m.

9 a.m.

10 a.m.

11 a.m.

Noon

1 p.m.

2 p.m.

3 p.m.

4 p.m.

5 p.m.

6 p.m.

Later evening

Time to relax?

February 11, 1928 was a big day for Ed Shoemaker and his cousin Edward Knabusch. On that day, they invented the La-Z-Boy reclining chair. Their first design was a slat porch chair made with a piece of plywood. Because the demand for the porch chair design was believed to be somewhat seasonal, the next year the two synchromarketing-minded entrepreneurs went on to design upholstered chairs for year-round indoor use.

What a brand name says

Much of a brand's potential marketing potency is lost when it's assigned an uninspiring or commodity-like name that says little to describe or differentiate the product or company -- such as Ed & Ed's Chair, or even worse, Chair Model 297. But "La-Z-Boy" communicates with prospective buyers -- reinforcing the relaxing, comfortable and casual nature of the brand. Note that many other successful brands also have names that communicate with buyers:

Huggies: diapers that fit close to prevent accidents.

Head & Shoulders: shampoo that controls dandruff to prevent embarrassing dandruff flakes from falling onto users' shoulders.

Mop 'n Glow: floor-cleaner that also leaves a shiny surface.

Happy birthday: Mary Quant

Born on February 11, 1934, Quant was a British fashion designer who recognized the potential of brands to have "personalities" and thus to evoke consumers' emotions. Sexuality-related emotions seemed to be the key emotions that Quant's designs evoked. Beginning in the late 1950s and continuing into the 1960s, Quant operationalized the notion that "less is more" as the women's skirts and shorts she designed ungrew shorter and shorter, which led some to credit her with the invention of the mini-skirt and "hot pants" (although some sources credit other designers with these innovations).

February 12, 2017
Sunday

Objectives & reminders

____

____

Appointments

Early morning

8 a.m.

9 a.m.

10 a.m.

11 a.m.

Noon

1 p.m.

2 p.m.

3 p.m.

4 p.m.

5 p.m.

6 p.m.

Later evening

Happy Birthday: Abraham Lincoln

Born in Hardin County, Kentucky on February 12, 1809, Lincoln went on to become the 16th President of the United States. His presidency (1861-1865) spanned the trying Civil War years. Some historians believe Lincoln was the country's greatest president, attributed in part to his superb human relations skills. For example, Lincoln once asserted, "He has a right to criticize, who has a heart to help."

Planning insights also applicable to businesses

At a news briefing on February 12, 2002, Donald H. Rumsfeld, then U.S. Secretary of Defense, offered the following insights regarding planning in the face of uncertainty:

> "Reports that say that something hasn't happened are always interesting to me, because as we know, there are *known knowns*; there are things we know we know. We also know there are *known unknowns*; that is to say we know there are some things we do not know. But there are also *unknown unknowns* -- the ones we don't know we don't know. And if one looks throughout the history of our country and other free countries, it is the latter category that tend to be the difficult ones."

On the same day 26 years earlier (February 12, 1976), the production of Red Dye #2 was banned in the U.S. The dye had been a fairly common ingredient in many food, drug and cosmetic products. Unfortunately, however, studies indicated that the ingredient was carcinogenic, which prompted the ban by the U.S. Food and Drug Administration. At the time, manufacturers may not have known that Red Dye #2 caused cancer, but those that recognized the possibility that ingredients could prove to be problematic for any of a variety of possible reasons ("known unknowns") were more likely to be prepared to substitute ingredients than those that assumed their product formulations were invincible ("unknown unknowns"). In other words, businesses are less likely to be taken by surprise and planning efforts are enhanced when as many of the "unknown unknowns" as possible are identified and, by doing so, move them into the "known unknowns" category.

February 13, 2017
Monday

Objectives & reminders

____

____

____

Appointments

Early morning

8 a.m.

9 a.m.

10 a.m.

11 a.m.

Noon

1 p.m.

2 p.m.

3 p.m.

4 p.m.

5 p.m.

6 p.m.

Later evening

February 13 Business Birthday Club

1933: Leeann Chin

Founder of the Chinese restaurant chain that bears her name, Leeann Chin, Inc. On the *importance of being in the market and involving employees*, Chin points out:

> "I travel, in [the United States] and in China, to develop new recipes and learn about new foods and changes in customer taste. I take our people on some of those trips with me. You can't just tell people things and expect them to learn, you have to show them."

1940: Robert J. Eaton

Former chairman and co-CEO of DaimlerChrysler Corp. Eaton weighs-in on the *distinction between management and leadership*:

> "I think people at the top of large corporations aren't -- or shouldn't -- be devoting very much time to management. Most of their time should be going toward leadership. ... [T]here isn't enough time for executives to manage, to control, to track results. You need to focus on vision and beliefs and values and inspiring people and breaking roadblocks for people to be able to accomplish more."

1947: Antony Burgmans

Former chairman of Unilever N.V., Burgmans uses a metaphor to explain why *companies should focus their resources* (after embarking on a program in 2003 to cut the number of Unilever brands from 1,600 to 400):

> "If you plant all the seeds you have in your garden... they will not grow well. With ample space... they will grow swiftly. The same applies to business. With less brands and use of more management resources for them, the brands are certain to grow."

February 14, 2017
Tuesday
Valentine's Day

Objectives & reminders

Remember to buy a box of Valentine's Day cards, the ones that say "you're the only one for me!" They're on sale this week... 12 cards for $1.89 !

Appointments

Early morning

8 a.m.

9 a.m.

10 a.m.

11 a.m.

Noon

1 p.m.

2 p.m.

3 p.m.

4 p.m.

5 p.m.

6 p.m.

Later evening

Businesses enjoy Valentine's Day

Some products and gift items are closely associated with specific holidays – turkeys and Thanksgiving, pumpkins and Halloween, fireworks on Independence Day, and so on. Today and the last few days leading up to Valentine's Day have generated much higher-than-average demand for the 53,000 flower shops in the U.S. If this Valentine's season resembles those of recent years, more than 150 million roses will be sold. It is not unusual for the typical florist's workload to increase seven to ten times during this period. In 2015, for example, 24 percent of U.S. adults bought flowers or plants as Valentine's Day gifts. Of these, nearly two-thirds purchased red roses.

However, businesses need not depend on flowers to tap into Valentine's Day. Other high-demand product categories include: candy/chocolate, stuffed animals, jewelry, greeting cards, and dining/entertainment. Creative possibilities are numerous. For example, restaurants offer free "kisses" today (made with Hershey's chocolate) and hotels offer "get-away" Valentine's Day mini-vacation packages.

Was St. Valentine a *young* Saint?
The correlation between age and Valentine's Day spending is a negative one. That is, younger adults tend to spend more money for Valentine's Day than do older consumers. On average, 18-to-34-year-olds plan to spend the most (about $140). Consumers in the 35-54 age category are less enthusiastic (about $60), followed by older consumers at least 55 years of age (less than $50).

Mixing politics, history and romance on Valentine's Day

Established in 1933, Martin's Tavern in Washington, D.C. has the inside track on Valentine's Day promotions. It seems that their booth #3 is where John F. Kennedy proposed marriage to Jacqueline Bouvier in 1953 (Kennedy was the 35th President of the U.S., from 1961 to 1963). To commemorate the event and allow other couples to share the Kennedy moment, the tavern accepts wedding proposal reservations for the same booth… and has plenty of champagne on hand.

February 15, 2017
Wednesday

Objectives & reminders

Adopt a stray dog for life today?

Appointments

Early morning

8 a.m.

9 a.m.

10 a.m.

11 a.m.

Noon

1 p.m.

2 p.m.

3 p.m.

4 p.m.

5 p.m.

6 p.m.

Later evening

Does advertising pay?

Apparently so. Campbell's soups were advertised for the first time on February 15, 1899. Eighty-eight years later at least one heir of the soup giant continued to receive dividends of $73,644 *daily*.

When to advertise? During "happy time," of course

American jeweler Charles Lewis Tiffany was born in Killingly, Connecticut on February 15, 1812. Today, marketers for the store he founded -- Tiffany's -- believe in advertising. For example, they advertise fine watches in *The Wall Street Journal* which include pictures of the watches displaying the time of approximately ten minutes after ten o'clock.

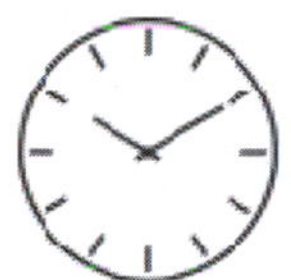

The 10:10 advertising practice is an industry-wide convention for featured time pieces with traditional "hands." The practice has to do with the nonverbal signals conveyed by time pieces' hand positions. In other words, nonverbal hand gestures and the inferences that others make from them are not strictly human phenomena. Examples: A watch set at 9:15 or 2:45 is too rigid or too corny. Those displaying 12:00 are too arrogant. Eight-twenty or 2:40? No, too negative. And, of course, 5:29 and 6:31 are ineffective too (too shy). It seems that from about 10:08 to 10:12 is the ideal period to be photographed if you're a watch or clock – that's when you're welcoming, optimistic, enthusiastic, and happy. What prospective buyer could resist a time piece with a predisposition like that!

Unannounced life transition points

"Sooner or later we all discover that the important moments in life are not the advertised ones, not the birthdays, the graduations, the weddings, not the great goals achieved. The real milestones are less prepossessing. They come to the door of memory unannounced, stray dogs that amble in, sniff around a bit and simply never leave. Our lives are measured by these." -- Susan B. Anthony, American reformer/suffragist, born on February 15, 1820

February 16, 2017
Thursday

Objectives & reminders

____

____

____

Appointments

Early morning

8 a.m.

9 a.m.

10 a.m.

11 a.m.

Noon

1 p.m.

2 p.m.

3 p.m.

4 p.m.

5 p.m.

6 p.m.

Later evening

Check this

February 16 marks the anniversary of the first known check, drawn on a British bank for £400 in the year 1659. The check appears remarkably similar to today's checks with the payer's and payee's names included along with the sum written in both words and figures. The oldest surviving *printed* check was issued 104 years later, in 1763.

Today, although checking systems are common in industrialized countries and checking accounts are among the first banking products American consumers obtain, checking does not exist everywhere around the globe. Cash is still king.

Thank you, Dr. Carothers

A patent was issued on February 16, 1937, to Dr. Wallace H. Carothers who worked for the American chemical company, E.I. du Pont de Nemours. The patent was for the first man-made fiber, called nylon. Over the years nylon proved to have several applications. The first commercial products using nylon were toothbrushes made with nylon bristles, introduced in 1938. Nylon yarn followed in late 1939; by mid-May 1940 several hosiery manufacturers throughout the United States introduced their brands of nylon stockings.

Happy birthday: Dick McDonald

Richard "Dick" McDonald, one of the original McDonald brothers -- of fast-food hamburger fame -- was born on February 16, 1909. Dick enjoys the distinction of having cooked the first McDonald's hamburger. Decades later, in 1984, he was honored in a ceremony in which he served the 50,000,000,000th McDonald's burger.

Any survivors? 
It is not known how many of those 50 billion burgers still exist today.

Today, the McDonald's Corporation knows that the success of the company is not about hamburgers, per se. The company recognizes the importance of the total customer experience with their four key watchwords: quality, value, cleanliness, and service.

February 17, 2017
Friday

Objectives & reminders

Appointments

Early morning

8 a.m.

9 a.m.

10 a.m.

11 a.m.

Noon

1 p.m.

2 p.m.

3 p.m.

4 p.m.

5 p.m.

6 p.m.

Later evening

Probably not *Star Wars*

What was possibly the first movie on a commercial airline flight was shown on February 17, 1929. Twelve passengers on the Universal Air Line flight from Minneapolis/St. Paul to Chicago watched the ten-reel motion picture as a technician operated the projector. Although the airline did not report the title of the film, it may have been a "talkie."

Today, movies and other entertainment options are common on commercial flights -- especially longer flights. On the surface, marketers know that movies can enhance passengers' perceived value of the flight. But they also recognize the marketing-relevance of some deeper psychological issues. First, movies help to distract anxious passengers who may fear flying. Less anxiety means a more positive flying experience, and thus a greater likelihood of future flights.

Second, although marketers know that consumers generally dislike waiting, there's not much marketers can do to shorten actual flight times, but they can shorten passengers' *perceived* flight time. Movies, magazines, and other entertainment, as well as food, drink and comfortable seats help the time to *seem* to pass more quickly -- thus enhancing passengers' flying experience.

Three other ways perceptions of waiting are affected

Mirrors placed next to elevators in tall buildings invite passengers to comb their hair, check their make-up, or adjust their attire -- thus distracting their focus from the length of the wait.

Pagers loaned to restaurant patrons waiting for tables make the waiting process more palatable than idly standing in line. The pagers grant patrons the freedom to stroll around the premises, or even off premises. The pagers summon customers when their tables are ready.

Interesting decor in any service environment stirs the senses and prompts customer-to-customer conversation, thus positively distracting customers and making the waiting process seem more reasonable.

February 18, 2017
Saturday

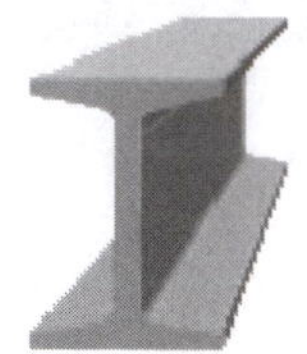

Objectives & reminders

____

____

Appointments

Early morning

8 a.m.

9 a.m.

10 a.m.

11 a.m.

Noon

1 p.m.

2 p.m.

3 p.m.

4 p.m.

5 p.m.

6 p.m.

Later evening

Happy birthday: Charles Michael Schwab

Born in Williamsburg, Pennsylvania on February 18, 1862, Charles M. Schwab became a key figure in the U.S. steel industry. He began his steel career working for industrialist Andrew Carnegie, eventually becoming president of Carnegie Steel Company in 1896. Shortly thereafter, the company's assets changed hands and emerged as U.S. Steel Corporation, which Schwab also ran (1901-1903). In 1903, Schwab left U.S. Steel to lead Bethlehem Steel Company (as president [1903-1913], and chairman [1913-1939]) which then grew to become a dominant force in the industry -- largely attributed to the company's development of the H-beam which spurred a building boom and made feasible the construction of skyscrapers.

Friendly advice
"Be friends with everybody. When you have friends you will know there is somebody who will stand by you. You know the old saying, that if you have a single enemy you will find him everywhere. It doesn't pay to make enemies. Lead the life that will make you kindly and friendly to every one about you, and you will be surprised what a happy life you will live."
-- Charles M. Schwab

Part of Schwab's success may be attributed to his visionary leadership. He dreamed big dreams and was willing to accept the accompanying risks, once noting, "if we are going bust, we will go bust big." Moreover, he recognized that dreams are only a starting point; dreams must be turned into plans and those plans implemented before success is realized.

So, Schwab's visionary approach to business included not only ambitious big pictures, but also many of the details necessary to develop the pictures into three-dimensional realities: "A man to carry on a successful business must have imagination. He must see things as in a vision, a dream of the whole thing."

February 19, 2017
Sunday

Objectives & reminders

____

____

____

Appointments

Early morning

8 a.m.

9 a.m.

10 a.m.

11 a.m.

Noon

1 p.m.

2 p.m.

3 p.m.

4 p.m.

5 p.m.

6 p.m.

Later evening

Nicolaus Copernicus: Not the center of the universe

On February 19, 1473, noted astronomer Nicolaus Copernicus was born. Copernicus advanced the proposition that the Earth orbits around the Sun annually while rotating on its axis daily. His contributions advanced our understanding of the cyclical aspects of nature's calendar and the leadership role nature plays in shaping buyers' and sellers' calendars. For example, understanding when the sun rises and sets each day influences the timing of indoor vs outdoor activities, as do seasonal changes in temperature and precipitation.

Copernicus's suggestion that the Earth was not the center of the universe was hard for many people of Copernicus's era to accept. Today it remains difficult for "ethnocentric" businesspeople to accept the notion that the Earth does not revolve around their domestic market. In the U.S., for example, some ethnocentric managers make business decisions from an American point of view; they consider the American market as primary and "foreign" markets as secondary – perhaps not realizing that more than 95 percent of the world's population lives *outside* of the U.S.

More consumer convenience created

To mass-produce and market his brand of ready-to-eat "corn flakes," Will Keith Kellogg incorporated the Battle Creek Toasted Corn Flake Company in Battle Creek, Michigan on February 19, 1906. In 1922, the name of the company was changed to the more familiar Kellogg Company. Today, Kellogg's Toasted Corn Flakes are still found on grocers' shelves, along with other popular Kellogg brands such as All-Bran (introduced in 1916), Rice Krispies (1928), and many others.

Kellogg not ethnocentric
Will Keith Kellogg was one of the first founders of an American consumer packaged goods company to recognize the potential of the *global* marketplace. He began selling corn flakes in Canada as early as 1914. A decade later, he built a manufacturing plant in Sydney, Australia -- followed by facilities in Manchester, England in 1938. Today, Kellogg brands are available in 180 countries around the world.

February 20, 2017
Monday
Presidents' Day

Objectives & reminders

____

____

____

Appointments

Early morning

8 a.m.

9 a.m.

10 a.m.

11 a.m.

Noon

1 p.m.

2 p.m.

3 p.m.

4 p.m.

5 p.m.

6 p.m.

Later evening

Presidents' Day

The third Monday of each February is set aside as Presidents' Day, on which all U.S. Presidents are honored. Because Presidents George Washington (1st President) and Abraham Lincoln (16th President) were born during the month of February (i.e., February 22 and 12, respectively), the holiday recognizes these great Presidents in particular.

Accordingly, Presidents' Day celebrations and promotions often incorporate images of Washington and Lincoln, as well as more general patriotic themes using images of the U.S. flag or red, white and blue color combinations (i.e., colors of the U.S. flag). Also, fireworks and the playing of the National Anthem are heard on Presidents' Day.

Presidents' Day is generally designated as a non-working holiday for U.S. federal employees -- one of about a dozen such holidays for federal workers set aside each year. State and local governments, as well as corporate America often follow the federal government's lead and close for the day – also granting their workers the day off. Thus, Presidents' Day is one of the most widely observed holidays during the year, at least in terms of consumers not reporting to their jobs.

Presidential consumer behavior

Two very general and commonsensical consumer behavior principles are particularly relevant on Presidents' Day. Both of these principles work to the advantage of marketers and event organizers who plan and promote alternative ways for consumers to spend their time and money.

P1 Employed consumers are more likely to shop on days they do not have to work. Similarly, these consumers also are more likely to pursue recreational, leisure and entertainment activities on days they do not have to work.

P2 Consumers are more likely to travel out of town for personal reasons during a three-day weekend than during a more routine two-day weekend.

February 21, 2017
Tuesday

Objectives & reminders

____

____

Appointments

Early morning

8 a.m.

9 a.m.

10 a.m.

11 a.m.

Noon

1 p.m.

2 p.m.

3 p.m.

4 p.m.

5 p.m.

6 p.m.

Later evening

"Plop, plop; fizz, fizz…"

Accompanied by heavy radio advertising, Alka Seltzer was introduced by Miles Laboratories on February 21, 1931. The antacid and headache remedy enjoyed moderate sales success for several years, but sales accelerated when advertising and packaging was used to increase users' rate of consumption. The new ad campaign always showed *two* Alka Seltzer tablets dropped into a glass of water -- implying that users too should use two tablets. The accompanying jingle reinforced the desired behavior: "Plop, plop; fizz, fizz. Oh, what a relief it is!" Similarly, packaging of Alka Seltzer tablets prompted increased consumption; *two* tablets were packaged in each foil.

Today, marketers use several techniques to encourage buyers to use more product and use it more frequently. Here are a few examples:

1. Larger serving sizes. For example, consumers tend to eat larger quantities of cookies when they are larger-sized.
2. Permission sizes. Implying that it's okay or normal to choose larger quantities prompts consumers to do so. For example, consumers gravitate toward larger soft drink sizes when the choices are "small," "*regular*," and "large," rather than when the same alternatives are referred to as "*regular*," "large" and "extra-large."
3. Perishability. If the unused portion of product is likely to spoil, we tend to go ahead and consume it.
4. Awkward packaging. If the package is destroyed when opened (like the packaging of some sandwich cookies), consumers may go ahead and use the entire amount rather than search for an alternative container to store the unused portion.
5. Discounts. If one item sells for a dollar, but three cost only two dollars, many consumers opt to buy three and then consume three.
6. Taste. When food products are tasty, larger quantities are frequently eaten.
7. Alternative uses. Like Alka Seltzer (antacid *and* headache remedy), multiple uses means more reasons to consume.
8. Variety. Additional flavors, colors, or styles help to avoid consumer boredom and stimulate additional consumption.

February 22, 2017
Wednesday

Objectives & reminders

____

____

____

Appointments

Early morning

8 a.m.

9 a.m.

10 a.m.

11 a.m.

Noon

1 p.m.

2 p.m.

3 p.m.

4 p.m.

5 p.m.

6 p.m.

Later evening

Happy birthday: Adolphe Quételet

Born in Belgium on February 22, 1796, Quételet was a numbers person. In particular, he was interested in probabilities. He learned that the distribution of values for many attributes of people and objects tended to fall in a predictable pattern clustered around the mean or average value of all the observations in the distribution, but that only a few values were actually "average." He referred to this phenomenon as the "law of deviation from an average" – what we now refer to as the "normal" distribution or curve.

Today, marketers interested in understanding buyers' purchase volume, frequency of store visits, income, age, or dozens of other helpful variables are seldom satisfied knowing the *average* values; they also want to know the *distribution* of these values. Thanks to Quételet's discovery, a sampling of values enables marketers to estimate the shape of the distribution.

Stat man: Did you know?
Quételet also coined the term "statistics." A *statistic* is an estimate derived from a sample of values taken from a larger population about which the researcher is interested in making inferences. *Statistics* is the study of such inferences, conducted, of course, by *statisticians*.

Young role models

"A Scout smiles and whistles under all circumstances." -- Sir Robert Baden-Powell, founder of the British Boy Scouts and the Girl Guides, born on February 22, 1857

Coincidentally, Sir Baden-Powell shared the same birthday with his wife, Olave St. Clair Baden-Powell, who was born in 1889. The two were married in 1912. Olave played an active role in the Girl Guides' movement.

Did you know it was probable?
As Adolphe Quételet might have pointed out, if 30 people are randomly selected, the probability is about 0.7 or 70 percent that two of them will share the same birthday (i.e., the same day of the year, but not necessarily the same year).

February 23, 2017
Thursday

Objectives & reminders

____

____

Appointments

Early morning

8 a.m.

9 a.m.

10 a.m.

11 a.m.

Noon

1 p.m.

2 p.m.

3 p.m.

4 p.m.

5 p.m.

6 p.m.

Later evening

Internal marketing first

The term "customers" usually refers to people and parties outside of the organization that buy the company's goods and services. Sometimes they are described as *external customers*. Clearly, the importance of external customers is undeniable; a business can not survive without external customers with whom to transact business.

Increasingly, however, marketers also consider the importance of *internal customers* -- employees who "buy" their jobs and job responsibilities. These employees must believe in the company and its products before they can convince external customers to do so. Internal marketing is particularly important in service organizations because customer-contact employees in these businesses don't simply *represent* the company to external customers; from external customers' point of view, these employees *are* the company.

One tool used to market to internal customers is the employee magazine. American Express claims to have launched the first such magazine on February 23, 1916, when their company's executive committee first appropriated $15,000 annually for the project.

The first issue of the employee magazine, called *American Express Service*, was born in May of the same year. Featured stories talked about company values, such as personal accountability and commitment. Articles also stressed the important roles that employees play throughout the company. Many of the themes are still relevant today and worth repeating to new generations of service employees.

Timeless insights
"A merchant selling shoes must depend for his business upon the quality of the shoes themselves, whereas an institution such as the American Express, selling service, must depend upon the quality of its [employees]… Upon the combined way in which each of us shoulders this responsibility, depends the success of the Company in merchandising its service." -- excerpt from the first issue of *American Express Service* (1916)

February 24, 2017
Friday

Objectives & reminders

____

____

____

Appointments

Early morning

8 a.m.

9 a.m.

10 a.m.

11 a.m.

Noon

1 p.m.

2 p.m.

3 p.m.

4 p.m.

5 p.m.

6 p.m.

Later evening

Back to basics and balance

Bombarded with deadlines and quotas to meet, meetings to attend, details to address, requests to consider, and job/family demands to balance, it's useful to periodically examine our priorities and evaluate whether the ways in which we invest our time are aligned with our priorities.

Several people share their insights on these matters. For example, Nike co-founder **Philip Knight**, who was born on February 24, 1938, points out that such conflicts are inevitable. He observes: "There is an immutable conflict at work, in life, and in business -- a constant battle between peace and chaos. Neither can be mastered, but both can be influenced. How you go about that is the key to success."

Retired educator **Donald P. Duncan**, who was born on February 24, 1916, offers more specific advice to manage the conflict. He emphasizes the value of distinguishing between the important and not-so-important: "The importance of any particular responsibility changes over time and the good judgment to distinguish at any given time between the important and the less important is paramount."

Steve Jobs, perhaps best known for co-founding Apple Computer, also was born on February 24, in 1955. He argues that people and companies are sometimes guilty of mismanaging their priorities to the point that important deadlines are missed. His philosophy was that "real artists ship," i.e., creative innovations and breakthrough designs are nice, but meeting deadlines is essential.

More recently, on February 24, 2005, **Steve Cruttenden**, marketing director for Rooster (British PR/marketing firm) commented on the tendency for businesses to become overly enamored with (distracted by?) technological possibilities on the Internet -- causing them to sometimes ignore important marketing fundamentals: "The Internet is the most cost-effective marketing tool when used correctly, yet… [m]any online strategies miss... marketing staples such as *creativity*, *key messages* and a *call to action*. We believe that companies willing to grasp the opportunities offered by the web can enjoy powerful results by going back to basics." (emphasis added)

February 25, 2017
Saturday

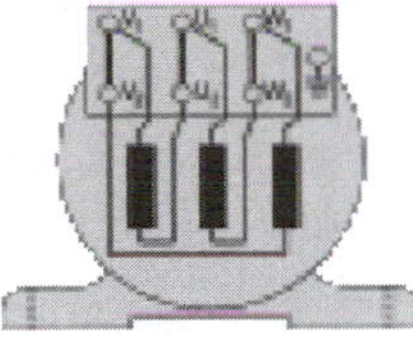

Objectives & reminders

____

____

Appointments

Early morning

8 a.m.

9 a.m.

10 a.m.

11 a.m.

Noon

1 p.m.

2 p.m.

3 p.m.

4 p.m.

5 p.m.

6 p.m.

Later evening

A taxing day

The ratification of the 16th Amendment to the U.S. Constitution was certified as "official" on February 25, 1913, after the required number of states approving the amendment was reached earlier in the month (February 3, 1913). The amendment paved the way for the introduction of a federal income tax.

Six years later, also on February 25, Oregon became the first state to levy a tax on gasoline -- one cent per gallon.

These and other taxes decrease the amount of money consumers have available to spend, thus increasing their sensitivity to prices. However, on the other hand, revenues generated by taxing authorities help to create enormous government markets for businesses to tap.

Power up!

February 25 marks the anniversary of the day in 1837 when a patent was issued to Thomas Davenport of Rutland, Vermont for the first practically-applied electric motor. One of his 50-pound motors was used that year to drill small holes up to ¼ inch in diameter. Another was used to turn hardwood. Both ran at a speed of 450rpm.

Although the motors performed needed functions, the extent to which they were genuinely practical for large-scale industrial applications is a debatable issue. That is, Davenport's motors were battery-powered, a power source that was -- at the time -- about 25 times more expensive than steam power.

The electric motor illustrates the dilemma faced when new products are developed but are not truly independent. That is, when an innovation depends on other products or on an infrastructure, the adoption of the innovation is likely to be slowed. Examples abound: Automobiles require roads and fueling stations. Airplanes need airports or airstrips to take-off and land. Computer hardware is useless without software. And, of course, electric motors need a cost-efficient source of power. Sometimes when businesspeople fear that an innovation may be "ahead of its time," it is the lack of availability or uneconomical nature of these accompanying products and infrastructure that concerns them.

February 26, 2017
Sunday

Objectives & reminders

____

____

Appointments

Early morning

8 a.m.

9 a.m.

10 a.m.

11 a.m.

Noon

1 p.m.

2 p.m.

3 p.m.

4 p.m.

5 p.m.

6 p.m.

Later evening

Food marketing day

"The best to you" on the morning of your birthday: John Harvey Kellogg

Kellogg was born on February 26, 1852, in Tyrone Township, Michigan. After studying medicine, he became a well-regarded surgeon, but soon developed an interest in the dietary needs of his patients at a sanitarium in Battle Creek, Michigan. His nutritionally-enhanced foods found a market which he and his brother Will tapped through their company, Sanitas Food Company. They produced and sold dry wheat, rice, and corn flakes positioned as a breakfast cereal.

Later, the brothers went their separate ways. Will formed the Kellogg Company to market cereals and John formed the Battle Creek Food Company to promote coffee substitutes and soy milk products. In addition to his food company, John Kellogg also authored about 50 nutrition-related books to promote healthy eating habits.

Longevity formula
"Eat half as much, sleep twice as much, drink three times as much, laugh four times as much, and you will live to a ripe old age." – John Harvey Kellogg

Happy Birthday: Fanny Cradock

On John Kellogg's 57th birthday (1909), another food marketer was born -- Phyllis Pechey. Pechey grew up in the United Kingdom and after World War II became known as the cooking guru Fanny Cradock. At least two of her cookbooks, *The Cook's Book* and *The Sociable Cook's Book* became best-sellers. According to one obituary, "she did much to awaken British regard for cooking after [World War II] and to improve the standards of commercial catering. Her aim was to make good cookery easy and fun for the postwar generation of housewives, who had grown up during the years of food shortages."

Sales cooks: Possible take-away
"A good salesman is like a good cook. He can create an appetite when the buyer isn't hungry." -- George H. Lorimer, American journalist and author

February 27, 2017
Monday

Objectives & reminders

____

____

____

Appointments

Early morning

8 a.m.

9 a.m.

10 a.m.

11 a.m.

Noon

1 p.m.

2 p.m.

3 p.m.

4 p.m.

5 p.m.

6 p.m.

Later evening

Skating on thin ice

The closing ceremonies of the Winter Olympics in Lillehammer, Norway were held on February 27, 1994, without U.S. ice skater Nancy Kerrigan, who had already left the Olympic Village for an appearance at Disney World. She was to receive more than $2 million from Disney and other companies for various appearances and endorsements. Unfortunately, while standing next to Mickey Mouse at her first appearance, she unwittingly said into a microphone, "I can't believe I'm doing this. This is so corny."

Happy birthday: Elizabeth Taylor

Academy Award winning actress Elizabeth Taylor was born in London on February 27, 1932. Taylor's acting career got an early start when she appeared in her first motion picture at the age of nine. As a child actress, she starred in *Lassie Come Home* (1943) and *National Velvet* (1944).

As an adult, she starred in many other movies and soon enjoyed an image of beauty and glamour that was well-suited for corporate America. However, she was very selective in terms of the products she endorsed or lent her name to. She did play a role in developing and endorsing a few perfume brands for perfume-maker Elizabeth Arden -- including White Diamonds and Black Pearls, among others.

Downside of celebrity spokespeople
Although the association with celebrities may have a positive impact on a brand or company, there are disadvantages. First, celebrities' credibility and sincerity are called into question when they have too many endorsements. Second, their image or appearance may change over time and grow to be a mismatch with the brand, company, or target markets. Even if the celebrities do not change, target markets may evolve to the point that they do not recognize or relate to the celebrity. Finally, celebrities are frequently in the media spotlight and are caught making comments that are not in the best interest of the companies and brands they supposedly endorse. Unlike advertising copy, what celebrities say and do cannot be controlled fully.

February 28, 2017
Tuesday

Objectives & reminders

____

____

Appointments

Early morning

8 a.m.

9 a.m.

10 a.m.

11 a.m.

Noon

1 p.m.

2 p.m.

3 p.m.

4 p.m.

5 p.m.

6 p.m.

Later evening

All aboard!

On February 28, 1827, B&O Railroad became the first railroad chartered to carry passengers in the United States. The railroad soon learned that transporting *people* is not the same business as transporting *cargo*.

Today, service businesses in a variety of industries recognize the same reality, i.e., different competencies are required to serve people than to serve objects. On balance, people tend to be more challenging. For example, people are inefficient; they require more space than similarly sized objects. They are not interested in simply being transported or otherwise being passive recipients of the service, but are conscious of the process or experience associated with the trip or service. They require amenities and expect to be comfortable. They require higher safety standards. Further, because each service customer is different, each one is likely to have a different set of expectations. And, unlike objects, people are more likely to notice service quality mishaps or deviations.

Ethical relief

"I went to [business school]... I was really torn... I had somehow picked up, as many people do... that there was something, not immoral, about business, but a sense that you had to play the edges in order to be successful. I think a lot of people feel that way. The business school was a tremendous release, because everything I was taught at the business school said that's not true. The way to be successful is to be straight." -- James E. Burke, former chairman and CEO of Johnson & Johnson, born on February 28, 1925

____

Don't stop with one idea

"The best way to have a good idea is to have a lot of ideas." -- Linus Pauling, chemist/physicist and Nobel Prize winner, born on February 28, 1901

_3___7___11___19___37___181_

The marketing race?

"If everything seems under control, you're just not going fast enough." -- Mario Andretti, professional race car driver, born on February 28, 1940

March 1, 2017
Wednesday

Objectives & reminders

More info…
Learn more about the *principle of round numbers* by reading Mississippi's bicentennial story on December 10 of this year.

Appointments

Early morning

8 a.m.

9 a.m.

10 a.m.

11 a.m.

Noon

1 p.m.

2 p.m.

3 p.m.

4 p.m.

5 p.m.

6 p.m.

Later evening

Happy sesquicentennial: Nebraska

Nebraska became the 37th U.S. state on March 1, 1867, so the "Cornhusker State" celebrates its sesquicentennial anniversary (i.e., 150th) today. For more than two years, organizers for "Nebraska 150 Celebration" have planned for the occasion – unveiling a special logo, introducing commemorative license plates and evaluating dozens of proposals from organizations throughout the state to determine the slate of events and programs dubbed "official."

Like most "round" anniversaries, Nebraska's 150th anniversary celebration this year is more celebratory than last year's 149th and probably more so than next year's 151st. So, while calendar-led marketers may be sensitive to the potential opportunities that any anniversary presents, they pay special attention to those that end in zero (e.g., 10th, 20th, 30th, 50th, 100th, 150th, etc.) – knowing that the celebratory momentum of these calendrical milestones are likely to open windows of marketing opportunity. Hopefully the sesquicentennial did not catch marketers in Nebraska by surprise.

Marketing opportunities in Nebraska: Invitation to discuss

Below are a few of Nebraska's demographic rankings among the 50 U.S. states. Consider the possible marketing implications of these rankings. For example, how might marketing programs be crafted or fine-tuned to increase their chances of being effective in the state?

- 11th in percentage of population age 65+ (13.6%)
- 13th in educational attainment (i.e., 89.8% of adult Nebraskans have graduated from high school)
- 22nd in median household income ($50,296)
- 29th in percentage of residents who live in urban areas (73.1%)
- 37th in total population (1.9 million)
- 42nd in percentage of households in poverty (i.e., 9.5%; only eight states have lower poverty rates)

March 2, 2017
Thursday

Objectives & reminders

____

____

Appointments

Early morning

8 a.m.

9 a.m.

10 a.m.

11 a.m.

Noon

1 p.m.

2 p.m.

3 p.m.

4 p.m.

5 p.m.

6 p.m.

Later evening

Happy birthday: Samuel Brannan

Born on March 2, 1819, Brannan became the first millionaire in the California gold rush of the late 1840s. He became wealthy not by mining for gold, per se, but by mining the miners.

Recognizing the importance of speed in seizing opportunities, he rushed from the site where gold had been discovered (near Coloma, California) to the nearby city of San Francisco. There, he bought every shovel he could find, then ran through the streets shouting, "Gold, gold from the American River!" Miners flocked to the golden location where they purchased shovels and other supplies -- at premium prices -- from Brannan's stores. Much of Brannan's success may be attributed to his quick reaction to the opportunity.

How do you like your *Green Eggs and Ham?*

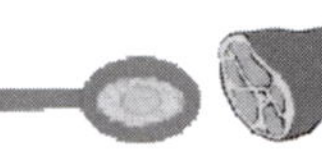

"Would you like them here or there?... Would you like them in a house? Would you like them with a mouse?... Would you like them in a box? Would you like them with a fox?... Would you? Could you? In a car? Eat them! Eat them! Here they are."– Sam-I-Am, the star in the popular children's book *Green Eggs and Ham* (1960), by Theodore Seuss Geisel who is better known as "Dr. Seuss."

The persistence of Sam-I-Am to entice a green-averse prospect to try the breakfast delicacy illustrates the persistence needed to be an effective salesperson. Sam-I-Am repeatedly tried to close the sale until the prospect finally tasted the green eggs and ham, and liked them.

By the way, Dr. Seuss's birthday is March 2, 1904. Before becoming a world-renowned children's author, Dr. Seuss wrote advertising cartoons.

Before *Green Eggs and Ham...*
There were green salespeople. Accordingly, in 1887 John Henry Patterson, the founder of the National Cash Register Company (NCR) put together a list of "don'ts" for his sales reps. Sam-I-Am may have found inspiration in one of Patterson's tips regarding persistence: "Don't stop calling on a man if he says he doesn't need one [a cash register] when you know he does."

March 3, 2017
Friday

FUTURE

Objectives & reminders

____

____

Appointments

Early morning

8 a.m.

9 a.m.

10 a.m.

11 a.m.

Noon

1 p.m.

2 p.m.

3 p.m.

4 p.m.

5 p.m.

6 p.m.

Later evening

First issue of *Time*

The first issue of *Time* magazine was published on 1923 – dated March 3. The initial issue was 32 pages in length. The concept behind the magazine was to give readers a weekly update of national and international news in a concise, convenient, yet intelligent way. At the time there were no truly national newspapers of general scope in the U.S., so *Time* attempted to fill this news void.

Planning as future time
"Business more than any other occupation is a continual dealing with the future; it is a continual calculation, an instinctive exercise in foresight." -- Henry R. Luce, founder and publisher of *Time* magazine

Technology and the human element

Advances in technology often lead to opportunities for marketers – opportunities for new products, new features, new improvements, new processes, and new efficiencies. However, we should not become so enamored with technology that we lose sight of the importance of the human dimensions of business. Lyndall Fownes Urwick is an early example of a businessperson who recognized these human factors.

Born in Malvern, Worcestershire on March 3, 1891, Urwick is a key British figure in the development of business management practices. As early as 1921, he advocated a professional approach to business, but recognized the importance of the human element. Despite the growing popularity of "scientific management," he maintained that workers should not be treated like machines. This philosophy extended to his thinking about customers.

By 1933 Urwick had pointed out the need for businesses to think differently about marketing, which he believed was much more than distribution. He urged businesses to listen intently to what customers wanted and *then* to determine how best to provide it for them -- a perspective that is well accepted today, but not at all common then. Within a year Urwick co-founded the first management consulting firm in the U.K. -- Urwick, Orr, & Partners.

March 4, 2017
Saturday

Objectives & reminders

____

____

Appointments

Early morning

8 a.m.

9 a.m.

10 a.m.

11 a.m.

Noon

1 p.m.

2 p.m.

3 p.m.

4 p.m.

5 p.m.

6 p.m.

Later evening

Being pithy on March 4

Leadership

"We are not enemies, but friends. We must not be enemies." -- Abraham Lincoln, 16th President of the United States. He said it during his inaugural address on March 4, 1861.

Economic urgency

"This nation asks for action, and action now... We must act and act quickly." -- U.S. President Franklin D. Roosevelt, regarding the Great Depression. He made this call for action during his inaugural address on March 4, 1933. Note that banks in 38 of 48 states were closed on March 4, 1933, as fearful depositors clamored to withdraw their money before the banking system collapsed.

Competition

"Everybody hates a monopoly unless they've got one." – James Barksdale, then chairman of Netscape Communications. His observation was reported in *The Wall Street Journal* on March 4, 1998.

The Internet as art?

"The beauty of the Internet is its openness. It cannot be controlled or dominated or cut off, because it is simply a constantly changing series of linkages. It is such a creative, living medium that no one yet fully comprehends its opportunities." -- Bill Gates, Microsoft's co-founder, reported in *The Wall Street Journal* on March 4, 1998

What's a "brand"?

"A brand offers a value that transcends the here-and-now. That value can be physical or emotional. Whether actual or perceived, however, that value must be overarching and unique. If it is, the brand can be adapted to other situations, and extended through time. For that's the definition of a well-run-brand. It is a big idea that is immortal." -- Cathleen "Cathie" Black, then President of Hearst Magazines, March 4, 1997

March 5, 2017
Sunday

Objectives & reminders

____

____

Appointments

Early morning

8 a.m.

9 a.m.

10 a.m.

11 a.m.

Noon

1 p.m.

2 p.m.

3 p.m.

4 p.m.

5 p.m.

6 p.m.

Later evening

Music of success 

Less than two years after migrating to the United States, Henry Englehard Steinway (then "Steinweg"), started a piano-making business with his sons -- in New York City, on March 5, 1853.

The Steinways developed a reputation for quality and innovation, believing piano-making to be a craft, not merely a business. Today, the company still exists as a family business owned by Henry E. Steinway's descendants.

Overcoming adversity

Many entrepreneurs face adversity. Some rise above it. Consider that faced by Henry E. Steinway growing up as a child in Germany. Several of his brothers were killed during the Napoleonic invasion and his family's house was burned to the ground. One brother survived the war, but was killed in a tragic accident, along with his father, when Henry was only 15 years old. Later, after moving to the U.S. and starting the family piano business with his sons, two of Henry's five sons died while still young men.

A more recent example of a successful entrepreneur overcoming adversity is that of media mogul Ted Turner. On March 5, 1963, 24-year-old Ted found himself at the helm of the family business under tragic circumstances. His father had committed suicide.

Turner went on to expand the business from outdoor (billboard) advertising and into television when he bought a small UHF station in Atlanta (WTCG, later renamed WTBS). Soon, he purchased the Atlanta Braves baseball team and later the city's basketball team (Hawks), both of which provided the television station with programming content. The station's audience continued to grow over the years.

Perhaps Turner is most noted for the successful 24-hour, all news network -- Cable News Network (CNN) – which he launched in 1980.

> **Strategic insight for small businesses**
> "When you are little, you have to do crazy things. You just can't copy the big guys. To succeed you have to be innovative." -- Ted Turner

March 6, 2017
Monday

Objectives & reminders

____

____

____

Appointments

Early morning

8 a.m.

9 a.m.

10 a.m.

11 a.m.

Noon

1 p.m.

2 p.m.

3 p.m.

4 p.m.

5 p.m.

6 p.m.

Later evening

Community norms relevant today?

In their quest to be unique and differentiate their products and brands from those of competitors, businesses sometimes face the risk of being *too* different if they counter established societal norms or existing consumer expectations. Marketers of women's fashions began to recognize this risk on March 6, 1921, when local officials in Sunbury, Pennsylvania decided to halt the rising tide of skirt lengths in response to several complaints from local citizens. An edict was issued requiring that skirts must extend at least four inches below the knees. Soon other communities passed their own dress codes.

Today, public dress codes tend to be more liberal than the Sunbury guideline of 1921, but marketers recognize that acceptable social norms do vary from community to community.

Happy birthday: Census Bureau

The U.S. Constitution requires that a census of the population be taken every ten years, largely to ensure political representation in Congress. Although the first census was taken in 1790, it was not until March 6, 1902 that the Bureau of the Census was established.

Today, the U.S. Census Bureau is the largest source of secondary data in the world. In addition to simple population counts (i.e., "nose" counts) the Bureau collects a wealth of data pertaining to consumer demographics (e.g., age, income, occupation, household size, race/ethnicity, etc.) and other variables, broken out by geographic areas as small as neighborhoods. The Census Bureau also collects data regarding businesses operating in each geographic area. The tabulated data are publicly available and are disseminated in a variety of ways. Many Census Bureau reports are routinely distributed to designated public and university libraries throughout the country.

Marketers find the census data useful for a variety of purposes -- to identify trends, pinpoint potential markets, estimate sales potentials, and establish sales territories. If the census data were not available, the time and expense of collecting comparable market data would be prohibitively expensive for most companies.

March 7, 2017
Tuesday

Objectives & reminders

____

____

____

Appointments

Early morning

8 a.m.

9 a.m.

10 a.m.

11 a.m.

Noon

1 p.m.

2 p.m.

3 p.m.

4 p.m.

5 p.m.

6 p.m.

Later evening

Happy birthday: Michael D. Eisner

Born in Mount Kisco, New York on March 7, 1942, Eisner grew to become one of the most influential people in the entertainment industry. Early in his career, he worked for television networks CBS and ABC, then for Paramount Pictures. He built a reputation for balancing the creative needs of the organization with traditional business needs such as staying within the budget.

In 1984, Eisner became the chairman and CEO of the Walt Disney Company, positions he would hold for the next 20-plus years. Under Eisner's leadership, Disney became a more diversified and much more profitable company.

Juggling is not a Mickey Mouse skill
"My job involves juggling multiple roles and finding common ground between conflicting impulses... I'm… an advocate for change but also a fierce protector of our brand. No tension is as great as the one between quality and commerce, balancing a passion for excellence with a commitment to containing costs and reaching a broad audience. There is a constant push-and-pull between tradition and innovation;… teamwork and individual accomplishment; logic and instinct; leading and letting go. When crises arise, it's almost invariably because an imbalance has occurred somewhere in this complex equation." -- Michael D. Eisner, *Work in Progress* (pp. x-xi)

It's a small world

One of the most significant technological advances of the 19th century -- the telephone -- was patented on March 7, 1876, by Alexander Graham Bell.

The telephone soon became a business tool used to connect businesses and their buyers. Like most advances in communication technologies, the telephone helped to shrink the world, i.e., it facilitated timely communication between people who were geographically separated.

Interestingly, the world shrank further on March 7, 1926, when trans-Atlantic telephone service began between New York and London.

March 8, 2017
Wednesday

Objectives & reminders

____

____

____

Appointments

Early morning

8 a.m.

9 a.m.

10 a.m.

11 a.m.

Noon

1 p.m.

2 p.m.

3 p.m.

4 p.m.

5 p.m.

6 p.m.

Later evening

International Women's Day

March 8 was first declared as International Women's Day in 1910 during an international conference of women in Helsinki, Finland. The occasion celebrates the social, political and economic accomplishments of women.

Despite the recognition of women on March 8, 1910, the relationship between women and March 8 goes back earlier than that. For example, on March 8, 1857, female garment workers in New York City staged a demonstration to demand better working conditions.

On March 8, 1884, Susan B. Anthony addressed the Judiciary Committee of the U.S. House of Representatives, "to ask that you will, at your earliest convenience, report to the House in favor of the submission of [an] amendment… that shall prohibit the disfranchisement of citizens of the United States on account of sex."

Gender equality in marketing: Is the glass 97 percent full or three percent empty?

Unlike in many professions, females in marketing tend to earn almost as much as their male counterparts. The marketing gender gap is only 3 percent, according to the findings of a survey conducted by the Chartered Institute of Marketing reported on March 8, 2005. In contrast, females in the legal profession earn an average of 36 percent less than males in comparable jobs, and in banking the gender gap is even wider -- 60 percent.

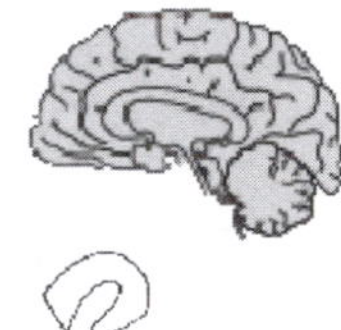

Advertising's perplexing question

"All advertising problems are subsidiary, in the last analysis, to the one main question, namely: by what means and in what manner may the mind of the potential customer be influenced most effectively?"

-- Daniel Starch, pioneer in the evaluation of advertising effectiveness, born on March 8, 1883

March 9, 2017
Thursday

Objectives & reminders

____

____

Appointments

Early morning

8 a.m.

9 a.m.

10 a.m.

11 a.m.

Noon

1 p.m.

2 p.m.

3 p.m.

4 p.m.

5 p.m.

6 p.m.

Later evening

Happy birthday: Beatrice Alexander Behrman

Long before Barbies and Beanie Babies, there were Madame Alexander dolls, created by Beatrice Alexander Behrman, who was born in Brooklyn, New York, on March 9, 1895.

Born as Bertha Alexander, she began her career as a child helping her father repair dolls in his porcelain repair shop (1st "doll hospital" in the U.S.?). At the time most dolls and doll parts were imported from Germany, but their importation was banned during World War I. So, Alexander made cloth dolls which she sold in her father's shop.

In 1923, Alexander obtained a bank loan of $5,000 and founded the Alexander Doll Company. Her dolls quickly became known for their quality workmanship and realistic details, such as eyes that opened and closed. Alexander's marketing team capitalized on this reputation by printing the firm's slogan on the dolls' boxes: "It's a Madame Alexander -- That's All You Need to Know."

In the 1930s, the company designed a Scarlett O'Hara doll, based on the character from the hugely popular novel and movie *Gone with the Wind*. This was the first time any doll manufacturer produced a doll based on a licensed character. "Madame Alexander" sold her company in 1988, but remained active as a design consultant for a short while before her death in 1990.

Protect children from advertising?

"[C]hildren are cognitively incapable of understanding all television commercials directed to them, and no amount of consumer education can do much to improve this natural age-based limitation... [H]ighly sugared foods and toys are the products most often advertised directly to children on television, and the average child spends an inordinate amount of time watching television programs and commercials targeted to him… [I]t is unrealistic to expect parents always to mediate between their children and television commercials, especially when the commercials are directed to the children." -- Peggy Charren, consumer activist and co-founder of Action for Children's Television (ACT) in 1968. Charren was born on March 9, 1928.

March 10, 2017
Friday

Objectives & reminders

___

___

___

Appointments

Early morning

8 a.m.

9 a.m.

10 a.m.

11 a.m.

Noon

1 p.m.

2 p.m.

3 p.m.

4 p.m.

5 p.m.

6 p.m.

Later evening

Surgeons are not style-conscious?

3M developed a non-woven fiber in the 1950s that was fashioned into a line of braziers which the firm launched with high hopes on March 10, 1958. Unfortunately for 3M, the bras were not well received in the marketplace, because, according to one source, they "had no style." Undaunted, 3M considered alternative uses and different markets and soon transformed the bra cups into surgical masks which were commercially successful.

Career advice on their birthday

Joseph L. Halberstein, a retired newspaper associate editor, born on March 10, 1923, offers this career insight: "Caring is what makes any endeavor a noble one."

Paul S. Drew, entrepreneur in northern Georgia, born on March 10, 1935, warns: "Don't make the same mistake *once*."

Shunning of conformity spells "opportunity" for marketers

"If... a dictator decreed feminine clothes to be illegal and that all women should wear barrels, it would not result in an era of uniformity, in my opinion. Very shortly, I think you'd find that one ingenious woman would color her barrel with a lipstick, another would pin paper lace doilies on the front of hers, and still another would decorate hers with thumbtacks. This is a strange human urge toward conformity, but a dislike for complete uniformity." -- Stanley Marcus, in a speech on March 10, 1959. Marcus was then the president of the department store chain that his father co-founded, Neiman-Marcus.

For Florida marketers

Conservationists have something to celebrate on March 10. On that date in 1903, U.S. President Theodore Roosevelt established a Federally-protected wildlife refuge on Pelican Island (on Florida's Indian River). The preserve would serve as a breeding ground for birds and was the first of 53 wildlife sanctuaries set aside as protected areas during Roosevelt's presidency. Roosevelt was a strong supporter of the conservation movement.

March 11, 2017
Saturday

Objectives & reminders

Appointments

Early morning

8 a.m.

9 a.m.

10 a.m.

11 a.m.

Noon

1 p.m.

2 p.m.

3 p.m.

4 p.m.

5 p.m.

6 p.m.

Later evening

Not so colorful publicity stunt?

Some business actions are done for no business reason other than to gain media attention or otherwise stir publicity. This may have been the case early in 2004 when Mars, Inc. stopped producing M&M's candies in their traditional familiar colors. Instead M&M's suddenly became black and white, and remained so for about ten weeks until the colorful candy reappeared on March 11, 2004.

The initial change did generate some limited media attention. Some consumers expressed regret for the colorless move, while others seemed puzzled or simply didn't care. When the colors were reintroduced on March 11, apparently the only celebration was the one staged in Los Angeles by the company itself.

The obvious stunt principle
Efforts to gain publicity are likely to fall flat when the media and customers perceive the attempt solely as a publicity stunt. Media prefer to publicize events that are newsworthy or otherwise of interest to their audiences.

Recognize me?

On a more positive publicity note for M&Ms, Yahoo! polled 600,000 consumers in the U.S. that same year (2004) and asked what their favorite advertising icons were. The Number 1 vote-getters were the M&M animated characters, followed by the AFLAC Duck (2nd), Mr. Peanut (3rd), the Pillsbury Doughboy (4th) and Tony the Tiger (5th).

Customer service is more than memorizing a script

"To give real service you must add something which cannot be bought or measured with money, and that is sincerity and integrity." -- Douglas Adams, British writer, born on March 11, 1952

March 12, 2017
Sunday

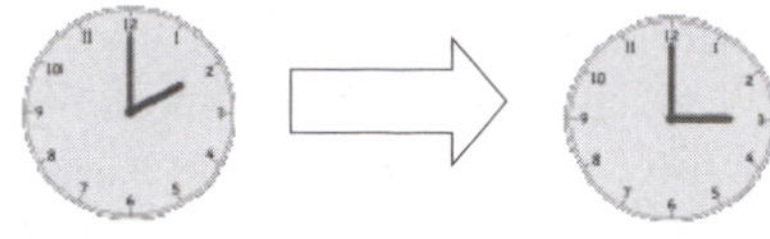

Objectives & reminders

Remember to adjust your clocks ahead today (e.g., 2:00 a.m. suddenly becomes 3:00 a.m.)

Appointments

Early morning

8 a.m.

9 a.m.

10 a.m.

11 a.m.

Noon

1 p.m.

2 p.m.

3 p.m.

4 p.m.

5 p.m.

6 p.m.

Later evening

Daylight Saving Time begins in most of United States

Consider the shorter- and longer-term marketing implications of Daylight Saving Time. For one, church attendance tends to drop temporarily from normal levels by about 15 percent today. Refer also to comments about Daylight Saving Time on the first Sunday in November (5th this year), when it ends.

Happy birthday: Clement Studebaker

Born in Pinetown, Pennsylvania on March 12, 1831, Studebaker gained valuable experience early in his life by helping in his father's blacksmith shop. After teaching school for a brief period, he and one of his brothers started their own blacksmith business in 1852. Then the two teamed with their other brothers in 1869 and founded the Studebaker Brothers Manufacturing Company which grew to become the world's largest producer of horse-drawn wagons and carriages. After Clement's death in 1901 the company diversified into automobiles, which the firm continued to produce until 1966.

The role of consumer expectations
Consumers are *satisfied* when they believe that the companies they deal with meet or exceed their expectations. But when consumers' perceptions of what they receive from a company fall short of those expectations, *dissatisfaction* is likely.

The Studebaker Brothers Manufacturing Company was one of the first firms to recognize the crucial role played by customers' expectations and multiple approaches to ensuring customer satisfaction. Accordingly, the firm's satisfaction-related motto was this: "Always give more than you promise."

March 13, 2017
Monday

Objectives & reminders

Appointments

Early morning

8 a.m.

9 a.m.

10 a.m.

11 a.m.

Noon

1 p.m.

2 p.m.

3 p.m.

4 p.m.

5 p.m.

6 p.m.

Later evening

Finding a way

Sometimes marketers are challenged with the task of persuading buyers to purchase. At other times buyers are convinced already, but they're short of money, so they can't buy -- or can they? Several business practices may facilitate purchase when buyers *want* to buy, but are short of money:

1. Accept credit cards. Credit cards create payment flexibility and consumers tend to feel less psychological discomfort when using a credit card than when parting with cash.

2. Extend credit. Although this can be a risky practice, consumers often believe that their financial situation will be better in the future than it is now.

3. Make the purchase more affordable. A no-frills model may help to drop the price into an affordable range. Also to lower costs and prices, consider asking the customer to supply part of the labor himself, e.g., are assembly, delivery, or other self-service options possible?

4. Consider barter. The customer may not have cash, but may have something else of value that could be accepted as partial or full payment. For example, on March 13, 1933 (during the Great Depression when consumers were cash-challenged), The Colonial Department Store in Detroit, Michigan agreed to "sell" clothing for farm products. Hay, eggs, honey, and livestock became acceptable payments. A 500-pound sow was worth three boys' suits, three pairs of shoes, or a dress.

A bad example?

An old saying reinforces the potent role that nonverbal behavior plays in the marketplace and in the workplace: "Your actions speak before you do." Apparently, one executive at The Coca-Cola Company was unaware of this wisdom on March 13, 1979, when he reportedly was caught drinking a Pepsi on The Coca-Cola Company's property. He never finished drinking it.

March 14, 2017
Tuesday

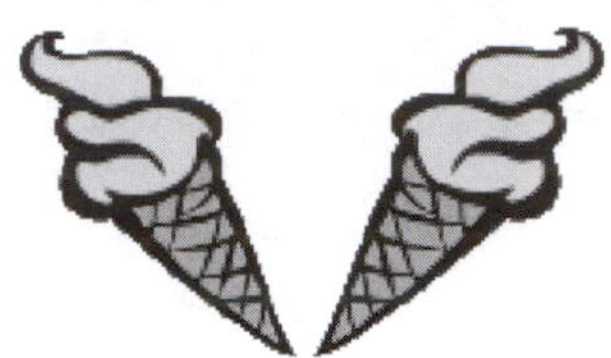

Objectives & reminders

____

____

Appointments

Early morning

8 a.m.

9 a.m.

10 a.m.

11 a.m.

Noon

1 p.m.

2 p.m.

3 p.m.

4 p.m.

5 p.m.

6 p.m.

Later evening

Quality is not about being lucky

On March 14, 1927, *Time* magazine reported an advertising first. The American Tobacco Company advertised a testimonial by singer Ernestine Schumann-Heink for *Lucky Strikes* cigarettes. Accompanying the testimonial and a picture of the singer, the ad stated unequivocally: "When smoking, she prefers *Lucky Strikes* because they give the greatest enjoyment and throat protection." This was the first time a cigarette manufacturer directly asserted that women smoke.

Unfortunately for the American Tobacco Company, there was somewhat of a glitch in the ad; Schumann-Heink refuted the testimonial: "I never smoked a cigarette in my life, and, although I don't condemn women who do, neither do I approve of it in them. Why, even my sons are not permitted to smoke in my presence on the days I sing." The error was blamed on the sloppy work of a "whippersnapper" and his bosses who failed to verify the legitimacy of the printed testimonial.

Quality is more than superior products and processes
It also has to do with performance excellence -- applying yourself -- as suggested by retired newspaper executive Paul A. Audet, who was born on March 14, 1923: "Whatever you do or you are, try to be the best. Somehow, some day, someone is bound to find out and you will be rewarded accordingly."

When quality is a tie, marketing is the tie-breaker

"If product quality is equal, people are going to select one brand or another based on marketing imagery – your ads, the color of your package, or your values. You're going to get only a slice of the market anyhow, whether it's the yellow package lovers or the people with progressive social values." – Ben Cohen and Jerry Greenfield, co-founders of Ben & Jerry's Homemade, Inc. (ice cream). Interestingly, Cohen and Greenfield were born only four days apart, and in the same hospital – Greenfield on March 14, 1951, followed by Cohen on March 18, 1951.

March 15, 2017
Wednesday

Objectives & reminders

____

____

Appointments

Early morning

8 a.m.

9 a.m.

10 a.m.

11 a.m.

Noon

1 p.m.

2 p.m.

3 p.m.

4 p.m.

5 p.m.

6 p.m.

Later evening

Ides of March: Good day or bad day?

Bad day for Caesar

Roman dictator King Julius Caesar was assassinated on March 15, 44 B.C. Poet William Shakespeare later made famous the warning Caesar received prior to his death: "Beware the ides of March." (in *Julius Caesar*, Act 1, scene 2)

Good day for Maine

Maine became the 23rd state on March 15, 1820. Maine is known for its picturesque coastline, lighthouses, lobsters and woodlands. Today, 90 percent of Maine is forested and is nicknamed the "Pine Tree State." In 2015, about 1.33 million consumers called Maine home.

Maine attraction
"Did you ever see a place that looks like it was built just to enjoy? Well this whole state of Maine looks that way." -- Will Rogers

---

Good day for London shoppers

Selfridge's department store ("Selfridge & Co., Ltd.") opened on Oxford Street in London on March 15, 1909. The store truly was a "department" store -- with 139 departments. The founder, H. Gordon Selfridge, had moved to London to launch his store after working for American retailer Marshall Field in Chicago. Working for Field, Selfridge developed a strong respect for customers which he summarized in the well-known, but debated assertion that "the customer is always right."

Good day for employees too
The "guide book" that H. Gordon Selfridge distributed to his employees in 1909 is filled with good advice that remains applicable. Employees were to "dress in good taste and thus be in harmony with the general tone of the business." Also, employees were expected to "treat each other with dignity and respect," and to be professional when representing the store: "Every promise to a customer is a pledge of the honour of this house."

March 16, 2017
Thursday

Objectives & reminders

____

____

____

Appointments

Early morning

8 a.m.

9 a.m.

10 a.m.

11 a.m.

Noon

1 p.m.

2 p.m.

3 p.m.

4 p.m.

5 p.m.

6 p.m.

Later evening

Happy birthday: Federal Trade Commission (FTC)

Charged with the responsibility of encouraging the free flow of international trade and curbing corporate actions that could interfere with competition, the U.S. FTC officially began operations on March 16, 1915.

Today, the FTC also monitors advertisements to ensure that ad claims can be substantiated and are not otherwise deceptive. The FTC has some authority over brand or product names too, i.e., the FTC can require a company to revise its brand name if the name misleads prospective buyers.

When it's okay to lose your marbles
An advertisement for vegetable soup showed a picture of the soup in a bowl containing, in addition to the soup itself, invisible glass marbles. The marbles (which sank to the bottom of the bowl and supported the vegetables) created the impression that the soup contained more vegetable stock than it actually had. In response, the FTC issued a cease and desist order to prohibit the deceptive use of marbles.

Managing a reputation for quality

Rolls-Royce was incorporated on March 16, 1906, by partners Charles Rolls and Henry Royce. Over the years the company has gone to great lengths to preserve the company's reputation for quality engineering and workmanship. At one point customers were contractually prohibited from having their malfunctioning vehicles towed. Apparently the public sight of a towed Rolls-Royce could jeopardize the brand's quality image. Instead, covered trucks were dispatched to transport downed Rolls-Royce vehicles to the service center for needed repairs.

Quality means never compromising
"Strive for perfection in everything we do. Take the best that exists and make it better. When it does not exist, design it. Accept nothing nearly right or good enough." – Henry Royce

March 17, 2017
Friday
St. Patrick's Day

Objectives & reminders

____

____

Appointments

Early morning

8 a.m.

9 a.m.

10 a.m.

11 a.m.

Noon

1 p.m.

2 p.m.

3 p.m.

4 p.m.

5 p.m.

6 p.m.

Later evening

St. Patrick's Day: Did you know?
The phrase heard on St. Patrick's Day, "Erin Go Bragh," means Irish forever.

First St. Patrick's Day parade

St. Patrick, the patron saint and missionary of Ireland, was not born on March 17; rather, he died on this day in the fifth century. On March 17, 1762, New York City staged the city's first parade in his honor. Today, the annual six-hour event features 150,000 marchers and attracts between 1.5 and 2.5 million onsite spectators, plus a television audience of four to five million viewers.

Marketing is expensive
Interested in advertising or sponsorship in the New York City St. Patrick's Day parade? The least expensive opportunities start at $10,000.

Traditionally, St. Patrick's Day was celebrated with a feast to honor St. Patrick who worked to convert Ireland to Christianity during the years of about 432 to 460. Irish immigrants brought the tradition of the feast with them to the U.S. Over time, the celebration evolved into a holiday to recognize and assert one's Irish heritage.

Although St. Patrick's Day is observed today in many parts of the world (e.g., Canada, Australia, Japan, Singapore, and Russia), in the United States, in particular, it has evolved into a secular and non-cultural celebration -- enjoyed regardless of whether one is Irish or not. Often St. Patrick's Day is celebrated with Irish green. Consumers observe the day by wearing green clothing and accessories, drinking green-colored beverages, wearing green make-up, adorning their homes and offices with green decorations, and so on.

Differentiate or Die

"Choosing among multiple options is always based on differences, implicit or explicit. Psychologists point out that vividly differentiated differences that are anchored to a product can enhance memory because they can be appreciated intellectually. In other words, if you're advertising a product, you ought to give the consumer a reason to choose that product. If you can entertain at the same time, that's great." – Jack Trout with Steve Rivkin, in *Differentiate or Die: Survival in Our Era of Killer Competition*, published on March 17, 2000

March 18, 2017
Saturday

Objectives & reminders

____

____

____

____

Appointments

Early morning

8 a.m.

9 a.m.

10 a.m.

11 a.m.

Noon

1 p.m.

2 p.m.

3 p.m.

4 p.m.

5 p.m.

6 p.m.

Later evening

Good day to fight complacency

Presidential Medal of Freedom

On March 18, 1992, only a few days before his death, Sam Walton -- founder of Wal-Mart -- was awarded the highest civilian award in the United States by President George H. Bush.

Walton was known for his strong work ethic and no-nonsense, yet aggressive approach to business. One way he guarded against complacency was to insist that Wal-Mart managers respect their competitors and continually watch what they were doing. Charlie Cate, a retired Wal-Mart store manager elaborated: "I remember [Sam Walton] saying over and over again: go in and check our competition. Check *everyone* who is our competition. And don't look for the bad. Look for the good. If you get one good idea, that's one more than you went into the store with, and we must try to incorporate it into our company. We're really not concerned with what they're doing wrong, we're concerned with what they're doing right, and everyone is doing something right."

Happy birthday: Lillian Vernon

Born in Leipzig, Germany as Lilly Menasche on March 18, 1927, Vernon migrated to the United States in 1937 to escape the Nazi persecution of Jewish Germans, including her own family. She went on to become one of the most successful pioneers in the American mail order business as founder and chairman of the Lillian Vernon Corporation.

In her 1997 autobiography, *An Eye For Winners*, Vernon explains how her early childhood memories in Nazi Germany have had a lasting effect on her personal and professional fight against complacency: "My parents and their friends always seemed to be on the brink of disaster. I think the atmosphere of imminent doom in which we lived during my formative years led to a lifelong sense of panic and anxiety. Will I be safe tomorrow? Will I survive? Overcoming those fears has been a lifelong battle, and many days -- even now -- I wonder if finally it will ever be won" (pp. 20-21).

March 19, 2017
Sunday

Objectives & reminders

____

____

____

____

Appointments

Early morning

8 a.m.

9 a.m.

10 a.m.

11 a.m.

Noon

1 p.m.

2 p.m.

3 p.m.

4 p.m.

5 p.m.

6 p.m.

Later evening

When is noon not noon?

Prior to 1918, the time displayed on clocks and watches could vary quite a bit from person to person and community to community. So the U.S. Congress addressed the issue on March 19 of that year by passing the Standard Time Act which established four standard time zones in the United States: Eastern, Central, Mountain, and Pacific.

Knowledge of time zones and their boundaries becomes increasingly important as marketers communicate with geographically dispersed audiences in real time. For example, if a customer in a distant city asks a sales rep to call her at noon, an opportunity may be lost if the rep doesn't understand time zones and calls at the wrong time.

Time zone confusion still exists
Some time-zone-related questions were included in the Calendar Literacy Survey. For example, when asked, "*If it is noon in New York City, what time is it in Los Angeles, California?*" 42 percent of the respondents did not know the correct answer (9:00 a.m.). New York (located in the Eastern Time zone) and Los Angeles (located in the Pacific Time zone) represent two of the largest population and business centers in the country.

If time zone confusion might exist where you work, consider noting the local times when communicating across time zones.

Speed demon

Increasingly, speed is becoming a key element of marketing and business strategy for many companies who continually ask: How can we adjust to the changing marketplace more quickly? How can we slash the amount of time to perform each job task? How can we reduce customers' waiting time? And so on.

Despite the potential competitive advantages gained by speed, a comment once made by former Kansan and lawman Wyatt Earp reminds us that the competitive advantages of speed are likely to be lost if quality is sacrificed for speed. "Fast is fine," said Earp, "but accuracy is everything." Earp was born on March 19, 1848.

March 20, 2017
Monday

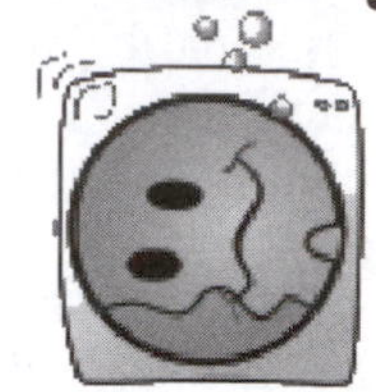

Objectives & reminders

____

____

Appointments

Early morning	6:29 a.m. EDT - Spring arrives in Northern Hemisphere
8 a.m.	
9 a.m.	
10 a.m.	
11 a.m.	
Noon	
1 p.m.	
2 p.m.	
3 p.m.	
4 p.m.	
5 p.m.	
6 p.m.	
Later evening	

Clean market research

On March 20, 1950, *Time* magazine reported some of the market research techniques used by Arthur Stanley Talbott, the advertising vice president of women's shoe manufacturer Joyce, Inc. Talbott would carry a bundle of laundry into self-service laundries and blend in with the rest of the customers, mostly female. He would initiate conversations with the women to learn their likes and dislikes. Often he would pull out a magazine and read ads to them to test the women's reactions to various words.

Over time, Talbott concluded that women find some words "repulsive" while others "appeal to women's hearts, emotions and vanities." Note examples of Talbott's findings in the accompanying boxes and consider the extent to which the same words are likely to be repulsive or appealing to women today.

Advertising words women found *repulsive*
habit
bra
leathery
parched
matron
clingy
model

Advertising words women found *appealing*
poise
charm
dainty
twinkle
blush
bloom
crisp
garden
bachelor

In another approach, Talbott showed photographs of shoe clerks to women to determine the characteristics of sales faces women preferred. His hypothesis was that "certain types of faces should be kept in the rear."

Insight for marketers who target children

"Play is often talked about as if it were a relief from serious learning. But for children play is serious learning. Play is really the work of childhood." – Fred Rogers, host of the internationally recognized children's television show, *Mister Rogers' Neighborhood* (1968-2001), born on March 20, 1928

March 21, 2017
Tuesday

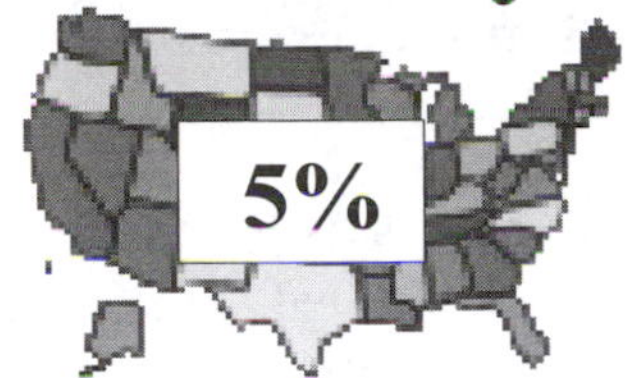

Objectives & reminders

____

____

Appointments

Early morning

8 a.m.

9 a.m.

10 a.m.

11 a.m.

Noon

1 p.m.

2 p.m.

3 p.m.

4 p.m.

5 p.m.

6 p.m.

Later evening

Markets, markets, everywhere

On March 21, 1992, the U.S. Census Bureau published the *World Population Profile.* According to the report, the world's population is projected to reach 8.2 billion by the year 2020 -- a 52 percent increase over 1992's population.

Since the 1992 report, worldwide population estimates for 2020 have been revised downward somewhat, but the growth rate remains substantial. As of 2015, the world's population was up to 7.3 billion, with China the most populous country in the world (1.38 billion consumers), followed by India (1.28 billion), the United States (0.322 billion, or 322 million), Indonesia (255 million), and Brazil (205 million). According to the U.S. Census Bureau, India's population will surpass that of China in the mid-2020s.

____

Get ready, get set, go!

As the world's population grows, so grows the attractiveness of an increasing number of markets around the world. For example, in the early to mid-1990s, Jack Welch, then chairman and CEO of General Electric commented on his company's commitment to pursue emerging opportunities in India and China. His observations are still relevant today as other companies follow GE's lead.

India

"India, with close to 125 million middle-class consumers and an exciting new government commitment to market liberalization, represents a vast opportunity for the [21st century]. Sure they are far away. Sure the cultures are different. And that's why only those passionately devoted to growth are going to share in the huge rewards of winning in these markets."
-- Jack Welch (1992)

China

"People say, 'You're taking too big a risk in China.' What are my alternatives? Stay out? China may not make it, and we may not make it in China. But there's no alternative to being in there with both feet, participating in this huge market, with this highly intelligent crowd of people."
-- Jack Welch (1994)

March 22, 2017
Wednesday

No fame in shame

Objectives & reminders

Appointments

Early morning

8 a.m.

9 a.m.

10 a.m.

11 a.m.

Noon

1 p.m.

2 p.m.

3 p.m.

4 p.m.

5 p.m.

6 p.m.

Later evening

"Most unworthy of American business"

On March 22, 1966, the president of General Motors, James M. Roche, appeared before a Senate committee on Traffic Safety and offered an apology to consumer advocate Ralph Nader.

In the previous year, Nader's controversial book had been published. Called *Unsafe at Any Speed*, the book criticized American automakers for their misguided design and marketing emphasis on style and power attributes while neglecting needed safety features. Nader's book was particularly critical of General Motors' Corvair models.

Apparently, the book angered "someone" at General Motors who authorized a campaign to discredit Nader. The campaign included an investigation of Nader's private life, including his sexual habits, political views, and attitudes toward Jews. Private detectives questioned dozens of Nader's friends and relatives. During the Senate committee proceedings, GM President Roche claimed he was unaware of the Nader investigation but offered an apology on behalf of his company -- agreeing with Senator Abraham Ribicoff that such a probe was "most unworthy of American business." Nader accepted Roche's apology but continued to maintain that GM should correct what he believed to be safety defects.

> **Invitation to discuss**
> Consider the extent to which Nader's and Drucker's concerns remain relevant today.

The battle between Nader and GM was one that helped launch the modern-day *consumerism* movement which asserts, in general terms, that businesses do not always act in the best interests of consumers, and because they don't, public policymakers and consumer interest groups must come to consumers' rescue. Unfortunately, the consumerism movement and some of the business actions that have prompted the movement pit consumers against businesses -- as adversaries, not allies. Thus, renowned business guru Peter Drucker referred to consumerism as the "shame of marketing" – suggesting that if businesses truly practice marketing, the consumerism movement and the anti-business sentiments that accompany it would not exist.

March 23, 2017
Thursday

Objectives & reminders

Appointments

Early morning

8 a.m.

9 a.m.

10 a.m.

11 a.m.

Noon

1 p.m.

2 p.m.

3 p.m.

4 p.m.

5 p.m.

6 p.m.

Later evening

The cover-up: A direct approach to bouncing back from one's mistakes

Bette Nesmith (later Bette Nesmith Graham) was born on March 23, 1934. She began her business career in the late 1940s as a secretary. Her job duties included typing letters and other documents.

The prevailing office technology of the day was the typewriter, but unfortunately Nesmith was not a very proficient typist; she made lots of typographical errors. To cover up her mistakes, she secretly began brushing white paint over them using a watercolor paintbrush. When other secretaries learned what she was doing, they insisted that she share the discovery, which she originally called "Mistake Out."

In 1956, Nesmith changed the name of her product to "Liquid Paper," applied for a trademark, studied business, and began working part-time to peddle a modest 100 bottles monthly. In the early 1960s, she was fired from her office job (one too many typing mistakes?) which prompted her to devote a full time effort to promoting her Liquid Paper business.

By 1968, annual sales reached 1 million bottles; by 1975, 25 million bottles! In 1979, she sold the company to Gillette Corporation for $47.5 million.

A Monkee's mother

While Bette Nesmith was promoting Liquid Paper, her son, Michael was making his mark in the entertainment business. In the mid-60s Michael Nesmith was a rock musician and one of the members of the Monkees. The Monkees not only played concerts and made records, but they also had their own television series. However, it's not clear whether the band was created to promote the TV series or whether the TV series was created to promote the band.

Fortunately for marketers, this is a very small group

"The only truly affluent are those who do not want more than they have." -- Erich Fromm, psychologist who studied the impact of society on individuals, born on March 23, 1900

March 24, 2017
Friday

Objectives & reminders

____

____

____

Appointments

Early morning

8 a.m.

9 a.m.

10 a.m.

11 a.m.

Noon

1 p.m.

2 p.m.

3 p.m.

4 p.m.

5 p.m.

6 p.m.

Later evening

The sun never sets on British influence

Today, 20 countries have a population that exceeds the United Kingdom's 65.6 million consumers (2016 estimates), including the U.S. which is about five times as large. However, these numbers greatly underestimate the important historical role the U.K. has played in the not-so-distant past.

For example, on March 24, 1906, the *Census of the British Empire* reported that 400 million people worldwide lived under British rule -- including its colonies, dependencies and protectorates. Of these 400 million, 41.5 million lived in the U.K. itself, 300 million in Asia, 43 million in Africa, seven million in the Americas, and five million in Australasia. With such a large worldwide presence, it is easy to understand the 19th century observation that "the sun never sets on the British Empire."

Although today's British "Empire" is only a fraction of its former size, as most of its former possessions are now independent, much of the influence of the former Empire's cultural, political and legal contributions remain. Global marketers can benefit by recognizing the British roots planted throughout the world.

No boundaries for marketing: Agree or disagree?

"If there was a market in mass-produced portable nuclear weapons, we'd market them too." -- Alan M. Sugar, British entrepreneur, billionaire, and founder of Amstrad plc (home electronics), born on March 24, 1947

Which comes first: chicken or egg?

"We can believe that we know where the world should go. But unless we're in touch with our customers, our model of the world can diverge from reality. There's no substitute for innovation, of course, but innovation is no substitute for being in touch, either." -- Steve Ballmer, then CEO of Microsoft Corporation (2000-2014). Ballmer was born in Detroit, Michigan on March 24, 1956. Today, he owns the Los Angeles Clippers of the National Basketball Association (NBA).

March 25, 2017
Saturday

Objectives & reminders

Appointments

Early morning

8 a.m.

9 a.m.

10 a.m.

11 a.m.

Noon

1 p.m.

2 p.m.

3 p.m.

4 p.m.

5 p.m.

6 p.m.

Later evening

Fire safety day

March 25 is a good day to audit fire prevention measures and review fire safety procedures with workers. It was on March 25, 1911, when a fire broke out in New York City in the ten-story building that housed the Triangle Shirtwaist Company factory. Sadly, 146 workers were killed.

Of course, any fire is a tragedy, but the tragedy of the Triangle Shirtwaist fire was magnified when investigators determined that the loss of life could have been prevented. Many workers were trapped inside the building. One of the exit doors was locked. Stair wells were cluttered, which slowed workers attempting to escape. Workers on the ninth floor did not hear a fire alarm. At least one of the fire extinguisher hoses that would have been used to fight the blaze had rotted and was useless. Nets used by firemen proved to be too weak and failed to break the fall of workers leaping from the burning building. Fire escapes also proved to be too weak, many breaking and collapsing under the weight of workers trying to escape.

The 1911 fire heightened government and business sensitivity to fire safety and resulted in considerable regulation and the formation of the New York Factory Investigating Commission. Apparently and unfortunately, however, additional fire safety lessons remained to be learned; on March 25, 1990, another fire engulfed a disco club in New York City, killing 87 people.

Management by walking around: Preventing other types of "fires"?

"I walk the properties. I visit the kitchen, the laundry, the housekeeping, the front office, the back office, the rooms, the parking lot, the receiving dock. What am I looking for? I want to know, is it clean? Is it sharp? What are our people like? Are they happy? Are they enjoying their work? What's the general manager like? How well does he know his people? My favorite general manager is the guy that can stand 50 yards away from an employee and say, 'Good morning, Sam. How's Joan, is she feeling better? And how's little Jimmy, is he still on the baseball team?'" -- J. Willard "Bill" Marriott, Jr., Executive Chairman and former CEO of Marriott International, Inc. (hotels), born in Washington D.C. on March 25, 1932

March 26, 2017
Sunday

Objectives & reminders

____

____

Appointments

Early morning

8 a.m.

9 a.m.

10 a.m.

11 a.m.

Noon

1 p.m.

2 p.m.

3 p.m.

4 p.m.

5 p.m.

6 p.m.

Later evening

Happy birthday: Condé Nast

Born in New York City on March 26, 1874, Nast became a successful advertising executive for *Collier's* magazine. He later purchased *Vogue* (1909) and *House and Garden* (1913). In 1914, he introduced *Vanity Fair*. While most other magazine publishers during this era focused their efforts solely on total circulation numbers, Nast realized that the ability to report a large number of subscribers, per se, was not necessarily in the best interest of advertisers. So, he introduced the concept of "class publications," closely related to what we now refer to as "target marketing." That is, he targeted reading audiences based on factors such as income level or common interest, knowing that he could persuade advertisers interested in reaching those groups to follow.

Choose your weapon: Shotgun or rifle
If you are a manufacturer of luxury products (say, gold watches), would you rather advertise in a media vehicle that reaches one million consumers with a median annual income of $30,000 or one that reaches only 100,000 consumers with a median annual income of $300,000? What additional information would you like to consider before deciding?

Thank you Popeye

On March 26, 1937, spinach growers expressed their gratitude for all that Popeye, the cartoon hero, had done to spur spinach sales. They erected a statue of the spinach-eating hero in Crystal City, Texas. After repeatedly witnessing Popeye's feats of strength attributed to his eating of spinach, American children asked their mothers to buy spinach at the grocery store. Sales soared.

The marketing lesson? Incorporating products into the content or setting of a printed story, broadcast, or cartoon is known as *product placement.* Relative to traditional advertising practices, product placement can be quite effective today, because consumers are exposed to so many blatant advertising messages that are ignored.

March 27, 2017
Monday

Objectives & reminders

____

____

Appointments

Early morning

8 a.m.

9 a.m.

10 a.m.

11 a.m.

Noon

1 p.m.

2 p.m.

3 p.m.

4 p.m.

5 p.m.

6 p.m.

Later evening

To sing or not to sing: Patty Smith Hill

Dr. Hill was a school teacher, principal, college professor and author best known for her contribution to the familiar song "Happy Birthday to You." Born on March 27, 1868, Hill co-authored the familiar melody with her sister Mildred.

The song was first published in 1893 as "Good Morning to All" – not as a birthday song, but as a song to welcome young children to school. Without authorization, the song was republished in 1924 with the lyrics revised to the now familiar theme. The song was essentially stolen and republished several times and by 1933 the title and lyrics had morphed into "Happy Birthday to You."

Disgusted by the extensive use of the song without permission and the corresponding absence of royalties, the Hill family took legal action to assert ownership of the melody. They won the right to receive royalties every time the song was sung *commercially*. As a result, companies stopped using the song. For example, Western Union who had sung "Happy Birthday to You" about 500,000 times as part of the company's birthday greeting services abruptly stopped using it.

In recent years, many restaurants and other businesses wishing to celebrate customers' birthdays have chosen to sing alternative birthday songs to avoid copyright infringement. After years of legal maneuvering, however, the song finally achieved public domain status in June 2016.

Is "first to market" always an advantage?

"It is better to be good than to be original."
-- Ludwig Mies van der Rohe, German architect, born on March 27, 1886

Why forecasting the future is difficult

"The trouble with the future is that there are so many of them." -- John Robinson Pierce, American communications engineer sometimes referred to as the "father of the communications satellite," born on March 27, 1910

March 28, 2017
Tuesday

Objectives & reminders

____

____

Appointments

Early morning

8 a.m.

9 a.m.

10 a.m.

11 a.m.

Noon

1 p.m.

2 p.m.

3 p.m.

4 p.m.

5 p.m.

6 p.m.

Later evening

Rethinking high-tech: Misplaced trust?

Fears of nuclear power were reignited on March 28, 1979, when the nuclear power facility on Three Mile Island (near Harrisburg, Pennsylvania) approached meltdown. Fortunately, a total disaster was avoided, but the incident prompted many to reconsider the desirability of nuclear energy.

Protests that followed the incident attracted thousands of concerned consumers -- many of whom believed their trust in big business and government had been misplaced; after all, it was big business and government that had previously assured them that nuclear facilities were safe. Safety-related questions led to broader questions regarding the country's adoption of the latest technology "without thought."

Low-tech opportunity on a stick

The media love to talk about the glamorous, cutting-edge world of high-tech -- so much so that one could be lulled into thinking that most innovations and most wealth are associated with high-tech. However, the reality is that the great majority of patents are for ordinary, not-particularly-high-tech things. Low-tech opportunities abound. This is true today, and it was true in the days before the emergence of California's "Silicon Valley."

For example, on March 28, 1927, *Time* magazine reported the success story of a low-tech innovation -- the Eskimo Pie, a brick of ice cream coated with chocolate and mounted on a stick. That week, the market value of the Eskimo Pie Corporation was estimated at $25 million, only six years after the invention of the Eskimo Pie. Licensees paid royalties of a nickel for each dozen Eskimo Pies they produced, giving the founders an income stream of $1 million annually.

Teamwork emphasis

"We've always stayed away from a star system. We've got very good people, but we're part of a team, and people work here because they like working with the other people at Goldman, Sachs." – Henry "Hank" Paulson, Jr., then chairman and CEO of Goldman, Sachs & Co. (investment banking), and later U.S. Secretary of Treasury. He was born in Palm Beach, FL on March 28, 1946.

March 29, 2017
Wednesday

Objectives & reminders

____

____

____

Appointments

Early morning

8 a.m.

9 a.m.

10 a.m.

11 a.m.

Noon

1 p.m.

2 p.m.

3 p.m.

4 p.m.

5 p.m.

6 p.m.

Later evening

Go Dow go!

On March 29, 1999, the Dow Jones Industrial Average (DJIA) -- an index of 30 large U.S. corporate stocks -- closed above 10,000 for the first time in its 103-year-old history (10,006.78, to be precise). Investors were not the only people thrilled with the milestone; marketers were excited too. A strong stock market creates a greater sense of wealth among stockholders, which tends to translate into a greater willingness to spend money on numerous products -- especially luxury products and durable goods.

____

The Wal-Mart Pledge

Each Wal-Mart employee takes the Wal-Mart pledge -- partially in honor of the company's founder, Sam Walton, who was born on March 29, 1918: "I solemnly swear and declare that every customer that comes within ten feet of me, I will smile, look them in the eye, and greet them, so help me Sam."

____

What is success?

"I would define success in terms of achieving something for the common good or above people's expectations of you.... The head of a major company who turns that company from poor results to being a world-beater is clearly successful, but so is someone who has great difficulty in learning to read but does so and then puts that to good use. His success is just as great." -- John Major, former British prime minister (1990-1997), born on March 29, 1943

____

"Crazy" entrepreneur born on March 29, 1819

Entrepreneurs are often "crazy" until their ideas are proven to be right. Then they become "geniuses," or wealthy, or both. In 1859 American oil entrepreneur Edwin L. Drake changed history when he successfully drilled for oil near Titusville, Pennsylvania. Of course, the technology to drill for oil is well-established and routinely used today, but not so in Drake's era. At the time, one of Drake's associates scoffed at the idea, "Drill for oil? You mean drill into the ground to try and find oil? You're crazy."

March 30, 2017
Thursday

Objectives & reminders

____

____

Apppp ointments

Early morning

8 a.m.

9 a.m.

10 a.m.

11 a.m.

Noon

1 p.m.

2 p.m.

3 p.m.

4 p.m.

5 p.m.

6 p.m.

Later evening

Correcting your own mistakes

Mistakes are a fact of business. That principle was apparent to Philadelphia's Hyman L. Lipman when he received a patent on March 30, 1858, for a pencil with an attached eraser. The invention was a big hit and soon became a common item in business offices.

Today, pencils with erasers reinforce the global nature of business. Not only are pencils used worldwide, but their manufacture also is international. For some pencil makers, for example, Sri Lanka and Mexico provide graphite. Germany and the state of Georgia supply the clay, which is mixed with the graphite to produce the pencils' "lead." The cedar surrounding the lead is grown in California's Sierra Mountains, but the wax-like substance used to coat the lead is from Brazil. The eraser-end consists of rubber from Malaysia and pumice from Italy. The job of bringing the raw materials together to produce the final product may be done somewhere else.

If such a "simple" product as a pencil has so many international ties, imagine the international web woven by producers of more complex products like automobiles or household appliances. Clearly, such businesses require many erasers.

Following through

"[W]hat you must never do is launch a new initiative and not follow it through really professionally, because the customers will come back to you very quickly indeed and say, 'Now listen, you've launched this but it's no good and I'm unhappy about it.'" -- Ian Charter MacLaurin, then chairman of Tesco Stores (largest chain of grocery stores in Great Britain, serving 12 million customers weekly), born on March 30, 1937

Lost your marbles? Try looking in West Virginia

Historically, West Virginia is to glass marbles as Texas is to oil, Nevada is to gambling, or Hawaii is to tourism. Recognizing this distinction, the West Virginia Marble Collectors' Club was formed on March 30, 2003. The Club promotes marble-collecting through club meetings (held in Parkersburg, WV), marble shows, a newsletter and other activities.

March 31, 2017
Friday

Objectives & reminders

____

____

Appointments

Early morning

8 a.m.

9 a.m.

10 a.m.

11 a.m.

Noon

1 p.m.

2 p.m.

3 p.m.

4 p.m.

5 p.m.

6 p.m.

Later evening

Turning a negative into a positive

The pharmaceutical and cosmetics giant Warner-Hudnut merged with Lambert Pharmacal Company on March 31, 1955, to become Warner-Lambert. Today, one of Warner-Lambert's most recognized brands is Listerine mouthwash -- a brand with a bad-tasting reputation. When consumers complained of Listerine's taste, its marketers could have reformulated the taste, but instead chose to promote the bad taste.

To convince consumers that an undesirable taste is a desirable attribute, Warner-Lambert implied that the bad taste is an integral part of Listerine's germ-killing potency. For example, one print ad in the early 1970s portrayed a consumer proclaiming, "I hate it, but I love it." The copy went on to say, "Anything that tastes that bad has gotta work... [Listerine] kills germs that can cause bad breath..."

Although it can be risky to tell customers to adjust their thinking, the ploy worked for Warner-Lambert's marketing of Listerine. Interestingly, Warner-Lambert used the opposite strategy to promote another one of its heavily advertised brands, Sugarless Trident gum. Stressing the gum's cavity-fighting and breath-freshening attributes, Trident ads bragged, "All that good stuff and *great taste too*." (emphasis added)

Happy Birthday: Andy Varipapa

Born in southern Italy on March 31, 1891, Varipapa's family soon moved to New York City where Andy proved himself to be quite an athlete and one of the first professional bowlers in the United States. He bowled competitively well into the 1950s and developed a repertoire of trick shots and stunts -- such as bowling simultaneously with two bowling balls, one in each hand. Varipapa amazed crowds assembled to see the exhibitions he conducted across the country to promote bowling.

In 2015, Wheaties' in-house marketing team for "the breakfast of champions" spliced together decades-old film footage of some of Varipapa's entertaining trick shots and included them in a nostalgic retro commercial to salute Varipapa and celebrate the brand's heritage. Particularly appealing to America's 46+ million bowlers, the ad aired during ESPN's Sunday telecasts of Professional Bowlers Association tournaments.

April 1, 2017
Saturday

Objectives & reminders

Call Al or L.E. today?

Appointments

Early morning

8 a.m.

9 a.m.

10 a.m.

11 a.m.

Noon

1 p.m.

2 p.m.

3 p.m.

4 p.m.

5 p.m.

6 p.m.

Later evening

Welcome to April!

"Isn't it appropriate that the month of the tax begins with April Fools' Day and ends with cries of May Day?" -- Anonymous

April Fools' Day (All Fools' Day)

It is not clear exactly when or why the tradition of designating April 1 as April Fools' Day began. Some believe the tradition started when the calendar was revamped and King James IV moved the New Year's holiday from April 1 to January 1.

Because gift-giving had been a tradition to usher in the New Year, some people clung to the idea of giving presents to others -- but others began giving mock presents on April 1 instead of serious gifts. Over time the day evolved into a celebration of frivolity, jokes and pranks. In 1752, for example, a tradition began in which young apprentices were sent on errands to find pots of striped paint or two-headed hammers.

Modern-day organizations have exploited the marketing potential of April Fools' Day. Late in March 1998, for example, Burger King promoted a new innovation -- a left-handed Whopper. After whopping publicity and customer requests for the sandwich, Burger King announced on April 1 that the entire promotion was an April Fools' joke.

Zoos are sometimes involved in April Fools' pranks when coworkers leave telephone messages for each other to call "Al E. Gater" or "L. E. Phant" with the local zoo's phone number attached. However, creative zoo fundraisers use the pranks to their advantage. When the calls pour in, they explain that the caller is the victim of an April Fools' prank. When the laughing subsides, the fundraiser asks the victim for the name and phone number of the prankster so a zoo representative can return the call and request a donation to support the zoo. Feeling somewhat guilty for involving the zoo in the prank, many pranksters agree to make a donation.

Foolish thought
"The first of April is the day we remember what we are the other 364 days of the year." -- Mark Twain

April 2, 2017
Sunday

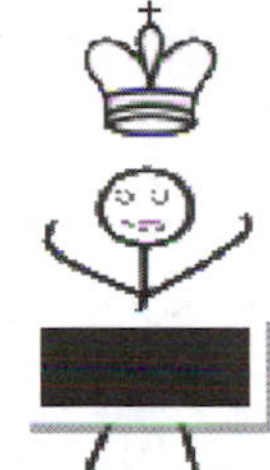

Objectives & reminders

____

____

Appointments

Early morning

8 a.m.

9 a.m.

10 a.m.

11 a.m.

Noon

1 p.m.

2 p.m.

3 p.m.

4 p.m.

5 p.m.

6 p.m.

Later evening

Happy birthday: Hans Christian Andersen

Born in Odense, Denmark on April 2, 1805, Andersen is one of the world's best known authors of children's fairy tales -- although he also wrote several plays, travel books, autobiographies, novels and poems. Today, his birthday is celebrated around the globe as International Children's Book Day.

One of Andersen's classic stories is "The Emperor's New Clothes." In it, scam artists pose as tailors and promise to make clothes for the king. When the king's advisors check the progress, the scam artists say that the clothes are visible only to those who are qualified to do their jobs. The clothes, they claim, are invisible to the inept. Not wanting anyone to think them incompetent, the king's advisors convince the king that the new garments are beautiful and befitting of a king.

The king's ego prevents him from seeing through the scam, so he pays the "tailors" their fee and then leads a procession through town while wearing his new suit of clothes. Finally, the scam is revealed when a small child watching the procession points out the naked truth, "the Emperor has no clothes."

> **Naked leadership**
> "This particular emperor expects to be told when he is naked." – Colin L. Powell, retired U.S. 4-Star General and Secretary of State (2001-2005)

Drawing from the lesson to be learned from "The Emperor's New Clothes," former Coca-Cola Company marketing director, Sergio Zyman, suggests that far too many advertising executives today are like the king's tailors. In effect, according to Zyman (in his book *The End of Advertising As We Know It*), advertising con men claim that, "[a]dvertising is an art and only artists and creative people get it. Stupid people won't be able to understand what we do" (p. 15).

Zyman warns businesspeople not to be duped by ad agencies that lose their focus of the bare purpose of advertising, which, he asserts, is to: "[s]ell more stuff to more people more often and for more money." Never be afraid to be the little kid along the parade route who is willing to point out the obvious.

April 3, 2017
Monday

Objectives & reminders

____

____

____

Appointments

Early morning

8 a.m.

9 a.m.

10 a.m.

11 a.m.

Noon

1 p.m.

2 p.m.

3 p.m.

4 p.m.

5 p.m.

6 p.m.

Later evening

Spending out of economic slumps

The U.S. was still suffering from the Great Depression in 1933. During such tough economic periods, spending plays a vital part in the recovery process, but consumers are not inclined to spend if they are unemployed or fear losing their jobs, as is often the case during economic downturns. Realizing this, President Franklin D. Roosevelt augmented sluggish consumer spending with government spending. Some companies so helped by encouraging their employees to spend, spend, spend. For example, on April 3, 1933, a notice to employees was posted at the Thomas A. Edison, Inc. plant in West Orange, New Jersey. It read:

> "President Roosevelt has done his part: now you do something. Buy something -- buy anything, anywhere; paint your kitchen, send a telegram, give a party, get a car, pay a bill, rent a flat, fix your roof, get a haircut, see a show, build a house, take a trip, sing a song, get married. It does not matter what you do -- but get going."

Buy Now

Speed kills. Costs & competing technology can kill too.

April 3 marks the anniversary of the Pony Express. On this day in 1860 the first rider headed west from St. Joseph, Missouri. The 19-year-old rider, Henry Wallace, carried 49 letters and a few special-edition newspapers. The almost 2,000-mile route to Sacramento, California took a series of riders about 10.5 days to complete, less than half the time it took stagecoaches to travel the same distance.

Unfortunately, the Pony Express service was never profitable. It cost the company about $16 to deliver a letter, but they charged "only" $5 per half-ounce. Nineteen months after the initial ride, the Pony Express went out of business, due to a combination of high costs, low volume, and the competing technology of the transcontinental telegraph. The speed of the service was a major point of differentiation relative to the snail mail of the day, but in consumers' minds, apparently the added benefit of speed did not justify the Pony Express' high prices.

April 4, 2017
Tuesday

Objectives & reminders

Appointments

Early morning

8 a.m.

9 a.m.

10 a.m.

11 a.m.

Noon

1 p.m.

2 p.m.

3 p.m.

4 p.m. What's planned for 4:44 on 4-4 ?

5 p.m.

6 p.m.

Later evening

4-4 or 4-4? No confusion today

Today is April 4 -- sometimes abbreviated in the U.S. as 4-4 (month-day). However, in many parts of the world such as Europe, the United Kingdom and Australia, today is 4 April, abbreviated as 4-4 (day-month). To avoid confusion when communicating internationally on other days this week, avoid the numerical abbreviations. For example, whereas "April 5" versus "5 April" is not likely to create confusion or misunderstanding, "4-5" versus "5-4" might.

4-4 promotion potential?

Because these days are easy to remember and schedule, consider the possibilities of staging promotions, events, celebrations, training sessions, employee parties, etc. whenever the day of the month corresponds with the month of the year, i.e., 4-4 (April 4), 5-5 (May 5), 6-6 (June 6), and so on.

Examples: Selected merchandise could be priced at "*four* for *four* dollars." Or, *four* mystery items scattered throughout the store might be sale priced for *four* dollars each. Or, *four* lucky customers could be selected to receive *four* gifts. And so on.

Such promotions could be further refined (restricted) to include the time of day, e.g., Any customer purchasing at least *four* items priced at *four* dollars or more after *four* p.m. receives a free gift. However, be sensitive to these times already "reserved" for other purposes, e.g., 11:00 a.m., November 11 commemorates the end of fighting in World War I and in many parts of the world is observed with a moment of silence.

John Cameron Swayze: Extreme time-keeping

Born in Wichita, Kansas on April 4, 1906, Swayze enjoyed a career as a news broadcaster before his 26-year reign as spokesperson for Timex watches.

During the long-running Timex campaign, Swayze used his broadcasting skills to "report" dozens of extreme uses (abuses) of the brand to dramatize the watches' durability. The slogan Swayze used to end each advertisement reinforced the durability message and became an iconic part of American culture: "It takes a licking and keeps on ticking."

April 5, 2017
Wednesday

Objectives & reminders

____

____

Appointments

Early morning

8 a.m.

9 a.m.

10 a.m.

11 a.m.

Noon

1 p.m.

2 p.m.

3 p.m.

4 p.m.

5 p.m.

6 p.m.

Later evening

Not just any birthday cake today!

Birthday cakes have been used to celebrate birthdays since the days of the ancient Greeks and Persians. In the 13th century, Germans added candles and used birthday cakes primarily to recognize children's birthdays. At dawn, they would present the cake, topped with lighted candles. The candles would burn until the family meal, at which time the cake would be eaten.

Today, it is not uncommon to recognize co-workers with birthday cakes, but because birthday cakes can be messy, alternatives such as individual cup cakes or cookies may be substituted. Another possible substitute is the Twinkie, which -- coincidentally -- was invented on April 5, 1930, by James A. Dewar. According to Dewar, the Twinkie was his all-time "best darn-tootin' idea."

Take this
"Celebration Pledge"
I, ______________________, promise never to miss an opportunity to celebrate the company's or co-workers' milestones and accomplishments. I understand that celebrations can be very beneficial; they recognize individuals and build a sense of team spirit. I know there is always something to celebrate if I will take the time to look for it.

Note: Apparently, Twinkie inventor James A. Dewar missed few celebrations; he ate two Twinkies each day!

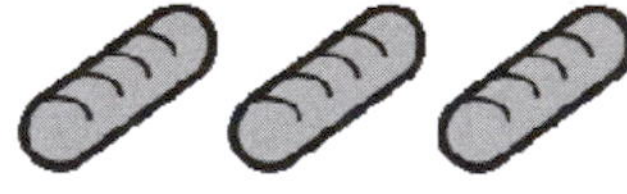

Leaders are simplifiers -- not simple-minded

"Great leaders are almost always great simplifiers who can cut through argument, debate and doubt, to offer a solution everybody can understand."
-- Colin L. Powell, retired four-star General, and U.S. Secretary of State from 2001 until 2005. Powell was born in New York City on April 5, 1937.

April 6, 2017
Thursday

STOP WARS

Objectives & reminders

____

____

____

Appointments

Early morning

8 a.m.

9 a.m.

10 a.m.

11 a.m.

Noon

1 p.m.

2 p.m.

3 p.m.

4 p.m.

5 p.m.

6 p.m.

Later evening

"The war to end all wars"

That was the hope on April 6, 1917, when the United States entered what we now refer to as World War I. U.S. allies France, Britain, and Russia had been fighting against Germany since 1914. The allies welcomed the two million U.S. troops who joined the effort. For three years prior to the U.S.'s formal declaration of war against Germany, President Woodrow Wilson had struggled to maintain neutrality.

As tragic as wars are, for businesspeople wars are about more than wars, per se. During times of wide-scale war, almost everything about the marketplace changes: public sentiments, economies, lifestyles, consumer buying habits, government priorities, competitive dynamics, access to raw materials, labor supply -- everything. When a war breaks out in a market, so should firms' contingency plans.

Limitation of marketing research

"Often people don't know what they want and can't describe it until they see it. If we'd done market research on the Macintosh [computer] prior to its introduction, and asked people to describe the ideal personal computer, they would have come up with something entirely different. But when we show people the Macintosh and say, 'Is this what you want?' they say, 'Yes.' You have to be able to make the abstract recognizable, because only then can people accept or reject it." -- John Sculley, former chairman and CEO of Apple Computer, born in New York City on April 6, 1939

Product design challenge is more difficult than making paper airplanes

"When the weight of the paperwork equals the weight of the plane, the plane will fly." -- Donald Wills Douglas, aircraft designer and founder of Douglas Aircraft Company in the early 1920s (the company merged with McDonnell Aircraft Company in 1967, then with Boeing in 1997), born on April 6, 1892

April 7, 2017
Friday

Objectives & reminders

____

____

____

Appointments

Early morning

8 a.m.

9 a.m.

10 a.m.

11 a.m.

Noon

1 p.m.

2 p.m.

3 p.m.

4 p.m.

5 p.m.

6 p.m.

Later evening

World Health Day

On April 7, 1948, the World Health Organization (WHO) was formed by the United Nations to prevent disease and promote health throughout the world. The organization's most ambitious goal was to reach every person in the world by the year 2000. Today, April 7 is celebrated annually as World Health Day.

Despite the noble cause and hard work of the WHO, health issues still challenge every community throughout the world. Consider how companies can augment the WHO's efforts in the communities they serve. For example, they might hire nurses and/or partner with local health clinics or nonprofit organizations to offer free screenings, literature and referrals for high blood pressure, diabetes, glaucoma, breast cancer or other all-too-common maladies.

Such efforts provide a valuable community service, attract media attention, and build goodwill, awareness and traffic for the business. The job is too big for the World Health Organization alone.

EEEEEEEEEEEEEEEEEEEEEE

Success factors: The two "E"s

"[T]he factors for success are summed up, it seems to me, in [these] words -- energy and enthusiasm. They carry with them the sense of conviction that what you're doing is the thing you want to do or that you believe in." -- David Frost, international broadcast journalist, born on April 7, 1939

Marbleous questions tactic

George David, former chairman and CEO of United Technologies Corporation (UTC), had a reputation for asking employees a lot of questions. As one senior executive at UTC (brutally?) put it, "He's like a college professor, and you'd better have done your homework." In response, David explained, "It's not that I want to know everything myself about everything. It's that I want to cause others to know everything." It may be that if David asks employees "What's up?" on April 7, they'll know enough to point out that it's David's birthday. He was born in Bryn Mawr, Pennsylvania, in 1942.

April 8, 2017
Saturday

Objectives & reminders

____

____

____

Appointments

Early morning

8 a.m.

9 a.m.

10 a.m.

11 a.m.

Noon

1 p.m.

2 p.m.

3 p.m.

4 p.m.

5 p.m.

6 p.m.

Later evening

Congratulations: "Hammering Hank" Aaron

It was April 8, 1974, when Atlanta Braves slugger Henry Aaron broke the Major League Baseball (MLB) record for career home-runs by hitting his 715th. Aaron hit another 40 home-runs before retiring from baseball in 1976. The previous MLB record-holder was Babe Ruth. Aaron's record stood until 2007 when San Francisco Giant Barry Bonds surpassed him. Today, Aaron is a businessman. Among other ventures, he's associated with a Toyota dealership and owns a Krispy Kreme franchise in the Atlanta area.

"Double-A" baseball: Aaron's advantage over Babe Ruth, Barry Bonds, & especially Dutch Zwilling
In addition to Aaron's appeal as a baseball icon and a classy guy, Aaron enjoys another distinct marketing advantage – the spelling of his name. That is, because "Aaron" begins with a double "a," any company name that features Aaron in its lead-off position is likely to be among the first firms listed in phone books or other alphabetically-organized directories where prospective customers are likely to search. Especially if the list of companies within a category is lengthy, prospective customers are more likely to notice the entries nearer the top of the list than those nearer the end.

Thank you: Tom Devlin

Tom Devlin, co-founder of the rent-to-own chain, Rent-A-Center, also hit a home run (so to speak) on April 8, when on that date in 1987 he made a $5 million pledge to Wichita State University. About 20 percent of the gift was earmarked for a new building -- Devlin Hall -- to house classrooms, offices, and WSU's Center for Entrepreneurship.

Plenty of market opportunities today...
"You just have to discover them. Start with the customer. How can you help him or her live a fuller life? How can you make life easier or better in some way? What is being overlooked in the marketplace? What services could be delivered better?" -- Tom Devlin

April 9, 2017
Sunday

Objectives & reminders

____

____

____

Appointments

Early morning

8 a.m.

9 a.m.

10 a.m.

11 a.m.

Noon

1 p.m.

2 p.m.

3 p.m.

4 p.m.

5 p.m.

6 p.m.

Later evening

Business-relevant lessons from the history of April 9

1667 The first public art exhibition was held at the Palais-Royale in Paris, France, by the Académie de Peinture. *Seeing is believing, and in marketing believing is usually a prerequisite for buying.*

1865 General Robert E. Lee surrendered his Confederate army to Union General Ulysses S. Grant, to end the U.S. Civil War (also known as the War Between the States). *(1) Sometimes decision-makers have to set aside their egos to make the decision that's best for the organization. (2) To cease fighting when it becomes apparent that victory is not possible frees valuable resources that can be productively applied elsewhere.*

1912 The "unsinkable" Titanic left Queenstown, Ireland -- bound for New York. The ship struck an iceberg and sank while speeding across the Atlantic in an attempt to make the trip in record time. *Speed often provides a competitive advantage in the marketplace, but not if other, more critical, attributes are sacrificed -- like safety and quality.*

1953 The first issue of *TV Guide* magazine was published – which, of course, would not have happened if television wasn't invented a few years earlier. *Every innovation opens the door for additional innovations and opportunities.*

1974 Ray Kroc, the legendary McDonald's entrepreneur, who also owned the poorly performing San Diego Padres baseball team addressed the crowd, "Ladies and gentlemen, I suffer with you. I've never seen such stupid baseball playing in my life." *Success in one industry does not ensure success in another. As successful companies or people move further away from what they know best, the less likely they are to duplicate their successes.*

April 10, 2017
Monday

Objectives & reminders

____

____

____

Appointments

Early morning

8 a.m.

9 a.m.

10 a.m.

11 a.m.

Noon

1 p.m.

2 p.m.

3 p.m.

4 p.m.

5 p.m.

6 p.m.

Later evening

Happy Birthday: John Daniel Hertz

Born on April 10, 1879, Hertz had several successes in the automobile industry -- selling automobiles, manufacturing them, and running a taxicab service. Today, his name is most often associated with the automobile rental firm he acquired in 1923 -- first named the Yellow Drive-It-Yourself Company, then changed to the more familiar Hertz Rent-A-Car in 1953.

Today, Hertz Corporation is the largest vehicle-renting company in the world -- with a fleet of 667,000 vehicles and more than 29,000 employees scattered across 145 countries.

The rationale behind Hertz's innovative concept of the Drive-It-Yourself taxicab is akin to self-service options available today in dozens of product and service categories. By substituting paid labor (e.g., paid taxicab drivers) for consumer labor, Hertz was able to drive-down operating costs, which enabled him to lower prices and thus expand the market.

Of course, not all customers prefer self-service and some are not able to perform the tasks required. However, since Hertz's self-service innovation, marketers have learned that many customers do opt for self-service – partially for price discounts, but for other reasons too.

When tasks are easy and familiar, customers may be able to provide the service more quickly themselves, e.g., looking up account information on the company's website at midnight rather than waiting until the next day to talk to a human service representative.

In other instances, customers may *perceive* self-service to be quicker, even if it isn't, i.e., if they are engaged in a self-service task rather than simply waiting, time seems to pass quickly.

When creativity or customization is involved, customers' self-service may be more in line with what they specifically want, such as preparing one's own salad at a salad bar. When more skill or time is required of self-service customers, an added degree of ownership pride may follow the self-provision of tasks, e.g., assembly of a bicycle or piece of furniture. Further, in the case of rental cars, customers may prefer the sense of privacy or control they feel when they drive themselves.

April 11, 2017
Tuesday

Objectives & reminders

____

____

____

Appointments

Early morning

8 a.m.

9 a.m.

10 a.m.

11 a.m.

Noon

1 p.m.

2 p.m.

3 p.m.

4 p.m.

5 p.m.

6 p.m.

Later evening

Goodbye to sexual harassment?

Although the problem still exists, a significant step against sexual harassment was taken on April 11, 1980, when the Equal Employment Opportunity Commission (EEOC) introduced regulations to ban the offensive practice in the workplace.

The EEOC defined "sexual harassment" broadly in terms of unwelcome sexually directed actions that create adverse employment conditions. More specifically, two general types of sexual harassment have emerged from EEOC guidelines and various court cases:

1. *Quid pro quo* exists when a supervisor makes a promotion, raise, or other employment outcomes conditional upon the subordinate's granting of sexual favors (e.g., "I will recommend you for promotion if you will...").
2. *Hostile environment* exists when sexual harassment unreasonably interferes with the worker's performance of his job or when the workplace is deemed to be intimidating or offensive (e.g., display of sexually-explicit pictures, use of sexually-related language, telling of "dirty" jokes).

Sexual harassment is also expensive
Estimates suggest that sexual harassment costs each larger firm about $6 million annually -- costs from higher employee turnover, increased absenteeism, and decreased productivity.

According to EEOC guidelines, companies should take proactive measures to protect themselves against charges of sexual harassment. Suggestions:

1. Develop a company policy against sexual harassment and distribute it to all personnel. Training programs to teach personnel about sexual harassment and the company's policy are also recommended.
2. Develop a process employees can use to report incidents of possible sexual harassment without fear of retaliation.
3. Ensure that sexual harassment complaints are taken seriously and investigated.
4. Discipline members of the organization who violate the company's policy against sexual harassment.

April 12, 2017
Wednesday

Objectives & reminders

Appointments

Early morning

8 a.m.

9 a.m.

10 a.m.

11 a.m.

Noon

1 p.m.

2 p.m.

3 p.m.

4 p.m.

5 p.m.

6 p.m.

Later evening

Happy birthday: Funny guys

One of the most popular American humorists of all time, Josh Billings, was born as Henry Wheeler Shaw on April 12, 1818. He was admired for his common sense wisdom and keen understanding of human behavior. When others would try to match his wit, people asked, "Are you 'Joshing' me?"

Limits to persuasion
"There is a great power in words, if you don't hitch too many of them together." – Josh Billings

Two other celebrities also born on April 12 made tens of millions of viewers laugh on late-night television -- retired talk show host David Letterman (1947) and American pop "singer" Tiny Tim (born in 1930 as Herbert Buckingham Khaury). Letterman is known for helping -- allowing -- people to laugh at themselves, at their own mistakes.

Credits to their professions?
"There's no business like show business, but there are several businesses like accounting." -- David Letterman

Tiny Tim was known for his comical attempts to sing "Tiptoe Through the Tulips" and other songs which somehow conveyed the idea that mistakes are more palatable if one is having fun in the process. Accordingly, he became a popular singer despite his inability to sing. As one observer put it, "As a singer only one thing stands between [Tiny Tim] and success -- complete and utter failure."

Multiple wishes
"I'd love to see Christ come back to crush the spirit of hate and make men put down their guns. I'd also like just one more hit single." -- Tiny Tim

Today, humor is a serious part of the marketplace and workplace as marketers and business leaders increasingly recognize its value. In advertising humor helps marketers break through the clutter to gain audiences' attention. Also, when ads make buyers laugh or smile, they are more likely to talk about the ads with other people, i.e., they spread word-of-mouth. In personal selling, a relaxed sense of humor can help put buyers at ease. In the workplace humor helps to alleviate stress, enhance creativity, and build a sense of team spirit.

April 13, 2017
Thursday

Objectives & reminders

____

____

Appointments

Early morning

8 a.m.

9 a.m.

10 a.m.

11 a.m.

Noon

1 p.m.

2 p.m.

3 p.m.

4 p.m.

5 p.m.

6 p.m.

Later evening

Happy birthday: Frank W. Woolworth

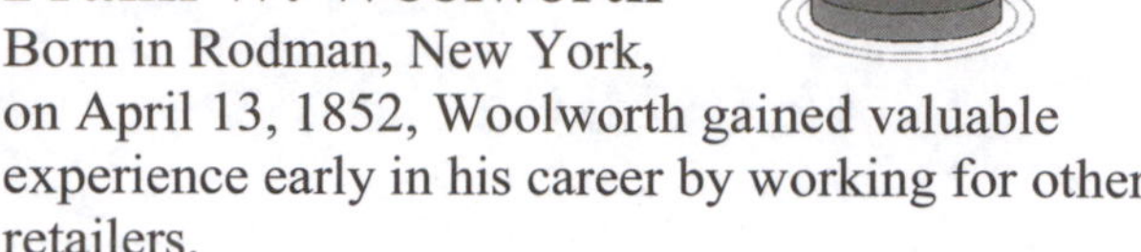

Born in Rodman, New York, on April 13, 1852, Woolworth gained valuable experience early in his career by working for other retailers.

Then, in 1879, with $350 in inventory, he opened his own retail store -- Great 5-Cent Store -- in Utica, New York. Unfortunately, the store's poor location forced the store to close only three months later. But within a month, Woolworth opened another store in Lancaster, Pennsylvania, which proved to be successful.

Soon, Woolworth added more stores as he began building his retail empire. In the early years, some stores proved to be profitable and others unprofitable. By 1911, Woolworth's chain had grown to more than 1,000 stores.

Noteworthy Woolworth innovations

Price lining. During the early days of Woolworth's, every item was priced at either 5-cents or 10-cents. Thus, Woolworth's and competitors who used the same concept became known as "five and dimes," and later as "dime stores."

Impulse buying. Before Woolworth's, retail clerks were typically stationed behind counters and retrieved merchandise that customers specifically requested. Woolworth deviated from the norm, however, when he placed merchandise on display tables for customers to browse and handle -- which led to a phenomenon that most of today's retail stores rely upon quite heavily, impulse buying.

Lay-away plan. Decades before credit cards were introduced, Woolworth helped shoppers facilitate purchases by holding merchandise for them in exchange for small deposits. Later, when buyers had enough money, they would pay the balance owed and take the merchandise.

April 14, 2017
Friday

9 7 5 3 1

Objectives & reminders

___

___

___

Appointments

Early morning

8 a.m.

9 a.m.

10 a.m.

11 a.m.

Noon

1 p.m.

2 p.m.

3 p.m.

4 p.m.

5 p.m.

6 p.m.

Later evening

New word enters language: Telescope

Although Galileo invented the instrument, Prince Federico Cesi was the first to describe the device as a "telescope" (or "telescopio" in Italian) in public -- on April 14, 1611, at a science banquet hosted by the Academy of Linceans in honor of Galileo's invention. The Prince used the term in christening the telescope. The word itself is derived from the combination of two Greek words, "tele" (far) and "scopeo" (to see).

Today, marketing researchers use the term in a different context, one that refers to a specific form of bias in survey research. For example, when consumers are asked to list the items they purchased during the past week, they frequently include on their lists items that were purchased during shopping trips earlier than the "past week," i.e., in the more distant past. In other words, their minds' eyes use telescopic lenses, so to speak, to make temporally distant (older) behaviors "appear" to be more recent.

Usually, this telescoping phenomenon is not an intentional bias on the part of respondents; rather it seems to be a part of human nature. Still, to avoid survey inaccuracies caused by the telescoping bias, marketing researchers are encouraged to use more objective data, such as items listed on cash register receipts or electronically recorded by stores' point-of-purchase technology.

Another approach that reduces but does not eliminate the problem, is to ask respondents to recall behavior from a more recent time frame, e.g., "What did you purchase *today*?" (rather than "...during the past *week*").

Keys to success: Hard work and persistence, not intelligence

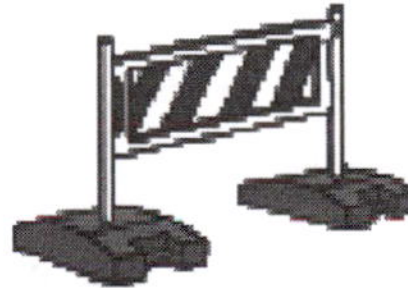

"Success in business does not depend upon genius. Any young man of ordinary intelligence who is morally sound and not afraid to work should succeed in spite of obstacles and handicaps if he plays the game fairly and keeps everlastingly at it." -- James Cash "J.C." Penney, who opened his first retail store at the age of 26 -- on April 14, 1902, in Kemmerer, Wyoming

April 15, 2017
Saturday

Objectives & reminders

____

____

____

Appointments

Early morning

8 a.m.

9 a.m.

10 a.m.

11 a.m.

Noon

1 p.m.

2 p.m.

3 p.m.

4 p.m.

5 p.m.

6 p.m.

Later evening

Not such a taxing day?

Although tax-payers can file for an extension, April 15 is the standard deadline in the U.S. for filing individual tax returns for the previous calendar year. Not surprisingly, accountants and tax preparation services have been busy during the last several days. Individuals as well may have little discretionary time available as they scramble to meet the deadline.

Most workers are required to file an annual income tax return, but because taxes are typically withheld from wage-earners' paychecks throughout the year, most U.S. consumers do not pay additional taxes in April. In fact, withheld taxes are usually more than enough to cover the tax burden and about 71 percent of U.S. tax-payers actually receive a tax refund -- a windfall that has averaged about $2,800 in recent years.

The Internal Revenue Service begins processing tax refunds as soon as the tax returns begin pouring in -- beginning as early as January. Some private companies speed the process by offering loans to tax-payers who anticipate tax refunds. With so many tax-payers receiving so much "extra" money this time of year, a wide variety of retailers are ready (already salivating?) with sale events and other incentives to attract a portion of it.

"Celebrating" taxes ☺
"I'm proud to be paying taxes in the United States. The only thing is, I could be as proud for half the money."
-- Arthur Godfrey, actor and comedian

Fruit bowl innovation

"[I]nnovation is not the consequence of a moment of brilliance. Rather, it is the fruit of an integrative approach -- the melding of strategy, marketing, R&D, production, and finance. Consequently, most successful corporations are becoming repositories and coordinators of intellect." -- Glen L. Urban, distinguished marketing scholar and former Dean of MIT's Sloan School of Management. Dr. Urban was born on April 15, 1940.

April 16, 2017
Sunday

Objectives & reminders

____

____

Appointments

Early morning

8 a.m.

9 a.m.

10 a.m.

11 a.m.

Noon

1 p.m.

2 p.m.

3 p.m.

4 p.m.

5 p.m.

6 p.m.

Later evening

Easter Sunday

Christians celebrate Easter to commemorate the resurrection of Jesus Christ. It is a "holiday" in the original sense of the word, i.e., a "holy day." In contrast to Good Friday (the Friday before Easter) which recognizes the crucifixion of Christ and is therefore a sad day for Christians, the miraculous resurrection is viewed as a joyous time. Church services are heavily attended on Easter, including sunrise services that coincide with the time of day Jesus was resurrected.

Over the years, more secular meanings and traditions have been associated with Easter. The decoration and exchange of Easter eggs has become a tradition in some families. Larger groups and communities organize Easter egg hunts for children. Because Easter is celebrated near the beginning of spring, Easter often is seen as the unofficial beginning of the new season -- prompting church-goers and others to don their new spring apparel.

The tradition of the Easter Bunny visiting children and leaving candy, eggs, and small gifts is widely observed in the U.S. While the Easter Bunny visits both Christian and non-Christian homes, many Christians are careful not to allow the Easter Bunny to upstage the original meaning of Easter (i.e., Christ's resurrection). Accordingly, they resist and some even resent the "excessive commercialization" of Easter.

Easter candy marketing facts

In terms of candy sales, Easter is second only to Halloween.

Easter-related candy sales tend to be lower when Easter falls in March rather than in April. Consider this when evaluating the effectiveness of promotional efforts.

Retail sales of Easter candy tend to increase when the candy is displayed with Easter toys (such as small stuffed animals) or when displayed near the card section or floral department.

Chocolate bunnies proliferate near Easter. Ninety million are made annually for the Easter season.

April 17, 2017
Monday

Objectives & reminders

____

____

____

Appointments

Early morning

8 a.m.

9 a.m.

10 a.m.

11 a.m.

Noon

1 p.m.

2 p.m.

3 p.m.

4 p.m.

5 p.m.

6 p.m.

Later evening

The "Good Hands" people

In 1931, the Great Depression was still wreaking havoc in America, but the promising future of the automobile spelled "opportunity" for Sears, Roebuck & Company's president and chairman General Robert E. Wood. He convinced the Board of Directors that they should back an automobile insurance concept. The Board agreed to fund the new project with $700,000.

So, on April 17, 1931, the Allstate Insurance Company was born. One month later, the new insurance company had its first policyholder. By the end of the year, 4,217 policies were in force. Today, Allstate is one of the largest insurance companies in the country, but has been independent from Sears since 1995.

Are you in good hands?
Allstate's advertising slogan, "You're in good hands," is one of the longest-running and best recognized. The slogan and accompanying iconic picture of a pair of open hands help to make the service more tangible and thus more easily understood.

Because services themselves are inherently intangible, consumers' mental images of a service can be fuzzy, abstract and vary greatly from one person to the next. As a result, services and service brands can be difficult to recognize and remember. Further, it is not always clear in customers' minds what a particular service entails. However, a tangible representation of the service -- like Allstate's "good hands" -- provides a memorable image upon which consumers can anchor their perceptions. When people think of Allstate, they immediately think of the good hands -- a symbol that reinforces the fundamental need-satisfying benefits of insurance: safety, security and protection.

Target marketing

"A well-charged pistol will do more execution than a whole barrel of gunpowder idly exploded in the air."
-- William Gilmore Simms, American writer, born on April 17, 1806

April 18, 2017
Tuesday

Builds goodwill?

True? Fair?

Beneficial to all?

Objectives & reminders

Appointments

Early morning

8 a.m.

9 a.m.

10 a.m.

11 a.m.

Noon

1 p.m.

2 p.m.

3 p.m.

4 p.m.

5 p.m.

6 p.m.

Later evening

Happy birthday: Herbert John Taylor

Born in Pickford, Michigan on April 18, 1893, Taylor was a religious and compassionate man interested in doing the "right thing."

In 1932, Taylor was put in charge of the struggling Club Aluminum company which was on the verge of bankruptcy. Saving the company appeared hopeless, but Taylor refused to let the company fold, knowing that the livelihood of 250 Club Aluminum employees was at stake. He sacrificed most of his own salary and invested personal funds to keep the company afloat long enough to enable him to turn it around.

His first priority was to change the ethical climate of Club Aluminum. He later explained, "If the people who worked for Club Aluminum were to think right, I knew they would do right. What we needed was a simple, easily remembered guide to right conduct -- a sort of ethical yardstick -- which all of us in the company could memorize and apply to what we thought, said and did." After praying about the matter, Taylor developed the guidelines that he called "The Four-Way Test."

An ethical yardstick: The Four-Way Test

1. "Is it the truth?"
2. "Is it fair to all concerned?"
3. "Will it build goodwill and better friendships?"
4. "Will it be beneficial to all concerned?"

-- Herbert John Taylor, 1932

Taylor proceeded to apply the Four-Way Test throughout the company. He used it to remedy the company's misleading advertising, to discourage salespeople from over-selling to dealers, to address vendor disputes in a mutually beneficial way, and to ensure that creditors were paid. Taylor and his application of the Four-Way Test helped to save the company. Within five years Club Aluminum was out of debt.

The application of the Four-Way Test did not end with Club Aluminum. In the early 1950s, Rotary International adopted the Test which was promoted around the world. Today, the Four-Way Test continues to be used as an ethical yardstick.

April 19, 2017
Wednesday

Objectives & reminders

Appointments

Early morning

8 a.m.

9 a.m.

10 a.m.

11 a.m.

Noon

1 p.m.

2 p.m.

3 p.m.

4 p.m.

5 p.m.

6 p.m.

Later evening

Remembering Oklahoma City

On April 19, 1995, a truck bomb exploded outside of the Alfred P. Murrah Federal Building in Oklahoma City, Oklahoma. The devastating blast destroyed the building, injured more than 500 people and killed 168 – including 17 children.

Remembering this event, as well as other man-made tragedies (e.g., Pearl Harbor attack of December 7, 1941, and the terrorist attacks of September 11, 2001) serves at least three purposes.

First, on a very basic human level, it reminds us how fragile life is and how quickly our individual worlds can change. Recognizing this we can express our deepest sympathies for the families and communities directly affected by the tragedy.

Second, as businesspeople, we're reminded of the realities of the world in which we live. Necessary steps to ensure the safety and security of employees and customers must be taken, and must be taken seriously.

Third, from a calendar planning perspective, some dates -- like this one -- may be handled best as "off limits" or "low profile" days. That is, to use another metaphor, allow the memory of the tragedy to remain "center stage." Especially in the local communities where memories of the tragedies are strongest, consider scheduling traditional sale events, grand opening celebrations, new product announcements, employee contests, and so on, on *other* days. Possible exceptions might be company efforts to participate in the community's observance/healing process, such as the distribution of free ribbons or arm bands to commemorate the event, or the use of company locations as collection points for food, clothing and other needed items to be given to victims. Higher-profile activities with obvious commercial intentions are likely to be regarded negatively.

Your community, your markets
What tragedies have occurred in your local community, or in the geographic markets your company serves that you may want to note on your calendar and in your business plans? What could your company do, not do, or reschedule to tastefully commemorate or otherwise respect the victims of those tragedies?

April 20, 2017
Thursday

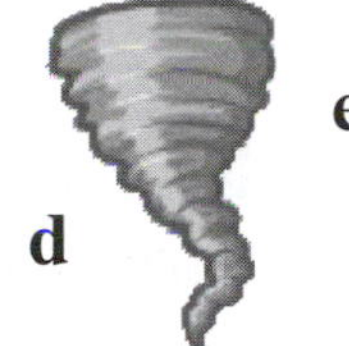

Objectives & remin rs

Severe weather drill possible today.

____

____

Appointments

Early morning

8 a.m.

9 a.m.

10 a.m.

11 a.m.

Noon

1 p.m.

2 p.m.

3 p.m.

4 p.m.

5 p.m.

6 p.m.

Later evening

Safety first: Take cover!

As part of Severe Weather Awareness Week, the U.S. National Weather Service recommends that *practice drills take place today* in preparation for seasonally severe weather that may follow in the weeks and months ahead.

Does your place of employment have an alarm or other system to alert workers and customers when severe weather is a threat? Does your organization have an established process for evacuating potentially dangerous areas and moving workers, customers and guests to safer areas -- such as basements or internal rooms? Are workers familiar with the process; do they know what to do in a weather emergency?

Tornados, in particular, are a concern in the U.S. as about 1,200 strike the country annually. Although they can occur in any state and in any month of the year, states east of the Rocky Mountains are most vulnerable and tornados are more likely to occur from March through June.

For communities on or near the coast, sensitivity to the approaching *hurricane* season (June through November) should be part of the awareness-raising efforts this week. Is your organization prepared?

For more information
For details and ideas regarding possible activities this week, visit the National Weather Service's designated website, http://www.weather.gov/mkx/awarenessweek and click on "Link to National Awareness Week Activities."

____

Happy Birthday: Stanley Marcus

On April 20, 1905, Stanley Marcus was born into a retailing family. He didn't realize it at the time but his life's story would be inseparably intertwined with that of the family business – Texas-based Neiman-Marcus department stores, co-founded by his father, Herbert Marcus. The younger Marcus began working in the "store" at age 21 and later became the retail chain's president and CEO.

The inescapable human element
"The human eye, the human experience, is the one thing that can make quality better -- or poorer." -- Stanley Marcus

April 21, 2017
Friday

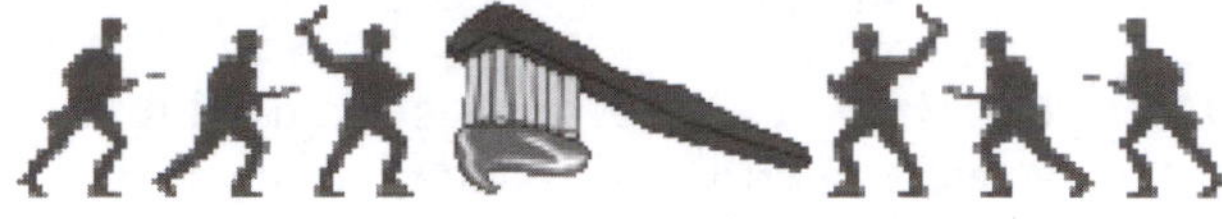

Objectives & reminders

____

____

____

Appointments

Early morning

8 a.m.

9 a.m.

10 a.m.

11 a.m.

Noon

1 p.m.

2 p.m.

3 p.m.

4 p.m.

5 p.m.

6 p.m.

Later evening

Accurate forecasts are a challenge

"If you have to forecast, forecast often." – Edgar R. Fieldler, American business economist who enjoyed a distinguished career in industry and federal government, born on April 21, 1929

Dual holiday in Brazil: Tiradentes Day, Brasília Day

April 21 is a national holiday in Brazil. First, the day commemorates a national hero -- Jose de Silva "Tiradentes" -- who was executed on April 21, 1789, while leading the fight for independence from Portugal.

> **A unique opportunity to promote Dental Hygiene Week?**
> Jose de Silva was not only a freedom fighter; he was a dentist. Other than Brazil, few countries (if any?) can claim dentists as national heroes.

One hundred and seventy one years later, on April 21, 1960, the city of Brasilia was dedicated as the new official capital of Brazil. Although citizens of the former capital, Rio de Janeiro, were generally not supportive of the move, President Kubitschek believed it was an essential change. The relocation of the capital and the numerous building projects associated with it helped to boost the economy of the interior of the country where Brasília is located.

Further, from a marketing perspective, the new buildings and modern infrastructure helped to market the country by making a positive impression on foreign businesspeople who visited Brazil to explore the possibilities of conducting business in the country.

Today, Brazil is the most populous country in South America (205 million consumers), and the fifth most populous country in the world -- behind China, India, United States, and Indonesia.

Good day for farming

"Prejudices, it is well known, are most difficult to eradicate from the heart whose soil has never been loosened or fertilized by education; they grow there, firm as weeds among stones." – Charlotte Brontë, British novelist, born on April 21, 1816

April 22, 2017
Saturday

Objectives & reminders

Help protect the "big blue marble" today, and every day.

Appointments

Early morning

8 a.m.

9 a.m.

10 a.m.

11 a.m.

Noon

1 p.m.

2 p.m.

3 p.m.

4 p.m.

5 p.m.

6 p.m.

Later evening

Earth Day

First celebrated in the United States on April 22, 1970, to increase public awareness of environmental problems throughout the world, Earth Day is observed in dozens of countries today.

Earth Day is an ideal time for companies to publicize their efforts and/or successes with regard to reducing or preventing pollution and conserving natural resources. Further, companies with strong environmental records often use Earth Day to heighten consumers' sensitivity to environmental issues and to stir their local communities to action by sponsoring recycling drives, clean-up projects, waste reduction campaigns, and other "green" initiatives.

Don't discard "disposal"

Northwestern University's distinguished marketing professor Philip Kotler has pointed out a largely ignored gap in consumer behavior research. He suggests that consumer behavior consists largely of three broad stages: (1) acquisition, (2) consumption, and (3) disposal. Most consumer behavior research and marketing practice focus on the first and second categories, i.e., how consumers go about making purchase decisions and acquiring products, and how they use products after purchase.

A small number of studies examine disposal-related issues -- e.g., how consumers get rid of the goods they buy (toss into the trash, hoard, burn, recycle, give to charity, trade-in, or other?), whether consumers insist on disposal of the old prior to the purchase of a replacement, to what extent consumers consider eventual disposal prior to the initial purchase, whether buyers consider and care about the environmental effects of disposed items, and so on.

Understanding and facilitating the disposal process could prove to be beneficial for marketers -- especially those that serve environment-conscious consumers.

April 23, 2017
Sunday

Objectives & reminders

____

____

____

Appointments

Early morning

8 a.m.

9 a.m.

10 a.m.

11 a.m.

Noon

1 p.m.

2 p.m.

3 p.m.

4 p.m.

5 p.m.

6 p.m.

Later evening

Cola war intensifies

On April 23, 1985, The Coca-Cola Company chairman Roberto Goizueta said, "the best has been made even better," when the company officially announced that it was changing Coke's formula. On the same day PepsiCo ran full page advertisements in major newspapers throughout the U.S. with PepsiCo's president, Roger Enrico, claiming that "the other guy just blinked" and their competitor was "reformulating brand Coke to be more like Pepsi [because] Pepsi tastes better than Coke." Protests by loyal Coke-drinkers pressured The Coca-Cola Company to reintroduce the original formula less than three months later.

The Pepsi Challenge:
Trick question, important point
Have Pepsi's taste tests found that consumers tend to prefer Pepsi over Coke? The temptation is to say "yes," but the correct answer is "no." While it may be true that more participants in the blind taste tests express a preference for the beverage made by PepsiCo than for the one made by Coca-Cola, keep in mind that the taste tests measure only taste. Pepsi and Coke are *brands* that include bundles of physical and image-related attributes that extend far beyond taste, per se. Accordingly, Pepsi ads are carefully worded to say that consumers prefer "the *taste* of Pepsi."

Hot brand!

Krispy Kreme (doughnuts) may have been the hottest brand in the United States in 2002. On April 23 of that year, the company opened a new store in Maple Grove, Minnesota. Four reporters from the Minneapolis *Star Tribune* were assigned to cover the grand opening event. During the first week of operation, the store's sales established a new company record of $480,693, which, of course, represents a lot of dough.

Since Krispy Kreme's glory days of a few years ago, the company has had its share of problems -- causing the company's stock price to plummet and its CEO to resign. In an effort to recover, the company has introduced a lower-calorie, whole wheat doughnut and expanded into markets outside of the United States, among other steps.

April 24, 2017
Monday

Objectives & reminders

____

____

____

Appointments

Early morning

8 a.m.

9 a.m.

10 a.m.

11 a.m.

Noon

1 p.m.

2 p.m.

3 p.m.

4 p.m.

5 p.m.

6 p.m.

Later evening

Happy birthday: Anthony Trollope

Trollope was one of the most successful and most prolific English novelists of the 19th century. He was born in London on April 24, 1815. Like many other successful authors, Trollope's keen insights into human nature provide guidance for aspiring business leaders. Examples are included in the accompanying boxes.

Customer as center of attention
"No man thinks there is much ado about nothing when the ado is about himself."

Reality of new product development
"To think of a story is much harder work than to write it."

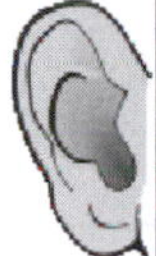

Listening
"It is very hard, that necessity of listening to a man who says nothing."

Leadership
"Little men in authority are always stern."

Competition
"Competition, that beautiful science of the present day, by which every plodding cart-horse is converted into a racer."

What to wear to work
"They are best dressed, whose dress no one observes."

Success is a journey, not a destination
"Success is the necessary misfortune of life, but it is only to the very unfortunate that it comes early."

April 25, 2017
Tuesday

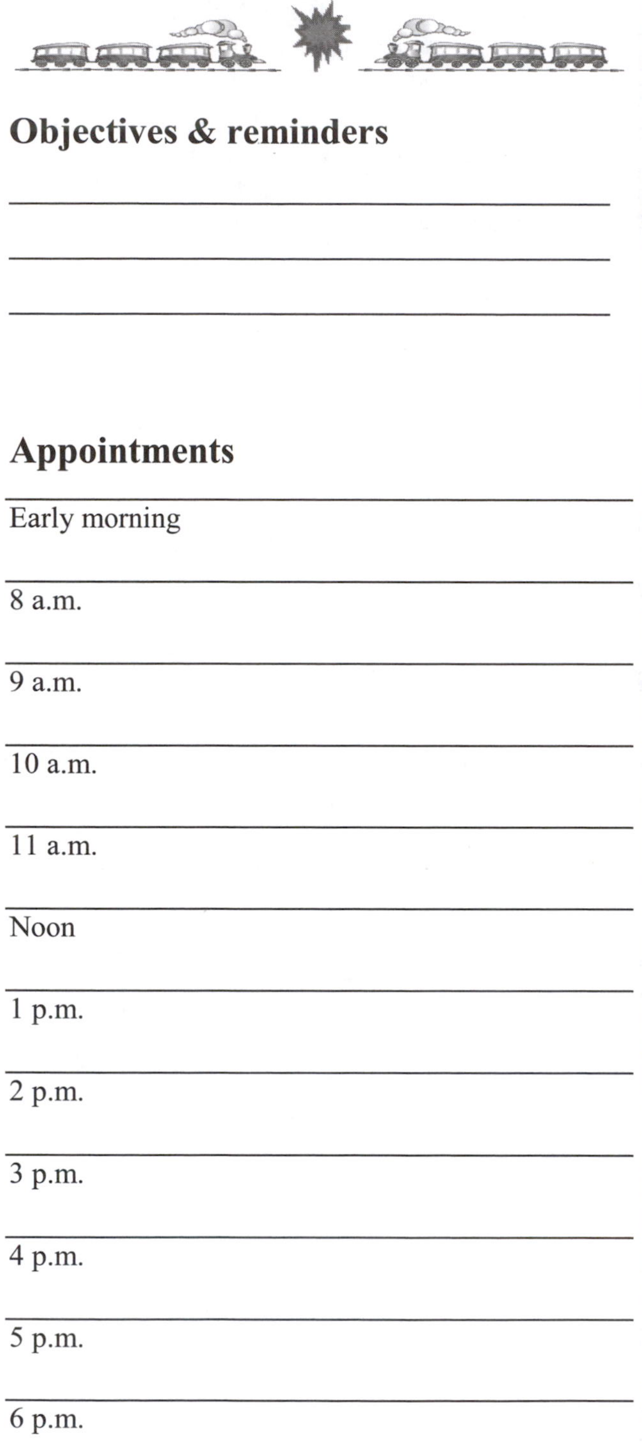

Objectives & reminders

Appointments

Early morning

8 a.m.

9 a.m.

10 a.m.

11 a.m.

Noon

1 p.m.

2 p.m.

3 p.m.

4 p.m.

5 p.m.

6 p.m.

Later evening

Possible conflicts of interest?

Two of the biggest advertising agency mergers in history occurred during the spring of 1986. The first, on April 25, combined three agencies from New York -- Doyle Dane Bernbach Group, Inc., Needham Harper Worldwide, and BBDO International, Inc. The second was consummated 17 days later when Ted Bates Worldwide was acquired by Saatchi & Saatchi. The two emerging super-sized firms suddenly became the biggest ad agencies in the world.

Mergers of large firms often raise questions about their effects on competition within the *merging companies' industry*, which is why antitrust legislation exists. However, the mergers of these ad agencies led to some particularly thorny questions about the competition within *clients' industries*. That is, when the agencies merged, clients of the new conglomerates found their accounts handled by the same firm that already handles their chief rival's account. Clients wondered: "Would competitors receive better service, lower prices or preferential treatment from the agency?" "Would confidential data or strategic plans shared with the agency be leaked to competitors?" And so on. Procter and Gamble and Colgate-Palmolive both expressed concerns about the mergers.

Consider the extent to which these or other ad agency mergers represent *actual* conflicts of interest, *potential* conflicts of interest, or *perceived* conflict of interest, and how they might jeopardize business relationships with clients. What, if anything, should merged *agencies* do to prevent or address clients' concerns? What courses of action might *clients* take?

Other conflicts of interest?

Can financial analysts make objective recommendations to "buy," "sell," or "hold" stocks when they or their firms serve as investment bankers hired to sell the stock of the companies they analyze? Are analysts' recommendations likely to be biased if they own the stock themselves? On April 25, 2002, these and other questions prompted the U.S. Security and Exchange Commission to launch a "conflict of interest" investigation of Wall Street analysts.

April 26, 2017
Wednesday

Objectives & reminders

____

____

Appointments

Early morning

8 a.m.

9 a.m.

10 a.m.

11 a.m.

Noon

1 p.m.

2 p.m.

3 p.m.

4 p.m.

5 p.m.

6 p.m.

Later evening

Administrative Professionals Day

Welcome to Administrative Professionals Day -- formerly known as Professional Secretaries Day.

Legendary basketball coach John Wooden once asserted that "the main ingredient of stardom is the rest of the team." Of course, his insight applies to business teams as well as to basketball teams. So, don't forget to show your office assistants and other teammates how valuable they are, *and...*

Although Administrative Professionals Day occurs only once a year (on Wednesday of the last full week in April), you don't have to make "thank you" an annual event. Instead, consider showing your appreciation on a daily basis.

Did you know?

- There are 4.1 million secretaries and administrative assistants in the United States. About one percent of them are male.
- "Administrative assistant" or similar title is now used to reflect the changing roles that secretaries once played, although "secretary" is still used in about 20 percent of the administrative workforce's job titles.

Better marketing by understanding consumers' usage behavior

Understanding how consumers use particular products often leads to improvements in those products or to ancillary or complementary products. Such was the case on April 26, 1892, when New Haven, Connecticut's Sarah Boone received a patent for an ironing board "having its edges curved to correspond to the outside and inside seams of a sleeve." Boone's firsthand ironing experience coupled with conversations with and observations of other ironers provided the insights needed for her innovative design that remains popular today.

April 27, 2017
Thursday

Objectives & reminders

____

____

____

Appointments

Early morning

8 a.m.

9 a.m.

10 a.m.

11 a.m.

Noon

1 p.m.

2 p.m.

3 p.m.

4 p.m.

5 p.m.

6 p.m.

Later evening

Improving hearing *and* listening

On April 27, 1880, Francis D. Clarke and M.G. Foster received the first patent in the United States for an electric "Device for Aiding the Deaf to Hear," i.e., a hearing aid. Unfortunately for the deaf, it would be another 21 years until hearing aids were commercially available.

Today, while *hearing* aids may improve people's ability to hear, *listening* involves a host of other issues. People who can hear may or may not be inclined to listen. Exactly 108 years after the hearing aid patent was issued -- i.e., April 27, 1988 -- Jack Welch, then chairman and CEO of General Electric, offered a suggestion for a *listening aid.* He recommended that businesses tear down the cumbersome and distracting bureaucracies that hinder listening. "Without all the din and prattle of bureaucracy," Welch asserted, "people listen as well as talk."

Three keys of leadership

"One, don't think you can ever ask anybody to do anything that you are not prepared to do yourself.... Two, it's essential that people know you care about them.... Three, you've always got to ask more of yourself and your people than either you or they think can be accomplished." -- David H. Komansky, former chairman and CEO of Merrill Lynch and Company, born on April 27, 1939

Leadership is bigger than the leader

"A leader is a person who has character and a purpose. That purpose has to be something that transcends one's own particular interest, something that benefits the whole of humanity... A leader has to have a vision, and has to be able to implement it." – Coretta Scott King, wife of slain civil rights leader Martin Luther King, Jr. and an influential leader herself. Ms. King was born in Marion, Alabama on April 27, 1927.

Timeless leadership tip

"Make it unquestionably clear what is expected of employees." – William Julian King, engineer (General Electric and Battelle Memorial Institute) and professor (Cornell U. and UCLA), born in Baton Rouge, Louisiana on April 27, 1902

April 28, 2017
Friday

Objectives & reminders

____

____

____

Appointments

Early morning

8 a.m.

9 a.m.

10 a.m.

11 a.m.

Noon

1 p.m.

2 p.m.

3 p.m.

4 p.m.

5 p.m.

6 p.m.

Later evening

Arbor Day

The first Arbor Day was celebrated by Nebraskans who planted more than one million trees on April 10, 1872. A few years later, Nebraska moved the celebration to April 22 to honor Julius Sterling Morton, a former governor and advocate of forestation who lobbied for several years for the tree-planting holiday. In the years that followed, other states began to celebrate Arbor Day too -- although at different times of the year.

Today, Arbor Day is generally recognized on the last Friday in April and represents the United States' oldest environmental holiday.

Arbor Day has been embraced by grade schools, in particular, who use the occasion to teach children about the techniques and virtues of planting trees. According to the *Farmers' Bulletin* (#1492):

> "Arbor Day has become associated all over the United States with patriotic and esthetic as well as economic ideas. It is at once a means of doing practical good to the community and an incentive to civic betterment.... The Arbor Day tree is not only a thing of beauty and utility in itself; it is also a symbol, standing for the recognition of the importance of the forest in the life of the Nation."

Trees

"I think that I shall never see
A poem lovely as a tree.

A tree whose hungry mouth is prest
Against the earth's sweet flowing breast;

A tree that looks at God all day,
And lifts her leafy arms to pray;

A tree that may in summer wear
A nest of robins in her hair;

Upon whose bosom snow has lain;
Who intimately lives with rain.

Poems are made by fools like me,
But only God can make a tree."

--Joyce Kilmer, American poet
who wrote "Trees" in 1913

April 29, 2017
Saturday

Objectives & reminders

Appointments

Early morning

8 a.m.

9 a.m.

10 a.m.

11 a.m.

Noon

1 p.m.

2 p.m.

3 p.m.

4 p.m.

5 p.m.

6 p.m.

Later evening

Marketing as a fishy profession

"If you want to catch more fish, use more hooks." -- George H. Allen, American football coach, born on April 29, 1922

Shifting focus

Many newspaper advertisements of the 1870s were little more than announcements: "We have this to sell, at this price, available at this location." Unlike astute advertisers today, few advertisers in the 1870s talked about user benefits; most were product-oriented because demand often outweighed supply. Notice the excerpts from the two newspaper ads in the accompanying boxes, both published on April 29, 1871, in the *Kennebec Reporter* (Gardiner, Maine). The ad for trusses was fairly typical for the period, whereas the ad for laundry soap is more reflective of an advertiser who is beginning to think about the product from the customer's point of view.

Truss this ad?
"The place to buy your TRUSSES, SUPPORTERS AND SHOULDER BRACES, And have them properly adjusted, is at Dr. A.F. Plimpton's Drug Store, Under the Evans Hotel, Water Street. Gardiner, ME."

Clean advertising
"NO MORE Boiling Clothes! -- NO STEAM In The House! -- LITTLE LABOR. WARFIELD'S Cold Water Soap! Saves boiling clothes; washes in *cold*, warm, hard or soft water; and is not so injurious to clothes as common soap. **For Sale by all Grocers**. JOHN DENNIS & CO., 77 Commercial St., Portland."

Gap analysis

"[T]here has always been a discrepancy between plans and performance." -- Hirohito, 124th Emperor of Japan (1928-1989), born on April 29, 1901

April 30, 2017
Sunday

Objectives & reminders

____

____

____

Appointments

Early morning

8 a.m.

9 a.m.

10 a.m.

11 a.m.

Noon

1 p.m.

2 p.m.

3 p.m.

4 p.m.

5 p.m.

6 p.m.

Later evening

Happy birthday: Bruce Henderson

Born in rural Tennessee on April 30, 1915, Henderson worked for his father's publishing business early in his business career, as a Bible salesman. He later worked for Westinghouse Corporation and then for the management consulting firm Arthur D. Little, before founding the consulting firm in 1963 that would become known as the Boston Consulting Group (BCG).

While at BCG, Henderson was instrumental in prompting companies to think more strategically about their businesses. For example, one of the underlying principles of what is probably the most well-known diagnostic tool his team developed -- the "Growth-Share Matrix" -- is that managers should not manage "strategic business units" (e.g., product lines, brands, stores, etc.) individually, but as a portfolio. Also reinforced by the Growth-Share Matrix, Henderson stressed the critical importance that a firm's relative market share and cash flow are to business success. This perspective forced managers to think more intently about longer-term planning, competition, and resource availability and allocation, while de-emphasizing what Henderson viewed as misleading measures of profitability.

Business strategy:
Built on competitive advantage

"[Strategy] is a deliberate search for a plan of action that will develop a business's competitive advantage and compound it. For any company the search is an iterative process that begins with a recognition of where you are and what you have now. Your most dangerous competitors are those that are most like you. The differences between you and your competitors are the basis of your advantage. If you are in business and self-supporting you already have some kind of competitive advantage no matter how small or subtle. Otherwise you would have gradually lost customers faster than you gained them. The objective is to enlarge the scope of your advantage..."
-- Bruce Henderson

Fast forward to 2014 and we find BCG with 82 offices in 46 countries, annual revenues of $4.55 billion, and more than 10,000 employees (including 6,200 consultants).

May 1, 2017
Monday

Objectives & reminders

____

____

____

Appointments

Early morning

8 a.m.

9 a.m.

10 a.m.

11 a.m.

Noon

1 p.m.

2 p.m.

3 p.m.

4 p.m.

5 p.m.

6 p.m.

Later evening

Postcards

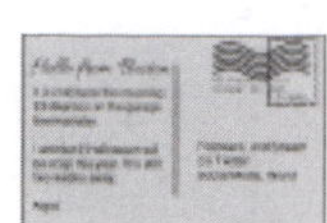

On May 1, 1873, the first U.S. postcard made its debut. Today, marketers often use postcards to send announcements, reminders, and other brief communications to customers. Because postcards are less expensive and less time-consuming to print, prepare and mail than letters with envelopes, they are a cost-efficient communication tool. Of course, they're not as cost-efficient as email, but because many people are bombarded with 100 or more emails weekly, the novelty effect of postcards increases the chances that they'll be noticed.

Professional service providers such as dentists, optometrists and physicians may lose revenue when clients miss appointments or fail to schedule them, so the staff use postcards as appointment reminders. One technique is to ask each clients to address a postcard to himself before leaving the service providers' office. Several weeks or months later, as the follow-up appointment approaches, the service provider mails the postcard to the client as a reminder. Recognition of their own handwriting grabs the recipient's attention.

The discount war begins!

The first Target store was opened on May 1, 1962, in Roseville, Minnesota. Also in 1962, S. S. Kresge opened the first Kmart (in Garden City, Michigan) and Sam Walton opened the first store (in Rogers, Arkansas) in what would later become the Wal-Mart chain.

The Great Exhibition

Long before there were Targets, Kmarts, Wal-Marts or shopping malls, there was London's Great Exhibition. Opened on May 1, 1851, 10,000+ exhibitors displayed a variety of goods from around the world along eight miles of tables. The exhibition remained open until October 1851. By then, six million people had visited the exhibition and made the venture a success -- paving the way for the hundreds of thousands of consumer and trade shows that would follow. Today, trade and consumer shows are effective and cost efficient ways for marketers to meet face-to-face with prospective customers who otherwise might be too geographically dispersed to contact economically.

May 2, 2017
Tuesday

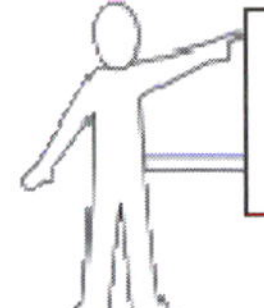

Marketing FAME
More than 15 minutes!

Objectives & reminders

____

____

Appointments

Early morning

8 a.m.

9 a.m.

10 a.m.

11 a.m.

Noon

1 p.m.

2 p.m.

3 p.m.

4 p.m.

5 p.m.

6 p.m.

Later evening

National Teacher Day

The first full week of May is Teacher Appreciation Week in the United States, and Tuesday of that week – today – is National Teacher Day. It's a great opportunity to honor local teachers and thank them for all they do for their students, their schools and their communities.

The promotion possibilities are numerous. For example, retail stores could set aside a display area to showcase thank you cards and small gift items for students to purchase and give to their teachers. Or, businesses could sponsor contests that solicit nominations of outstanding teachers in the area – with awards, certificates of appreciation, gift cards, and other recognition or prizes bestowed upon the nominees and winners.

For international marketers
At least 90 countries set aside one or more days to honor their teachers. These dates are scattered throughout the year, but October 5 seems to be the single most popular date – recognized as World Teachers' Day.

Happy birthday: *Good Housekeeping*

Founded by Clark W. Bryan, a journalist and businessman, *Good Housekeeping* was born on May 2, 1885. The magazine soon became one of the most popular women's magazines, reaching a circulation of 300,000 by 1911. Today, *Good Housekeeping* has about 4.3 million subscribers.

Good Housekeeping contributed to consumer and business interests when the magazine began sponsoring an "Experiment Station" in 1900 to test consumer products and offer recommendations for the benefit of the magazine's readers. This evolved into the Good Housekeeping Institute and a practice of awarding its "Seal of Approval" to selected items. By the 1920s the Seal of Approval became the "Guaranty Seal," used as a screening device to prevent ads for inferior products from reaching the pages of *Good Housekeeping*.

"This is Your Guaranty"
"Every article advertised in *Good Housekeeping* carries with it a money-back guaranty..." -- *Good Housekeeping*, Feb. 1926 issue

May 3, 2017
Wednesday

Objectives & reminders

____

____

____

Appointments

Early morning

8 a.m.

9 a.m.

10 a.m.

11 a.m.

Noon

1 p.m.

2 p.m.

3 p.m.

4 p.m.

5 p.m.

6 p.m.

Later evening

Happy birthday: Karl Abraham

Born in Germany on May 3, 1877, Abraham was one of many psychologists over the years to investigate the tremendous influence that childhood experiences have on people later in life. Not surprisingly, consumer researchers who followed Abraham (such as Lester Guest and James McNeal) have found that consumption experiences and loyalties toward brands, product categories and stores often form early in life. That's one reason why businesses increasingly cater to children and teens.

What do you get when you cross a Ford Explorer with a Firestone tire?

In 2000, you got rollover accidents and tragic fatalities, followed by lots of finger-pointing and Ford Motor Company's decision to stop using Firestone tires for the first time in decades. The negative publicity associated with the auto accidents and feud with Bridgestone-Firestone contributed to Ford's $6.4 billion in losses in 2001 and 2002.

Forty-three years earlier, however, when a Ford was crossed with a Firestone, you got William Clay Ford, Jr. -- born on May 3, 1957. That is, Jr's father was William Clay Ford (son of Ford Motor Company's founder, Henry Ford), while his mother was Martha Firestone (from Harvey Firestone's tire family dynasty). Partially in response to the tire debacle, William Clay Ford, Jr. was named Ford's CEO in October 2001.

What CEOs say when they inherit a financially-challenged company
"We need to get our focus back on the basics of our business..."
-- William Clay Ford, Jr.

____

Titles are impressive: Agree or disagree?

"It is not titles that honor men, but men that honor titles." -- Niccolò Machiavelli, Italian statesman, born on May 3, 1469

May 4, 2017
Thursday

"Only" $24?

Objectives & reminders

Appointments

Early morning

8 a.m.

9 a.m.

10 a.m.

11 a.m.

Noon

1 p.m.

2 p.m.

3 p.m.

4 p.m.

5 p.m.

6 p.m.

Later evening

From good buy to goodbye

$24 good buy Manhattan

On May 4, 1626, Dutch colonist Peter Minuit first landed on an island in present-day New York, called Manhattan. Representing the Dutch West India Company, Minuit's job was to look after the company's trading interests and colonization efforts throughout the Hudson River region. Accordingly, he bought the entire island from the Algonquin Indians for about $24.

Today, $24 will not buy one square inch of Manhattan where apartments routinely sell for more than $1 million each. However, before assuming that Minuit received the better end of the transaction, consider how much that $24 might be worth in 2017 had it been placed in a modest investment to earn a compounded annual return of 7 percent – about $6.5 trillion, or enough to buy 6.5 million apartments priced at $1 million each. It's not surprising that today's investment counselors urge their clients to take a long-term view of investing.

$25 goodbye to Indianapolis

With $25 in his pocket, 25-year-old professional bowler Dick Weber said "goodbye" to Indianapolis, Indiana, on May 4, 1955. He was headed to St. Louis to join the now legendary Budweiser's bowling team. His bowling career blossomed as Weber became one of the best three bowlers of all time, winning professional titles in each of six consecutive decades!

Shortly after joining the Budweiser team, Weber agreed to be a spokesman for bowling manufacturer AMF. His relationship with AMF would continue for 48 years until Weber's death in 2005 -- perhaps the longest continuous endorsement relationship of any professional athlete.

"On a scale of 1 to 10, a 300"
In 2005, AMF saluted Dick Weber: "Athlete of rare gifts. Ambassador for bowling worldwide. A human being of warmth, generosity and good humor. A partner with AMF for over 48 years, Dick Weber was as good as it gets. We will all miss him."

May 5, 2017
Friday

Objectives & reminders

____

____

____

Appointments

Early morning

8 a.m.

9 a.m.

10 a.m.

11 a.m.

Noon

1 p.m.

2 p.m.

3 p.m.

4 p.m.

5 p.m.

6 p.m.

Later evening

Cinco de Mayo

Mexico gained its independence by defeating French invaders at the Battle of Puebla de Los Angeles (a small town in east-central Mexico) on May 5, 1862. Accordingly, Cinco de Mayo is a national holiday in Mexico and celebrated annually on May 5 with a variety of cultural festivities such as fairs, parades, food, dancing, and so on.

Breakfast Defectors Day
In 2015, Taco Bell, the U.S.-based Mexican fast food chain, capitalized on the public attention drawn to Cinco de Mayo to promote its breakfast menu and challenge McDonald's breakfast customers to defect to Taco Bell. On May 5 that year, from 7:00 to 11:00 a.m., Taco Bell gave customers free breakfast tacos.

Cinco de Mayo is also widely recognized and celebrated in the U.S. to promote the heritage and culture of the Hispanic community. About 17 percent of the U.S. population is Hispanic -- making it the largest and one of the fastest-growing ethnic groups in the nation. A disproportionately large number of Hispanics live in the Southwestern U.S., California, and southern Florida.

Cultural branding gone too far: Agree or disagree?

"The effect, if not always the original intent, of advanced branding is to nudge the hosting culture into the background and make the brand the star. It is not to sponsor culture but to be the culture. And why shouldn't it be? If brands are not products but ideas, attitudes, values and experiences, why can't they be culture too?" -- Naomi Klein, Canadian journalist, author and frequent critic of marketing practices, born in Montreal, Quebec on May 5, 1970. This quotation – worthy of consideration on Cinco de Mayo and other culturally-relevant holidays – is from page 30 of her thought-provoking 2002 book, *No Logo.*

Objectives & reminders

Appointments

Early morning

8 a.m.

9 a.m.

10 a.m.

11 a.m.

Noon

1 p.m.

2 p.m.

3 p.m.

4 p.m.

5 p.m.

6 p.m.

Later evening

The cold facts

The first U.S. patent for a refrigerator was granted on May 6, 1851, to John Gorrie. Although it was several years before refrigerators were commonplace, their gradual adoption spurred consumption of food products as consumers became less concerned about spoilage. That is, larger quantities of food were purchased and prepared knowing that unused portions could be saved in the refrigerator and eaten later. Generally, whenever larger quantities of food or other consumable items are readily available in consumers' homes, the rate of consumption increases.

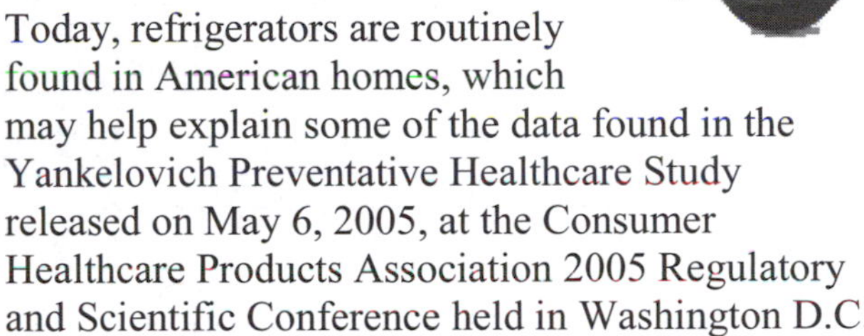

Perhaps refrigerators should be banned?

Today, refrigerators are routinely found in American homes, which may help explain some of the data found in the Yankelovich Preventative Healthcare Study released on May 6, 2005, at the Consumer Healthcare Products Association 2005 Regulatory and Scientific Conference held in Washington D.C.

The study of 6,000 consumers found that 72 percent of Americans were overweight and 39 percent were obese. Curiously, however, only 30 percent of the surveyed respondents reported efforts to lose weight. Frequently cited barriers to attaining and maintaining a healthy weight include:

- "Dislike exercise" (22%)
- "Enjoy junk food too much" (21%)
- "Inability to afford a successful weight loss program" (20%)
- "Lack of will power to stick to a plan" (15%)
- "Inability to figure out the best way to lose weight" (14%)

Consider how food and fitness businesses could use these findings when developing and promoting their products and services. For example, to counter consumers' dislike for exercise, fitness centers could promote their supportive social atmosphere and fun games and sports, rather than "exercise," per se. Or, food producers could develop snack foods that are both good tasting and nutritious.

May 7, 2017
Sunday

Objectives & reminders

___

___

Appointments

Early morning

8 a.m.

9 a.m.

10 a.m.

11 a.m.

Noon

1 p.m.

2 p.m.

3 p.m.

4 p.m.

5 p.m.

6 p.m.

Later evening

Shaping globalization

"Globalization is led by businesses that are scanning the world for the best place to produce and sell their products. This process is going to continue, no matter what governments decide."
-- Lester C. Thurow, economist and former dean of the MIT Sloan School of Management, born on May 7, 1938

Happy birthday: Edwin Herbert Land

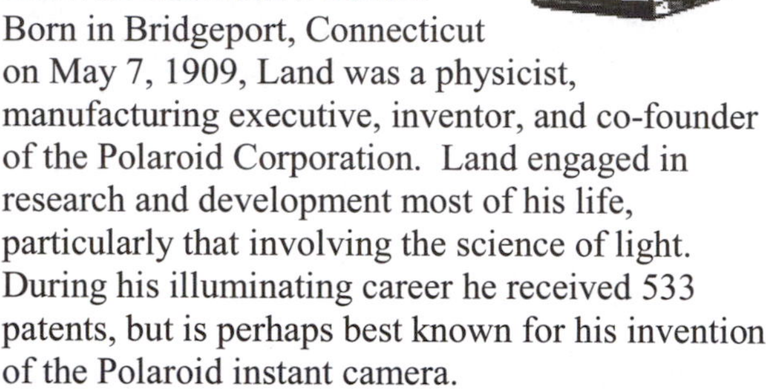

Born in Bridgeport, Connecticut on May 7, 1909, Land was a physicist, manufacturing executive, inventor, and co-founder of the Polaroid Corporation. Land engaged in research and development most of his life, particularly that involving the science of light. During his illuminating career he received 533 patents, but is perhaps best known for his invention of the Polaroid instant camera.

Clearly, Land was an "idea" person. He had a reputation for identifying ideas with commercial application and then following through with their development. Interestingly, many of his ideas came to him not during formal planning or idea-generation sessions, but during the course of everyday life. For example, Land enjoyed walking. Ideas for innovative products or solutions to technical problems often came to him as he freed his mind from day-to-day distractions during long walks.

In one particularly serendipitous moment in the early 1940s, Land's creative genius was sparked when his three-year-old daughter asked why she had to wait to see the photographs he had just taken. Four years later he was marketing the Polaroid camera and his daughter no longer had to wait for more than a few seconds to see photographs. By the late 1960s, about half of all U.S. households had a Polaroid camera.

Thinking out of the box
According to Edwin H. Land, significant progress in innovation is always "taken by some individual who has freed himself from a way of thinking that is held by friends and associates who may be more intelligent, better educated, better disciplined, but who have not mastered the art of the fresh, clean look at old, old knowledge."

May 8, 2017
Monday

Objectives & reminders

____

____

____

Appointments

Early morning

8 a.m.

9 a.m.

10 a.m.

11 a.m.

Noon

1 p.m.

2 p.m.

3 p.m.

4 p.m.

5 p.m.

6 p.m.

Later evening

Happy birthday: Leon Festinger

Born in Brooklyn, New York on May 8, 1919, Festinger's research contributed greatly to the fields of psychology and marketing. Perhaps he is best known in marketing for his development of theories of cognitive dissonance which are detailed in two of his books, *A Theory of Cognitive Dissonance* (1957), and *Conflict, Decision, and Dissonance* (1964).

A consumer might experience cognitive dissonance (i.e., psychological tension or discomfort) when two or more cognitive elements (such as beliefs, attitudes, knowledge of the environment) seem to be incompatible. For example, cognitive dissonance might surface when a consumer becomes aware that she is eating a box of cookies on the same day she's pledged to diet. When dissonance occurs, she is likely to eliminate or minimize the inconsistency by altering one or more of the cognitive elements, e.g., "A few cookies won't hurt my diet" or "I don't really need to diet today.").

The phenomenon is highly marketing-relevant because cognitive dissonance can alter consumers' purchase intentions ("I must stop buying cookies"). Marketers can help themselves as well as consumers by providing ammunition to help consumers cope with cognitive dissonance. A cookie manufacturer, for example, might stress that one cookie contains only seven grams of fat, or that they are "reduced fat," or "sugar free." Or, portraying slim cookie-eating models in advertising may subtly imply dieting and cookies are not incompatible.

One important subset of the cognitive dissonance phenomenon sometimes occurs after buyers make a purchase and then wonder if they might have made a mistake -- e.g., purchased the wrong brand, the wrong size, paid too much money, etc. This form of cognitive dissonance is known as *post-purchase dissonance* or *buyers' remorse*. To address it, marketers follow-up the sale with communications that reinforce the wisdom of the purchase decision. In addition, salespeople can help customers cope with buyers' remorse by contacting them a few days after the purchase to make sure that promised benefits have materialized. The failure to address customers' concerns quickly may magnify the dissonance and jeopardize future sales.

May 9, 2017
Tuesday

Objectives & reminders

____

____

____

Appointments

Early morning

8 a.m.

9 a.m.

10 a.m.

11 a.m.

Noon

1 p.m.

2 p.m.

3 p.m.

4 p.m.

5 p.m.

6 p.m.

Later evening

Even *before* reality television

It was May 9, 1961, when the chairman of the Federal Communications Commission, Newton N. Minow, criticized the relatively new medium of television. He called it a "vast wasteland" – a phrase that still remains in TV critics' vocabularies.

Certainly in terms of retaining customers

"I think that American salesmanship can be a weapon more powerful than the atomic bomb." -- Henry J. Kaiser, American industrialist (construction, ship-building, automobiles, aircraft, insurance), born on May 9, 1882

Advertising reinforces good quality, but doesn't offset poor quality

"The quality of the product is number one; our advertising is number two... In advertising you have to tell people why they should buy your product, meaning you have to make the best product in your field." -- Frank Perdue, former president of Perdue Farms (the first chicken producer to successfully brand chickens -- a product category that had been considered a commodity), born on May 9, 1920

Career advice to love

"Know what you love and do what you love. If you don't do what you love, you're just wasting your time." -- Billy Joel, singer and songwriter who loves music, born on May 9, 1949

The leadership stretch

"Leadership is about calling people to do things beyond themselves." – David R. Gergen, American political consultant and television commentator, born on May 9, 1942

May 10, 2017
Wednesday

Objectives & reminders

____

____

____

Appointments

Early morning

8 a.m.

9 a.m.

10 a.m.

11 a.m.

Noon

1 p.m.

2 p.m.

3 p.m.

4 p.m.

5 p.m.

6 p.m.

Later evening

Happy birthday: Sir Thomas Lipton

Born in Glasgow, Scotland on May 10, 1850, Lipton sailed for America as a teenager, but returned to Glasgow after only a few years where he opened a grocery store at the age of 24. Within another six years, he was running a chain of grocery stores and was quite wealthy.

In America, Lipton is perhaps best known for the tea he branded when he founded the Lipton Tea Company. He was one of the first food marketers to recognize the value of branding and brand-name advertising.

During Sir Lipton's era, many food products were not branded and quality varied considerably. Branding was a way for producers of consistently high quality goods to differentiate themselves from lower-quality producers. The practice of branding increased as more and more consumers began to request specific brands.

Sir Lipton also was among the first to incorporate humor in advertising. He reasoned that if customers were in a good mood, they would be more inclined to spend their money. Today, marketers recognize multiple effects of humor.

> **No time for a cup of tea?**
> "Work hard, deal honestly, be enterprising, exercise careful judgment, advertise freely but judiciously." -- Sir Thomas Lipton

---

Happy birthday: Nancy Walker

Born in Philadelphia, Pennsylvania as Anna Myrtle Swoyer on May 10, 1922, Walker was a successful American actress who appeared in both movies and television. One of her most remembered roles was Ida Morgenstern who was Rhoda's mother on *The Mary Tyler Moore Show* and its spinoff *Rhoda* in the 1970s and 1980s.

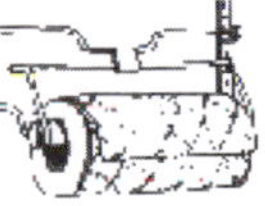

However, advertising buffs may remember Walker as "Rosie the Waitress" in a long-running television campaign for Bounty paper towels. The campaign was launched in the 1970s and continued into the 1990s, during which Rosie frequently cleaned spills and reminded audiences that Bounty was "the quicker picker upper."

May 11, 2017
Thursday

Objectives & reminders

____

____

Appointments

Early morning

8 a.m.

9 a.m.

10 a.m.

11 a.m.

Noon

1 p.m.

2 p.m.

3 p.m.

4 p.m.

5 p.m.

6 p.m.

Later evening

Marbleous firms are resilient

A fire destroyed the original Neiman-Marcus department store in Dallas on May 11, 1913. The retailer bounced back, and 17 days later the store reopened in a new temporary location. In Chicago, the Marshall Field's department store also burned down -- twice -- but was quickly rebuilt each time. In Liverpool, England, Lewis's department store suffered from fires on two separate occasions and a bombing in World War II, but they too rebuilt.

> **If you're in retailing, connect the dots…**
> By the way, the first fire insurance policy in the U. S. was issued on May 11, 1752.

The birth of CRM

Many companies, industries and professions have their own acronyms, abbreviations or sets of initials that confuse or have little meaning to newcomers or outsiders. To orient newcomers, large firms sometimes publish glossaries of the language shortcuts used in the organization. Still, confusion exists when the same acronyms are claimed by more than one organization or group. For example, the AMA is the American Marketing Association, but it is also the American Medical Association. ADA refers to the Americans with Disabilities Act, but it is also the American Dental Association and a small town in Oklahoma.

> **When in doubt, spell it out**
> Avoid confusion by specifying the words an acronym stands for, at least when you *first* use the acronym in a communication.

One set of initials that has gained considerable attention over past two decades is CRM, which commonly refers to ***c***ustomer ***r***elationship ***m***anagement (essentially, using computer technology to help build relationships with customers). Before that, however, CRM referred to ***c***ause-***r***elated ***m***arketing (e.g., "we'll donate a dollar to this charitable cause every time a customer makes a purchase") and ***c***ardiac ***r***hythm ***m***anagement (ask your physician). And, if we track CRM all the way back to the early 1930s, we find that the initials represented those of distinguished marketing scholar ***C***laude ***R***. ***M***artin, Jr., who was born on May 11, 1932. Martin was a Professor at the University of Michigan.

May 12, 2017
Friday

Objective or reminder

Appointments

Early morning

8 a.m.

9 a.m.

10 a.m.

11 a.m.

Noon

1 p.m.

2 p.m.

3 p.m.

4 p.m.

5 p.m.

6 p.m.

Later evening

Limerick Day

Today is Limerick Day to celebrate the birthday of comic poet Edward Lear. Born in London on May 12, 1812, Lear popularized limericks with the publication of his *Book of Nonsense* in 1846. Consider the fun employees and customers can have writing limericks for promotional events.

Marketing for All the Marbles
There once was a marketing rep
At selling marbles he was adept.
With all buyers in town
He'd routinely knuckledown.
And the marbles he won, he kept.

Speaking of corny

"For me, P&L stands for ***P***eople and ***L***ove. It's corny, but it works." -- Mary Kay Ash, founder of Mary Kay cosmetics, born on May 12, 1918 (some sources say 1915 or 1916)

Gender victory

Some barriers that had perpetuated gender-related job discrimination in the United States fell on May 12, 1971, when the U.S. Civil Service Commission disallowed "for men only" or "for women only" designations for most federal jobs. The ban prompted private firms to reconsider the appropriateness of gender specifications used in their hiring practices as well.

Lost his marbles?

"When you come to a fork in the road, take it." But... "You've got to be very careful if you don't know where you're going, because you might not get there." Otherwise admit... "We made too many wrong mistakes."
-- Yogi Berra, former baseball player and manager of the New York Yankees, born on May 12, 1925

American brand: Agree or disagree?

"If a man is going to be an American at all let him be so without any qualifying adjectives; and if he is going to be something else let him drop the word American from his personal description."
-- Henry Cabot Lodge, American, ***or*** Republican statesman and historian, born on May 12, 1850

May 13, 2017
Saturday

Objectives & reminders

Appointments

Early morning

8 a.m.

9 a.m.

10 a.m.

11 a.m.

Noon

1 p.m.

2 p.m.

3 p.m.

4 p.m.

5 p.m.

6 p.m.

Later evening

Aviation-related milestones today

Increased emphasis on speed

On May 13, 1918, the "air mail" stamp was introduced in the United States at what was then a premium price -- 24 cents. Mail sent from city to city by air would arrive at its final destination sooner, the Post Office promised, than standard trucked mail.

Today, service businesses often seek ways to speed service. When speedy service is important to customers, some businesses create a competitive advantage by promoting their speed of service, e.g., FedEx, Domino's and Speedy Print.

Avoid mailing leaky packages

Transporting mail can be challenging enough, but transporting people can be even more challenging. The mail doesn't care about riding in comfort and is not concerned about the total experience, but these matters are relevant to people passengers.

Apparently marketing-oriented Russian Igor Sikorski was sensitive to passengers' comfort in 1913 when he designed a large Russian passenger transport plane -- Russky Vitiaz -- with a lavatory. On May 13, 1913, the lavatory idea first flew.

Didn't they have lavatories?

On May 13, 1982 -- exactly 69 years after Russia made history -- Braniff International Corporation filed for bankruptcy. Until then Braniff had been the eighth largest airline in the U.S. They became the first, but certainly not the last, major U.S. airline to file for bankruptcy.

More milestones for aviation marketers

England's Royal Flying Corps was formed on May 13, 1912. Thirty years later, on May 13, 1942, a helicopter first flew from coast to coast (U.S.). Seven years after that, on May 13, 1949, the Canberra made its first test flight. The Canberra was the first British jet bomber.

May 14, 2017
Sunday

Objectives & reminders

Telephone Mom ______________________

____

____

Appointments

Early morning

8 a.m.

9 a.m.

10 a.m.

11 a.m.

Noon

1 p.m.

2 p.m.

3 p.m.

4 p.m.

5 p.m.

6 p.m.

Later evening

Mother's Day

As the name of the holiday implies, Mother's Day is a day to celebrate and honor Moms and motherhood -- to say "thank you," to ease Mom's workload a bit (breakfast in bed?) and otherwise brighten her day. In the United States, Mother's Day is celebrated on the second Sunday in May, as it is in Australia, Belgium, Canada, Denmark, Finland, Italy, Japan and Turkey. Several other countries celebrate Mother's Day on May 10, while a few celebrate the occasion on other dates.

> **Mom's job is critical**
> "The hand that rocks the cradle is the hand that rules the world."
> -- William Ross Wallace, 19th century American poet

Mother's Day data

Several studies provide marketing-relevant insights about Mother's Day. Here are some of the findings:

1. 83 percent of surveyed consumers plan to celebrate Mother's Day.
2. 79 percent of those surveyed report sending cards to Mom on Mother's Day. About four-fifths of the cards are purchased within one week of Mother's Day. Sixty-three percent of surveyed mothers say they keep the cards they receive (only 12 percent claim to throw *all* of the cards away after Mother's Day; 24 percent "keep some.")
3. Mother's Day is the most popular holiday to dine out. Thirty-eight percent of surveyed consumers report celebrating Mother's Day at a restaurant.
4. Of the consumers who plan to celebrate Mother's Day, $123 is the average amount of money they expect to spend. On average, male respondents expect to spend about 20 percent more, females about 20 percent less.
5. Most popular gift categories? Cards, flowers, gift cards, gardening items, clothing, jewelry, books, CDs, candy, perfume.
6. Most popular Mother's Day shopping destinations? Specialty stores (35%), department stores (27%), and discount stores (14%).

May 15, 2017
Monday

Objectives & reminders

____

____

Appointments

Early morning

8 a.m.

9 a.m.

10 a.m.

11 a.m.

Noon

1 p.m.

2 p.m.

3 p.m.

4 p.m.

5 p.m.

6 p.m.

Later evening

Kansas featured today!

Happy birthday: Lyman Frank Baum

Author of *The Wonderful Wizard of Oz*, Baum was born on May 15, 1856, in Chittenango, New York. Baum is best known for his "Oz" classic and other best-selling books, but his career also included marketing-relevant jobs. For example, he was a merchandiser responsible for arranging window displays. He also served as a retail store manager.

> **It's a 24-year journey from Bingley, England (home offices of Emerald Publishing Group) back to Kansas**
> "Come along, Toto," [Dorothy] said, "We will go to the Emerald City and ask the Great Oz how to get back to Kansas."
> -- L. Frank Baum, from Chapter 3 of *The Wonderful Wizard of Oz*

Not everyone reads textbooks

Several computerized and process-oriented techniques are available to help marketers, entrepreneurs and authors find names for their brands, companies and settings. Some are covered in business textbooks, but not everyone reads them.

When Lyman Frank Baum was struggling to think of a name for Dorothy's mythical and magical destination, he didn't use a formal approach to figure it out. Instead his eyes glanced around his office and happened to fixate on the label on the bottom drawer of his alphabetized file cabinet. It read, "O-Z."

In a more recent Kansas-related example, brothers Dan and Frank Carney of Wichita, Kansas were preparing to open their first pizza restaurant in the late 1950s. They had settled on a rather lengthy name for the new business -- something like "The Pizza Emporium." But, like most new entrepreneurs, the Carneys did not have an unlimited supply of money, so they jumped at the opportunity when Pepsi offered to give them a *free* sign to hang outside the building. When the Carneys realized the sign was too small to include all of the letters in "The Pizza Emporium," they quickly shortened the name and dubbed their new business, "Pizza Hut." Today, the original sign remains affixed to the original Pizza Hut building.

May 16, 2017
Tuesday

Objectives & reminders

____

____

____

Appointments

Early morning

8 a.m.

9 a.m.

10 a.m.

11 a.m.

Noon

1 p.m.

2 p.m.

3 p.m.

4 p.m.

5 p.m.

6 p.m.

Later evening

Congress chose the nickel

On May 16, 1866, the U.S. Congress authorized the minting of a new 5-cent coin, to become known as the "nickel." The new nickel replaced the previously used half-dime silver coin. Today, the relative size of U.S. nickel and dime coins are potentially confusing in that although a dime is worth more than a nickel (i.e., 10 cents vs. 5 cents), the dime is smaller and thinner.

For astute marketers, nickels are worth more than dimes

Understanding the potentially confusing size discrepancy between nickels and dimes, a grandfather who lived near Nashville, Tennessee, reached into his pocket and pulled out a nickel and a dime each time his five-year-old grandson visited. He held out the coins and explained to the child, "You can have either coin, but not both. Do you want the big, fat, shinny, pretty nickel, *or* the scrawny, thin, ugly dime?" Grinning at the opportunity, the boy consistently chose the nickel, after which his grandfather consistently broke into a hearty laugh.

This ritual continued several times until the youngster's older and presumably smarter brother pulled him aside and explained, "You dummy, don't you understand that a dime is worth *twice* as much as a nickel? That means you can buy more candy with a dime than with a nickel. Even if you don't like the looks of a dime, you can take the dime to the store and trade it for *two* nickels. Take the dime next time!"

"No," responded the defiant five-year-old as he shook his head in rejection of his brother's suggestion. "I know the dime is worth more," he went on to explain, "but as soon as I pick the dime, Grand-Dad will stop playing the game."

Was the five-year-old really a "dummy," as his older brother asserted? No, the child realized that although one dime is worth more than one nickel, a continuous stream of nickels over time is worth much more than a single dime. In much the same way, astute marketers are careful not to maximize short-run sales revenue if it risks alienating potentially loyal customers. They would rather have repeat "nickel" customers than one-time "dime" customers.

May 17, 2017
Wednesday

Objectives & reminders

____

____

Appointments

Early morning

8 a.m.

9 a.m.

10 a.m.

11 a.m.

Noon

1 p.m.

2 p.m.

3 p.m.

4 p.m.

5 p.m.

6 p.m.

Later evening

An American dream

On May 17, 1848, a young boy and his family from Glasgow, Scotland set sail for America. Their ten-week journey would eventually end in Pittsburgh, Pennsylvania. The boy was Andrew Carnegie. Although he did not know it at the time, in another 52 years he would be the wealthiest man in America.

Rich perspective
"At the end, the acquisition of wealth is ignoble in the extreme. I assume that you save and long for wealth only as a means of enabling you the better to do some good in your day and generation."
-- Andrew Carnegie

"Is that your final answer?"

Long before *Who Wants to Be a Millionaire?* became a hit television show, there was a radio panel-type quiz show called *Information Please*. It was the first broadcast show of its kind, first aired on May 17, 1938.

The popularity of *Information Please* and the dozens of "me-too" radio and television shows that followed proved that a significant proportion of the public has an interest both in trivia and in knowledge-based contests. Today, we also know that people tend to be more engaged when listening to or viewing such shows than when attending to most other types of programs. So, the attentive audiences may mean that marketers get a better return on their money when they advertise on knowledge-based contest shows. To further capitalize on the public's interest in trivia, creative marketers can develop their own trivia contests for customers.

Take pleasure in knowing that tomorrow is Russell's birthday
"There is much pleasure to be gained from useless knowledge."
-- Bertrand Russell, American philosopher

May 18, 2017
Thursday

Objectives & reminders

___

___

___

Appointments

Early morning

8 a.m.

9 a.m.

10 a.m.

11 a.m.

Noon

1 p.m.

2 p.m.

3 p.m.

4 p.m.

5 p.m.

6 p.m.

Later evening

Happy birthday: Jules Dupuit

Born in Fossano, Italy on May 18, 1804, Dupuit moved to France with his family at the age of ten where he studied engineering and later developed an interest in economics. As a self-taught economist, Dupuit advanced the concept of *consumer surplus*, which was developed further by Alfred Marshall.

Consumer surplus defined
Consumer surplus is the buyer's economic gain from a transaction, i.e., the positive difference between the amount the buyer actually paid for something and the maximum amount he or she *would* have been willing to pay.

Although the concept of consumer surplus is rather straightforward, several difficulties surface when marketers try to quantify it and reflect the concept in their marketing programs. First, there's the question of whether the business objective should be to increase consumer surplus or decrease it. Increasing it means the consumer probably will perceive greater value or a better "deal," so he or she might be more inclined to continue to purchase and to encourage other buyers to do the same. So, long-term profitability might increase with increased consumer surplus stemming from the repeat purchases and positive word-of-mouth. However, short-term profits may be sacrificed if the price paid in the transaction at hand is much lower than the maximum price that the customer would have been willing to pay.

Second, the amount buyers are willing to pay (and thus the size of the consumer surplus) varies from customer to customer and can be highly situational. A consumer who has trudged across the desert for several days without anything to drink would be willing to pay much more for a bottle of water than would an ordinary customer under ordinary circumstances. More routinely, perhaps, is the consumer's knowledge of what competitors charge for comparable products, i.e., the "going rate" affects the maximum price the buyer is willing to pay, and thus the size of the consumer surplus.

These and other considerations make it nearly impossible for a firm to approach maximum profitability by charging a single price for all customers and across all situations.

May 19, 2017
Friday

Objectives & reminders

____

____

____

Appointments

Early morning

8 a.m.

9 a.m.

10 a.m.

11 a.m.

Noon

1 p.m.

2 p.m.

3 p.m.

4 p.m.

5 p.m.

6 p.m.

Later evening

Classify this

It was May 19, 1657, when Thomas Newcome's *Publick Adviser* was first published. It was unique in that it was the first English paper to contain only advertising. Moreover, it was the first paper in which classified advertising appeared. Today, classified ads provide an inexpensive way for individuals and businesses to offer goods and services for sale, but the audience tends to be limited to buyers already actively searching for the advertised items.

For Sale: Shameless promotion
Calendar-related appointment books, with rich content. Plan promotional calendar to coincide with holidays and cultural events. Recognize business milestones. Link history with present day. Learn from yesterday's and today's business leaders. Identify peaks and valleys in demand. Lots of information for conversation-starters. Plenty of marbles to be found. Reasonably priced. Read twice for no extra charge; use in multiple courses.

High cost of e-mail failure

On May 19, 2005, the results of a study regarding e-mail failure were released. Commissioned by CipherTrust, Inc. the study surveyed marketing and IT directors in organizations with at least 200 employees. Surveyed marketing directors estimated that the cost of not being able to send or receive e-mails cost their companies an average of about $122,000 (or £68,000) *per day.* Respondents most frequently cited virus attacks as the key external reasons for e-failures.

E-mail failure as inferential springboard
"An e-failure raises doubts in the mind of the customer about the fundamental capability of the organization. If the company can't keep a communication system such as e-mail up and running, how are they going to handle my business?"
-- Stephen Martin, Market Clarity

May 20, 2017
Saturday

Objectives & reminders

____

____

____

Appointments

Early morning

8 a.m.

9 a.m.

10 a.m.

11 a.m.

Noon

1 p.m.

2 p.m.

3 p.m.

4 p.m.

5 p.m.

6 p.m.

Later evening

Armed Forces Day

On the third Saturday of May, we salute the men and women in all branches of the U.S. military. The first Armed Forces Day was celebrated on May 20, 1950. Since then, parades, open houses, air shows, and receptions have been part of local celebrations. Businesses sometimes stage special events or offer discounts to military personnel, veterans and their families as a way of recognizing and thanking them for their service.

Catering to tough customers

In the early 1850s miners toiled long hours in hopes of striking it rich in the gold mines of northern California. Some of the people who hit it biggest though, were not miners, but businessmen who sold supplies to the miners. That was the intention of merchant Levi Strauss when he arrived in San Francisco with a boat-load of canvas. He had planned to make tents with the canvas and sell them to miners, but unfortunately his supply of canvas far exceeded the demand for tents.

Listening to the miners complain that pants were not durable enough, Strauss began selling trousers made from the heavy canvas material. The innovation was well received and miners, ranchers and farmers bought the trousers. Then, in 1872, a customer and tailor explained that the pants' durability could be further improved by reinforcing the stress points with copper rivets. Strauss liked the idea, refined it, and received a patent for copper-riveted jeans on May 20, 1873. He even gave the customer a job as production manager.

Two learning principles from Levi's

Change: Rarely should plans be irreversible or inflexible. Strauss was willing to change directions when he realized the demand for durable pants was much greater than that for canvas tents.

Listening: Listening to customers makes good sense (and dollars). Strauss first sensed the potential demand for canvas pants when listening to customers. Later, he learned to improve the pants by listening to another customer who suggested copper rivets.

May 21, 2017
Sunday

Objectives & reminders

___

___

Appointments

Early morning
8 a.m.
9 a.m.
10 a.m.
11 a.m.
Noon
1 p.m.
2 p.m.
3 p.m.
4 p.m.
5 p.m.
6 p.m.
Later evening

Thank you: Clara Barton

It was May 21, 1881, when 59-year-old Clarissa "Clara" Harlowe Barton founded the American branch of the Red Cross, about 18 years after the International Red Cross was formed in Europe. In addition to raising money for the organization and leading relief workers, Barton was a lobbyist. She successfully advocated for the inclusion of the "American amendment" to the 1884 Geneva Convention so that the Red Cross would be permitted to provide relief during wartime and following natural disasters and other calamities.

Barton headed the American Red Cross until 1904. Prior to the formation of the American Red Cross, Barton served as the superintendent of nurses for the Army of the James who cared for soldiers wounded in the Civil War.

Non-profit appeal
An *appeal* is a communication that motivates an audience to act. Consider the appeal below used in an ad for the American Red Cross. Is it likely to be effective?

"Every year, your heart pumps 2,625,000 pints of blood. Surely, you can spare a few."

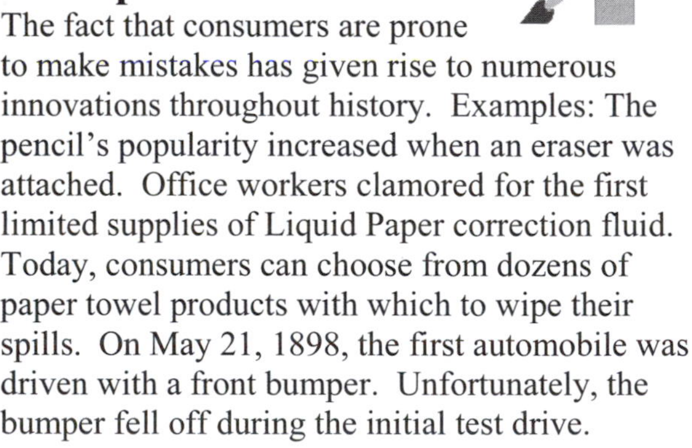

Marketing opportunity: Anticipate human error

The fact that consumers are prone to make mistakes has given rise to numerous innovations throughout history. Examples: The pencil's popularity increased when an eraser was attached. Office workers clamored for the first limited supplies of Liquid Paper correction fluid. Today, consumers can choose from dozens of paper towel products with which to wipe their spills. On May 21, 1898, the first automobile was driven with a front bumper. Unfortunately, the bumper fell off during the initial test drive.

What other products or product features are closely associated with the reality that people make mistakes? What opportunities exist for new "anti-mistake" innovations? In addition to product development, how else can marketers reduce the likelihood of customer mistakes or minimize the consequences of mistakes?

May 22, 2017
Monday

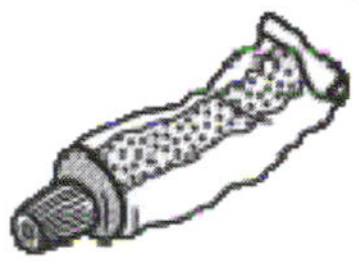

Objectives & reminders

____

____

____

Appointments

Early morning

8 a.m.

9 a.m.

10 a.m.

11 a.m.

Noon

1 p.m.

2 p.m.

3 p.m.

4 p.m.

5 p.m.

6 p.m.

Later evening

More about consumer mistakes

Discussed yesterday (see May 21), the automobile bumper is an example of an innovation that helps to reduce the negative consequences of the human factor involved in using a product. Other innovations seem to be less forgiving of consumer mistakes and serve to increase consumption or waste when consumers make mistakes. Such an innovation emerged on May 22, 1892, when Dr. Washington Sheffield invented the collapsible metal toothpaste tube. Sheffield was a dentist from New London, Connecticut.

If you're not convinced of the increased usage of toothpaste associated with consumer error, try squirting too much toothpaste onto your toothbrush and then putting the excess amount back into the tube for later use! If you are successful with toothpaste, try putting excess shaving cream, hair spray, and deodorant back into their containers.

Windows to the world

Surrounded by considerable publicity, Microsoft introduced Windows 3.0 on May 22, 1990. Within four months, the software had sold one million copies. Later that year, Microsoft's net revenues passed the $1-billion-mark for the first time.

Happy birthday: Sir Arthur Conan Doyle

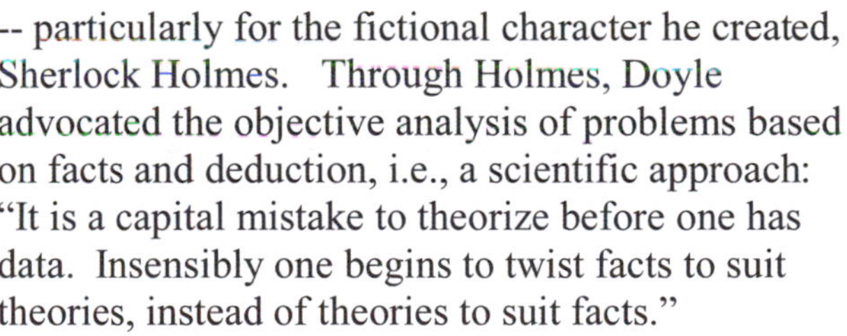

Born in Edinburgh (UK) on May 22, 1859, Doyle was a Scottish physician, but is better know as a novelist -- particularly for the fictional character he created, Sherlock Holmes. Through Holmes, Doyle advocated the objective analysis of problems based on facts and deduction, i.e., a scientific approach: "It is a capital mistake to theorize before one has data. Insensibly one begins to twist facts to suit theories, instead of theories to suit facts."

Learn to succeed

"You have to serve many apprenticeships throughout your life. Show me somebody who won't serve an apprenticeship, and I'll show you somebody who won't go very far." -- T. Boone Pickens, Jr., founder, president and chairman of Mesa Petroleum (1956-1996), and chairman of BP Capital Management, born in Holdenville, Oklahoma on May 22, 1928

May 23, 2017
Tuesday

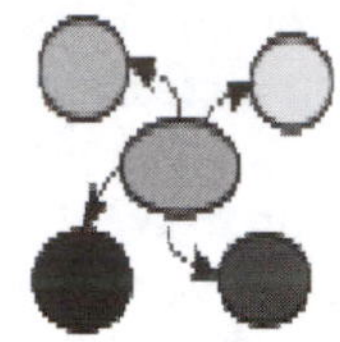

Objectives & reminders

___

___

___

Appointments

Early morning

8 a.m.

9 a.m.

10 a.m.

11 a.m.

Noon

1 p.m.

2 p.m.

3 p.m.

4 p.m.

5 p.m.

6 p.m.

Later evening

Time pressures afflict the young

Many new products and services appeal to consumers' interest in convenience or saving time. Apparently realizing this, Cliff Notes, Inc. began publishing condensed versions of time-consuming tomes. The mini-books were first used in schools on May 23, 1953.

Happy birthday: Michael Porter

Born in Ann Arbor, Michigan on May 23, 1947, Michael Porter is a professor at Harvard University and one of the leading thinkers on the topic of business strategy. Three of his books, in particular, have influenced business practitioners, government policy-makers, and scholars: *Competitive Strategy* (1980), *Competitive Advantage* (1985), and *The Competitive Advantage of Nations* (1990). As the titles imply, Porter considers the determinants of competitive advantage as fundamental building blocks of business strategy. That is, to build an effective business strategy, firms must understand their relative competitive advantages.

Strategic doing
"The essence of strategy is choosing to perform activities differently than rivals do."
– Michael Porter

One of Porter's contributions is his "five forces" model that helps firms understand the competitive environment and make pricing, distribution and other marketing-relevant decisions. Rather than considering only existing rivals in the industry as competitors, Porter encourages businesses to think more expansively about the competition. For example, possible competitive threats include potential new entrants to the industry or new entrants to the market from other industries. Buyers and suppliers must be considered as potential competitors as well; if they are not able to negotiate favorable prices, they may enter the market as direct competitors. Finally, substitute products or services also represent a competitive threat (e.g., beef vs. tuna producers; airlines vs. rental car firms).

Marketing decisions: Consider competition
"Cutting prices is usually insanity if the competition can go as low as you can."
-- Michael Porter

May 24, 2017
Wednesday

Objectives & reminders

____

____

Appointments

Early morning

8 a.m.

9 a.m.

10 a.m.

11 a.m.

Noon

1 p.m.

2 p.m.

3 p.m.

4 p.m.

5 p.m.

6 p.m.

Later evening

Happy Birthday: Queen Victoria

Born in London on May 24, 1819, Alexandrina Victoria rose to the British monarchy in 1837 and served as Queen until her death in 1901 -- thus becoming the longest-reigning monarch in British history. The "Victorian era" was characterized by British expansion.

Throughout Great Britain and the former British Empire, Queen Victoria's birthday is celebrated variously as "Victoria Day," "Commonwealth Day," or "Empire Day." In Canada, Victoria Day is observed as a legal holiday and celebrated on the Monday before May 25.

Illuminating innovation

On May 24, 1935, the Cincinnati Reds hosted the Philadelphia Phillies in the first baseball game played at night. Thanks to the innovation of outdoor electrical lighting, the players could see well enough to play the game and the fans could see well enough to watch it.

For baseball and countless other activities and organizations, outdoor lighting is good for business. Not only are well-lit areas considered safer than their darker counterparts, outdoor lighting offers scheduling flexibility by essentially extending the day into the night -- thus creating opportunities to create additional demand and shift some demand to night-time hours. By the way, the Reds won.

Bridge-building

On May 24, 1862, the Westminster Bridge opened over the River Thames in London. Exactly 21 years later, on May 24, 1883, the Brooklyn Bridge opened over the East River in New York. Today, far less majestic bridges are regularly opened in both large and small market areas. And when they are, consumer shopping patterns and market boundaries tend to change. In effect, what was a distant destination may be much closer and more convenient after a new bridge is opened. It follows that new bridges often represent opportunities for brick-and-mortar marketers to attract new groups of customers while also representing the challenges of dealing with a new mix of competitors.

May 25, 2017
Thursday

Objectives & reminders

____

____

Appoin m

Early morning

8 a.m.

9 a.m.

10 a.m.

11 a.m.

Noon

1 p.m.

2 p.m.

3 p.m.

4 p.m.

5 p.m.

6 p.m.

Later evening

The truth about mousetraps

"If you build a better mousetrap the world will beat a path to your door." Presumably, although there is some doubt, this popularized mousetrap advice was penned by one of America's most famous philosophers and essayists, Ralph Waldo Emerson, who happened to be born on May 25, 1803.

Although product quality is highly relevant to business success, the "better mousetrap" quotation implies that quality is not only *the* salient purchase criterion, but that buyers agree as to what constitutes quality, will recognize the high quality upon seeing it, will magically know that the better mousetrap is available, will know where to find it, will have the money to pay for it, and will willingly spend the money for a better mousetrap instead of buying food and clothing for their children. Builders of better mousetraps have learned that mousetrap marketing is much more involved than simply making a good product.

In 1899 an effective mousetrap was built -- by John Mast, of Lititz, Pennsylvania. His patent was for the familiar snap-trap design that remains popular today. The design releases a heavy spring-steel wire to crush the mouse when the victim nibbles on the cheese-baited trigger mechanism.

Media-paved highways
"If you make a product good enough, even though you live in the depths of the forest the public will make a path to your door, says the philosopher. But if you want the public in sufficient numbers, you would better construct a highway. Advertising is that highway." – William Randolph Hearst (1863-1951), American media magnate

However, what about *better* mousetraps and paths beaten to manufacturers' doors? Since Mast's patent more than 4,400 mousetrap patents have been issued by the U.S. Patent Office. Another 400 patent applications are filed annually. Many of these competing mousetraps are arguably "better." Some are less violent, while others hide the dead mouse from view, won't hurt family pets, or don't have to be baited. But, it seems that few buyers are beating very many paths to very many mousetrap producers' doors. According to one estimate, only 20 or so of the post-Mast mousetrap designs have been profitable.

May 26, 2017
Friday

Objectives & reminders

____

____

Appointments

Early morning

8 a.m.

9 a.m.

10 a.m.

11 a.m.

Noon

1 p.m.

2 p.m.

3 p.m.

4 p.m.

5 p.m.

6 p.m.

Later evening

Happy birthday: John Wayne

John Wayne, one of the most popular actors of all time, was born as Marion Michael Morrison on May 26, 1907. Wayne began his movie career in 1926 as an assistant prop man, which led to small roles as an extra, then to larger roles. In 1939 his career began to take off after playing the role of a hero in *Stagecoach*. In most of the dozens of movies that followed, Wayne's hero-like characters displayed admirable values such as compassion, honesty, decency, patriotism and courage. Throughout his career, John Wayne served as a role model to millions of fans.

Heroes never lie. Heroes know best.
"Nobody should come to the movies unless he believes in heroes." -- John Wayne

Today, actors, athletes and other celebrities continue to serve as powerful role models and subtly or not-so-subtly let their fans know what style of clothes to wear, what automobile to drive, which brand to drink, and so on. Knowing this, marketers actively enlist celebrities as spokes-people for their brands. Well known actors tend to be more effective at getting the audiences' attention than unknown spokespeople. Some firms simply give celebrities merchandise in hopes that they will be seen or photographed using it.

Is "Pitch No-More" a brand?
After repeated exposures, celebrity spokespeople can become closely associated with the brands or companies they represent. After winning the prestigious Cy Young baseball award in 1987, Philadelphia Phillies pitcher Steve Bedrosian commented on the endorsement opportunities he had received: "I was offered a spot in an ad for neutering pets. Not exactly what I had in mind."

In other instances, marketers lobby or contract with movie studios to have their brands included in a movie (known as *product placement*). For example, they might pay one fee if a soft drink vending machine with a brand's logo appears in the background of a scene. A higher fee might be paid if the scene shows the actor buying the brand from the machine. Still higher fees might be involved if the actor is shown drinking the brand.

May 27, 2017
Saturday
Clearly, too big of a day for this calendar!

Objectives & reminders

____

____

____

Appointments

Early morning

8 a.m.

9 a.m.

10 a.m.

11 a.m.

Noon

1 p.m.

2 p.m.

3 p.m.

4 p.m.

5 p.m.

6 p.m.

Later evening – Celebrate, of course, but responsibly.

Be your own marbleous graduate!
"A graduation ceremony is an event where the commencement speaker tells thousands of students dressed in identical caps and gowns that 'individuality' is the key to success." -- Robert Orben

Congratulations graduates!

Graduation from high school or college is a joyous occasion for graduates and their families. Each year in the U.S., more than five million students earn high school diplomas or college degrees. Most graduate about this time of year. For businesses interested in capitalizing on the graduation phenomenon, there are at least two levels of marketing opportunities to consider: (1) the graduation ceremonies themselves and accompanying celebrations, and (2) the transition market.

Graduations and celebrations. The graduation event itself represents obvious marketing opportunities for caps, gowns, invitations, and so on, but there are also opportunities for marketers of food, decorations, and entertainment that accompany the celebration parties. A demand bubble for travel and hospitality also accompanies graduation as out-of-town friends and families travel to attend the festivities. And, of course, there's the market for a wide variety of gifts which neither graduates nor marketers want to miss.

The transition market. Intertwined with graduation gift-giving and reinforced by graduation speeches that talk about "going out into the world," is the transition phenomenon associated with graduation. Almost by definition "graduation" means "completion," and when one thing is completed another begins. Soon after the ceremony and hoopla subside, most graduates move on to a new set of goals, new aspirations, and a new lifestyle. For some, that means more schooling (e.g., from high school to college, or college to graduate school). For others, it may mean a new job to launch a new career, which could also mean moving to a new community.

Many graduates who made a habit of postponing purchases and lifestyle changes while in school find themselves spending heavily immediately after graduation. They may invest in cars, houses, furniture, wardrobes, and so on. They may delay marriage, babies, and/or moving to distant communities until after they graduate. And recent graduates may find themselves suddenly in the market for insurance, utilities, and other things that Mom and Dad previously purchased for them.

All of these changes imply tremendous opportunities for businesses that catch graduates in transition. And businesses that are first to reach consumers in transition tend to have an advantage over those that introduce themselves later.

May 28, 2017
Sunday

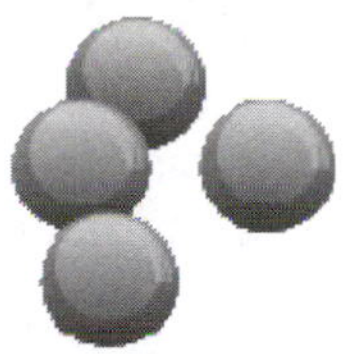

New **users** and new **uses** for marbles?

Objectives & reminders

____

____

Appointments

Early morning

8 a.m.

9 a.m.

10 a.m.

11 a.m.

Noon

1 p.m.

2 p.m.

3 p.m.

4 p.m.

5 p.m.

6 p.m.

Later evening

Staying focused

"It's necessary to know what adds true value to a product, and what does not. Who are the value creators and who are the value destroyers?" -- Alexander M. Cutler, chairman and CEO of Eaton Corporation (diversified manufacturer of automotive parts, hydraulic equipment, aerospace equipment, etc.), born in Milwaukee, Wisconsin on May 28, 1951

Early pull strategy

Jello-O brand dessert gelatin was introduced on May 28, 1897. Although gelatin had been invented 52 years earlier, Jell-O was somewhat unique in that it was available in four fruit flavors: lemon, orange, raspberry and strawberry. Still, early sales of Jell-O were sluggish until about 1904 when the new owners of Jell-O -- Genesee Pure Food Co. -- began using an innovative *pull strategy* to generate demand and secure distribution. A team of sales reps would enter a town and distribute hundreds of free Jell-O recipe booklets door-to-door. Then they would go to area grocers and advise them to stock their shelves with Jell-O because consumers would ask for it soon.

> **Pull principle**: Retailers want to stock what *their* customers want to buy.

Today, recipes continue to play an important role in the marketing of Jell-O. There are over 700 Jell-O recipes to keep consumers from becoming bored with the brand. According to Kraft Foods, which owns the brand, 95 percent of American consumers recognize the Jell-O brand name, and 66 percent eat Jell-O regularly. About 300 million boxes of Jell-O gelatin are sold annually in the United States.

> **Two recipes to increase demand**
> 1. Find new *users*
> 2. Find new *uses*

Problems? Yes. Surprises? No.

"Encountering problems is to be expected, but failing to mention problems, or worse, covering them up, should not be tolerated." -- Rudolph "Rudy" W. Giuliani, former mayor of New York City, born on May 28, 1944

May 29, 2017
Monday
Memorial Day

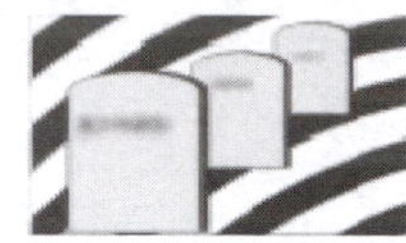

Objectives & reminders

___

___

___

Appointments

Early morning

8 a.m.

9 a.m.

10 a.m.

11 a.m.

Noon

1 p.m.

2 p.m.

3 p.m.

4 p.m.

5 p.m.

6 p.m.

Later evening

Memorial Day: Final Monday in May

Like many holidays, Memorial Day is observed in a variety of ways, but often consists of a mixture of both public and personal elements. The public side may feature military parades, cemetery ceremonies, prayers for peace, and the reading of Lincoln's Gettysburg Address. On a personal level, flowers and flags may be placed on graves with much of the day spent in prayer, sharing memories of the deceased, and personal reflection.

Another "sale" event won't do
"[Memorial Day] is the most beautiful and sacred of our national holidays, and its observance is of a dignified, reverent nature." -- Mary E. Hazeltine, historian

Understandably, for people who have suffered the loss of loved ones to war, the day can be quite emotional. These people, and many others, insist that the spirit of Memorial Day be preserved. That's why during late May many newspapers print editorials and letters to the editor reminding citizens to remember the "true" meaning of Memorial Day. They point out that just because the Monday observance creates a three-day weekend for many workers, Memorial Day should not be viewed solely in terms of an extra opportunity to take a mini-vacation or go shopping. Accordingly, to avoid creating ill-will, marketers should be sensitive to linking their marketing efforts with Memorial Day in a tasteful and respectful way.

No promotions today: Agree or disagree?

Dare to differentiate and be creative

"Conformity is the jailer of freedom and the enemy of growth." -- John F. Kennedy, 35th President of the U.S. (1961-1963), born in Brookline, Massachusetts 100 years ago on May 29, 1917

Marketers discover what's interesting

"There is no such thing on earth as an uninteresting subject; the only thing that can exist is an uninterested person." -- Gilbert Keith "G.K." Chesterton, British writer and social critic/philosopher, born on May 29, 1874

May 30, 2017
Tuesday

Objectives & reminders

____

____

____

Appointments

Early morning

8 a.m.

9 a.m.

10 a.m.

11 a.m.

Noon

1 p.m.

2 p.m.

3 p.m.

4 p.m.

5 p.m.

6 p.m.

Later evening

May 30: The "real" Memorial Day

The first national Memorial Day (then called "Decoration Day") in the U.S. was designated as May 30, 1868, and continued to be observed on May 30 until 1971 when the observance was moved to the last Monday in May. Since 1971 many veterans and other citizens have protested the move. They insist that scheduling Memorial Day on Monday is simply an excuse to create a three-day weekend which detracts from the holiday's original patriotic meanings. So, some people continue to observe Memorial Day on May 30.

Rush actions, rash actions
"[L]awmakers moved the holiday to the last Monday in May in order to give Federal workers a three-day weekend... I don't know for sure, but it was probably done at midnight on the last day Congress was in session." -- Thelly Reahm

Salute to Abraham Lincoln

May 30 was Memorial Day in 1922 – a fitting day to dedicate the Lincoln Memorial in Washington D.C. The sculpture of Lincoln (16th president of the U.S., 1861-1865) sitting in an armchair while pondering something was dubbed "Seated Lincoln" by its creator, Daniel Chester French. Surely business students at Lincoln Memorial University in northeastern Tennessee already knew that.

Lighter than air?

Not quite. At 3.5 tons, the not-so-cleverly named "SR-N1" wasn't lighter than air, but it did float on air, sort of. The innovation launched on May 30, 1959, in Cowes, England was a hovercraft designed by Christopher Cockerell. The hovercraft concept was subsequently borrowed by other boat-builders in the years to follow.

Inspired by Cockerell's hovercraft, Swedish inventor Karl Dahlman used the concept to develop the first hover lawn mower -- the Flymo -- in 1963. The Flymo was lightweight, easy to use, and earned high marks from European consumers. The Flymo is a good example of how a technology developed for one application or product category may be adapted to another.

May 31, 2017
Wednesday

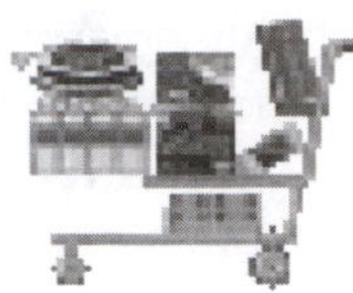

All natural ingredients!

Objectives & reminders

____

____

Appointments

Early morning

8 a.m.

9 a.m.

10 a.m.

11 a.m.

Noon

1 p.m.

2 p.m.

3 p.m.

4 p.m.

5 p.m.

6 p.m.

Later evening

Happy birthday: Joe Namath

"Broadway Joe" was born in Beaver Falls, Pennsylvania on May 31, 1943. Namath first captured the attention of football fans in the 1960s when he was named the AFL's Rookie of the Year (1965) and Player of the Year (1968). He also received the Most Valuable Player award for his outstanding performance in Super Bowl III (1969).

> **Winning perspective**
> "When you win, nothing hurts."
> -- Joe Namath

Although Namath may be best remembered for his career as a football quarterback for the New York Jets, his career as an advertising spokesperson is noteworthy too. Namath pitched several products -- even pantyhose. In one TV campaign promoting Noxzema shaving cream, he used a razor to rhythmically strip away the whiskers on his face while gyrating to a striptease "take-it-off" melody. Unintentionally proving the effectiveness of advertising, hundreds of men injured themselves while imitating Joe Namath's shaving antics.

Birth of an advertising vehicle

The first issue of *Parade* was sold on May 31, 1941. At 5 cents per copy, 125,000 copies of the first issue were sold. Today, the weekly Sunday publication is inserted in 700+ newspapers around the U.S., giving it a circulation of more than 32 million and making it one of the most widely distributed and read publications in the country.

Happy birthday: Walt Whitman

Walter Whitman was born on May 31, 1819, on Long Island, New York. He is best known for his poetry, but he also was a journalist and a bookstore proprietor, among other things. In "New Themes Entered Upon," Whitman points out the universal and enduring appeal of nature:

> "After you have exhausted what there is in business, politics, conviviality, and so on -- have found that none of these finally satisfy, or permanently wear -- what remains? Nature remains."

Consider how marketers use nature to enhance the appeal of their products, services, and physical environments.

June 1, 2017
Thursday

Objectives & reminders

____

____

____

Appointments

Early morning

8 a.m.

9 a.m.

10 a.m.

11 a.m.

Noon

1 p.m.

2 p.m.

3 p.m.

4 p.m.

5 p.m.

6 p.m.

Later evening

Clothes make the child?

On June 1, 1999, interviews with 1,172 children were completed in 25 U.S. cities. Among the findings, 44 percent of the 12- to 14-year-olds said that "clothes" are among "the most important things that kids at [their] school use to decide who fits in." "Popularity" was the second most frequently mentioned response (37%), followed by "being good-looking" (34%) and "being a good friend" (33%).

Invitation to discuss
What are the marketing implications of this study's findings?

This man needs the vacation

On June 1, 1993, a disgruntled customer reportedly seized a vacuum cleaner company's repair van in retaliation for the company's failure to give him the free plane ticket promised in a promotional offer. Essentially, the offer promised free plane tickets with the purchase of vacuum cleaners. Although there were thousands of customers who apparently felt cheated when the company failed to honor its commitment, this was the only customer who took such drastic action. Others simply sued.

Three take-away promotion principles

1. Once a promotional offer is made, the commitment should guide the company's behavior; it's no longer a matter of profit and loss.
2. If customers' response rate to a promotional offer is uncertain, the promotion should be tested on a limited basis first. Or, if the promotion includes free or bonus goods and services, a cap on the number of freebies should be considered and disclosed.
3. The greater the value of a "free" promotional item, the greater the likelihood that the freebie will upstage the featured core product -- thus diluting the perceived value of the core item. Here, did consumers think they were getting a free plane ticket with the purchase of a vacuum cleaner, or a free vacuum cleaner with the purchase of a plane ticket?

June 2, 2017
Friday

Objectives & reminders

____

____

____

Appointments

Early morning

8 a.m.

9 a.m.

10 a.m.

11 a.m.

Noon

1 p.m.

2 p.m.

3 p.m.

4 p.m.

5 p.m.

6 p.m.

Later evening

Musical milestone

Steinway & Sons launched their piano-making business in 1853. On June 2, 1988, the company celebrated its 135th anniversary by unveiling its 500,000th piano. Reflecting on the company's history, Henry Steinway attributed some of the company's original success to his grandfather, William Steinway (one of the "Sons" in Steinway & Sons), who used a *negative appeal* to suggest that piano lessons play an integral role in one's cultural education. As the young Steinway put it in 1988: "The idea that your daughter is a schlumpf unless she plays the piano -- William did more to invent that than anybody."

+ - + - + - + - + - +

Appeals to motivate buyers to act may be broadly classified as either positive or negative. A *positive appeal* suggests that something desirable will happen if you buy the product or otherwise take the prescribed action, e.g., you'll look better, feel better, be the envy of your friends, save time or money, and so on. In contrast, a *negative appeal* emphasizes the undesirable consequences of *not* buying or acting, e.g., friends will shun you, you'll pay more in the long run, you won't be popular, or you may become a "schlumpf" if you don't learn to play the piano. Negative appeals may arouse intense feelings of fear, guilt, self-consciousness, or even shame that buyers wish to avoid.

II III II III II III II III

Success + values = greater success

"In the pursuit of opportunity and success, we all need a greater adherence to principles and values in guiding our behavior and actions. I owe a great part of my success in business to a simple, personal philosophy: I believe you can be the most determined competitor, totally focused on winning, which I am, but you can do it with integrity, grace, and always treating people with respect and dignity." -- Kenneth Chenault, chairman and CEO of American Express Company, born in Mineola, New York on June 2, 1951

June 3, 2017
Saturday

Objectives & reminders

____

____

____

Appointments

Early morning

8 a.m.

9 a.m.

10 a.m.

11 a.m.

Noon

1 p.m.

2 p.m.

3 p.m.

4 p.m.

5 p.m.

6 p.m.

Later evening

Computer's fault: Agree or disagree?

On June 3, 2015, administrators at Wichita State University (WSU) in south central Kansas scrambled to mend relationships with 67 senior citizens who received letters informing them that they had failed the courses they had enrolled in and were being "placed on financial aid suspension." In reality, the seniors were only auditing the courses, so they did not fail and no financial aid was involved. The potentially offensive letters were blamed on a "computer glitch."

In a service recovery effort to address the mistake, WSU personnel drove to the seniors' homes to personally deliver letters of apology and small bars of chocolate. Apparently WSU's gestures had a positive impact; not only were the seniors not offended by the mishap, many reported an interest in auditing additional courses in the future.

Service recovery principle
When an organization or its employees make mistakes that involve customers, customers' ultimate satisfaction or dissatisfaction may hinge more on the organization's *response* to the mishap than on the original *mishap* itself. Handled well, customers may be quite forgiving and walk away happy. Handled poorly, what was one mishap becomes two!

The unwork ethic

"I really would like to stop working forever – never work again… and do nothing but write poetry and have leisure to spend the day outdoors and go to museums and see friends." – Allen Ginsberg, poet and social critic, born on June 3, 1926

Could he have been talking about marketing?

"The subject itself is of no account; what matters is the way it is presented?" – Raoul Dufy, French artist, born on June 3, 1877

June 4, 2017

Sunday

Objectives & reminders

____

____

____

____

Appointments

Early morning

8 a.m.

9 a.m.

10 a.m.

11 a.m.

Noon

1 p.m.

2 p.m.

3 p.m.

4 p.m.

5 p.m.

6 p.m.

Later evening

Observation and innovation

The potential to learn from customers is huge -- by asking them questions, listening to their questions and comments, and observing their behavior.

Indeed, observation was the informal learning technique that Sylvan Goldman, the Humpty Dumpty supermarket manager in Oklahoma City used when he noticed that many female customers would bring their own shopping baskets into the store. They would walk around the store, fill their baskets, and then leave the store. Rarely would they purchase more than their baskets would hold.

To make the shopping experience a little easier for customers and to encourage a higher volume of purchases, Goldman asked handyman Fred Young to design a shopping cart. Young made several carts by attaching two baskets on a metal folding chair and then mounting the chair on casters.

The shopping carts were first placed near the store's entrance on June 4, 1937. But, because the innovation clashed with existing customer behavior, customers tended not to use them.

Understanding the psychology involved in the adoption of new tools and new behaviors, Goldman hired people to push filled shopping carts around the store. Seeing other people use the carts prompted customers to do the same. Today, the use of shopping carts is widespread.

Alternative uses

Innovations can serve multiple purposes. In Bratislava, Slovakia, for example, some grocery stores use shopping carts as a method of crowd control. Because stores and aisles are smaller than those typically found in the U.S., only a limited number of customers are allowed in the store to shop at the same time. To control the customer flow, shoppers are expected to use a basket or cart provided by the store. So, the stores limit the number of customers in the store by limiting the number of carts and baskets available. During busy periods, customers wait next to the check-out aisles to recycle the baskets and carts given up by exiting customers.

June 5, 2017
Monday

Objectives & reminders

____

____

____

Appointments

Early morning

8 a.m.

9 a.m.

10 a.m.

11 a.m.

Noon

1 p.m.

2 p.m.

3 p.m.

4 p.m.

5 p.m.

6 p.m.

Later evening

World Environment Day (WED)

Celebrated annually on June 5, World Environment Day is sponsored by the United Nations. Consumers and businesses throughout the world are encouraged to preserve and enhance the environment. The UN designated June 5 for WED at their Conference on the Human Environment, held on June 5, 1972, in Stockholm, Sweden.

One small European company, Redeem Plc, marries its marketing efforts with WED by promoting its mobile telephone and printer cartridge recycling services. Urging people to recycle, Redeem estimates that there are 90 million unwanted mobile phones in the U.K. alone. They dramatize this large number by suggesting that if all 90 million phones were "[p]laced end-to-end... they would extend along the length of the Great Wall of China nearly five times."

Dow wow!

Investors had something to bark about on June 5, 1950, when the Dow Jones Industrial Average (DJIA), an index of large-company stocks headquartered in the United States, reached 222.57 -- the highest level in almost 20 years. The day's rally was sparked by the news that General Motors had reached a five-year contract with the United Auto Workers union.

Not only do investors like to hear positive news about the stock market, but marketers do too. When investments appreciate, investors (who are also consumers) feel wealthier, and when they feel wealthier, they are more inclined to spend. The key for marketers, of course, is to contact investors who feel wealthy *before* the stock market heads south and opposite feelings are evoked.

Marketing distinguishes humans

"Man is an animal that makes bargains; no other animal does this -- one dog does not exchange a bone with another." -- Adam Smith, Scottish political economist and author of the highly influential book, *The Wealth of Nations* (1776). Smith was baptized on June 5, 1723, probably about three days after his birth.

June 6, 2017
Tuesday

Objectives & reminders

____

____

____

Appointments

Early morning

8 a.m.

9 a.m.

10 a.m.

11 a.m.

Noon

1 p.m.

2 p.m.

3 p.m.

4 p.m.

5 p.m.

6 p.m.

Later evening

Another promotional coup

On June 6, 1988, Southwest Airlines scored a publicity and promotional hit when they painted one of their 737 planes to resemble a killer whale. Why? To create awareness, garner media attention, and stimulate word-of-mouth for the fact that they had just become the official airline of San Antonio's aquatic theme park, Sea World.

Happy birthday: Robert B. Englund

Born in Glendale, California on June 6, 1949, actor Englund is best known for his role as Freddy Krueger in the horror movie, *A Nightmare On Elm Street*, and the several sequels that followed.

In his 2001 book, *Marketing Outrageously*, Jon Spoelstra suggests that far too many companies look to Freddie Krueger as a cost-cutting role model. According to Spoelstra, the "Freddie Krueger Approach" increases short-term profits, but is messy: "They crank up the chainsaws and cut away some fat, along with a lot of muscle and gizzard and bone. Wall Street loves this approach. The more blood on the floor, the better."

Cost-cutting is only short term solution
It is true that cutting unnecessary costs will increase profitability, but a Krueger-like obsession with slashing costs can distract managers and marketers from the essential profit-generating activity of exploiting opportunities in the marketplace. In short, a business cannot "save" its way into prosperity; it takes money to make money.

Happy birthday: Samuel Ferber

Former promotion manager, advertising manager, and publishing executive, Samuel Ferber was born in New York City on June 6, 1920. He offers these insights regarding the planning of change: "[O]ne should 'never leave well enough alone.' When things are progressing smoothly is the precise moment to plan the evolutionary change that insures progress and vitality. In my time, I have seen pillars of industry... fall by the wayside because their emphasis has been on self-preservation rather than innovation."

June 7, 2017
Wednesday

Objectives & reminders

______

______

______

Appointments

Early morning

8 a.m.

9 a.m.

10 a.m.

11 a.m.

Noon

1 p.m.

2 p.m.

3 p.m.

4 p.m.

5 p.m.

6 p.m.

Later evening

Happy birthday: Brooks Stevens

Born in Milwaukee, Wisconsin on June 7, 1911, Stevens was an industrial designer of home appliances. He did design work for several U.S. automakers and for Harley-Davidson motorcycles too. In 1954, he popularized the product-related concept called *planned obsolescence,* which he defined as, "instilling in the buyer the desire to own something a little newer, a little better, a little sooner than is necessary."

Since the 1950s, "planned obsolescence" has been used in connection with an array of intentional design and promotion tactics to shorten the useable life of products and therefore force, manipulate or coax buyers into purchasing replacements earlier than necessary. Some manufacturers have been accused of engineering poor quality so products will not be durable, or designing products that can not be serviced or repaired easily or inexpensively.

But not all obsolescence is necessarily planned or manipulative, and the consequences are not always costly or otherwise undesirable for buyers. For example, it is beneficial that grocers take unsafe or marginally safe food off their shelves; expiration dates on perishable items provide useful information to prevent buyers from purchasing unsafe food. Or, new product models that are introduced with technological innovations (such as computers with faster microprocessors or extended memory) promise additional benefits to justify and encourage replacement of outdated models.

In support of planned obsolescence: Agree or disagree?
"Some have an idea that the reason we in this country discard things so readily is because we have so much. The facts are exactly the opposite -- the reason we have so much is simply because we discard things so readily. We replace the old in return for something that will serve us better."
-- Alfred P. Sloan, Jr., past president and chairman of General Motors

Fortunately, for value-conscious buyers who do not feel compelled to always own the newest or most advanced model, there are competitors in most product categories that have positioned their brands as high-quality and durable alternatives, backed by strong warranties and service networks committed to supporting buyers after purchase.

June 8, 2017
Thursday

Objectives & reminders

____

____

____

Appointments

Early morning

8 a.m.

9 a.m.

10 a.m.

11 a.m.

Noon

1 p.m.

2 p.m.

3 p.m.

4 p.m.

5 p.m.

6 p.m.

Later evening

Speed and content trump visuals: Agree or disagree?

"Web users ultimately want to get at data quickly and easily. They don't care as much about attractive sites and pretty design." -- Tim Berners-Lee, inventor of the World Wide Web and director of the 408-member World Wide Web Consortium (W3C) that oversees the "Web's" development. Berners-Lee was born in London on June 8, 1955.

Sour grapes?

"The market is not an invention of capitalism. It has existed for centuries. It is an invention of civilization." -- Mikhail Gorbachev, then General Secretary of the Communist Party of the Soviet Union, June 8, 1990

People as brands

What's the name of Stephen King's publisher? What is the name of Martha Stewart's company? When a single individual becomes a product's most salient attribute or when that person is so closely associated with the company or product that buyers are more aware of the individual than the company or its products, the individual may become, in effect, the brand. That's beneficial as long as the person maintains a good reputation and continues to capture public attention.

However, when the individual becomes the brand, there's always the risk of confusion or diluting the value of the brand when other individuals with the same or similar name enter the market. One of the first ways to address this concern was implemented on June 8, 1903, when the famous inventor and businessman Thomas A. Edison signed an agreement with his son, Thomas A. Edison, *Jr.* The two agreed that Junior would not use his own name in any business venture. In return, Senior would give the younger Edison a weekly allowance of $35. Not surprisingly, few people today are familiar with Junior's business career.

Don't be an expert

"An expert is a man who has stopped thinking. Why should he think? He is an expert." -- Frank Lloyd Wright, highly influential American architect, born on June 8, 1867

June 9, 2017
Friday

Objectives & reminders

____

____

Appointments

Early morning

8 a.m.

9 a.m.

10 a.m.

11 a.m.

Noon

1 p.m.

2 p.m.

3 p.m.

4 p.m.

5 p.m.

6 p.m.

Later evening

The Pre-President President

What was President Woodrow Wilson's title *before* he became the 28th president of the U.S. in 1913? President. That is, before serving as the U.S. President, Wilson served as President of Princeton University, elected on June 9, 1902 (he also served as Governor of New Jersey for a brief time between presidencies). Wilson is the only U.S. president to have earned a doctoral degree, but not the only Princeton president to do so.

After serving as Princeton's president for almost eight years, Wilson commented on the role and potential of higher education in a 1910 address to the alumni:

> "While attending a recent Lincoln celebration I asked myself if Lincoln would have been as serviceable to the people of this country had he been a college man, and I was obliged to say to myself that he would not. The process to which the college man is subjected does not render him serviceable to the country as a whole... The American college must become saturated in the same sympathies as the common people."

Consider the extent to which Wilson's comments remain applicable today. In particular, what does it mean and how important is it for businesspeople to be "serviceable to the country" (marketplace?)? To what extent (if any?) does the college experience "saturate" business students "in the same sympathies as the common people"?

Exercising marketing caution
Warning: Marketers are not always members of the market segments they target. Products, prices, promotions and channels that *personally* appeal to marketers may be irrelevant to targeted customers. Separating one's personal perceptions and preferences from those of targeted customers is one of the most difficult challenges marketers face. The greater the gaps between marketers and the customers they serve or seek to serve, the greater the marketing challenge. But, effective marketers are able to step out of their own shoes, so to speak, and into the shoes of their customers.

June 10, 2017
Saturday

Objectives & reminders

____

____

____

Appointments

Early morning

8 a.m.

9 a.m.

10 a.m.

11 a.m.

Noon

1 p.m.

2 p.m.

3 p.m.

4 p.m.

5 p.m.

6 p.m.

Later evening

It pays to listen to international consumers

"[F]oreign consumers provide useful information for product development, so exporting actually helps local producers improve their product's quality. In the emerging markets of India, Poland, or Mexico, local customers may ask manufacturers one question about their product; in Singapore, Britain, or Canada, customers ask ten questions. Every question gives the emerging-markets' CEO another view of what needs to be done." -- Rahul Bajaj, chairman of Bajaj Auto Ltd. (India), born on June 10, 1938. In 1975, Bajaj received the Man of the Year Award from the National Institute of Quality Assurance.

Fine line between success and failure

"Always remember this: There are only 18 inches between a pat on the back and a kick in the rump." -- Hattie McDaniel, first African-American actress to win an Academy Award, born on June 10, 1895

Office innovations on June 10

1902 Americus F. Callahan received a patent for the time-saving innovation he called the "outlook" envelope -- what we now refer to as the see-through or window envelope.

1943 Lasalo Biro, from Budapest, Hungary patented the ballpoint pen. The next year, ballpoint pens were mass produced in Britain, then in Argentina and the U.S. in 1945.

1952 DuPont registered a trademark for Mylar® -- a polyester film stronger than cellophane and used in a variety of applications, including packaging.

1977 Apple shipped its first Apple II computer, five days after the Apple II went on sale.

Marketing insight: Consumer behavior changes over time

"When a man opens the car door for his wife, it's either a new car or a new wife." -- Prince Philip, Duke of Edinburgh, born on June 10, 1921

June 11, 2017
Sunday

Objectives & reminders

____

____

____

Appointments

Early morning

8 a.m.

9 a.m.

10 a.m.

11 a.m.

Noon

1 p.m.

2 p.m.

3 p.m.

4 p.m.

5 p.m.

6 p.m.

Later evening

Kamehameha Day

The first King of Hawaii -- King Kalani Kamehameha -- was born on June 11, 1737. Hawaiians celebrate the day with festivities including parades and pageants depicting Hawaii's rich history.

Evil media: Agree or disagree?

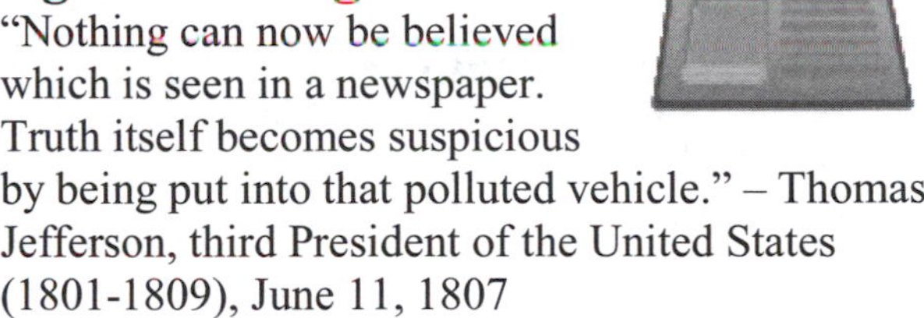

"Nothing can now be believed which is seen in a newspaper. Truth itself becomes suspicious by being put into that polluted vehicle." – Thomas Jefferson, third President of the United States (1801-1809), June 11, 1807

What might happen if a modern-day president made such a comment? Do you think an aspiring president could become one if he or she made such a comment during the election campaign?

Five tips to beat Jefferson at media relations

Avoid complaining about minor errors or misprints. Instead, next time provide *written* information; it's less likely to lead to errors. Whenever possible, anticipate reporters' questions and try to have information ready for them.

Don't play favorites with media reps. If they sense an intentional bias and are blocked from getting the information they request, they may not work as hard to get the story right.

Avoid making "off the record" comments. Reporters may not be able to remember which comments were "off the record." Instead, assume that whatever you say may be quoted; be careful, accurate and concise when speaking with media representatives.

Always be frank and honest with media reps. Evasiveness may prompt them to talk to your critics.

Don't be critical of editors or reporters when a company story is omitted or when a long story is condensed. Understand that their space or air time is limited.

June 12, 2017
Monday

Objectives & reminders

____

____

____

Appointments

Early morning

8 a.m.

9 a.m.

10 a.m.

11 a.m.

Noon

1 p.m.

2 p.m.

3 p.m.

4 p.m.

5 p.m.

6 p.m.

Later evening

Reality check for sports marketers

Nicole Brown Simpson and her friend Ron Goldman were found brutally stabbed to death in Brentwood, California on June 12, 1994. The chief suspect was Ms. Simpson's ex-husband, O.J. Simpson -- former football player for the Buffalo Bills who turned spokesperson and endorser for several brands and firms after ending his football career. In the highly publicized investigation and courtroom proceedings that followed, O.J. Simpson was acquitted in a criminal trial, but found responsible in a civil suit and ordered to pay $33.5 million.

Not surprisingly, corporations that O.J. Simpson had pitched for almost immediately began to distance themselves from the accused killer as the public's association between Simpson and football was marred by Simpson's new association with murder. The incident reminded corporate advertisers that scandals or negative publicity that tarnish the reputation or image of spokespeople also can jeopardize the reputation or image of the companies or brands pitched. Unlike spokes*characters* (e.g., Pillsbury Doughboy, Tony the Tiger, Jolly Green Giant), spokes*people* are not completely controllable.

Business for Social Responsibility formed

On June 12, 1992, representatives from 54 companies crowded into a hotel room in Washington D.C. to launch a new organization, "to help companies implement responsible business policies and practices." The new organization was dubbed Business for Social Responsibility (BSR) and soon grew to include many large firms such as AT&T, Starbucks, Time Warner, Federal Express, Reebok, and Hallmark, to name a few. Today more than 250 companies are BSR members.

Good for business

"Conducting your business in a socially responsible way is good business. It means that you can attract better employees and that customers will know what you stand for and like you for it." -- M. Anthony Burns, former CEO of Ryder Systems

June 13, 2017
Tuesday

Objectives & reminders

____

____

____

Appointments

Early morning

8 a.m.

9 a.m.

10 a.m.

11 a.m.

Noon

1 p.m.

2 p.m.

3 p.m.

4 p.m.

5 p.m.

6 p.m.

Later evening

FREE book !

5 businessmen + 2 Harbors = 3M

June 13, 1902, changed Minnesota's history. That's the day Henry S. Bryan, Hermon W. Cable, John Dwan, William A. McGonagle, and Dr. J. Danley Budd founded Minnesota Mining and Manufacturing -- 3M -- in Two Harbors, Minnesota. The company struggled during the early days to mine a mineral that could be used for grinding-wheel abrasives. Soon, the company's focus changed to sandpaper products.

Within a few years, the company was on a success trajectory and in 1916 was able to pay its first dividend. The company's legacy for innovation was well under way by the 1920s when 3M invented a waterproof sandpaper and masking tape. Dozens of other adhesive and abrasive innovations followed, including cellophane tape and more recently, Post It Notes. Today, 3M is one of the largest firms in the U.S. with 88,000 employees and annual revenues in excess of $30 billion.

Much of 3M's history, philosophy, and dozens of marketing insights are professionally presented in the 248-page book, *A Century of Innovation: The 3M Story* -- available FREE online: http://multimedia.3m.com/mws/media/171240o/3m-coi-book-tif.pdf. Quoted in the boxes below are three of the many "*t*ime-*t*ested *t*ruths" developed in the book. As you read the book and the three 3Ts below, consider the book's multiple audiences and what impact the book is likely to have on them.

Planned obsolescence revisited
"Be the first to make your own best products obsolete. Give people a product that's better than they have -- or one they didn't know they needed, until they tried it."

Think "partnerships"
"The best customer is a partner. 3M is innovative when it gives its customers solutions to their problems."

Becoming one with the customer
"Being 'customer intimate' means getting out with your customers, 'living' with them and seeing what they see. Know your market well enough to anticipate your customers' wants and needs... even before they do."

June 14, 2017
Wednesday

Objectives & reminders

____

____

____

Appointments

Early morning

8 a.m.

9 a.m.

10 a.m.

11 a.m.

Noon

1 p.m.

2 p.m.

3 p.m.

4 p.m.

5 p.m.

6 p.m.

Later evening

Flag Day

It was June 14, 1777, when the Continental Congress approved the stars and stripes design for the American flag, but it wasn't until 1916 that President Woodrow Wilson proclaimed that the occasion be commemorated annually. Thus June 14 became Flag Day -- a day to proudly display the flag and reflect upon its meaning.

Stars and Stripes decided
"Resolved, that the Flag of the thirteen United States shall be thirteen stripes, alternate red and white; that the Union be thirteen stars, white on a blue field, representing a new constellation."
-- *Journals of the Continental Congress*, June 14, 1777

Celebrating flags around the world

"There is hopeful symbolism in the fact that flags do not wave in a vacuum." -- Arthur C. Clark, English scientist and writer

Waving his own flag: Now "President" Trump?

Born in New York City on June 14, 1946, Donald Trump, a.k.a., "The Donald" is a self-promoting, outspoken, risk-taking real estate developer, entrepreneur, author (e.g., *Art of the Deal* and *The Way to the Top*), host of the business competition television show *The Apprentice*, and at the time of this printing, the 2016 Republican Party nominee for President of the United States. His flamboyant, high-rolling leadership style is reflected by his philosophy of "thinking big."

Thinking big!

- "I like thinking big. As long as you're going to be thinking anyway, think big."
- "People may not always think big themselves, but they can still get very excited by those who do."

June 15, 2017
Thursday

Objectives & reminders

____

____

____

Appointments

Early morning

8 a.m.

9 a.m.

10 a.m.

11 a.m.

Noon

1 p.m.

2 p.m.

3 p.m.

4 p.m.

5 p.m.

6 p.m.

Later evening

The U.S. Agricultural Marketing Act

President Herbert Hoover signed the Agricultural Marketing Act on June 15, 1929, to establish the Federal Farm Board. The Board's challenge was to assist agricultural cooperatives in the promotion and sale of *farm commodities*. Money was set aside to fund various commodity programs. Further, to help stabilize prices, the Act allowed the government to buy surplus agricultural products and then sell them to other countries.

Big ideas re (non)commodity marketing

By definition, commodities are undifferentiated products. Although some are graded, generally distinctions are not made between one producer's commodity products and another's. Accordingly, there are several implications and principles associated with commodity marketing; here are a few…

Commodity-producers are price-takers. They must accept the going market price. Rarely can a single producer affect the market price.

However, the collective efforts of many commodity producers in a product category can have a limited effect on demand and prices. Governmental actions can impact price too.

Given the limited ability of individual commodity marketers to influence prices and demand, strategies of scale or efficiency are often pursued to improve profit margins.

Another approach to improve profit margins is to forecast commodity prices and time production to coincide with peak prices.

Perhaps the most marketing-oriented approach is to move away from commodities altogether by *meaningfully* differentiating and branding the firm's outputs so they are not considered commodities. That's what the founders of Quaker Oats did with oatmeal near the middle of the 19th century and what Perdue Farms did with chickens a century later. When buyers recognize the uniqueness or superiority of a meaningfully differentiated brand, they're likely to develop a preference for it and may be willing to pay a premium price.

June 16, 2017
Friday

Objectives & reminders

____

____

____

Appointments

Early morning

8 a.m.

9 a.m.

10 a.m.

11 a.m.

Noon

1 p.m.

2 p.m.

3 p.m.

4 p.m.

5 p.m.

6 p.m.

Later evening

The pre-Coke, pre-Pepsi era

Long before there was Coca-Cola, Pepsi Cola, or other cola-flavored soft drinks, there were chocolate drinks made with cocoa, potato starch, and lots of flour to absorb the cocoa butter grease (yuck!). One of the first of these was advertised in the *Publick Adviser* on June 16, 1657:

> "[On] Bishopsgate Street... at a Frenchman's house, is an excellent West India drink called 'Chocolate' to be sold, where you may have it ready at any time, and also unmade at reasonable rates."

Spencer would be proud

Coca-Cola's script logo featuring the now familiar Spencerian handwriting was first introduced in an advertisement on June 16, 1887. Although the logo has evolved over the years, characteristics of the original script are clearly recognizable in today's Coca-Cola logo. A few years later, Pepsi Cola introduced its logo as part of the company's trademark which it registered on June 16, 1903. Like Coca-Cola, Pepsi Cola's logo also had ***elements of a script style.***

Today, companies innovate to keep pace with competitors and maintain an up-to-date image. Not only are their logos subject to change, but their brand names, promotions, packaging, and product designs may change as well. But, if too many changes are introduced too quickly or if the changes are too drastic, long-standing relationships with customers may be jeopardized. When customers have become familiar with a brand throughout their lives, sudden changes may evoke a sense of loss or even betrayal, or nostalgic sentiments may be aroused as previously loyal customers long for "the way the brand used to be in the good ole days." Also potentially problematic are extreme packaging or name changes that could make it difficult for buyers to recognize the brand on store shelves.

Consequently, companies often try to balance the need to introduce changes with the value of long-term customer relationships. They may do this by introducing the changes gradually -- sometimes over a period of several years or decades -- carefully ensuring that not all elements of the familiar are cast aside to make room for the new.

June 17, 2017
Saturday

Objectives & reminders

____

____

Appointments

Early morning

8 a.m.

9 a.m.

10 a.m.

11 a.m.

Noon

1 p.m.

2 p.m.

3 p.m.

4 p.m.

5 p.m.

6 p.m.

Later evening

Happy birthday: Barry Manilow

Born in Brooklyn, NY on June 17, 1943, Manilow has been a popular songwriter, musician and singer for more than four decades. "Mandy" (1974), his first big hit, was followed by dozens of others.

However, before Manilow cracked the music charts with regularity, he wrote numerous advertising jingles. Many of Manilow's jingles have become hits themselves: "You Deserve a Break Today" (McDonald's), "Like a Good Neighbor, State Farm Is There" (State Farm Insurance), "Get a Bucket of Chicken (Kentucky Fried Chicken), "Most Original Soft Drink" (Dr. Pepper), and "We're the Pepsi People Feelin' Free" (Pepsi Cola), to name a few.

Four advantages of advertising jingles

1. Jingles break through the clutter (*get* audience's attention).
2. Jingles entertain audience (*keep* audience's attention).
3. Messages often easier to remember with jingles (musical qualities prompt listeners to replay jingles in their minds).
4. Jingles stir word-of-mouth (jingles may be shared when facts are not).

II III II III II III II III

Leadership 101: Leverage strengths

"I believe that you've got to manage to people's strengths. Everybody's got weaknesses. And if you focus on his or her weaknesses, you're just going to make everybody unhappy. Focus on their strengths. If you gradually understand that their weaknesses are more profound than their strengths, then you have to reassign them. But if you have good people and focus on what they do well, and kind of work around their weaknesses, they'll be happy and do better and so will the company."
-- William "Bill" Steere, Jr., former chairman and CEO of Pfizer, Inc. (world's third-largest pharmaceutical firm), born on June 17, 1936

June 18, 2017
Sunday

Objectives & reminders

____

____

____

Appointments

Early morning

8 a.m.

9 a.m.

10 a.m.

11 a.m.

Noon

1 p.m.

2 p.m.

3 p.m.

4 p.m.

5 p.m.

6 p.m.

Later evening

Father's Day

Since a presidential proclamation in 1972, Father's Day has been celebrated annually in the U.S. on the third Sunday in June. Today, Father's Day is celebrated or acknowledged by 72 percent of Americans. It's a day for families to honor fathers and to thank them for all they do for their families. Father's Day celebrations often include honoring fathers with gifts, cards, telephone calls or personal visits, family meals, and efforts to make the day a little easier or more enjoyable for Dad.

Father's Day facts for marketers
When surveyed "only days before Father's Day," 53 percent of gift-givers had not yet decided what gift to purchase.

Most popular gift categories for Father's Day: cards (60%), apparel (41%), dinner (38%), sporting goods (22%), home improvement items (18%), electronics (17%), and gardening tools (12%).

No such thing as average: Agree or disagree?

"The average family exists only on paper and its average budget is a fiction, invented by statisticians for the convenience of statisticians." -- Sylvia Porter, economist and personal finance columnist, born on June 18, 1913

Free the creative: Agree or disagree?

"There is too much administration of everything creative. It distorts our society and its character. The solution is to select competent, well-qualified people and give them freedom and support to pursue their creative gifts." -- Jerome Karle, physicist and co-winner of the Nobel Prize in chemistry, born on June 18, 1918

It's fun-damental: Agree or disagree?

"Fun is a stimulant to people. They enjoy their work more and work more productively." -- Herb Kelleher, co-founder of Southwest Airlines. Southwest's first flight was on June 18, 1971. Today, the company's 46,000 employees have fun with 3,800 flights daily.

June 19, 2017
Monday

Objectives & reminders

____

____

Appointments

Early morning

8 a.m.

9 a.m.

10 a.m.

11 a.m.

Noon

1 p.m.

2 p.m.

3 p.m.

4 p.m.

5 p.m.

6 p.m.

Later evening

Juneteenth

A milestone in African-Americans' struggle for freedom occurred on June 19, 1865, when slaves in Texas first learned of their freedom.

Although President Abraham Lincoln had issued the Emancipation Proclamation almost two and a half years earlier -- while the Civil War was still raging -- the Confederate states did not recognize Lincoln's authority at the time, so many southern slaves did not know they were free, and those that did could not safely exercise their freedom.

This changed shortly after the war, when Union soldiers led by General Gordon Granger informed slaves of their freedom. In December 1865, slavery was officially outlawed in the U.S. by the ratification of the 13th Amendment to the Constitution.

Today, Juneteenth (a hybrid combination of "*June*" and "nine*teenth*") is celebrated primarily in the southern U.S. and primarily by African-Americans. In Texas the day is observed as a state holiday and also is referred to as "Emancipation Day." Juneteenth provides businesses with an excellent opportunity to recognize the contributions of African-Americans throughout their community and express appreciation for their African-American customers.

Integrity matters

"If you have integrity, nothing else matters. If you don't have integrity, nothing else matters."
-- Evelle J. Younger, former U.S. Attorney General, born on June 19, 1918

Integrity *and* health matter

"If you don't have your health and your integrity, you don't have much to offer." -- James J. Mulva, chairman and CEO of ConocoPhillips (petroleum), born in De Pere, Wisconsin on June 19, 1946

No substitute for the extraordinary

"One machine can do the work of fifty ordinary men. No machine can do the work of one extraordinary man." -- Elbert Hubbard, American philosopher, writer, and observer of human behavior, born on June 19, 1856

June 20, 2017
Tuesday

Objectives & reminders

____

____

____

Appointments

Early morning

8 a.m.

9 a.m.

10 a.m.

11 a.m.

Noon

1 p.m.

2 p.m.

3 p.m.

4 p.m.

5 p.m.

6 p.m.

Later evening

Welcome aboard: West Virginia

West Virginia became the 35th U.S. state on June 20, 1863. For most of the last century, the state's economy has depended heavily on coal and the state continues to be one of the country's leading coal producing states.

Today, in addition to coal, West Virginia has become somewhat of a retirement mecca, with the state's mountains and forests attracting many retirees.

Tourism also is a growth industry in the state, thanks to the state's scenic mountains, forests, rivers, and 33 state parks which collectively provide tourists with ample opportunities to enjoy outdoor activities such as camping, hiking and white water rafting.

Historically, the mountainous terrain in much of the state has left many regions isolated, which has given rise to several unique cultural traditions (e.g., music, furniture making, quilting and other arts) that are celebrated today in a number of fairs and festivals held throughout the state.

Did you know?
West Virginia's flower is the rhododendron. The state's bird is the cardinal, and it's motto is "Montani Semper Liberi" (Mountaineers are always free).

Cultural influence

What has been described as, "the most popular and influential variety show in television history," premiered on June 20, 1948, on CBS television – *Toast of the Town,* later renamed *The Ed Sullivan Show.* For 23 years, the show introduced American audiences to most major performers and helped propel the careers of many, including Elvis Presley and the Beatles.

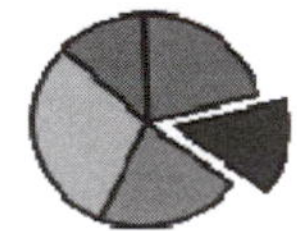

In the late 1960s, however, the show's ratings dropped as audience demographics began tilting toward older Americans. As a result, advertisers began losing interest in the show, so it was canceled in 1971.

June 21, 2017
Wednesday

Almost the first full day of summer in the Northern Hemisphere

Objectives & reminders

____

____

Appointments

Early morning	12:24 a.m. EDT: Summer arrives
8 a.m.	
9 a.m.	
10 a.m.	
11 a.m.	
Noon	
1 p.m.	
2 p.m.	
3 p.m.	
4 p.m.	
5 p.m.	
6 p.m.	
Later evening	

Summer is here!

Today marks the beginning of summer in the Northern Hemisphere – the year with the most daylight hours, generally accompanied by warm or hot temperatures for the three-month summer season that follows.

For seasonal products and businesses, shifts in demand are likely to coincide with changes in the seasons. Obviously, sales demand for swim-wear, lawn and garden equipment, air conditioners, family vacations (while children are out of school), and many outdoor sporting activities are higher in summer than in winter. For many products, however, seasonal variation in demand can be much less apparent, but real nonetheless. That's why it is useful to examine a company's or product category's historical sales records to identify seasonal peaks and valleys in demand.

Once seasonal demand patterns are detected, appropriate actions may be taken. These may include efforts to:

1. Adjust inventory levels to match forecasted demand.
2. Accelerate the arrival of the selling season and beat competitors to customers by promoting and displaying seasonal items prior to the start of the season.
3. Extend the buying season by identifying and promoting alternative product uses that are less seasonally-related (e.g., positioning hats as fashion statements).
4. Extend the buying season by pointing out the customer benefits associated with buying during the off-season (e.g., fewer crowds, easier parking, personalized services).
5. Alter the product mix throughout the year to include items likely to be in high demand during the current season.
6. Smooth peaks and valleys in demand by adding non-seasonal merchandise to the product mix.
7. Time activities not directly tied to sales to coincide with lull periods of demand (e.g., plant/equipment maintenance, training).
8. Accelerate the start of the buying season with "seasonal dating," e.g., offer to ship items to retailers in May but not bill them until August.

June 22, 2017
Thursday

Objectives & reminders

____

____

____

Appointments

Early morning

8 a.m.

9 a.m.

10 a.m.

11 a.m.

Noon

1 p.m.

2 p.m.

3 p.m.

4 p.m.

5 p.m.

6 p.m.

Later evening

Instinctive "drive" motivates us: Agree or disagree?

Born on June 22, 1871, William McDougall was a psychologist who studied social behavior and motivation. In particular, he coined the term *hormic psychology*, which includes his theory of motivation that asserts that people are often motivated by inherited instincts that drive them to achieve and to pursue their goals. According to McDougall, people often are unaware of these instinctive drives or their potency. Many of McDougall's ideas are summarized in his book, *An Introduction to Social Psychology* – first published in 1908 and revised several times since then.

Sign of the zodiac: Cancer

On the zodiac calendar, people born from June 22 to July 22 fall under the sign of Cancer or The Crab. Astrologists consider them to be family-oriented, cautious, imaginative, detail-oriented, and interested in history.

Whether or not astrological configurations affect anyone's personality, behavior or experiences is debatable. However, people who do believe in astrology and follow their horoscope religiously may alter their plans and behavior in very tangible ways – ways that could affect their behavior in the workplace or marketplace.

Is it worthwhile for sales reps to follow customers' horoscopes?
Consider the effect that the following horoscopes (by astrologist Linda C. Black) might have on a buyer's behavior if he or she is a strong believer in astrology.

1. "Over the next few days, you'll be too busy to do much research. If there's something you have to find out, ask for help."
2. "Be careful with your money. It'll be easy to think you have more than you do. Don't give away a secret, either."
3. "Don't get too wafty or over-enthusiastic in your expectations. A certain amount of good old common sense is required."

June 23, 2017
Friday

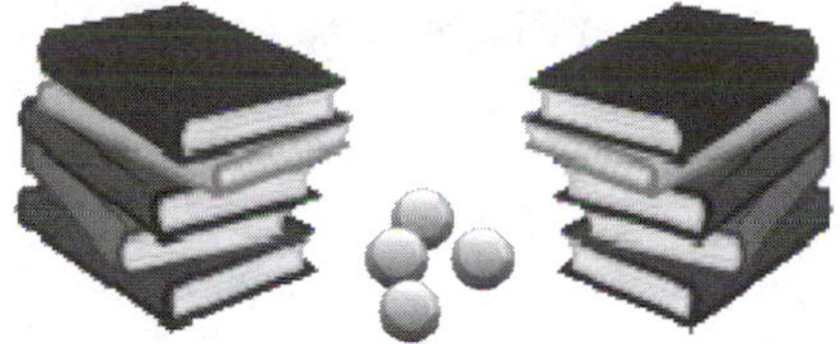

Objectives & reminders

____

____

____

Appointments

Early morning

8 a.m.

9 a.m.

10 a.m.

11 a.m.

Noon

1 p.m.

2 p.m.

3 p.m.

4 p.m.

5 p.m.

6 p.m.

Later evening

June 23 in publishing history

1696 The first evening newspaper was published in London, *Dawks's News-Letter*. Publisher Ichabod Dawks differentiated his paper not only by publishing the evening edition, but also by opting for an italic script that resembled handwriting – probably in an effort to appeal to older readers whose nostalgic memories still cherished the days of handwritten newsletters that were circulated before newspapers were commonly printed.

1775 The first book published in the U.S. was advertised in Philadelphia by publisher Story & Humphreys. The book, *Impenetrable Secret*, was touted as "printed with types, paper and ink manufactured in this Province."

1860 The U.S. Congress established the Government Printing Office (GPO). Today, the GPO publishes hundreds of free or nominally-priced pamphlets and books, many of which deal with business- and consumer-relevant issues. Visit the GPO's website, www.gpo.gov, or telephone the GPO's toll-free number in the U.S.: 866-512-1800.

1868 Working with Carlos Glidden, printer/publisher Christopher Latham Sholes received a patent for the typewriter. They sold the rights to investor James Densmore, who commercialized the invention. The innovation in word processing soon became known as the Remington type-writer. Mark Twain earned the distinction of being the first author to submit a typewritten book manuscript to a publisher.

1879 William Ewert Berry was born. In 1901, Berry launched *Advertising World* and served as both editor and advertising manager of the publication. Partnering with his brother, Seymour, Berry went on to launch or acquire several other publications in Great Britain, including the *Sunday Times* and the *Financial Times*.

June 24, 2017
Saturday

Objectives & reminders

____

____

Appointments

Early morning

8 a.m.

9 a.m.

10 a.m.

11 a.m.

Noon

1 p.m.

2 p.m.

3 p.m.

4 p.m.

5 p.m.

6 p.m.

Later evening

Grand opening: Marbleous event!

On June 24, 1902, the *Minneapolis Journal* reported the opening of George Draper Dayton's first Goodfellow Store. Dayton's organization later launched Dayton's department stores, followed by Target discount stores.

> "Thousands of men and women were present at the auspicious formal opening of the new [store]... They made purchases, listened to a splendid orchestra and looked with delight at the beautiful goods and beautiful decorations... Well-dressed and happy-looking clerks were behind the spacious counters ready to answer every query. There are tall glass showcases instead of old-style shelving and the counter cases are all of glass, fitted with electric lights." – *Minneapolis Journal*

Baby lesson

Stores, products and innovations are like people in that they often attract more attention in their infancy -- when they are new. New stores, new products, and new babies are news that media and consumers are interested in seeing and talking about.

But, the extra attention doesn't necessarily materialize automatically; the opportunities must be seized. So, companies plan grand opening events, ribbon-cutting ceremonies, high-profile demonstrations, and mail lots of invitations to announce the arrival of their newborns.

Association of National Advertisers

On June 24, 1910, 45 companies met in a Detroit hotel to form what is now known as the ANA -- one of the advertising industry's oldest trade organizations. Among other objectives, the organization sought to establish standards and mechanisms to enable advertisers to verify media vehicles' circulation statistics. In 1914, the Audit Bureau of Circulation was founded and shares some of the same objectives. Today, the ANA's headquarters are in New York and its 600 member companies represent 10,000 brands and spend more than $250 billion annually on advertising and other marketing communications.

June 25, 2017
Sunday

Objectives & reminders

____

____

____

____

Appointments

Early morning

8 a.m.

9 a.m.

10 a.m.

11 a.m.

Noon

1 p.m.

2 p.m.

3 p.m.

4 p.m.

5 p.m.

6 p.m.

Later evening

Happy birthday: Jan Carlzon

Born in Nyköping, Sweden on June 25, 1941, Jan Carlzon began his career in 1967 as a product manager for a tour operator. This experience helped him to understand that service businesses face a set of business challenges that are somewhat different from those that manufacturers face.

By the late 1970s Carlzon was gaining experience in the airline industry, eventually becoming CEO and president of Scandinavian Airlines System (SAS) in 1981. Industry analysts credit Carlzon with greatly improving SAS's performance and developing more of a service-oriented culture throughout the organization.

One of the focal points of Carlzon's service initiative was the concept of "moments of truth" – which is also the title of the English edition of his 1987 book. Moments of truth are interpersonal episodes between employees and customers, e.g., when a passenger telephones an airline representative to inquire about flight schedules or order a ticket, when the passenger obtains a boarding pass from a ticketing agent, when the passenger accepts a soft drink from a flight attendant, and so on. For any given passenger for any given flight, there may be a dozen or more moments of truth that collectively contribute to the passenger's flight experience.

Every time an employee interacts with a customer, Carlzon reasoned, the potential exists to build-up or tear-down the company's relationship with the customer. A smile, a speedy response, a thoughtful answer to a customer's question, a proactive gesture, and a "thank you," are just a few of the infinite number of ways employees could build customer relationships during moments of truth.

Although any single moment of truth may appear to be insignificant, the collective power of these relationship-building opportunities became apparent when Carlzon estimated that 68,000+ of them occur daily at SAS. So he took action to improve the quality of moments of truth, which included empowering employees with information. As Carlzon noted in his book, "An individual without information cannot take responsibility; an individual who is given information cannot help but take responsibility." (p. 35)

June 26, 2017
Monday

Objectives & reminders

____

____

____

Appointments

Early morning

8 a.m.

9 a.m.

10 a.m.

11 a.m.

Noon

1 p.m.

2 p.m.

3 p.m.

4 p.m.

5 p.m.

6 p.m.

Later evening

African independence

The early 1960s was a period of substantial political change for the continent of Africa, as predicted by British Prime Minister Harold Macmillan only five weeks into the decade: "The wind of change is blowing through the continent." In 1960 alone, 16 African countries gained their independence and joined the United Nations. In particular, on June 26 of that year Somalia (then British Somaliland) and Madagascar (then Malagasy Republic) broke from British and French rule, respectively. Today, June 26 is celebrated as these countries' Independence Day or National Day.

Perception creates reality

After sinking his life's savings into the development and introduction of a practical plow made of cast iron, Charles Newbold of Chesterfield, New Jersey received a patent for his invention on June 26, 1797. Unfortunately, farmers feared what they perceived to be the harmful effects of the iron on their fields, so they rejected the innovation (note that the farmers' fears were not justified; iron plows do not harm the soil).

Invitation to be a marketing consultant
Suppose Mr. Newbold had hired you as a marketing consultant before the introduction of his new plow. Describe the marketing research you might have done to identify farmers' attitudes toward cast iron plows. Assuming that Mr. Newbold decided to introduce the plow after he learned about farmers' plow perceptions, what suggestions might you have offered to him to increase farmers' acceptance of his plow?

Leader of the pack

"Unless you have some goals, I don't think there's any way to get above the pack. My vision was always well beyond what I had any reason to expect." -- John B. Fuqua, former chairman of Fuqua Industries ($2 billion conglomerate), born on June 26, 1918

June 27, 2017
Tuesday

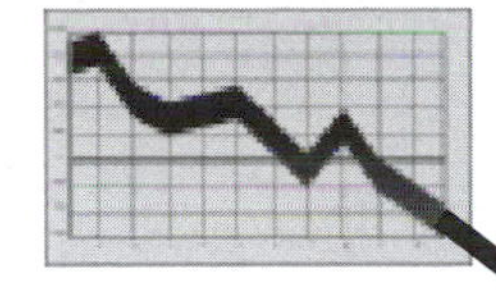

Objectives & reminders

____

____

____

Appointments

Early morning

8 a.m.

9 a.m.

10 a.m.

11 a.m.

Noon

1 p.m.

2 p.m.

3 p.m.

4 p.m.

5 p.m.

6 p.m.

Later evening

Economic downturns

For advance planners, the stock market serves as an indicator of public sentiment and possible swings in the economy. That was certainly the case on June 27, 1893, when the New York stock market crashed, triggering 642 bank failures and the collapse of more than 16,000 businesses. Railroads were hit particularly hard.

Swings in the economy affect businesses, in general, and marketers, in particular. When the economy is booming, customers and prospective customers are more inclined to spend. But when the economy plunges or when buyers fear tough times are ahead, they're more likely to hold onto their money. Although individual marketers can not control the ups and downs in the economy, there are several things they can do to make downturns more palatable for their firms and for their customers. For example:

1. Build strong relationships with customers *before* the economy sours. There are no guarantees, but if customers have to slash their budgets during a financial crisis, they're less likely to cut ties with people and businesses they like.

> **Friend-building**
> "It's easier to say 'no' to a stranger or acquaintance than to a good friend. Be a friend." – I said that

2. Maintain a positive outlook. Customers notice. Enthusiasm and confidence are contagious.

3. Explore creative financing alternatives. Customers may want to buy, but may be short of cash. Low-interest financing, delayed payment options, low down-payment requirements, or leasing alternatives may enable customers to buy.

4. Stress long-term value. Remind customers of durability. Look beyond the recession and encourage customers to do the same.

5. In general, keep marketing. Even if some customers don't buy during the economic downturn, when the tough times end they're more likely to remember firms that remembered them.

June 28, 2017
Wednesday

Objectives & reminders

____

____

____

Appointments

Early morning

8 a.m.

9 a.m.

10 a.m.

11 a.m.

Noon

1 p.m.

2 p.m.

3 p.m.

4 p.m.

5 p.m.

6 p.m.

Later evening

Remembering the "Great War"

On June 28, 1914, Archduke Ferdinand of Austria and his wife, Sofia, were assassinated by a Bosnian Serb in Sarajevo. The assassinations led to a chain of events that started World War I, referred to at the time as the "Great War." Exactly five years later, on June 28, 1919, the War formally ended when Germany agreed to the terms of the Treaty of Versailles, in Versailles, France.

The Monday Holiday Law

It was June 28, 1968, when U.S. President Lyndon B. Johnson signed Public Law 90-363 which moved several holiday observances to Monday, including: George Washington's birthday (later Presidents' Day), Memorial Day, Labor Day, Columbus Day and Veterans Day (although Veterans Day was later moved back to its original observance date, November 11). The new Monday holidays went into effect in 1971.

The Monday Holiday Law created several new three-day weekends for government employees as well as workers of other organizations that recognized the holidays. The extended weekends work to the advantage of marketers of tourism, hospitality and travel-related services as consumers often take mini-vacations or otherwise travel out of town during three-day weekends. Retail stores also find an influx of consumers willing to shop during the three-day weekends, which is why they often time "sales" and other promotional events to coincide with the three-day weekends.

Work or shop?

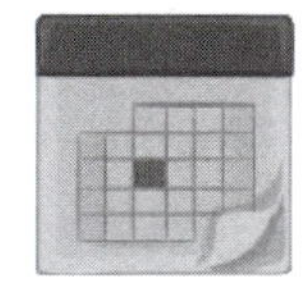

Consumers are more likely to shop -- especially for discretionary goods -- on days they do not have to work at their jobs.

Success is hard work

"[T]here are plenty of people in this company who are better educated than I am. But the reason I am sitting in the president's seat and they aren't is because I am gutsy, I am tenacious, I stir things up, and I am a very, very hard worker." – Kathy Taggares, founder and President of K.T.'s Kitchens, Inc. (multi-million-dollar food processing firm), born on June 28, 1952

June 29, 2017
Thursday

Objectives & reminders

____

____

Appointments

Early morning

8 a.m.

9 a.m.

10 a.m.

11 a.m.

Noon

1 p.m.

2 p.m.

3 p.m.

4 p.m.

5 p.m.

6 p.m.

Later evening

1st² National?

The first First (1st² ?) National Bank opened on June 29, 1863, in Davenport, Iowa. Today, if banks wish to differentiate themselves from competitors and occupy their own unique position in the marketplace, why do so many call themselves the First National Bank? If the answer is that being "first" is prestigious and is associated with being a winner, then why are so many other banks content to have "Second," "Third," "Fourth," or even "Fifth" in their names? Even more baffling, how does one explain the name of Cincinnati, Ohio's "Fifth Third Bank"? Some sort of a tie?

Quality principle: Less expensive to get it right the first time

In his 1979 book, *Quality Is Free*, Philip B. Crosby asserts that contrary to what many people think, upgrading product quality does not, in the long-term, raise costs. Rather, Crosby makes the case that quality improvements pay for themselves in a number of ways. For example, businesses with high quality products need to spend fewer resources correcting defects and placating customers negatively affected by the defects.

> **The cost of quality**
> "Quality is... the expense of nonconformance – the cost[s] of doing things wrong. These costs... are a result of not doing things right the first time.... [I]t is always cheaper to do things right the first time." – Philip B. Crosby, *Quality is Free*, pp. 15-16

An example of the expensive quality recovery phenomenon became evident on June 29, 1972, when Ford Motor Company recalled more than four million cars and trucks it had manufactured during the previous two years.

> **Big idea**
> It is almost always less expensive to correct engineering or production mistakes *before* the products leave the factory, but it's even less expensive than that to prevent mistakes from occurring in the first place.

June 30, 2017
Friday

Objectives & reminders

____

____

____

Appointments

Early morning

8 a.m.

9 a.m.

10 a.m.

11 a.m.

Noon

1 p.m.

2 p.m.

3 p.m.

4 p.m.

5 p.m.

6 p.m.

Later evening

Clearly for marketers, words matter

"Words well chosen have the power to awe, inspire, motivate, alienate, subjugate, even alter something as significant as the course of history, or as cosmically minute as the buying habits of consumers... The expressions that are memorable, persuasive, and have the greatest impact are more than slogans and taglines – they are powerlines." – Steve Cone, Chief Marketing Officer for Epsilon, former advertising executive and author of *Powerlines: Words that Sell Brands, Grip Fans, and Sometimes Change History*, published on June 30, 2008

Key criterion for targeted markets

Willie Sutton was born in Brooklyn, New York on June 30, 1901. During his infamous 30-year career as a criminal, he robbed almost 100 banks. In 1952, Sutton was captured and imprisoned at Attica State Prison in New York. When asked why he robbed banks, he explained, "Because that's where the money is."

Soon after his release from prison in 1969, Sutton starred in a television commercial for the Bank and Trust Company of New Britain, Connecticut to promote the bank's new photo credit cards. As an increasing number of Americans acquired credit cards during the early 1970s, clearly plastic was where the money was.

Good day for feedback

The 26th Amendment to the U.S. Constitution was ratified on June 30, 1971, giving 18-year-olds the right to vote. Congratulations! Before the amendment, the legal voting age was 21.

www.MarketingMarbles.com

To celebrate the occasion, please take a moment to use the "Contact" page of our website to vote for what you like or don't like about *Marketing FAME*. If you have any suggestions to improve future editions, pass them along. Your vote counts!

July 1, 2017
Saturday

Objectives & reminders

___

___

___

Appointments

Early morning

8 a.m.

9 a.m.

10 a.m.

11 a.m.

Noon

1 p.m.

2 p.m.

3 p.m.

4 p.m.

5 p.m.

6 p.m.

Later evening

Welcome to July!

July is the seventh month on the Gregorian calendar, but was fifth on the Roman calendar. Previously known as "Quintilis," the month was renamed by the Roman Senate in honor of Julius Caesar.

Canada Day

With the passage of the British North America Act, Canada became a self-governing entity on July 1, 1867. Formerly known as "Dominion Day," Canadian consumers continue to celebrate the holiday on July 1 each year (except when July 1 is a Sunday; then the legal holiday is observed on Monday, July 2). In addition to proudly displaying the Canadian flag and singing the national anthem, "O Canada," Canadians celebrate the holiday with parades and fireworks.

The Lincoln Highway

On July 1, 1913, the Lincoln Highway Association (LHA) was formed to satisfy public demand for a coast-to-coast paved road that would connect New York City with San Francisco -- a 3,400-mile stretch. The LHA solicited both private and corporate donations for the ambitious project. Within a few years, public demand for more roads pushed the federal government into the business of building roads to connect other cities throughout the U.S.

More than four decades later, in 1956, the U.S. Federal Aid Highway Act was passed. The Act paved way to pay for the construction of more than 41,000 miles of the U.S. interstate system. Today, modern commerce depends heavily on highway networks.

All jobs involve personal selling: Agree or disagree?

"I have never worked a day in my life without selling. If I believe in something, I sell it, and I sell it hard." -- Estée Lauder, founder of the cosmetics company that bears her name, born on July 1, 1906 (Note sources disagree as to the year of Lauder's birth; some say 1907, while others report 1908, 1909 or 1910).

July 2, 2017
Sunday

☐ Excellent
☐ Good
☐ Mediocre
☐ Poor

Objectives & reminders

____

____

Appointments

Early morning

8 a.m.

9 a.m.

10 a.m.

11 a.m.

Noon

1 p.m.

2 p.m.

3 p.m.

4 p.m.

5 p.m.

6 p.m.

Later evening

Happy birthday: Dave Thomas

Born on July 2, 1932, in Atlantic City, New Jersey, Rex David "Dave" Thomas began dreaming of running his own restaurant at the age of eight. When he was 12, he landed his first job in a restaurant. In the 10th grade (age 15), he dropped out of school and worked full time in the food service business. He gained additional experience in the Army managing an enlisted-men's club. Then he became one of the first Kentucky Fried Chicken franchisees.

It's never too late
Thomas dropped out of high school at the age of 15, but in 1993 (at the age of 61), he earned his GED from Coconut Creek High School in Fort Lauderdale, Florida.

Next, in Columbus, Ohio in 1969, Thomas opened the first of what would become a chain of more than 1,000 Wendy's restaurants within less than a decade. Although Thomas removed himself from day-to-day operations in 1982, he continued to play a cheerleader role for the company -- visiting stores and espousing his philosophy of hard work and his principles of business success:

1. "Quality is our recipe."
2. "Do the right thing."
3. "Treat people with respect."
4. "Profit is not a dirty word."
5. "Giving back."

From 1989 until his death in early 2002, Thomas personally appeared in more than 800 television commercials for Wendy's. By then, the company (Wendy's International) had grown to more than 6,000 restaurants in North America. Today, his image continues to be used in Wendy's signage and promotional materials.

Dave on advertising and quality
"Some of these advertising gurus come up with fancy ideas that don't really make sense. You can do a lot of fancy commercials, but if you don't provide a quality product, the commercials just don't work. When people see a commercial of any kind, they want to be sure that what they see is what they'll get. That's the same with any product." – Dave Thomas

July 3, 2017
Monday

Objectives & reminders

____

____

____

Appointments

Early morning

8 a.m.

9 a.m.

10 a.m.

11 a.m.

Noon

1 p.m.

2 p.m.

3 p.m.

4 p.m.

5 p.m.

6 p.m.

Later evening

Debut of *Science*

A new publication was introduced on July 3, 1880: *Science: A Weekly Journal of Scientific Progress.* With the help of journalist John Michaels, inventor Thomas A. Edison founded the new journal. The publication provided a channel for scientists to disseminate the findings of their research, thereby enabling researchers to learn from each other and build upon the scientific work already developed.

Today, business leaders are interested in mechanisms that facilitate learning in their organizations. All too often an experienced salesperson, for example, will develop a keen understanding of product applications, the market, or specific customers' needs, but may not have a way of effectively and easily transmitting that knowledge throughout the organization. In many instances, there may be no personal incentive for a knowledgeable salesperson to share what he or she has learned. Consequently, new sales reps may be forced to "reinvent the learning wheel," so to speak, possibly spending years to develop the same level of knowledge their more experienced counterparts have amassed already.

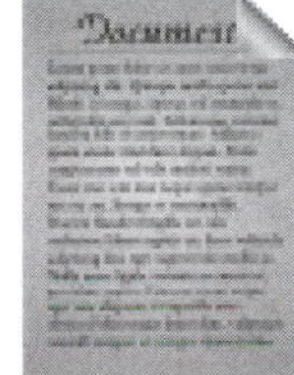

It's not surprising that companies able to harness and disseminate the collective knowledge and experience of their workforce are likely to gain a competitive advantage. Some use company newsletters or "house organs" to communicate with workers; many of these feature interviews with experienced or creative workers who share their insights. Some organizations involve experienced personnel in training programs for the less experienced. Still others implement formal or quasi-formal coaching or mentoring programs in which experienced personnel share their knowledge with newer employees with whom they are matched.

There's much to be said for informal approaches too -- such as social gatherings, periodic luncheons, and simply locating the offices or workstations of the experienced near those of the less experienced. Such informal approaches bring people into contact with each other, and when that happens, useful information is exchanged.

July 4, 2017
Tuesday
Independence Day

Objectives & reminders

____

____

Appointments

Early morning

8 a.m.

9 a.m.

10 a.m.

11 a.m.

Noon

1 p.m.

2 p.m.

3 p.m.

4 p.m.

5 p.m.

6 p.m.

Later evening

Declaration of Independence

In Philadelphia, Pennsylvania the Second Continental Congress unanimously voted in support of the Declaration of Independence on July 4, 1776. As one of the most important documents in the history of the country, the document proclaimed the United States' freedom from Great Britain's rule. However, it took almost four decades for the occasion to be widely celebrated. It took another 120-130 years before Congress finally declared (in 1941) that July 4 would be a federal legal holiday.

Today, Independence Day is considered the country's birthday and is one of the most celebrated secular holidays in America -- characterized by picnics, cookouts, family gatherings, patriotic parades, flag-waving, speeches, fireworks, and a day away from the job.

Excerpt from one of America's most treasured documents
"We hold these truths to be self-evident, that all men are created equal, that they are endowed by their Creator with certain unalienable rights, that among these are life, liberty, and the pursuit of happiness. That, to secure these rights, governments are instituted among men, deriving their just powers from the consent of the governed. That whenever any form of government becomes destructive of these ends, it is the right of the people to alter or to abolish it, and to institute new government..."
– Declaration of Independence

Market to their aspirations

"The poor wish to be rich, the rich wish to be happy, the single wish to be married..." -- Ann Landers, American advice columnist, born on July 4, 1918

Profits are essential

"Civilization and profits go hand in hand."
-- Calvin Coolidge, 30th President of the United States (1923-1929), born in Plymouth Notch, Vermont on July 4, 1872

July 5, 2017
Wednesday

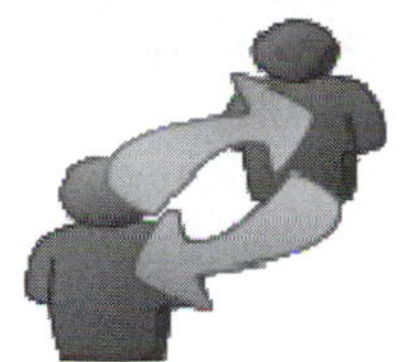

Objectives & reminders

____

____

____

Appointments

Early morning

8 a.m.

9 a.m.

10 a.m.

11 a.m.

Noon

1 p.m.

2 p.m.

3 p.m.

4 p.m.

5 p.m.

6 p.m.

Later evening

Time for a Declaration of In*ter*dependence?

"Independence" has become an ideal, a cause and a rallying cry – a patriotic theme embraced by Americans who salute veterans and fallen soldiers that unselfishly fought to attain and preserve it.

To challenge the notion of independence may seem outrageous, but it may be useful to reconsider the time-honored ideal of independence and the extent to which it should be a goal.

It is true that businesses are independent in that they are somewhat autonomous units or possibly a collection of autonomous units free to choose among a variety of strategic options, and they are free to allocate their resources largely as they see fit. Employees too may be independent in the sense that they are often "empowered" or granted freedom to meet their job challenges.

So, independence has its place in business, but a business cannot be completely independent. By definition, a business must engage in exchanges with customers outside of the business; otherwise it cannot survive in the long-term. The ideal is to recognize the need to move beyond independence and embrace in*ter*dependence -- i.e., involvement in mutually beneficial relationships in which each party contributes to the relationship and in return receives benefits contributed by other parties in the relationship.

While in*ter*dependence is an important and necessary goal for businesses, it's highly relevant for individuals too. Successful individuals recognize that they can not possibly have all of the experience and skills needed to be truly independent. That's why they join organizations and why smart entrepreneurs reach out for assistance from others. People need the assistance of others, with whom they exchange information, expertise and support.

Even top business leaders routinely recognize their own personal limitations and think in terms of surrounding themselves with a *team* whose members contribute to the team and in return benefit from his or her membership on it. Because team members are in*ter*dependent, the team is able to accomplish what individuals can not.

July 6, 2017
Thursday

Objectives & reminders

____

____

Appointments

Early morning

8 a.m.

9 a.m.

10 a.m.

11 a.m.

Noon

1 p.m.

2 p.m.

3 p.m.

4 p.m.

5 p.m.

6 p.m.

Later evening

Happy birthday: Roger Ward Babson

Born in Gloucester, Massachusetts on July 6, 1875, Babson was an engineer and investment banker early in his career, but he achieved the success for which he is known as an entrepreneurial business statistician who compiled investment-related information, developed economic and corporate forecasts, and then sold the information and insights to subscribers. The business information company he founded in 1904 as Babson's Statistical Organization survived for almost 100 years -- finally closing its doors in 2001 when it was known as Babson's Reports.

Did you know that he knew?
Although some of the theories and tools Babson used to develop his forecasts have since been shown to be of questionable validity, Babson was one of the few forecasters to correctly predict the stock market crash of October 1929 and the Great Depression that followed.

Babson was also known for his philanthropic efforts. In 1919 he founded the Babson Institute (now Babson College) in Wellesley Hills, Massachusetts -- an institution well regarded today for its leadership in the field of entrepreneurship. Then, in 1927 he founded Webber College (now Webber International University) in Babson Park, Florida.

Simulated business experience
To simulate a business-like environment, some of the first cohorts of Babson's students were required to dress professionally and keep regular working hours (8:30-5:00 Monday-Friday, 8:30 to noon on Saturday). To ensure compliance, a time clock was used by students who "punched in" and "out" each day. Babson's business students also had their own desks and were supplied with telephones, typewriters, adding machines and dictating recorders. Also, personal secretaries typed the students' assignments for them.

July 7, 2017
Friday

Objectives & reminders

Appointments

2:00 a.m.
3:00 a.m.
4:00 a.m.
5:00 a.m.
6:00 a.m.
7:00 a.m.

8 a.m.

9 a.m.

10 a.m.

11 a.m.

Noon

1 p.m.

2 p.m.

3 p.m.

4 p.m.

5 p.m.

6 p.m.

Later evening

Good day to schedule breakfast with a client

As Benjamin Franklin first noted in *Poor Richard's Almanac* on July 7, 1757, "The early bird gets the worm."

Dubious distinction

In 1932 the Great Depression was a sobering reality for millions of unemployed and underemployed Americans. More than 20 percent of the workforce was not working, and millions more were concerned about their financial futures. As a result, consumers tended to be extremely careful about how they spent the little money they had, which meant businesses suffered too.

Reflecting the poor business climate, on July 7 of that year the Dow Jones Industrial Average (DJIA) reached a record low: 41.2. The DJIA is an index of large "blue chip" U.S. stocks. In sharp contrast to 1932, since March 1999 the DJIA has generally stayed above 10,000.

Beyond crisis management

July 7, 1997, became a day of horror for the Starbucks coffee empire when three Starbucks employees were murdered during a robbery attempt at a Washington D.C. Starbucks location.

When Starbucks' chairman Howard Schultz heard the bad news at 5:00 a.m., he immediately chartered a plane and flew to Washington D.C. where he stayed for a week to visit the store where the tragedy took place, work with police, meet with the victims' families, and attend the victims' funerals. He then announced that all future profits from the store would be donated to organizations committed to victims' rights and the prevention of violence. Don Graham, CEO of the *Washington Post*, praised Schultz for his prompt and compassionate response to the tragedy: "You cannot do better in a crisis than he did in that instance. He went way beyond the normal bounds."

July 8, 2017
Saturday

Objectives & reminders

____

____

Appointments

Early morning

8 a.m.

9 a.m.

10 a.m.

11 a.m.

Noon

1 p.m.

2 p.m.

3 p.m.

4 p.m.

5 p.m.

6 p.m.

Later evening

Happy Birthday: *The Wall Street Journal*

The first issue of *WSJ* appeared on Monday, July 8, 1889. The four-page debut issue cost readers two cents. Charles Henry Dow (who three years earlier had formulated the Dow Jones Industrial Average) served as the Editor of the newspaper.

Today, *WSJ* covers a wide variety of business-relevant news, including developments pertaining to consumer behavior, social trends, and lifestyles. With a global audience of more than four million (including 1.4 million in the U.S. alone), its influence in the business community is undeniable.

Happy birthday: Austin B. Hill

Hill was a medical statistician born in London on July 8, 1897. One of his biggest contributions to the research field was his introduction of the *clinical trial* concept involving two groups of test subjects -- one receiving the treatment of interest (e.g., a new medication), while the other group unknowingly received a dummy treatment or placebo (e.g., a harmless pill containing no medication). By comparing changes in the test subjects across the two groups, researchers using the clinical trial method are better able to assess the extent to which changes in the subjects should be attributed to the treatment or to other factors not specifically tested.

Today, marketing researchers utilize essentially the same concept, although they are not likely to refer to "clinical trials" (instead they talk about *treatment groups* and *control groups,* or *test stores* and *control stores*). For example, a manufacturer interested in measuring consumers' perceptions of product performance involving a new technology might distribute product samples to groups of prospective users -- with some samples including the new technology and others excluding it. The consumers receiving the samples with the new technology would be referred to as the *treatment group*, while those receiving samples without it would represent the *control group*.

Then the findings of follow-up surveys used to measure users' perceptions could be adjusted to account for any positive or negative biases that may cloud some users' perceptions.

July 9, 2017
Sunday

Objectives & reminders

______

______

______

Appointments

Early morning

8 a.m.

9 a.m.

10 a.m.

11 a.m.

Noon

1 p.m.

2 p.m.

3 p.m.

4 p.m.

5 p.m.

6 p.m.

Later evening

Bowling for Dollars

According to *Forbes* magazine on July 9, 1989, Wal-Mart founder Sam Moore Walton was the richest man in the United States -- worth a reported $8.7 billion ($8,700,000,000). Reported less frequently than his wealth, Walton was quite an athlete as a teen. He quarterbacked his high school football team and met his wife, Helen, while bowling at a local bowling center.

Perhaps the $8.7 billion is a rounding error?
"Nowadays, you hear a lot about fancy accounting methods, like LIFO and FIFO, but back [in the early days of Wal-Mart] we were using the ESP method, which really sped things along when it came time to close those books. It's a pretty basic method: if you can't make your books balance, you take however much they're off by and enter it under the heading ESP, which stands for Error Some Place." -- Sam Walton

Inventors born on July 9

1766 Jacob Perkins: In addition to several other inventions during his life, at the age of 24 he invented a machine for cutting and heading nails.

1802 Thomas Davenport: Invented the first electric motor (using direct current) that proved to be commercially successful, patented in 1837 (see February 25 story).

1819 Elias Howe: Invented the sewing machine in 1846.

1856 Nikola Tesla: Invented the first alternating current induction motor in 1883.

1894 Percy Le Baron Spencer: Invented the microwave oven shortly after the second World War.

1971 Marc Andreessen: Invented the graphical Web browser (also co-founded Netscape).

July 10, 2017
Monday

What could have been?

Objectives & reminders

____

____

Appointments

Early morning

8 a.m.

9 a.m.

10 a.m.

11 a.m.

Noon

1 p.m.

2 p.m.

3 p.m.

4 p.m.

5 p.m.

6 p.m.

Later evening

Happy birthday: Harvey R. Ball

Ball was born on July 10, 1921, and went on to become a commercial artist. One day Ball was approached by an insurance company needing something to help boost office morale. In only ten minutes he designed the now familiar yellow "smiley face," for which he was paid $45. The popularity of the design caught on and the design was used on signs, notepads, buttons, balloons, marbles and numerous other objects. In one year alone (1971), 50 million smiley face buttons were sold. Unfortunately, Ball never trademarked the good-natured design so he received no royalties for it. Today, Wal-Mart uses the smiley face design in signage and advertising.

What if...?

Can we say with certainty what might have happened if Harvey Ball had trademarked the smiley face design? Would he have been a wealthy man before his death in 2001? Or, would the trademark protection have restricted the design's use and therefore limited its popularity? Had the design been trademarked might other artists have designed around the original smiley face to create competing and possibly equally popular smiling designs?

Reintroduction of Coca-Cola "Classic"

"Some critics will say Coca-Cola made a mistake. Some cynics will say that we planned the whole thing. The truth is we are not that dumb and we're not that smart."-- Don Keough, then COO of The Coca-Cola Company, during a press conference on July 10, 1985, when it was announced that the company would bring back the original Coca-Cola formula. Only a few months earlier the company had modified Coke's formula and taste which created a public and media uproar – thus prompting the decision reversal on July 10.

July 11, 2017
Tuesday

Objectives & reminders

Appointments

Early morning

8 a.m.

9 a.m.

10 a.m.

11 a.m.

Noon

1 p.m.

2 p.m.

3 p.m.

4 p.m.

5 p.m.

6 p.m.

Later evening

Five billion anniversary

On July 11, 1987, the world's population reached the five billion mark. Today, it is more than seven billion. More than 95 percent of the world's consumers live outside of the United States. More than half of them are under the age of 28 and 60 percent do not use the Internet. Of those at least 15 years old, 14 percent cannot read and write. An estimated 28 percent of the world's population lives in poverty, on less than $3.11 per day.

Given that so many consumers around the world are poor, consider the following tips for increasing marketing effectiveness when serving low-income market segments. Also, consider that when marketers in more affluent countries learn to serve the poor in their own domestic markets they are well poised for international expansion.

1. Knowing that the poor often have little or no savings to draw from, offer goods in smaller, more affordable, quantities. Example: Sell *one* disposable razor rather than a package of *one dozen*.

2. Knowing that the poor may have difficulty traveling to distant stores, make goods available in local neighborhood stores if possible. Also, retailers could consider locating their stores near public transportation or providing transportation for customers, such as a shuttle service to/from the bus route.

3. Make purchases more affordable with creative financing arrangements, such as rent-to-own or lay-away plans, or by spreading credit card payments over two or more months.

4. Include some "upscale" items in the product mix to allow customers to splurge. The poor may believe that they will never own a mansion or a luxury automobile, but know they can occasionally afford a small piece of "the good life" by buying a bottle of the highest quality and most prestigious brand of mustard -- the same brand affluent people purchase.

5. Recognize that being poor may be only a temporary condition. Building relationships with low-income consumers and treating them respectfully may be profitable in the long-term as they climb the economic ladder.

July 12, 2017
Wednesday

Objectives & reminders

Be prepared for a trick question from instructor.

Appointments

Early morning

8 a.m.

9 a.m.

10 a.m.

11 a.m.

Noon

1 p.m.

2 p.m.

3 p.m.

4 p.m.

5 p.m.

6 p.m.

Later evening

Etch-A-Sketch

The first Etch-A-Sketch was sold on July 12, 1960. Since that initial sale, more than 100 million units have been sold worldwide.

Whenever a "hit" product comes along, it's useful for marketers to examine the reasons behind its success -- with the intent of incorporating portions of the success formula in future products in the same, related, or different product categories. For the Etch-A-Sketch, consider these pluses:

1. The Etch-A-Sketch was novel. At the time it was developed, there was no other item on the market quite like it.
2. The product concept is easy to understand: Turn the knobs and create your own picture. Easily understood concepts are easy to convey in advertising and easy to demonstrate in the stores. The name itself – "Etch-A-Sketch" – also helps make the product concept easy to understand.
3. Further, the Etch-A-Sketch is easy to play with initially, yet more difficult to master. Children can enjoy it right away, but not get bored with continued use. Even adults are challenged by the Etch-A-Sketch.
4. Playing with an Etch-A-Sketch stirs creativity -- another factor that prevents boredom and one that parents appreciate.
5. The Etch-A-Sketch is self-contained. There are no extra parts or game pieces to be lost, no batteries to be replaced, and no electrical outlets needed.
6. It's a clean and convenient toy -- no messy crayons, nothing to spill, easy to carry.
7. The Etch-A-Sketch is gender neutral. Being neither a "girl'" toy nor a "boy" toy, the size of the market potential is not halved and children can share the toy with their siblings.

Your turn
Can you name another popular toy that shares the characteristics of the Etch-A-Sketch's success formula?

July 13, 2017
Thursday

Objectives & reminders

___

___

Appointments

Early morning

8 a.m.

9 a.m.

10 a.m.

11 a.m.

Noon

1 p.m.

2 p.m.

3 p.m.

4 p.m.

5 p.m.

6 p.m.

Later evening

Happy birthday: Erno Rubik

Rubik was born in Budapest, Hungary on July 13, 1944. He was a mathematician at the Academy of Applied Arts and Crafts in Budapest, but is best known for inventing the "Rubik's Cube" in 1974 -- a toy with 26 small colorful cubes that rotate around a central axis to form a larger cube of cubes.

The play objective of the Rubik's Cube is to twist the smaller cubes around the outer face of the cube such that only small cubes of the same color remain on each of the six outer faces of the cube -- a challenging task given that there are 43.2 quintillion possible cube configurations.

Originally available only in Hungary, the Rubik's Cube was brought to the United States late in 1979 and quickly became one of the hottest selling "toys," appealing to both children and adults.

Since its initial introduction, more than 350 million Rubik's Cubes have been sold throughout the world. Today, Erno Rubik is involved in the development of other engaging games and puzzles. More information about the Rubik's Cube may be found at www.rubiks.com.

The success formula revisited
Note that the characteristics attributed to the success of the Etch-A-Sketch (see July 12) also help to explain the popularity of the Rubik's Cube.

Wells Fargo opens for business

It was 1852 when Henry Wells, William G. Fargo and their associates founded the Wells Fargo financial empire. On July 13 of that year, they began banking operations in San Francisco and Sacramento, California.

Chrysler rolls back

After U.S. federal loans bailed out struggling Chrysler Corporation a few years earlier, the company finished paying back the loans on July 13, 1983. At the time, CEO Lee Iacocca publicly asserted, "We at Chrysler borrow money the old fashioned way. We pay it back."

July 14, 2017
Friday

Objectives & reminders

____

____

____

Appointments

Early morning

8 a.m.

9 a.m.

10 a.m.

11 a.m.

Noon

1 p.m.

2 p.m.

3 p.m.

4 p.m.

5 p.m.

6 p.m.

Later evening

Hello President Ford

Born in Omaha, Nebraska on July 14, 1913, Gerald R. Ford was a partner in a law firm in the 1940s before his 24-year membership in the U.S. House of Representatives. In 1973 he became the vice-president of the United States and then served as the nation's 38th President from 1974 until 1977.

Taking responsibility
"Responsibilities abandoned today return as more acute crises tomorrow." – Gerald R. Ford

Farewell Ford President

Apparently Lee Iacocca did not have Gerald Ford's political skills while Iacocca was the president of Ford Motor Company. Consequently, he "resigned" on July 14, 1978, but soon landed the top job at Chrysler and accepted the challenge of turning around the struggling company. Iacocca proved to be effective at Chrysler and was known as a straightforward, no-nonsense, get-things-done business leader who believed in the free enterprise system but insisted on a "level playing field" for U.S. firms to compete against non-U.S. firms.

Iacocca on...

Planning
"The discipline of writing something down is the first step toward making it happen."

Cost control
"Unless you know the costs, you'll be noncompetitive."

Listening
"You have to be able to listen well if you're going to motivate the people… [T]hat's the difference between a mediocre company and a great company. The most fulfilling thing for me as a manager is to watch someone the system has labeled as just average or mediocre really come into his own, all because someone has listened to his problems and helped him solve them."

Communication
"[I]f people understand what you want them to do, and it makes sense, they'll do it."

July 15, 2017
Saturday

Objectives & reminders

____

____

____

Appointments

Early morning

8 a.m.

9 a.m.

10 a.m.

11 a.m.

Noon

1 p.m.

2 p.m.

3 p.m.

4 p.m.

5 p.m.

6 p.m.

Later evening

Time to plan for Christmas?

Clement Moore was born on July 15, 1779. Perhaps he is best known for the poem he originally penned for his children, "A Visit from St. Nicholas" (which begins "Twas the night before Christmas, and all through the house...").

Although July may be a bit early for some businesses to plan for the upcoming Christmas season, for most retailers it's not at all too early. But it will be too late to capitalize upon the gift-giving tradition of the season if retailers procrastinate until the *night* before Christmas.

T'was the *Summer* Before Christmas

T'was the summer before Christmas
and all through the store,

Managers were planning each nook of
the floor.

The "buy" orders were placed and
mailed with care,

In hopes that merchandise soon would
be there.

Decision-making consideration

"Reason itself is fallible, and this fallibility must find a place in our logic." – Nicola Abbagnano, Italian philosopher, born on July 15, 1900

What explains this phenomenon?

"[E]xecutives are able to understand each other with very few words when discussing essential problems of organization, provided that the questions are stated without dependence upon the technologies of their respective fields. This is strikingly true, in fact chiefly observable, when men of radically different fields discuss such questions. It is not due to any common nomenclature or general study of organization systems." – Chester I. Barnard, *The Functions of the Executive* (pp. vii-viii), July 15, 1938

July 16, 2017
Sunday

Objectives & reminders

Appointments

Early morning

8 a.m.

9 a.m.

10 a.m.

11 a.m.

Noon

1 p.m.

2 p.m.

3 p.m.

4 p.m.

5 p.m.

6 p.m.

Later evening

Happy birthday: Orville Redenbacher

Born in Brazil, Indiana on July 16, 1907, Redenbacher was a successful businessman who challenged the assumption that popcorn is a commodity. His company successfully differentiated popcorn, and then branded and promoted "gourmet" popcorn. Doing so enabled his company to command a premium price.

In his company's early days (mid-1960s), Redenbacher was like most entrepreneurs in that he did not have access to unlimited piles of money with which to grow the business. But he was creative, so he pursued a strategy of substituting creativity for money. Redenbacher had his grandson, Gary, personally deliver autographed jars of popcorn to radio announcers at Chicago Cubs baseball games. The announcers enjoyed the popcorn so much that they began to talk about the brand throughout the game, which prompted others to talk -- and to sample gourmet popcorn for themselves. Sales started popping in response to this almost-free publicity.

Are publicity & word-of-mouth "free"?
While it is true that publicity generated by influencers (such as radio announcers) and comment spread by ordinary consumers are not paid for, per se, there may be some expense and proactive effort involved to stimulate the freebies. Had Redenbacher simply waited for publicity and word-of-mouth to materialize by themselves, he might have waited for a long time.

The public as a key stakeholder

"The public must be taken into the company's confidence when changes in policies and procedures are introduced if good public relations are to be maintained... Even when the corporation has the legal right to do something, it is better to do it with public approval than without." – Ivy L. Lee, co-founder of one of the first public relations firms in the U.S. (in 1904) and considered by many to be the founder of modern public relations. Lee was born in Cedartown, Georgia on July 16, 1877.

July 17, 2017
Monday

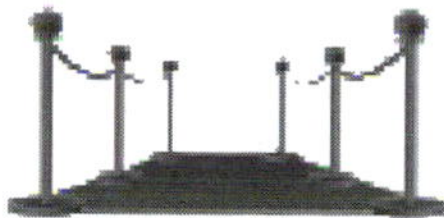

Objectives & reminders

____

____

____

Appointments

Early morning

8 a.m.

9 a.m.

10 a.m.

11 a.m.

Noon

1 p.m.

2 p.m.

3 p.m.

4 p.m.

5 p.m.

6 p.m.

Later evening

Mickey Mouse project

On July 17, 1954, construction began on a new theme park in Anaheim, California -- Disneyland. The 160-acre project was the dream of founder Walt Disney who wanted a tangible location for Mickey Mouse, Donald Duck, and his other animated creations to live – and a place where Mickey and Donald could "receive guests."

> **The larger vision**
> "Disneyland is dedicated to the ideals, the dreams and the hard facts that have created America – with the hope that it will be a source of joy and inspiration to all the world."
> – Walt Disney, July 17, 1955

Exactly one year after construction began – on July 17, 1955 – Disneyland opened for business. Although skeptics questioned the park's viability, Disneyland was an immediate success. More than a million guests visited the park during the first six months of operation. Magically, the park earned almost $200 million during its first decade. Today, more than 16 million guests visit Disneyland annually.

Although there are many reasons for Disneyland's success, three keys include the company's...

1. Commitment to quality. Walt Disney insisted on doing things right. He also recognized that much of quality was found in the details. In the early days of Disneyland, Mr. Disney himself was found replacing plants that had been trampled by guests.

2. Reverence for guests. Prospective Disneyland employees at Disneyland University are taught that "every guest receives VIP treatment." Walt Disney believed that a friendly atmosphere was essential.

3. Manager-employee relations. "Walt" insisted that the Disney family be on a first-name basis. He believed the informality would facilitate better communication.

July 18, 2017
Tuesday

Objectives & reminders

____

____

Appointments

Early morning

8 a.m.

9 a.m.

10 a.m.

11 a.m.

Noon

1 p.m.

2 p.m.

3 p.m.

4 p.m.

5 p.m.

6 p.m.

Later evening

SPAM milestone

The first can of SPAM meat product was manufactured in Austin, Minnesota in 1937. On July 18, 2002, Hormel Foods, makers of SPAM, produced the six billionth can. Today, 122 million cans of SPAM are sold annually in the U.S. alone. On a per capita basis, SPAM is most popular in Hawaii, Alaska, Arkansas, Texas and Alabama.

Outside of the United States, SPAM is sold in 40 countries, although the brand's marketing mix varies. In the United Kingdom, for example, a television commercial for SPAM suggests the meat product makes for an ideal wedding anniversary meal – an ad that probably would be ineffective in the United States.

Store design as marketing tool

"A good storefront is one of your best salesmen. On its dignity and good taste people will base their opinions of your entire business." – Victor Gruen, commercial architect who is sometimes described as the "father of the modern American shopping mall," born in Vienna, Austria on July 18, 1903 (moved to the U.S. in 1938). In a review of Gruen's biography, *Mall Maker* (2003), Richard Longstreth describes Gruen as one of the first American architects "to immerse himself in the intricacies of retailing and then seek dramatically new environments to improve the retail business."

Plans improve the odds of success

"No plan can prevent a stupid person from doing the wrong thing in the wrong place at the wrong time – but a good plan should keep a concentration from forming." – Charles E. Wilson, past president of General Motors, born on July 18, 1890

Timing and calendar-led marketing

"Watch for opportunities of doing things, for there is nothing well done but what's done in season." -- Aesop, fabulist who wrote "The Tortoise and the Hare" and dozens of other business-relevant fables about 2,700 years ago. On July 18, 2002, a collection of his fables was published in a book dubbed *Aesop's Fables*, translated by Laura Gibbs.

July 19, 2017
Wednesday

Objectives & reminders

____

____

Appointments

Early morning

8 a.m.

9 a.m.

10 a.m.

11 a.m.

Noon

1 p.m.

2 p.m.

3 p.m.

4 p.m.

5 p.m.

6 p.m.

Later evening

Business birthdays on July 19

1842 Charles Woodward. In addition to being a farmer and politician during his life, Woodward was also a merchant. After gaining some experience operating small retail stores, Woodward launched a mail order business in 1896, then opened the first Woodward's Department Store in 1903, in Vancouver, Canada. Over the years, the western Canada chain grew to 29 stores. In 1993, Hudson's Bay Company acquired Woodward's assets.

1892 Sir Frederic Collins (Eric) Hooper. Keeping one foot in industry and one foot in government service, Hooper played a key role in bridging business and government interests. He advocated improved British business-government relations, as well as business-labor relations.

As a business consultant, Hooper enjoyed playing with words to create advertising. When working for Schweppes (mineral water firm), for example, he redesigned maps of England to include a new county, called "Schweppeshire." And, near the end of the year, he asked consumers, "How many Schwepping days until Christmas?"

1953 Howard Schultz. After joining the Sales and Marketing Department of Starbucks Coffee Company in 1982, Schultz found that the company's owners resisted his innovative ideas regarding the retailing of coffee, so he bought the company within five years and became its chair and CEO. Since then, Starbucks has opened thousands of coffee shops around the world under Schultz's leadership.

Coffee as an experience
"Starbucks has become what I call the third place. The first place is home. The second place is work. We are the place in between. It's a place to feel comfort. A place to feel safe. A place to feel like you belong." – Howard Schultz

July 20, 2017
Thursday

Objectives & reminders

____

____

____

Appointments

Early morning

8 a.m.

9 a.m.

10 a.m.

11 a.m.

Noon

1 p.m.

2 p.m.

3 p.m.

4 p.m.

5 p.m.

6 p.m.

Later evening

U.S. National Lollipop Day

Celebrated on July 20 each year, Lollipop Day recognizes the history and pervasive presence of lollipops.

While hard candy has existed for centuries, it wasn't until 1908 that George Smith came up with the idea of mounting the candy on a stick. At the time, Smith's other money-making interests were in race horses. So, Smith decided to name his candy creation after his favorite horse -- Lolly Pop. He did trademark the name "Lolly Pop," but it fell into the public domain in the 1930s after Smith stopped producing them.

Lollipop promotions with multiple objectives

Free lollipops are long-standing and inexpensive benefits for customers of banks, retail stores, and other businesses. Beyond the obvious gesture that customers and their children appreciate, consider the less apparent ways that the businesses benefit too.

First, if customers' children know that lollipops are waiting for them at the business, they are less likely to object to their parents visiting the business. The larger principle is this: Children can and do influence their parents' shopping decisions -- where to shop, when to shop, how much time to spend shopping, and so on.

Second, because lollipops help occupy children's time, children are less likely to interrupt conversations between parents and employees, or otherwise create mischief. Talking assumes a lower priority for children who have lollipops in their mouths. Consider the larger principles: (1) Distractions steal buyers' attention and distracted buyers are less likely to make satisfactory purchase decisions, and (2) While waiting is generally a more difficult task for children than for adults, waiting is more palatable for everyone when the time is filled with pleasant (good-tasting) activities.

July 21, 2017
Friday

Objectives & reminders

____

____

____

Appointments

Early morning

8 a.m.

9 a.m.

10 a.m.

11 a.m.

Noon

1 p.m.

2 p.m.

3 p.m.

4 p.m.

5 p.m.

6 p.m.

Later evening

Too harsh a view of advertising: Agree or disagree?

"Ours is the first age in which many thousands of the best-trained individual minds have made it a full-time business to get inside the collective public mind. To get inside in order to manipulate, exploit, control is the object now. And to generate heat not light is the intention. To keep everybody in the helpless state engendered by prolonged mental rutting is the effect of many ads and much entertainment alike." – (Herbert) Marshall McLuhan (1951), Canadian-born researcher and writer with a particular interest in the effect of communication on culture, born on July 21, 1911

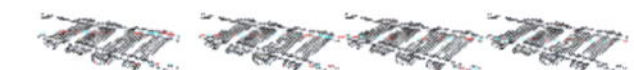

Economic boosts of July 21

Throughout history, major public works projects have played a key role in the economic transformation of individual communities and, as the following examples suggest, entire regions.

1904 The Trans-Siberian Railway was completed after 13 years of construction. As the longest railway in the world, the 4,607 miles of track provided an economic boost to the area by linking European Russia with the Pacific coast and opening up Siberia to colonization.

1970 Egypt's Aswan High Dam was completed after 11 years of construction. The two-mile, $1 billion project across the Nile River put an end to the area's annual flood-drought cycle and increased the productivity of almost a million acres of farm land -- leading to a tripling of the country's agricultural income. The huge 300-mile long and at some points 10-mile wide reservoir -- Lake Nasser (named after President Gamal Abdel Nasser) -- created by the dam ensured a reliable and year-round source of water for the region. Further, the electric power generated by the dam provided electricity throughout the country -- including remote areas that previously had gone without.

Explain, & discuss marketing implications
Dam-building is an effort to replace nature's calendar with mankind's calendar.

July 22, 2017
Saturday

Objectives & reminders

Appointments

Early morning

8 a.m.

9 a.m.

10 a.m.

11 a.m.

Noon

1 p.m.

2 p.m.

3 p.m.

4 p.m.

5 p.m.

6 p.m.

Later evening

Drive-in theaters

On July 22, 1957, *Newsweek* magazine reported the popularity and growth of drive-in theaters. The concept involved moviegoers parking their cars to face a large movie screen in outdoor amphitheaters, attaching speakers to the inside of their cars and watching movies from the comfort and privacy of their own cars. Although drive-ins began springing up in the 1920s, the concept grew rapidly in the 1940s and early 1950s. By 1952 there were an estimated 3,300 drive-in theaters in the United States. Today, less than 400 remain.

Consumers enjoyed the privacy, appreciated being able to dress casually, felt comfortable bringing the children along, and liked the prices that were usually lower than those of traditional movie theaters. Drive-in theater operators liked the concept too. Being outdoors, operating costs tended to be lower for drive-ins than for traditional indoor theaters. The fact that customers brought their own seats lowered operating costs further.

The evolution of business concepts
Business concepts seem to come and go. Like fix-it shops, bookmobiles, and home delivery of milk, drive-in theaters still exist but are less common today than in the past.

Discuss the reasons for the rising popularity of drive-ins in the 1940s and 1950s, and why few drive-ins exist today. What roles have social trends, demographics, technology, costs, competing concepts, and other factors played in the decline of drive-in theaters?

Happy birthday: Alexander S. Calder

Born in Lawnton, Pennsylvania on July 22, 1898, Calder was a painter and sculptor who perhaps is best known for creating the mobile in the early 1930s. A *mobile* is a sculpture with delicately balanced components typically suspended from a central point. Since Calder pioneered the art form, retailers have realized the aesthetic and attention-getting benefits of mobiles, as well as their efficient use of space. Consequently, mobiles are used today in a variety of ways, such as for in-store signage and merchandise displays.

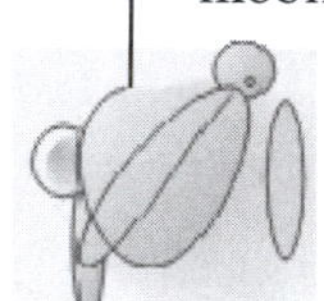

July 23, 2017
Sunday

Objectives & reminders

Appointments

Early morning

8 a.m.

9 a.m.

10 a.m.

11 a.m.

Noon

1 p.m.

2 p.m.

3 p.m.

4 p.m.

5 p.m.

6 p.m.

Later evening

Parents' Day

First proclaimed by President William J. Clinton in 1994, Parents' Day is celebrated annually in the United States on the fourth Sunday in July. The law creating Parents' Day established the day for "recognizing, uplifting, and supporting the role of parents in the rearing of children."

What it's all about
"On Parents' Day, America honors our mothers and fathers for their extraordinary devotion and for the great sacrifices they make to provide a hopeful and promising future for their children." – President George W. Bush (2001-2009)

Although the holiday is relatively new and not yet widely publicized in the U.S., business opportunities to promote and link with the occasion abound. The promotion of cards and gifts to recognize, honor and thank parents are obvious examples. Another approach is to position family outings (e.g., dining out, visiting an amusement park, etc.) as an opportunity for children to give their parents a break from the day-to-day routine of cooking, housework, yardwork and other chores.

Invitation to discuss:
Which target market?
What is the target market for Parents' Day – parents, children or both? Consider alternate ways businesses might market Parents' Day directly to parents or indirectly to parents' children. How might Parents' Day communications vary depending upon the targeted market?

Perhaps, but a collection of falsehoods can be made to appear in even more ways

"One of the most untruthful things possible... is a collection of facts, because they can be made to appear so many different ways." – Karl A. Menninger, psychiatrist and founder of the Menninger Clinic, born on July 23, 1893

July 24, 2017
Monday

Objectives & reminders

___

___

___

Appointments

Early morning

8 a.m.

9 a.m.

10 a.m.

11 a.m.

Noon

1 p.m.

2 p.m.

3 p.m.

4 p.m.

5 p.m.

6 p.m.

Later evening

Marble marketers celebrate

Akron, Ohio made history on July 24, 1886, when Sam C. Dyke made the first mass-produced marbles, which also may have been the first mass-produced toys. Dyke's new factory was able to turn out one million marbles daily which helped to drive down the per-unit manufacturing costs and therefore retail prices. The retail price of a single marble prior to mass-production was about the same as a handful of mass-produced marbles.

Customization versus standardization
Marketing managers' preferences may conflict with those of production operation managers. Marketers may argue for short production runs and more customized items to satisfy the exacting tastes of individual customers, while operations people may advocate longer production runs of more standardized items to drive production costs down.

Different companies in the same industry may resolve this debate quite differently, depending on their technology, the size and preferences of the markets they serve, and their competitors' strategies.

Prices and consumer behavior

Economics 101 points out an inverse relationship between prices and demand, i.e., when prices go up, sales volume goes down. Such an inverse relationship may exist in many (most?) situations, but there are plenty of exceptions; sometimes demand increases when price increases. For example, higher prices often imply higher quality, so raising the price can sometimes stimulate demand among quality-conscious consumers -- especially when competing brands in the same category are known to vary in terms of quality and/or when little objective information about a particular brand's quality is available.

In other instances, a hike in price may be interpreted as a signal that shortages exist and supply may be disrupted soon. Apparently, that's what happened in 1950, when on July 24 *Time* magazine reported a huge jump in demand for nylon stockings in stores that had recently increased prices from $1.35 to $2.00 per pair.

July 25, 2017
Tuesday

Objectives & reminders

Appointments

Early morning

8 a.m.

9 a.m.

10 a.m.

11 a.m.

Noon

1 p.m.

2 p.m.

3 p.m.

4 p.m.

5 p.m.

6 p.m.

Later evening

Publicity as "a breath of fresh air" for non-adopted innovation

It was July 25, 1916, when an explosion ripped through a tunnel being built under Lake Erie by Cleveland Waterworks. The explosion injured and/or trapped dozens of workers. Sadly, the smoke and gas in the tunnel prevented early responders from reaching the trapped tunnelers.

Learning of the accident, inventor Garrett A. Morgan rushed to the scene with his brother and several gas inhalators he had patented four years earlier. Donning the gas masks, the Morgans and a few volunteers entered the tunnel and managed to rescue 32 workers who probably would have perished if not for Morgan and his gas masks.

Morgan's act of heroism, coupled with the amazing performance of his gas mask invention, propelled Morgan and his gas mask into the national media spotlight. Although Morgan had generated little interest (and fewer sales) prior to the Cleveland tunnel accident, the favorable publicity that followed ignited an explosion of orders from fire departments around the country.

Selected gas mask marketing principles

P1 Successful product demonstrations conducted under "real world" conditions can be more persuasive than more scientifically defensible laboratory tests.

P2 New products perceived to significantly influence people's lives (or *save lives* in the case of Morgan's gas masks) have a greater potential for generating media publicity than more mundane innovations.

P3 Confidence is contagious. Morgan's personal willingness to trust the gas mask with his life inspired others to do the same.

Soon another market for Morgan's gas masks emerged when chemical warfare was resorted to during World War I. The gas masks protected soldiers from deadly chlorine fumes and saved many more lives.

July 26, 2017
Wednesday

Objectives & reminders

____

____

____

Appointments

Early morning

8 a.m.

9 a.m.

10 a.m.

11 a.m.

Noon

1 p.m.

2 p.m.

3 p.m.

4 p.m.

5 p.m.

6 p.m.

Later evening

July 26 birthdays galore!

Apparently July 26 is one of the most popular days on which to be born. Here's a list of a few people to recognize on their birthdays.

1799 Isaac Babbitt -- American entrepreneur and inventor of a friction-reducing alloy -- babbitt's metal -- used in bearings. When in his mid-20s, Babbitt founded Reed & Barton -- the oldest independent silversmith company in the country.

1894 Aldous L. Huxley – British author of several books, including *Brave New World* (1932) and *The Perennial Philosophy* (1945). His career advice is worth considering: "Experience is not what happens to a man. It is what a man does with what happens to him."

1935 Charlotte Beers -- former president of Ogilvy & Mather Worldwide (advertising agency), and former chair of J. Walter Thompson (advertising agency). From 2001 until 2003, Beers worked as under secretary for public affairs and diplomacy at the U.S. State Department where she marketed America: "It is almost as though we have to redefine what America is. This is the most sophisticated brand assignment I have ever had."

1937 "Chainsaw" Al Dunlap -- former chairman and CEO of Scott Paper and Sunbeam who developed a reputation (obsession?) for massive employee layoffs. Dunlap seemed to perceive his role as an outsider hired to fix broken companies: "For the most part, I don't believe a company can fix itself solely from the inside. Management has too many friends, too many vested interests, too much baggage. If a correction is too painful, the managers won't have the backbone to do it."

1943 Mick Jagger -- of the Rolling Stones. Had Jagger been trained as a marketing scholar, he might have sung the group's 1965 hit as, "I always experience a negative disconfirmation of expectations," rather than, "I can't get no satisfaction."

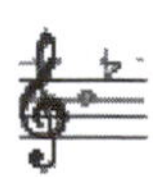

July 27, 2017
Thursday

Objectives & reminders

____

____

____

Appointments

Early morning

8 a.m.

9 a.m.

10 a.m.

11 a.m.

Noon

1 p.m.

2 p.m.

3 p.m.

4 p.m.

5 p.m.

6 p.m.

Later evening

Happy birthday: Bugs Bunny

Bugs made his debut in a film called *A Wild Hare* on July 27, 1940. The animated rabbit was both smart and mischievous. Bugs quickly became a celebrity and continues to amuse audiences today.

Cartoon animation began in France in 1908, but within a year the technique was adopted by U.S. film-makers. Cartoon characters such as Gertie the Dinosaur in the early 1910s were followed by several Disney creations in the 1920s and 1930s, including Mickey Mouse, Sleeping Beauty, and Snow White.

Today, the entertainment world is well aware of the appeal of cartoon animation -- especially to children. Small children are more likely to recognize and identify cartoon characters than adult actors. Further, children have learned to equate cartoon characters with fun.

Recognizing these marketing advantages, many businesses have adopted cartoon characters as central elements in their campaigns to appeal to children. Children's breakfast cereals have utilized animated characters for decades. Manufacturers of toys, children's clothing, and a variety of food products also utilize cartoon characters they've created, while others seek licensing/endorsement contracts from well established and influential cartoon personalities like Bugs Bunny, Mickey Mouse and Dora the Explorer.

Customer comments:
"They're (not always) GRRREAT!"
Astute marketers are usually in favor of any mechanism that will generate feedback from customers. Without feedback, businesses don't know what customers like and don't like, and what needs to be changed.

Accordingly, packages of Kellogg's Sugar Frosted Flakes once included a toll-free telephone number for consumers to offer comments. Unfortunately, the practice had to be discontinued. It seems that Kellogg's call center was flooded with calls from children wanting to speak to Tony the Tiger.

July 28, 2017
Friday

Supper Bowl Weekend?

Objectives & reminders

____

____

Appointments

Early morning

8 a.m.

9 a.m.

10 a.m.

11 a.m.

Noon

1 p.m.

2 p.m.

3 p.m.

4 p.m.

5 p.m.

6 p.m.

Later evening

Happy birthday: Earl Tupper

Born into a farming family in Berlin, New Hampshire on July 28, 1907, Tupper was an inventor at heart. Throughout his life he had dozens (perhaps hundreds) of ideas for new products or for the improvement of existing products.

Typically, Tupper's inventive ideas were not technological breakthroughs but represented incremental improvements of ordinary low-tech items that promised to improve consumers' daily lives. Accordingly, the invention that most bolstered his career and started a new category of household items was the "wonderbowl" -- a flexible plastic container with a patented "burping" seal that Tupper developed after World War II.

Innovation reality
Despite the publicity and "buzz" generated by high-tech innovations, most new products are low-tech.

Although innovative in design, Tupper's wonderbowls and other Tupperware items did not sell very well in retail stores. So, in 1951, Tupper hired Brownie Wise who reinvented the company's marketing efforts by pioneering a new direct sales approach now known as *in-home sales parties.* That is, Wise hired an army of aspiring saleswomen to demonstrate the virtues of Tupperware products during relaxed, in-home presentations "hosted" by other women who invited their friends to the "parties."

The in-home parties proved to be quite effective; Tupperware sales and profits soared. Noticing the in-home Tupperization phenomenon, dozens of other direct marketing companies have since copied Wise's in-home sales party concept.

The pal principle: One reason for the success of in-home sales parties
People are more likely to purchase (and more likely to purchase in larger quantities) when shopping with friends than when shopping alone.

July 29, 2017
Saturday

Objectives & reminders

____

____

____

____

Appointments

Early morning

8 a.m.

9 a.m.

10 a.m.

11 a.m.

Noon

1 p.m.

2 p.m.

3 p.m.

4 p.m.

5 p.m.

6 p.m.

Later evening

Happy birthday: NASA

On July 29, 1958, the United States officially entered the "space race" when Congress approved legislation to form the National Aeronautics and Space Administration (NASA) -- an organization to coordinate and focus U.S. space initiatives.

The birth of NASA was partially in response to the prior year's success by the Soviet Union in launching the first satellite to orbit the earth -- *Sputnik*. The Soviet Union leveraged their success with *Sputnik* to promote their technological capabilities to underdeveloped "Third World" countries who were looking beyond their borders for scientific and technological help. Because the U.S. could not afford to allow the Soviet Union's bragging rights to go unchallenged, the country entered what became known as the "space race."

Less than three years later, after some NASA successes (including *Explorer I*'s orbit of the earth), President Kennedy challenged NASA and the country to send a man to the moon and return him safely by the end of the decade (1960s). After fulfilling Kennedy's ambitious vision in July 1969, NASA moved on to the space shuttle and other projects.

Space enthusiasts market
Perhaps bolstered by science fiction writers, movies and television shows, NASA's efforts have captured the interest of devoted space enthusiasts -- which targeted media have followed.

SpaceDaily (www.spacedaily.com), for example, claims to reach over 850,000 readers monthly. Their audience demographics are skewed upscale -- e.g., readers' median income is about $75,000, 69 percent have at least one college degree, and 71 percent own their own home.

Similarly, *Universe Today* (www.universetoday.com) claims to reach a sizeable audience -- 20,000 page-views daily. *Universe Today*'s audience is upscale too, significantly international (40.3% outside the U.S.) and predominantly male (79.4%).

July 30, 2017
Sunday

Objectives & reminders

____

____

____

Appointments

Early morning

8 a.m.

9 a.m.

10 a.m.

11 a.m.

Noon

1 p.m.

2 p.m.

3 p.m.

4 p.m.

5 p.m.

6 p.m.

Later evening

Happy birthday: Another marbleous marketer

W.W. "Foots" Clements was born in Windham Springs, Alabama on July 30, 1914. He began his marketing career as a student at the University of Alabama in 1935 when he landed a job as a route salesman for Dr. Pepper. Thirty-four years later he was named President and CEO of the company -- then Chairman five years after that. During his 60 years at the company, Clements was instrumental in Dr. Pepper's significant growth and international expansion.

Although considerable power accompanied his top level positions, Clements retained the values he had learned early in life, including the considerate regard for others. To promote and reinforce these values, he kept a supply of marbles inscribed with the Golden Rule, which he gave to people with whom he interacted.

The Golden Rule
Do unto others as you would have them do unto you. – *The Holy Bible*, Luke 6:31

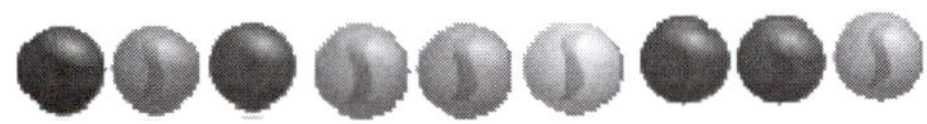

Birthday celebrity brush with marketing

Born in Ottawa, Canada on July 30, 1941, Paul A. Anka was a successful singer in the late 1950s and 1960s who staged a comeback in 1975 when he sang a song called "Times of Your Life" for an ad campaign for Kodak. Not only was the ad campaign successful for Kodak, but Anka went on to record the song for national distribution. When the song became a top-ten hit, Kodak continued to benefit through consumers' association of the song with the company.

A Kodak moment:
Excerpt from "Times of Your Life"
"Gather moments while you may
Collect the dreams you dream today.
Remember, will you remember
The times of your life?" – written by
Roger Nichols and sung by Paul Anka

July 31, 2017
Monday

Objectives & reminders

____

____

Appointments

Early morning

8 a.m.

9 a.m.

10 a.m.

11 a.m.

Noon

1 p.m.

2 p.m.

3 p.m.

4 p.m.

5 p.m.

6 p.m.

Later evening

Marketing not necessary: Agree or disagree?

"I think marketing is a dirty word. I've never liked it. Get it right, and the product will sell itself." – Howard Head, an engineering major in college who later founded (and, of course, headed) Head Ski Co. in 1948. After selling his ski business in 1969, Head took up tennis and soon developed the Prince tennis racquet which debuted in 1976. Head was born in Philadelphia on July 31, 1914.

Convenience is key: Agree or disagree?

"Make your product easier to buy than your competition, or you will find your customers buying from them, not you." – Mark Cuban, American billionaire entrepreneur (founder of HDNet and owner of the Dallas Mavericks NBA basketball team), born in Mt. Lebanon, Pennsylvania on July 31, 1958

Career consideration

"My philosophy... when you leave this world it should be better because you have lived." – William C. Portman II, entrepreneur and business leader (founder and chairman of the Portman Equipment Co., material handling distributor), born on July 31, 1922

Who's in charge of consumer protection?

"Many people want the government to protect the consumer. A much more urgent problem is to protect the consumer from the government." – Milton Friedman, highly influential American economist and Nobel Prize winner (1976), born in Brooklyn, New York on July 31, 1912

August 1, 2017
Tuesday

Marbleous day to compete!

Objectives & reminders

____

____

Appointments

Early morning

8 a.m.

9 a.m.

10 a.m.

11 a.m.

Noon

1 p.m.

2 p.m.

3 p.m.

4 p.m.

5 p.m.

6 p.m.

Later evening

Controlling the competition

Much has been written about how companies can or should cope with competitors. In a competitive environment, business decisions and plans are greatly influenced by the actions of competitors. Actions of Competitor A are likely to evoke a reaction by Competitor B, which, in turn, may prompt Competitor A to rethink and revise its actions, possibly evoking further reactions by Competitor B, and so on. The process may never end as companies realize that they cannot control their competitors.

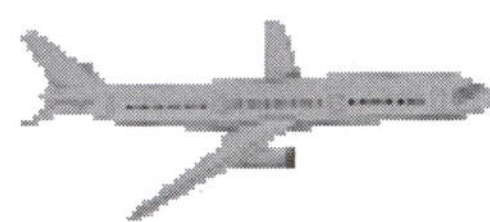

Or can they? The Boeing Company, aircraft-maker, learned how to control its arch-rival McDonnell-Douglas. On August 1, 1997, Boeing simply purchased McDonnell-Douglas. Now Boeing has one less competitor to cope with.

Competing by inventing a new category

"You do not merely want to be considered just the best of the best. You want to be considered the only ones who do what you do."
-- Jerry Garcia, former musician in the rock band and category creator, the Grateful Dead. Garcia was born on August 1, 1942.

Competing with integrity

"A business of high principle generates greater drive and effectiveness because people know they can do the right thing decisively and with confidence. They know that any action that is even slightly unprincipled will be generally condemned. It attracts high-caliber people, thereby gaining a basic competitive edge. It develops better and more profitable relations with customers, competitors and the public because it can be counted on to do the right thing at all times." -- Marvin Bower, former managing director of McKinsey & Company (management consulting firm), born on August 1, 1903. Bower is considered the "father of modern management consulting."

August 2, 2017
Wednesday

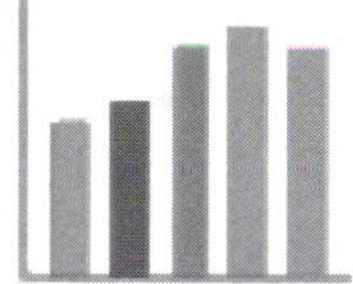

Objectives & reminders

____

____

____

Appointments

Early morning

8 a.m.

9 a.m.

10 a.m.

11 a.m.

Noon

1 p.m.

2 p.m.

3 p.m.

4 p.m.

5 p.m.

6 p.m.

Later evening

Happy birthday: Harrington Emerson

Born in Trenton, New Jersey on August 2, 1853, Emerson was a noted engineer, management consultant and author in the late 1800s and early 1900s. Somewhat like many management experts of the day, Emerson was greatly concerned with the concept of efficiency. He believed that improved efficiency was a key to business success.

Somewhat *un*like many of his contemporaries, however, Emerson considered the concept of efficiency at many levels. That is, he recognized that potential (in)efficiencies of organizations extended beyond the exclusive domain of individual workers and maintained that the organization of a business also contributed to its degree of efficiency.

Many of the ideas Emerson developed in his 1913 book, *The Twelve Principles of Efficiency*, are still relevant today. For example, he stressed the importance for organizations to:

1. Understand and articulate their goals and values, as well as their relationships with society.
2. Instill in workers a sense of self-discipline and commitment to the organization's systems. Unless workers willingly conform to the systems, efficiencies are not likely to materialize.
3. Always treat workers fairly to increase the odds that they will participate in company efforts to improve efficiency. Further, when workers do contribute to efficiency improvements they should be rewarded for doing so.
4. Keep accurate and timely records of time and productivity. Otherwise organizations will not know whether efficiencies are being achieved and which programs or workers are achieving them.

Efficiency versus effectiveness

In the latter half of the 1900s, management guru Peter Drucker observed that managers should not be content only with *"doing things right"* (efficiency), but should also think in terms of *"doing the right things"* (effectiveness).

August 3, 2017
Thursday

Spain's flag today

Objectives & reminders

____

____

Appointments

Early morning

8 a.m.

9 a.m.

10 a.m.

11 a.m.

Noon

1 p.m.

2 p.m.

3 p.m.

4 p.m.

5 p.m.

6 p.m.

Later evening

Sailing Columbus

Italian explorer Christopher Columbus left the Spanish port of Palos on August 3, 1492, with three ships and a crew of 90. His objective? To discover a western sea route to India and China. In October of the same year he landed in the Bahamas and later the same day sighted Cuba which he believed to be mainland China. In December he landed on Hispaniola (Haiti and Dominican Republic) which he confused with Japan. The next year he returned to Spain with what he thought were seven "Indian" captives.

Did Columbus fail?

On the original 1492 expedition and three follow-up expeditions, Columbus never reached his stated objective of finding a western route to the Far East. However, he did bring gold and other riches from the New World back to Spain and began the colonization process which helped usher in a century-long period of wealth and global power for Spain.

So, to what extent was Columbus a failure? How does hindsight -- the perspective of time -- potentially alter one's evaluation of Columbus? What modern day "failures" could be argued to be successes in disguise? Are managers, entrepreneurs and business critics sometimes too quick to label an outcome as a "failure"?

Selling yourself

"You'll never sell any product that is as important as yourself, so you want to do it right. Selling yourself – in job interviews, in your performance on the job so you can earn a promotion, and in working with outsiders so you can make yourself attractive to other companies and thus increase your career progress and your earning power – is your most basic selling skill." – Larry King, American broadcast journalist and former television talk-show host (*Larry King Live*), in his book, *How to Talk to Anyone... Anywhere*, second edition published on August 3, 2004

August 4, 2017
Friday

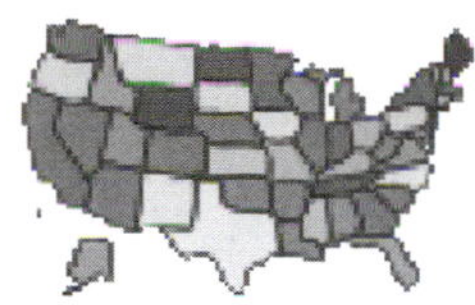

Objectives & reminders

______

______

______

Appointments

Early morning

8 a.m.

9 a.m.

10 a.m.

11 a.m.

Noon

1 p.m.

2 p.m.

3 p.m.

4 p.m.

5 p.m.

6 p.m.

Later evening

State sales tax "holidays"

To help families cope with the back-to-school financial burden, almost one third of U.S. states now call time-out on sales taxes for qualified back-to-school items purchased on two to seven designated days. Qualified purchases vary from state to state, but often include clothing items, school supplies, backpacks, books and computers. These sales tax holidays most often occur in August; and within August, most begin on the first weekend – beginning today. In anticipation of the sales tax holidays and the annual media attention they attract, many retailers time their back-to-school sale events to coincide with the holidays.

States with sales tax holidays in August
Alabama, Arkansas, Connecticut, Florida, Georgia, Iowa, Maryland, Massachusetts, Missouri, New Mexico, Oklahoma, South Carolina, Tennessee, Texas

Questions?
State-by-state dates, lists of qualified purchases and other useful details regarding sales tax holidays may be found at www.taxadmin.org

Back-to-school scoop
For more info about the back-to-school shopping season, read the fact-filled entry for the 8th of August.

365 sales tax holidays
As one of only five states without a general state sales tax, New Hampshire lured back-to-school shoppers in 2005 with an ad campaign targeting consumers in nearby Massachusetts, a state that designates only two sales tax holidays.

The New Hampshire ad campaign took jabs at its southern neighbor by pointing out, "365 vs. 002... Tax-Free Shopping Days (for those of you keeping score)." New Hampshire's marketing-minded governor at the time, John Lynch, added, "There is no need for shoppers to pack all of their shopping into two days during a beautiful summer weekend, when every day is a sales tax holiday in New Hampshire."

August 5, 2017
Saturday

Objectives & reminders

Appointments

Early morning

8 a.m.

9 a.m.

10 a.m.

11 a.m.

Noon

1 p.m.

2 p.m.

3 p.m.

4 p.m.

5 p.m.

6 p.m.

Later evening

Happy birthday: Bruce F. Barton

Born on August 5, 1886, in Robbins, Tennessee Barton enjoyed a multi-faceted career as a religious author and Congressman, but is perhaps best known as one of the most innovative and effective advertising executives of the 20th century. As founder of the advertising agency BBDO, Barton is credited with the creation of the character/symbol Betty Crocker. Many of Barton's business and advertising insights are revealed in his popular 1924 book -- *The Man Nobody Knows* -- that describes the life of Jesus in business terms.

Today, BBDO Worldwide employs more than 15,000 people in its 289 offices located in 80 countries.

Good advertising
= (respect x intelligent audiences)
+ (belief x meritorious products)
"Much brass has been sounded and many cymbals tinkled in the name of advertising; but the advertisements which persuade people to act are written by men who have an abiding respect for the intelligence of their readers, and a deep sincerity regarding the merits of the goods they have to sell." – Bruce Barton

When to advertise
"In good times, people want to advertise; in bad times, they have to." -- Bruce Barton

Advertising winks when life stinks

On August 5, 1837, an article in *The Town* described Robert Warren as being "suckled amid scenes repulsive to the growth of mind." Despite his challenging background, Warren rose above his circumstances to become a British manufacturer with a marketing vision. That is, Warren's company was among the first British firms to advertise its household products nationally. His approach to advertising used poetry first to capture prospective buyers' attention -- then to entertain, inform, and persuade them. One poet who worked for the firm, Alexander Kemp, claimed to have written two hundred of these advertising poems.

August 6, 2017
Sunday

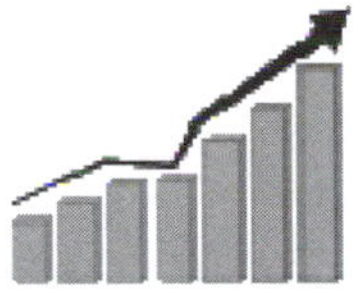

Buyers' expectations

Objectives & reminders

Appointments

Early morning

8 a.m.

9 a.m.

10 a.m.

11 a.m.

Noon

1 p.m.

2 p.m.

3 p.m.

4 p.m.

5 p.m.

6 p.m.

Later evening

From "extra" to "expected"

One of the most challenging aspects of business is keeping up with customers' rising expectations. Product attributes, prices and business practices that might have been good enough to satisfy or even thrill yesterday's customers may meet only minimal expectations of today's customers. This phenomenon of rising expectations often begins when a business tries to gain a competitive advantage by introducing something new, different, better or extra for the benefit of its customers. At first customers may appreciate the innovation, thereby giving the business the desired competitive advantage. But then competitors start offering the same or similar "innovation" and customers start to expect what was once a bonus, so the business tries another innovation and the process is repeated.

Keeping score

A business cannot keep up with customers' expectations if they don't know what those expectations are and when they change. That's why periodic surveys, toll-free "hotlines," customer comment cards, day-to-day face-to-face contact with customers and other approaches for cultivating customer feedback are so useful.

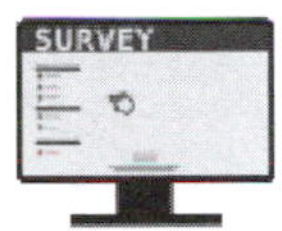

Plenty of examples in the hospitality field illustrate the phenomenon. Hotels that installed television sets for their guests in the early 1950s gained a competitive advantage. Today, guests not only expect a television, they are likely to be dissatisfied if it is not a *color* TV equipped with *remote control* and multiple *cable* channels.

A clean advantage

On August 6, 1889, the Savoy Hotel opened with a novel attribute for hotels -- *private* bathrooms. The closest competitor at the time (Hotel Victoria) had four bath-rooms for up to 500 guests to share. The incredulous builder of the Savoy Hotel was so stunned by the idea of so many bathrooms, he asked the proprietor if the expected guests were amphibious.

August 7, 2017
Monday

Objectives & reminders

____

____

____

Appointments

Early morning

8 a.m.

9 a.m.

10 a.m.

11 a.m.

Noon

1 p.m.

2 p.m.

3 p.m.

4 p.m.

5 p.m.

6 p.m.

Later evening

Happy birthday: Jenny Craig

Entrepreneur and business executive Jenny Craig was born as Genevieve Guidroz -- in New Orleans, Louisiana on August 7, 1932. Her fitness-related career began in 1959 when she joined a fitness center to lose weight, then accepted a job to help the gym's other customers also lose weight. Over time, she managed several fitness centers, but saw the need and the business potential for a broader weight loss concept -- a combination of fitness, diet and other lifestyle changes, facilitated by

trained counselors and psychologists. When the partners in the fitness chain she worked for weren't particularly receptive to the idea, Jenny Craig and her husband Sid, started their own company in Australia -- Jenny Craig Weight Loss Centres. Today, the company operates more than 700 centres in the United States, Canada, Australia and New Zealand.

Product/service differentiation
To achieve a distinct position in a competitive marketplace and add customer value to the product mix, Jenny Craig introduced frozen planned meals in the late 1980s which not only were convenient for customers to prepare, but were convenient in that they eliminated the need for dieters to count calories or grams of fat -- if they stuck to the Jenny Craig plan.

Forget the carbohydrates: Higher business purpose can energize business

Like many entrepreneurs, Jenny Craig's business interests were driven by a purpose greater than simply "making money." She wanted to help people live healthier lives -- coming to that realization after her mother and four of her five siblings -- all overweight -- died before reaching their 50th birthdays. Looking back on her family's eating habits, Craig realized the difference some sort of intervention might have made: "Everything we ate involved butter and fat, with lots of starches. I just figured that was the way to eat."

August 8, 2017
Tuesday

Objectives & reminders

____

____

____

Appointments

Early morning

8 a.m.

9 a.m.

10 a.m.

11 a.m.

Noon

1 p.m.

2 p.m.

3 p.m.

4 p.m.

5 p.m.

6 p.m.

Later evening

Hi-ho, hi-ho...

"It's off to school we go." About this time of the year, 82 million school children in the U.S. from kindergarten through high school (i.e., K-12) prepare for the impending nine-month school year. For most students and their parents, that means shopping for school supplies, clothing, shoes, computers, calculators, cell phones, lunch boxes, back-packs, and a variety of other items.

For the retailers that serve the back-to-schoolers, the back-to-school shopping season is one of the busiest and most lucrative of the year -- typically second only to the Christmas shopping season. Discount retailers such as Wal-Mart and Target tend to benefit the most during the back-to-school season, although specialty stores that cater to teens and young adults also tend to do well.

Estimates vary in terms of how much money students and their parents spend on back-to-school items. For households with one or more K-12 children, the median in 2015 was about $630 per household. For college-bound students, the median was much higher – about $900 per student. For K-12 students, the National Retail Federation breaks spending into four major categories, with clothing commanding the largest share of the back-to-school budget (46%), followed by electronics and computer-related equipment (19%), shoes (19%), and school supplies (16%).

Why buy?

A survey of more than 35,000 consumers conducted by the NPD Group found five factors that most influenced back-to-school purchases:

1st "Value"
2nd "Required by school"
3rd "Child wanted it"
4th "Replacement item"
5th "Fashionable & trendy"

Schools help merchandise planning

66 percent of surveyed consumers with school-age children said that back-to-school shopping lists provided by the school exert considerable influence on back-to-school spending. Knowing this, many retailers ask for advance copies of such lists to plan their merchandise mix accordingly.

August 9, 2017
Wednesday

Objectives & reminders

____

____

____

Appointments

Early morning

8 a.m.

9 a.m.

10 a.m.

11 a.m.

Noon

1 p.m.

2 p.m.

3 p.m.

4 p.m.

5 p.m.

6 p.m.

Later evening

Creative pricing tip: Change the unit priced

Pricing decisions can involve redefining the basis of what is priced -- to help attract different market segments or change customers' behaviors.

That's what happened in 1968, when *Time* magazine reported on August 9 that the New York Hilton (Manhattan's largest hotel) had introduced an alternative pricing scheme -- renting rooms by the hour. Hilton's "Day-Hour Plan" was targeted toward business people who often visited the city without staying overnight, but needed a place to relax for a short while nonetheless.

Other creative pricing examples abound and collectively illustrate how changing the unit priced affects target markets.

- A rural Nevada hotel appeals to truckers by charging for 12-hour blocks of time, beginning when guests check in. Because truckers' driving schedules are erratic, truckers appreciate what amounts to the ultimate in flexible check-in times.
- Long-distance carriers charge telephone customers on a per call basis, but to encourage a higher call volume they also offer package prices that allow customers an unlimited number of calls for a single monthly rate.
- Many bowling centers offer time bowling specials to attract price-sensitive customers. That is, rather than paying by the game, bowlers are charged by the hour or time-block. Typically, the time-based pricing means less wasted time between frames for bowlers interested in getting their money's worth.
- Grocers learned decades ago that pricing canned goods or other items for "five for a dollar," for example, leads to higher purchase volumes than "20 cents each." The multiple pricing tactic conveys a sense of value and prompts shoppers to stock-up.
- Appliance repair services may charge an hourly labor rate or a set amount for each type of repair. The latter approach helps customers gauge their pricing expectations and reduces the anxiety associated with unknown prices.

August 10, 2017
Thursday

Objectives & reminders

Appointments

Early morning

8 a.m.

9 a.m.

10 a.m.

11 a.m.

Noon

1 p.m.

2 p.m.

3 p.m.

4 p.m.

5 p.m.

6 p.m.

Later evening

Happy birthday: The Dean of Sausage

Born into a poor family on August 10, 1928, Jimmy Dean was determined to succeed – to "pull myself up by my bootstraps and go out and make something of myself." He did, twice. First, Dean enjoyed a successful career in the entertainment business as a country singer and star of the television show *Town and Country Time.* Then, he entered the food processing business and parlayed Jimmy Dean's Sausage into a multi-million dollar company and one of the most recognized brands in the industry.

Sausage company motto
"Do what you say you're going to do, when you say you're going to do it, and try to do it a little better than you said you would." -- Jimmy Dean

A telling calendrical twist was incorporated into the sausage company's 2015 television advertising campaign for its line of breakfast croissant sandwiches. Audiences were promised that the croissants make "every day taste like the weekend" – implying that weekends have a special meaning that distinguish them in a positive way from weekdays. By associating croissants with the desirable attributes and sentiments of weekends, it is likely that the ad campaign enhanced the appeal of the croissants.

Relevant questions for calendar-led marketers' brand positioning efforts

- When do buyers purchase and consume the brand? Consider time-of-day, day-of-week, day/period-of-month, and day/period-of-year. When do/would they *prefer* to purchase and consume it?
- What behaviors and sentiments are associated with each calendrical period? For example, which periods are known for relaxation or stress, work or leisure, biological cravings for hot vs. cold food, and so on?
- What are buyers' most (least) favorite calendrical periods? Why?

August 11, 2017
Friday

Objectives & reminders

____

____

Appointments

Early morning

8 a.m.

9 a.m.

10 a.m.

11 a.m.

Noon

1 p.m.

2 p.m.

3 p.m.

4 p.m.

5 p.m.

6 p.m.

Later evening

Automobiles, brands & brand names

Toyota stumbles with "pet" vehicle

The Japanese auto-maker, Toyota, rolled its first entry into U.S. markets on August 11, 1957. The "Toyopet" was clearly a Japanese car -- small, small, small -- too small for American consumers to accept. Further, the "pet" name wasn't particularly appealing to American auto-buyers seeking to "express themselves" with the vehicles they drove. Anti-Japanese sentiments that lingered after World War II also might have played a role in Toyota's weak reception in the U.S. So, Toyota's effort to break into the U.S. failed -- resulting in heavy financial losses. However, rather than giving up, Toyota redoubled its efforts, studied American tastes more closely, redesigned its offerings, and later reentered the market successfully.

Happy birthday: comrade, pal, chum

Exactly nine years after the U.S. entry of the Toyopet, the first Chevy Camaro rolled off the assembly line in General Motors' Norwood, Ohio plant -- on August 11, 1966. Although the design and technical attributes of the Camaro were carefully planned and tested over an extended period of time, surprisingly the name "Camaro" was chosen in haste only a few weeks before the automobile's introduction. According to Elliot Estes, the manager responsible for naming the Camaro, "I went into a closet, shut the door and came out with the name." In French, Camaro means "comrade, pal, or chum." Fortunately for GM, the Camaro was well received.

Although GM may have been more fortunate (luckier?) with their naming of the Camaro than Toyota was with the Toyopet, choosing a brand's name as an afterthought can prove to be a costly mistake. Marketing scholar Philip Kotler points out the importance of carefully selecting brand names by reminding us of a study involving pictures of two young women. Upon viewing the two pictures, study participants were evenly divided in their perceptions of which woman was more attractive. However, when another group of participants viewed the same pictures labeled as "Gertrude" and "Jennifer," only 20 percent claimed Gertrude was more attractive; 80 percent voted for Jennifer.

August 12 2017 Saturday

Objectives & reminders

Reserve bowling lane

Appointments

Early morning

8 a.m.

9 a.m.

10 a.m.

11 a.m.

Noon

1 p.m.

2 p.m.

3 p.m.

4 p.m.

5 p.m.

6 p.m.

Later evening

Bowling for Marketing FAME

National Bowling Day

Timed to coincide with the start of the new eight- to nine-month bowling season, the second Saturday in August is National Bowling Day (NBD). The occasion focuses the industry's, media's and public's attention on one of the most popular sports and recreational activities in the country – enjoyed annually by more than 46 million Americans.

In celebration, expect bowling centers in your community to host special events, circulate bowling coupons and otherwise promote the sport. On NBD in 2015, for example, Bowlmor AMF offered free bowling in all of its U.S. bowling centers from 10:00 a.m. until noon.

If you're a marketer for a non-bowling business, consider the potential for capitalizing on the NBD upsurge in bowling traffic with tie-in or cross promotions. For example, if you're a marketer for a local pizza restaurant, you might swap coupons with marketers of nearby bowling centers – agreeing to distribute their bowling coupons in your restaurant in exchange for their distribution of pizza coupons in their bowling centers. It's an inexpensive and easy promotion device that benefits both businesses and consumers.

Bowling marketing strikes

A key objective in bowling is to knock down as many pins as possible with each roll of the ball. Toppling all ten pins on the first roll – called a "strike" – is the ideal. However, as shown in the center lane to the left, it's not the ball, per se, that strikes all ten pins. On a perfect strike, the ball touches only four pins (the darker ones on the lane) – propelling those pins into others to generate "pin action" and the resulting strike.

In much the same way, metaphorically thinking of marketers as bowlers, marketing efforts as bowling balls, and buyers as bowling pins, it's not uncommon for the best marketing shots to directly touch only a few buyers. It is largely through the pin action of those buyers – known to marketers as "word-of-mouth" communications – that leads to many marketing strikes.

August 13, 2017
Sunday

Objectives & reminders

______

______

______

Appointments

Early morning

8 a.m.

9 a.m.

10 a.m.

11 a.m.

Noon

1 p.m.

2 p.m.

3 p.m.

4 p.m.

5 p.m.

6 p.m.

Later evening

Happy birthday: Alfred Hitchcock

Hitchcock was born in London on August 13, 1899. His career as a film-maker produced 50 feature-length movies including *Strangers on a Train* (1951), *Vertigo* (1958), *North by Northwest* (1959), *Psycho* (1960), and *The Birds* (1963). Hitchcock's movies had a reputation of using suspense to arouse audiences' emotional responses of fear. His popular 1960s television series, *Alfred Hitchcock Presents*, also kept viewers in suspense. According to Hitchcock, "Seeing a murder on television can help work off one's antagonisms. And if you haven't any antagonisms, the commercials will give you some."

Fear as a marketing appeal
Although fear appeals may catch buyers' attention and arouse their emotions, prospects are likely to turn away from extreme uses of fear. Ethical considerations also come into play when fear appeals are too extreme. It might be effective and acceptable for a life insurance salesperson to ask a family's bread-winner to consider, "what would become of your family if something were to happen to you?", but ineffective, distasteful and alienating to reinforce the question by showing graphic pictures of a neighbor recently killed in an automobile accident.

Fear as an employee motivator
Some managers believe that fear can be used to motivate employees (e.g., "You'll be fired if you *fail* in this task."), but its effectiveness tends to be short-lived and less effective than more positive appeals (e.g., "If you *succeed* in this task, you will be rewarded."). According to Tom Morris, author of the book, *If Aristotle Ran General Motors*, "fear is an acid that will eat away corporate spirit as fast as anything on earth. And I believe that artificially constructed fear, the policy of scaring people by issuing threats, misrepresenting the market, and manipulating emotions, [is] just plain wrong... [and] creates more problems than it solves" (p. 197).

August 14, 2017
Monday

Objectives & reminders

___

___

___

Appointments

Early morning

8 a.m.

9 a.m.

10 a.m.

11 a.m.

Noon

1 p.m.

2 p.m.

3 p.m.

4 p.m.

5 p.m.

6 p.m.

Later evening

The meaning of soup

Born in Vienna, Austria on August 14, 1907, Earnest Dichter played an influential role in moving marketers to think about consumer psychology and behavior more deeply. Although not all of his observations were backed-up with hard data, his basic thesis was accurate, important and certainly thought-provoking: i.e., he believed that superficial "nose counting" analyses of consumer behavior are inadequate in a competitive marketplace.

Dichter argued that seemingly ordinary products have "magic meanings and mysterious origins" that, if understood, could give marketers an edge in the marketplace. Accordingly, Dichter is sometimes referred to as the "father of motivation research." To illustrate, in his 1964 classic book, *Handbook of Consumer Motivations: The Psychology of the World of Objects*, Dichter explores the meaning of soup:

> "Soup is endowed with magic power in the folklore of many countries. It is the brew of the good fairy, satisfying a hunger that is not merely of the body. It protects, heals, and gives strength, courage, and the feeling of belonging. Magic arises from the brewing together of special ingredients... As an elixir formed of all the nourishing virtues of the original foods, it is akin to blood or marrow" (pp. 67-68).

"Friendly" tone of advertising
"When the consumer feels that the advertiser speaks to him as a friend or as an unbiased authority, creating the atmosphere of word of mouth, the consumer will relax and tend to accept the recommendation." -- Ernest Dichter

The best place to eat soup

"It's very important for us to connect with folks. And one of the greatest places to do that is in the cafeteria. I get to see folks from all walks of life, and the people who really make the company work." – Robert "Bob" A. Eckert, former chairman and CEO of Mattel, Inc. (toy- and game-maker), born on August 14, 1954

August 15, 2017
Tuesday

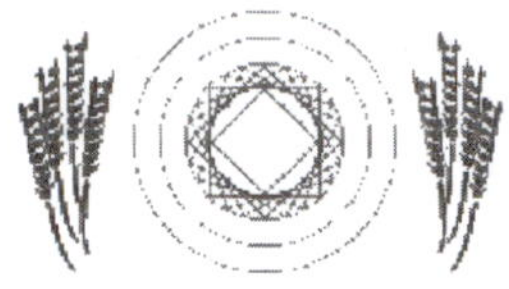

Objectives & reminders

____

____

____

Appointments

Early morning

8 a.m.

9 a.m.

10 a.m.

11 a.m.

Noon

1 p.m.

2 p.m.

3 p.m.

4 p.m.

5 p.m.

6 p.m.

Later evening

Publicity stunt, for breakfast?

For marketing-challenged communities not blessed with spectacular mountains or canyons, or with the world's deepest hand-dug well or the largest ball of twine on earth, fortunately there are crop circles to generate publicity.

The modern-day history of crop circles dates back to August 1972 when the first crop circle was reported. Since that year, August has been the most popular month of the year for crop circle sightings. Crop circles have been spotted in more than a dozen countries including the United States, Canada, Australia, Japan, Russia, and especially Southern England. Moreover, they've been reported in hundreds of media stories and sparked serious scientific research to assess their origin.

To capitalize on the public's fascination with crop circles, entrepreneurs Gary and JoAnn Chambers filed for a copyright and trademark for their proposed innovation -- Crop Circle Cereal – on August 15, 1997. As of July 2016, their apparently not-yet-implemented marketing plan for the out-of-this-world breakfast cereal remained on their website, www.cropcirclecereal.com. According to the website:

> "The marketing concept for this product is in synchronistic alignment with the current global fascination of the paranormal -- particularly UFOs, aliens and extraterrestrial activity. The mass market is currently being exposed to all types of unexplained phenomena throughout various forms of media, which creates a timely marketing opportunity to promote a product with the name of one of the most fascinating of all these anomalies -- Crop Circles.... Because the true nature of this enigmatic phenomenon can neither be explained nor denied, it presents a wide-open creative format based on fact, fantasy, mystery and science fiction."

Success formula for aspiring crop circle hoaxers & other professionals

"I can give you a six-word formula for success: 'Think things through -- then follow-through.'" -- Sir Walter Scott, Scottish historical novelist, born on August 15, 1771

August 16, 2017
Wednesday

$100 = $1,372?

Objectives & reminders

____

____

____

Appointments

Early morning

8 a.m.

9 a.m.

10 a.m.

11 a.m.

Noon

1 p.m.

2 p.m.

3 p.m.

4 p.m.

5 p.m.

6 p.m.

Later evening

Inflation ramps up

In August 1948, inflation was on the rise as the Consumer Price Index (CPI) reached a record high. The price of a typical package of goods that had cost U.S. consumers $100 only three years earlier (at the end of World War II) had risen to $135. So, on August 16, 1948, the Federal Reserve System attempted to curb inflation by slowing consumer spending by discouraging the use of installment credit. To do that, they simply raised interest rates. Apparently, the Fed's move helped, as consumer prices remained at or below the August 1948 levels for another two years. In the longer-term, however, inflationary forces have proven to be stronger than the Fed's anti-inflation forces. By August 2017, the same package of goods that had cost consumers $100 in 1948 was priced at $1,372.

Consumer spending tends to be relatively high when...

- Credit is readily available,
- Interests rates on credit are relatively low,
- Unemployment is relatively low and is expected to remain low,
- Consumer confidence in the economy is relatively high, and
- The value of consumers' houses and/or investment portfolios has risen recently and consumers feel "wealthy."

Customer-focus is less than ideal: Agree or disagree?

"Customers buy products and services to help them get jobs done.... When companies focus on helping the customer get a job done faster, more conveniently, and less expensively than before, they are more likely to create products and services that the customer wants. Only after a company chooses to focus on the job, not the customer, are they capable of reliably creating customer value."
-- Anthony Ulwick, founder and CEO of Strategyn, and author of *What Customers Want*, published on August 16, 2005

August 17, 2017
Thursday

Objectives & reminders

____

____

____

Appointments

Early morning

8 a.m.

9 a.m.

10 a.m.

11 a.m.

Noon

1 p.m.

2 p.m.

3 p.m.

4 p.m.

5 p.m.

6 p.m.

Later evening

Happy birthday: Lawrence J. Ellison

Born in the Bronx, New York on August 17, 1944, Larry Ellison showed a strong aptitude for math and science as a college student at the University of Illinois and at the University of Chicago. Ellison dropped out of college and gained work experience in a variety of technical jobs before co-founding his own consulting company in 1977, Software Development Labs. Later the name of the company was changed to Oracle, with Ellison as the CEO. Today, Oracle is the second largest software company in the world (2nd to Microsoft) and Ellison remains with the company as its Executive Chairman and CTO.

Personality and success

"The most important aspect of my personality, as far as determining my

success goes, has been my questioning conventional wisdom, doubting the experts, and questioning authority. While that can be very painful in relationships with your parents and teachers, it's enormously useful in life... Think things out for yourself. Come to your own judgments. Don't simply conform to conventional ways of thinking, to conventional ways of dressing, conventional ways of acting. A lot of things are based on fashion, even morality at times is based on fashion." -- Larry Ellison

Fear revisited, reconsidered

"I think most great achievers are driven, not so much by the pursuit of success, but by the fear of failure. Unless failure gets very close, that fear doesn't reach profound levels, but it drives us. It drives me to work very hard. It drives me to make sure that my life is very orderly, that I'm in control of my company, or in control of the airplane or boat or what-have-you, so that I'm not at risk of failure. Whenever I feel even remotely close to being at risk of failure, I can't stop working."
-- Larry Ellison

August 18, 2017
Friday

Objectives & reminders

____

____

____

Appointments

Early morning

8 a.m.

9 a.m.

10 a.m.

11 a.m.

Noon

1 p.m.

2 p.m.

3 p.m.

4 p.m.

5 p.m.

6 p.m.

Later evening

A "Field" day for women!

Forget birthday cakes today. Have a cookie instead -- to celebrate Marshall Field's birthday. Field was born on a farm near Conway, Massachusetts on August 18, 1834, and soon began his career in retailing -- first as a 16-year-old delivery boy, and then as a sales clerk. In his early 20s, he moved to Chicago and quickly became a partner in a wholesale business. Soon, he ventured into a business partnership and opened one of the first department stores in the country in 1868. In 1881, Field bought out his partner and changed the name of the firm to Marshall Field and Company.

Much of Marshall Field's success may be attributed to the company's recognition of the importance of serving female customers. As Mr. Field often told male clerks, "Give the lady what she wants."

Fast forward to August 18, 1977, and continue the field day by having another celebratory cookie -- one from Debra J. Fields, also known as "Mrs. Fields." It was on that day that 20-year-old Fields opened her first cookie store, in Palo Alto, California.

By noon on that first day, Fields had not sold one cookie. Somewhat in desperation, she walked onto the sidewalk in front of the store and began giving away free cookies. The freebies swayed the cookie votes in her direction and became an important part of her marketing programs for several years. Today, customers enjoy cookies at about 400 of Mrs. Fields' franchise locations; about three-fourths are in the United States.

Biting the cookie that feeds you!
In the early days of Mrs. Fields' cookie business, one chocolate supplier hung up on Debra Fields (after calling her "Sweetheart") when she telephoned to inquire about doing business with him. As a result, Fields has been loyal to *another* supplier for several years. The snubber lost the opportunity to compete for what became a $7 million account! Principle: People are committed to companies and other people who are committed to them.

August 19, 2017
Saturday

Objectives & reminders

____

____

____

Appointments

Early morning

8 a.m.

9 a.m.

10 a.m.

11 a.m.

Noon

1 p.m.

2 p.m.

3 p.m.

4 p.m.

5 p.m.

6 p.m.

Later evening

Good Advice Day

Truth in employee evaluations

"[O]ne of the things that leaders forget is that people look to us to tell them the truth in terms of how they're doing.... As management, we must tell people what we expect. And if they don't meet the expectations we have to tell them, and tell them why, so they can improve. Maybe it's something we can work on together. It's so important to be brutally honest with your people. People respect that." – Charles Wang, founder and former chairman and CEO of Computer Associates International, Inc. (1976-2002), born on August 19, 1944

Perhaps the best strategy is in the tactical details

"[S]trategy is easy, it's tactics that are very difficult. Many people have a lot of strategies, but only good people can execute them. It takes a step-by-step approach, and the ability to execute." -- Arthur Rock, Silicon Valley venture capitalist (Arthur Rock & Company), born on August 19, 1926

Technology not a complete substitute

"I have witnessed a whole succession of technological revolutions. But none of them has done away with the need for character in the individual or the ability to think." -- Bernard M. Baruch, American economist, financier, stock market speculator, and presidential advisor, born on August 19, 1870

Be indispensable by being dispensable

"All too often we say of a man doing a good job that he is indispensable.... In business, a man can come nearest to indispensability by being dispensable in his current job. How can a man move up to new responsibilities if he is the only one able to handle his present tasks? It matters not how small or large the job you now have, if you have trained no one to do it as well, you're not available; you've made your promotion difficult if not impossible." -- Malcolm S. Forbes, business analyst and former publisher of *Forbes* magazine (founded by his father, B.C. Forbes). Malcolm Forbes was born on August 19, 1919.

August 20, 2017
Sunday

Second Most Marbleous

Objectives & reminders

Appointments

Early morning

8 a.m.

9 a.m.

10 a.m.

11 a.m.

Noon

1 p.m.

2 p.m.

3 p.m.

4 p.m.

5 p.m.

6 p.m.

Later evening

The Customer Comes Second

The revised edition of Hal Rosenbluth's best-selling book, *The Customer Comes Second*, was published on August 20, 2002. In the book, Rosenbluth maintains that employers should insist on hiring "nice people" -- especially for jobs that require interaction with customers and other employees. Unlike many other desirable characteristics that employers would like to see in prospective employees, "niceness" is not a trait that can be easily trained into a person. So, applicants should show evidence that they are already nice.

Old play on words still rings true
"It's nice to be important, but it's more important to be nice." -- William "Bud" Loveall, friend and team-oriented leader

The rationale behind niceness has to do with teamwork and customer service. In short, nice people are more likely to function collaboratively and cooperatively in team environments. And, in a multitude of ways, nice people are more likely to make a positive impression on the customers with whom they interact. Of course, niceness isn't the only trait employers should seek, but it is one that paves the way for effectiveness in many jobs.

Demonstrating niceties:
Checklist for job interviews

1. Does applicant hold the door for others?
2. Is applicant nice to people not directly involved in the hiring decision -- e.g., secretaries, wait staff at restaurant, doormen, etc.?
3. How often does the applicant smile?
4. Does the applicant clean-up after himself/herself or offer to do so, e.g., wipe table and rinse out cup after coffee?
5. Are "please" and "thank-you" prominent parts of applicant's vocabulary?
6. Are applicant's behaviors proactively nice? Example: Does he/she ask about others' comfort, the well-being of their families, and so on?

August 21, 2017
Monday

Objectives & reminders

Appointments

Early morning

8 a.m.

9 a.m.

10 a.m.

11 a.m.

Noon

1 p.m.

2 p.m.

3 p.m.

4 p.m.

5 p.m.

6 p.m.

Later evening

Happy birthday: Walter Wilson

Born in Glasgow, Scotland on August 21, 1849, Wilson began his career early in life -- first as a hosiery agent at age 14, then as a hat-manufacturing entrepreneur by the time he was 20. Before the age of 30, Wilson stopped making hats but used his experience to buy hats from other manufacturers in his new hat store. His store -- The Colosseum -- stocked 25,000 hats and employed 150 assistants. By the time Wilson was 40 years old, his company had almost 500 employees and had evolved from a hat store into more of a department store with 23 departments.

Wilson's business flourished, largely due to his creative flair for advertising, promotion, and publicity. Many of his tactics were quite innovative at the time. For example, he advertised heavily in local newspapers using unusual, attention-getting layouts. He also used coded texts in his ads to test the effectiveness of various words and appeals. During an economic downturn in 1886, he hired as many as 2,000 unemployed workers to stroll through the community wearing sandwich boards. The next year he chartered five steamers and took 16,000 underprivileged children for an outing. In 1889 he distributed circulars from the top of Paris's Eiffel Tower.

A related key to Wilson's success was his understanding that shopping could be more than simply an activity to acquire goods, although that's what shopping often was at other stores in those days. Rather, Wilson recognized the potential for shopping to be an entertaining, enjoyable experience. So, his store frequently featured novelty acts, shows and other in-store attractions to build store traffic and spread word-of-mouth.

No fear of rejection

Marketers may hear "no" several times before hearing "yes," but those that rise to the top neither fear rejection nor are they discouraged by it. Walter Wilson was that way. Once he offered to supply uniforms for the local police force in Glasgow, Scotland in exchange for printing the name of his store on their helmets. Unfortunately for Wilson, the police declined the offer. Undaunted, Wilson quickly moved on to pursue other promotional ideas.

August 22, 2017
Tuesday

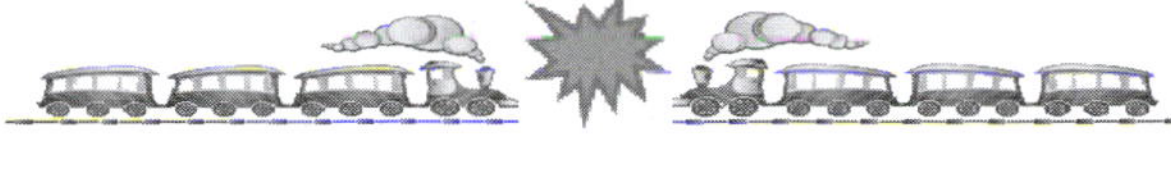

Objectives & reminders

Appointments

Early morning

8 a.m.

9 a.m.

10 a.m.

11 a.m.

Noon

1 p.m.

2 p.m.

3 p.m.

4 p.m.

5 p.m.

6 p.m.

Later evening

Napa Valley Wine Train (NVWT)

Given the impact on customer (dis)satisfaction and patronage behavior, marketers of retail stores and many service businesses are sensitive to employees' encounters with customers. However, also highly-relevant are customer-to-customer (C2C) encounters. When customers share the same physical environment, their verbal and non-verbal behaviors can enhance or detract from the experience of other customers.

The relevance of C2C encounters was certainly apparent on August 22, 2015, when 11 members of a book club were removed from the NVWT in Northern California for allegedly loud and boisterous behavior. Reports of the incident vary, but apparently the book club members' party-type behavior disturbed other passengers who expected a quiet, peaceful train experience. Acting on other passengers' complaints, the train's employees repeatedly asked the book club members to "tone it down." When the book club members failed to comply, the train's police got involved and the alleged perpetrators were escorted past several other passengers and ejected from the train.

Although the company later offered an apology, book club members threatened a lawsuit -- arguing that they were not louder than other passengers on the train and that they were humiliated victims of discrimination. In the aftermath, it seems clear that the incident led to considerable negative publicity for the NVWT and created a wake of customer dissatisfaction -- for both the ejected passengers and those disturbed by their behavior.

Three ways to avoid C2C train wrecks

- Practice target marketing. C2C compatibility is likely to be higher when the customer mix is homogeneous.
- Communicate expectations to customers. Acceptable behavior in one service setting may be unacceptable in another (e.g., shouting at a sporting event vs. in a public library).
- Manage the physical facilities, e.g., provide a spacious environment so customers can avoid others with whom they're incompatible, install acoustical ceilings to absorb noise and smoke-eaters to clean the air, and so on.

August 23, 2017
Wednesday

Objectives & reminders

____

____

____

Appointments

Early morning

8 a.m.

9 a.m.

10 a.m.

11 a.m.

Noon

1 p.m.

2 p.m.

3 p.m.

4 p.m.

5 p.m.

6 p.m.

Later evening

Month of Virgos

According to zodiac followers, those of us born between August 23 and September 22 are classified as Virgos, or Virgins. Accordingly, Virgos are purported to be conservative and shy, prudish, skeptical, concerned with health, and often introverted. According to one horoscope for Virgos in 2017, "You will have more new opportunities than last year… [and your] professional activities will be subject to changes that will affect your overall organization" (www.divinologue.com).

Astrology is nonsense: Agree or disagree? Whether you agree or not is only partially relevant if those you work with -- including customers -- believe in astrology. If they follow their horoscopes and adjust their decisions and behavior accordingly, they could affect you.

Customer satisfaction: More than an abstract concept

"Customer satisfaction is the most important measure to me, and if you really believe that, then you've got to tie it to your reward system, to your management practices, and we do.... We measure customer satisfaction every way imaginable. We measure it, on a scale of one to five, after every customer visit. We track every problem by how well we respond to it and I review how well we are doing with every critical account every night. The measurements are not only done in absolute terms, but relative to our key competitors as well. Once a year we total all these results and we pay managers based on how well they score." -- John T. Chambers, former computer salesman for IBM who became the CEO of Cisco Systems in 1995 and now serves as Cisco's Executive Chairman. He was born in Cleveland, Ohio on August 23, 1949.

Independence versus in*ter*dependence

"There is no such thing as a self-made man. We are made up of thousands of others. Everyone who has ever done a kind deed for us, or spoken one word of encouragement to us, has entered into the make-up of our character and of our thoughts, as well as our success." -- George Matthew Adams, American author and president of Adams Newspaper Service (renamed George Matthew Adams Service in 1916), born on August 23, 1878

August 24, 2017
Thursday

Objectives & reminders

____

____

____

Appointments

Early morning

8 a.m.

9 a.m.

10 a.m.

11 a.m.

Noon

1 p.m.

2 p.m.

3 p.m.

4 p.m.

5 p.m.

6 p.m.

Later evening

Tough day for crisis managers

August 24 should serve to remind businesspeople of the constant threat of a variety of crises waiting to harm the business environment and jeopardize the future of their businesses. As the following historical events of August 24 show, some crises are man-made while others are "acts of God." Although individuals or individual companies may not be able to prevent many crises, by anticipating the unanticipated, firms can prepare contingency plans to lessen the devastating effects of crises.

79 a.d.

Italy's Mount Vesuvius erupted, destroying the cities of Pompeii and Herculaneum, and killing several thousand people. Lasting for 18 hours, the eruption buried Pompeii under 14-17 feet of pumice and ash. Sixty feet of mud and volcanic debris buried Herculaneum. Today, Vesuvius remains active (last eruption in 1944) and is expected to erupt again in the near future; 700,000 people now live around the base of Vesuvius.

1857

Ohio Life Insurance & Trust Company's New York branch failed, leading to a financial panic and one of the most devastating economic crises in the history of the U.S. Almost 5,000 firms failed that year. Within two years, another 8,000 businesses collapsed. Over speculation in real estate and railway securities was largely to blame for the crisis.

1992

Hurricane Andrew first smashed its way onto the coast of Florida. The storm raged for three days in Florida and Louisiana, forcing the evacuation of a million residents. Andrew was the biggest natural disaster in the U.S. that year and, at the time, the most devastating storm in decades in terms of property damage.

August 25, 2017
Friday

Objectives & reminders

____

____

____

Appointments

Early morning

8 a.m.

9 a.m.

10 a.m.

11 a.m.

Noon

1 p.m.

2 p.m.

3 p.m.

4 p.m.

5 p.m.

6 p.m.

Later evening

Business births on August 25

1819 Allan Pinkerton, founder of the Pinkerton National Detective Agency. His agency's logo included the "All-Seeing Eye," from which today's generic reference to private detectives as "private eyes" comes.

1880 Joshua Lionel Cowen, founder of the Lionel Corporation which became the largest toy train manufacturer in the U.S. At the age of 22 Cowen invented an electric model train that he used as an attention-getting device in a store window display. He launched the manufacturing company when numerous customers asked to buy the toy train.

1910 Arnold Neustadter, who in 1940 invented the alphabetized, rotating card file known as the Rolodex. Throughout his career, Neustadter also invented several other office-related products.

Debut of *Father Knows Best*

Playing the role of a married father of a son and two daughters, actor Robert Young began dispensing his fatherly wisdom on August 25, 1949, on the radio show that would evolve into one of the most popular sit-coms of all-time. In 1954, the show moved to television where it continued until 1963.

While *Father Knows Best* may bring back nostalgic memories (for your parents!), the show's efforts to portray what was then a "typical" middle-class American household reflected what is not so typical today. During the *Father Knows Best* era, about half of U.S. households consisted of a married couple plus one or more children under the age of 18. Today, this profile describes less than one of five households. Further, while consumers in the middle-income groups still dominate, higher percentages of consumers today are now found in either high-income or low-income categories.

So, in terms of household composition, income, and in many other ways, it has become increasingly difficult to define what it means to be "typical" -- which is why astute marketers today think in terms of market segmentation and target marketing. The one-size-fits-all approach to marketing has become increasingly ineffective since *Father Knows Best.*

August 26, 2017
Saturday

Objectives & reminders

____

____

____

Appointments

Early morning

8 a.m.

9 a.m.

10 a.m.

11 a.m.

Noon

1 p.m.

2 p.m.

3 p.m.

4 p.m.

5 p.m.

6 p.m.

Later evening

Happy birthday: Barbara Ehrenreich

Born in Butte, Montana on August 26, 1941, Ehrenreich is a journalist and author. In addition to 18 books, she's written for numerous publications such as *Time* magazine and *The New York Times*. Ehrenreich's best-selling 2001 book, *Nickel and Dimed: On (Not) Getting By in America*, provides a revealing and thought-provoking examination of the lifestyles and challenges faced by the working poor. To gain perspective and empathize with the working poor, Ehrenreich abandoned her middle-class existence and most of her resources for several months. She worked in various entry-level jobs in an effort to support herself, including two restaurant jobs, a job as a dietary aide in a nursing home, a maid for a cleaning franchise, and an on-floor job at Wal-Mart. In her final assessment, Ehrenreich failed to achieve a sustainable lifestyle.

Expensive to be poor
What do Ehrenreich and others mean when they observe that it is expensive to be poor? What are the possible marketing implications (opportunities?) of this phenomenon?

Although the book is somewhat controversial, many of Ehrenreich's observations and experiences are consumption-related, so the book should be of interest to marketers who want to gain a richer understanding (or alternative perspective) of this substantial market segment and learn how to reach and serve it more effectively.

How large is the "working poor" market segment? According to 2010 and 2012 data from the U.S. Bureau of Labor Statistics (BLS), about two-thirds of those in poverty in the U.S. do work at least part time. Of American consumers below the poverty line, about 10.6 million are employed. However, many analysts have challenged BLS data for many years and suggest that the working poor segment is much larger. For example, in 2004 *Business Week* magazine gauged the size of the segment to be about 28 million consumers -- which includes workers over the age of 18 who are employed, but earn $9.04 an hour or less. The same year, consumer advocate Ralph Nader estimated that the working poor consisted of 47 million Americans who "do not make a living wage for themselves, much less for their families."

August 27, 2017
Sunday

Objectives & reminders

____

____

____

Appointments

Early morning

8 a.m.

9 a.m.

10 a.m.

11 a.m.

Noon

1 p.m.

2 p.m.

3 p.m.

4 p.m.

5 p.m.

6 p.m.

Later evening

Happy birthday:
Margaret Wolfe Hungerford

Born in Ireland on August 27, 1850, Hungerford was a popular novelist who, in her 1878 novel *Molly Brown*, observed that "beauty is altogether in the eye of the beholder."

Today, astute businesspeople recognize that beauty isn't the only perceptual attribute that's in the eye of the beholder. Most perceptions are highly subjective and can vary in an increasingly diverse society. Although impossible to master, the ability to view the world through the eyes of others is one of the most valuable business and life skills one can attain.

What is a "beautiful" price?
When several shoppers see discounted price tags on merchandise, some conclude that the store is rewarding valued customers with a great price, while another pats himself on the back for finding such a great bargain. Other shoppers conclude that the merchandise is out of season or of inferior quality. Another assumes that at such low prices the store's customer satisfaction policy must not apply. Some believe the merchandise is likely to remain at the low price for quite a long time, while others grab items and rush to the cash register before the price rises. One customer wants all of her friends to know how little she paid, while another prefers to have her friends think she paid full price. Indeed, the beauty of price is in the eye of the beholder.

Beauty may be in the eye of the beholder, but promotion is in the eye of your supervisor

"Dress for the position you want, not for the position you are currently in." -- Lynn Deckinger, communications manager for the Greater Wichita (Kansas) Convention and Visitors Bureau, born exactly 119 years after Ms. Hungerford, on August 27, 1969

August 28, 2017
Monday

PPPP

Objectives & reminders

____

____

____

Appointments

Early morning

8 a.m.

9 a.m.

10 a.m.

11 a.m.

Noon

1 p.m.

2 p.m.

3 p.m.

4 p.m.

5 p.m.

6 p.m.

Later evening

August 28 in the history of the marketing mix's "four Ps"

Product: 1898

North Carolina pharmacist Caleb D. Bradham began using a trademark and assigned a name to the beverage he had concocted -- Pepsi-Cola. Over the next 100-plus years, 200 other cola brands were introduced, but Pepsi survived and became one of the leaders in the category.

Place (distribution): 1907

Two teens from Seattle, Washington – Jim Casey and Claude Ryan – started a messenger service that would become the largest package delivery service in the world -- United Parcel Service (UPS).

Promotion: 1922

The first radio advertisement aired on New York's station WEAF. The $50, 10-minute spot lectured listeners on the appeal of living away from the hustle and bustle of the big city -- to promote "Hawthorne Court," a new apartment complex opening in New York's Jackson Heights area.

Price: 1986

General Motors began luring customers with an attractive and unprecedented new-vehicle loan rate of 2.9 percent (at a time when major banks' "prime rate" was 7.5%). The company recognized that price is a multi-dimensional "p" for buyers of "big ticket" items such as automobiles. That is, auto-buyers consider not only the sticker price, but also the down-payment, trade-in allowance, operating costs (e.g., gasoline mileage), insurance and property taxes, and the price of financing. The low interest rate helped make the other pricing elements more palatable.

August 29, 2017
Tuesday

Objectives & reminders

____

____

____

Appointments

Early morning

8 a.m.

9 a.m.

10 a.m.

11 a.m.

Noon

1 p.m.

2 p.m.

3 p.m.

4 p.m.

5 p.m.

6 p.m.

Later evening

Eating your Wheaties

August 29, 1939, was a key day in the history of sponsorship. That's when General Mills became the first commercial sponsor of a televised sports broadcast. Their Wheaties brand of ready-to-eat breakfast cereal sponsored a local baseball game in New York City between the New York Dodgers and the Cincinnati Reds. At the time, about 500 households in New York owned television sets.

Today, the concept of television sponsorship has been extended to include *title sponsorships* (i.e., having the name of the event named after the sponsor), *category sponsorships* (e.g., the event's official soft drink, official camera, etc.), and *feature sponsorships* (e.g., "The half-time report is brought to you by..."), among others.

If it's not implemented, it's not a good strategy: Agree or disagree?

"Implementation is a bigger issue in being successful than most strategies are. I'm not saying that you don't have to know which is the right hill to take. But knowing which hill to take is only part of the battle. You've got to get your people to want to take the hill. And if you know how to do that, you're going to be successful. You can always get someone to help you with the strategy part... But you better be able to talk straight to people and get them to want to help you."
-- Gordon Bethune, recently retired chairman and CEO of Continental Airlines who is credited with dramatically turning around the ailing company. Bethune was born on August 29, 1941.

Market motivation

"If a man goes into business with only the idea of making a lot of money, chances are he won't. But if he puts service and quality first, the money will take care of itself. Producing a first-class product that meets a real need is a much stronger motivation for success than getting rich." -- Joyce C. "J.C." Hall, founder of Hallmark Cards, Inc., born on August 29, 1891. Today, the company's President and CEO is J.C.'s grandson, Donald J. Hall, Jr.

August 30, 2017
Wednesday

Objectives & reminders

Appointments

Early morning

8 a.m.

9 a.m.

10 a.m.

11 a.m.

Noon

1 p.m.

2 p.m.

3 p.m.

4 p.m.

5 p.m.

6 p.m.

Later evening

Hot line installed

August 30, 1963, was a key date in the easing of tense relations between the United States and the Soviet Union. That's when the so called "hot line" was installed to connect the White House in Washington D.C. to the Kremlin in Moscow. The objective was to provide a communications link between the two governments so leaders could talk directly to each other in the event of an international crisis (such as the Cuban missile crisis that had occurred the previous year).

Recognizing the value of direct communications and easy access to decision-makers, businesses soon began installing hot lines so customers could speak directly with managers or with the home office. In the U.S., the spread of hot lines was greatly aided by the advent of toll-free WATS lines in 1967, essentially the forerunner of today's toll-free 1-800 and 1-866 telephone numbers.

Hot communication principles in support of hot lines or other forms of direct communication

P1 Companies are not likely to improve unless they knows what is important to customers and they understand how customers perceive their products and services. The most difficult complaints to address are those never voiced.

P2 The more convenient it is for customers to offer comments to a company, the more likely they are to do so.

P3 Customer comments received by front-line personnel (e.g., retail clerks) are often stifled. That is, these employees may hear customer comments but never forward them to supervisors or managers.

P4 The more times a message (such as a customer comment) is passed from one party to another, the greater the likelihood that the message will be distorted or otherwise miscommunicated. A *direct* line of communication is less likely to be plagued with such communication maladies.

August 31, 2017
Thursday

Objectives & reminders

Appointments

Early morning

8 a.m.

9 a.m.

10 a.m.

11 a.m.

Noon

1 p.m.

2 p.m.

3 p.m.

4 p.m.

5 p.m.

6 p.m.

Later evening

Comparing apples and oranges

Price comparisons can be difficult for consumers when competing product alternatives are not directly comparable, as when alternatives are in different forms or involve different technologies. Such comparisons are further complicated when choices vary in terms of the length of their expected useful lives, maintenance and operating costs, labor costs, storage costs, insurance, taxes, and so on.

The challenge of evaluating the price of competing alternatives was evident in the early 1900s when consumers began considering whether to trade in their horses and buggies for automobiles. To make the case for automobiles, on August 31, 1916, one "motorcar" dealer used a technique that remains effective today. He analyzed all of the costs involved in owning and operating a horse and buggy versus those for owning and operating an

automobile, and broke the total costs into smaller and more directly comparable increments, i.e., average costs per mile. His conclusion: "An automobile beats a horse and buggy in many ways, not only in speed and its range, but also in the cost of travel per mile."

The best value?

As buyers become better educated and more sophisticated in their purchase decisions, increasingly they look beyond the price tag to determine which purchase alternative is the best value. As a salesperson, what "value" considerations would you remind buyers to consider in the following circumstances?

? A couple contemplating the purchase of their first washer and dryer.

? A recent college graduate wondering if he should trade in his very old and unreliable automobile for a newer model.

? A small business owner considering whether to invest in a photo copier of her own, rather than driving three miles to use the nearest public photo copier.

September 1, 2017
Friday

Objectives & reminders

____

____

____

Appointments

Early morning

8 a.m.

9 a.m.

10 a.m.

11 a.m.

Noon

1 p.m.

2 p.m.

3 p.m.

4 p.m.

5 p.m.

6 p.m.

Later evening

Wasting no time

Sam Walton is well known as the founder of Wal-Mart, but the early days of Walton's career included service in the military during World War II. When the war ended, Walton was discharged from the military and immediately began exploring career options. With some prior experience in retailing, Walton stumbled upon the opportunity to buy a Ben Franklin (variety store) franchise which he seized with the help of a loan from his father-in-law. Within days -- on September 1, 1945 -- while still in his 20s, Walton opened the store in Newport, Arkansas. Although Walton did not agree with all of Ben Franklin's policies and practices, he used the experience to shape his vision for what would later become Wal-Mart.

Allen pilots Boeing

On the same day that Sam Walton began selling toy planes in his new Ben Franklin franchise, William M. Allen accepted the controls of The Boeing Company -- makers of full-size aircraft. That is, Allen became the company's president on September 1, 1945, and continued to lead Boeing until 1972.

During his reign, Allen was not afraid to take calculated risks. He could see the direction that technology was heading and took steps to ensure that Boeing would be a part of that future. Accordingly, he helped move Boeing from propeller-driven aircraft into the jet age, and then into aerospace technology. Later, near the turn of the century, business analyst and consultant Jim Collins studied American business leaders and concluded that Allen was among the most effective in the history of the nation.

The vision of a leader

"Paths open for the future are paths of opportunity for the aggressive, capable company in the aerospace field, offering multiple choices of endeavor... The years ahead promise to be at least as challenging and revolutionary as those through which we have come." -- William M. Allen

September 2, 2017
Saturday

Objectives & reminders

____

____

____

Appointments

Early morning

8 a.m.

9 a.m.

10 a.m.

11 a.m.

Noon

1 p.m.

2 p.m.

3 p.m.

4 p.m.

5 p.m.

6 p.m.

Later evening

Shopology

Beginning on September 2, 2001,the BBC aired a documentary that examined the psychological aspects of shopping and consumerism in industrialized countries such as the United States, Britain and Japan. Named *Shopology*, the program featured psychologists who considered the potential psychological health risks associated with shopping and consuming today. Some of the concerns expressed include:

* It is now possible for consumers to "buy" a lifestyle. For many consumers, consumption patterns define who they are.
* The emphasis on branding exerts social pressure for consumers to buy the right brands to "fit in."
* For many consumers, the pressure to consume increases stress. Some consumers attempt to cope with this stress by further increasing their levels of consumption.
* Increased consumption can increase consumer debt, which can place hardships on families.

●●●●●●●●●●

Business key

"The most important thing in running a successful business is to have customer confidence. You've got to satisfy your customers, and most important, you've got to give your customers their money's worth." – William T. Dillard, Sr., founder of Dillard's Inc. department stores, born on September 2, 1914

Fear is healthy: Agree or disagree?

"It's fear that gets you out of comfortable equilibrium, that gets you to do the difficult tasks... [it is] healthy, like physical pain is healthy. It warns your body that something is wrong."
– Andrew S. Grove, former chairman and CEO of Intel Corporation and author of the best-selling book, *Only the Paranoid Survive* (1996). Grove was born on September 2, 1936.

September 3, 2017
Sunday

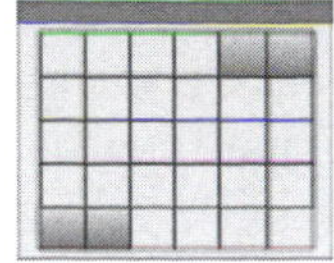

Objectives & reminders

____

____

____

Appointments

Early morning

8 a.m.

9 a.m.

10 a.m.

11 a.m.

Noon

1 p.m.

2 p.m.

3 p.m.

4 p.m.

5 p.m.

6 p.m.

Later evening

Avoiding Labor Day confusion

Labor Day is a U.S. federal holiday observed on the first Monday in September -- tomorrow. Given that almost all federal employees and about 19 of 20 workers at large U.S. firms enjoyed a paid day away from their jobs on Labor Day in 2015, it's not surprising that Sirloin Stockade would invite customers to spend part of their free time dining at their restaurants.

Accordingly, the evening before Labor Day in 2015, Sirloin Stockade sent email invitations to customers inviting them to, "Join us for a Labor Day Breakfast… Monday, September 6th from 8 a.m.--11 a.m."

Hopefully confusion was avoided by including "Monday" in the invitation, but Labor Day fell on the 7th of September that year -- not the 6th. It may have been that the company simply used the same announcement they had used in an earlier year, but forgot to update the occasion's date for 2015.

Findings from the Calendar Literacy Survey indicated that most surveyed American college students did not know or had difficulty recalling when one or more U.S. holidays occur. About one of every eight respondents failed to correctly indicate that Labor Day falls on a Monday.

So, to avoid confusion, noting both the day-of-week and the specific date on holiday invitations and other promotional materials is a good idea, as Sirloin Stockade attempted to do. But then it's important to proofread the copy and check the day and date against the calendar for accuracy. Typically for holidays, either the day-of-week and/or the date changes slightly from year to year. For holidays based on the lunar calendar, such as Islamic and Jewish holidays, both the day-of-week and date can change substantially when converted to the Gregorian calendar.

Learning from experience

"Experience may be hard but we claim its gifts because they are real, even though our feet bleed on its stones. We seek progressive advancement through the transformation of daily experience.... Experience can both guide and guard us. Foolish indeed are those who do not bring oil to its burning." – Mary Parker Follett, management consultant and writer, born on September 3, 1868

September 4, 2017
Monday

Labor Day

Objectives & reminders

___

___

Appointments

Early morning

8 a.m.

9 a.m.

10 a.m.

11 a.m.

Noon

1 p.m.

2 p.m.

3 p.m.

4 p.m.

5 p.m.

6 p.m.

Later evening

Labor Day

First observed in 1882, Labor Day was intended to honor workers' efforts and accomplishments. The original celebration included a parade in New York by the Knights of Labor. Thanks largely to the increasing size and clout of the labor movement during those early years, a Congressional bill in 1894 made "Labor's Holiday" a legal holiday for Federal workers. Most states soon followed Congress's lead and recognized the holiday as well.

Today, Labor Day is celebrated in the United States and Canada on the first Monday of September. It is one of the most widely observed holidays in the U.S. in terms of the number of employers who give workers the day off, with pay.

Labor Day celebrations still acknowledge the contribution of labor and the labor movement with parades, speeches, and other ceremonies. However, as the unofficial end of summer, many people also view the holiday as their last opportunity of the season to engage in outdoor activities such as picnics and cookouts, swimming, camping, and boating. Further, because Labor Day always falls on Monday, the three-day weekend prompts people to travel. In 2015, for example, AAA estimated that about 11 percent (35.5 million) of the U.S. population traveled during the weekend – most (30.4 million) by automobile, making the weekend one of the busiest of the year for highways.

Labor Labor Day
About 10,000 American women *doubly* recognize Labor Day by spending the day... in labor.

Labor Day shopping
Much like other holidays on which consumers don't have to report for work, many consumers choose to shop on Labor Day. Retail stores that remain open tend to report sales that are 20 to 30 percent higher than typical Mondays. Many retailers capitalize on Labor Day by timing the introduction of fall-related merchandise to coincide with the Labor Day weekend.

September 5, 2017
Tuesday

Objectives & reminders

____

____

____

Appointments

Early morning

8 a.m.

9 a.m.

10 a.m.

11 a.m.

Noon

1 p.m.

2 p.m.

3 p.m.

4 p.m.

5 p.m.

6 p.m.

Later evening

Forecasting shoe prices

Often the forces that influence prices are debated and not at all obvious. This is true for the stock market as well as for most consumer and industrial products. Yet, the difficulty of the task doesn't keep economists, market researchers and others from trying to determine why prices fluctuate.

That was the case on September 5, 1927, when *Time* magazine reported accusations by the National Shoe Retailers' Association. The NSRA pointed to vegetarians' eating habits to help explain the recent 15-20 percent increase in the price of shoes. The organization claimed that the recent growth in the number of vegetarians had negatively affected the demand for beef, which meant that fewer cattle had been slaughtered and therefore, there was less leather available for the manufacture of shoes. The leather shortage, in turn, drove leather prices up, and the increases were passed along to shoe buyers.

Happy birthday: Paul A. Volcker

On the same day the NSRA reportedly blamed vegetarians for the increasing prices of shoes – September 5, 1927 – financial economist Paul A. Volcker was born in Cape May, New Jersey.

Although it is not clear whether Volcker was a vegetarian, he probably did wear shoes when he began his career in 1953 as an assistant in the Securities Department of the Federal Reserve Bank of New York, followed by a five-year stint in commercial financial services. Volcker returned to public service in 1962 -- working in various positions for the Treasury Department and the Federal Reserve Bank. In 1979 he was a shoe-in for the job of chair of the Federal Reserve System's Board of Governors. He remained in that role until 1987.

Economics 101

"[The federal budget] deficit decreases savings. The lower the savings, the lower the investment you have, the more costly your investment will be; the lower the investment you have, the lower the growth; the lower the productivity of the economy, the lower the growth of the economy. It's as simple as that." -- Paul A. Volcker

September 6, 2017
Wednesday

Objectives & reminders

____

____

____

Appointments

Early morning

8 a.m.

9 a.m.

10 a.m.

11 a.m.

Noon

1 p.m.

2 p.m.

3 p.m.

4 p.m.

5 p.m.

6 p.m.

Later evening

Happy birthday: Joseph P. Kennedy, Sr.

Born in Boston on September 6, 1888, Joseph Kennedy was an ambitious and successful businessman, as well as the patriarch of the widely publicized Kennedy family. By the time he was 25 years old Kennedy already was the president of a small bank. Subsequent business ventures included investment banking, alcohol, movie theaters and film production. By the age of 30, Kennedy was a millionaire.

The senior Kennedy used his business skills to help his son -- John F. "Jack" Kennedy -- get elected to Congress in 1946. In planning the campaign, Joseph Kennedy remarked, "We're going to sell Jack like soap flakes." The younger Kennedy not only won that election, but in 1961 went on to become the 35th President of the United States.

Power negotiations
"Whenever you're sitting across from some important person, always picture him sitting there in a suit of long red underwear." -- Joseph P. Kennedy, Sr.

Branding as a promise and a vision: Much more than a name

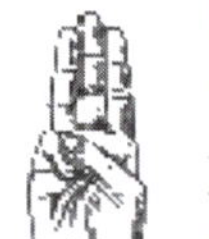

"Ultimately, strong branding is not just a promise to our customers, to our partners, to our shareholders and to our communities; it is also a promise to ourselves... in that sense, it is about using a brand as a beacon, as a compass, for determining the right actions, for staying the course, for evolving a culture, for inspiring a company to reach its full potential." – Carly Fiorina, former CEO of Hewlett-Packard and 2016 U.S. presidential candidate, born on September 6, 1954

Don't just *talk* about it

"Action indeed is the sole medium of expression for ethics." – Jane Addams, American social reformer who co-founded the Hull House in Chicago, in 1889, to assist needy families and children. Addams was born on September 6, 1860.

September 7, 2017
Thursday

Objectives & reminders

____

____

____

Appointments

Early morning

8 a.m.

9 a.m.

10 a.m.

11 a.m.

Noon

1 p.m.

2 p.m.

3 p.m.

4 p.m.

5 p.m.

6 p.m.

Later evening

Packard's Law

Born in Pueblo, Colorado on September 7, 1912, David Packard co-founded the Hewlett-Packard Company in 1939 with a whopping $538 investment.

He and his partner, William Hewlett, immediately went about the task of growing the company into the multi-billion dollar electronics and IT firm that it is today. Along the growth path, Packard recognized the folly of trying to grow H-P -- or any firm -- faster than the company's pool of human resources.

This realization became known as "Packard's Law," articulated by Jim Collins in his best-selling 2001 book, *Good to Great*: "No company can grow revenues consistently faster than its ability to get enough of the right people to implement that growth and still become a great company. If your growth rate in revenues consistently outpaces your growth rate in people, you simply will not -- indeed cannot -- build a great company" (p. 54).

Recognizing Packard's Law
"I spend a lot of time making sure we have the right people in place for succession planning, training and development." -- Patrick J. Moore, chairman, CEO and president of Smurfit-Stone Container Corporation, born in Chicago, Illinois on September 7, 1954

Developing employees
One important element of preparing employees for company growth is keeping them informed of company happenings. In a study released on September 7, 2005, by Knexus Consulting, apparently most companies fail to communicate adequately with their employees, in that "only four in ten employees are satisfied with internal corporate communication." Further, the study found that internal communication and overall job satisfaction were strongly correlated.

September 8, 2017
Friday

Objectives & reminders

____

____

Appointments

Early morning

8 a.m.

9 a.m.

10 a.m.

11 a.m.

Noon

1 p.m.

2 p.m.

3 p.m.

4 p.m.

5 p.m.

6 p.m.

Later evening

International Literacy Day

September 8 is recognized by the United Nations (UN) as International Literacy Day (ILD) to celebrate and promote literacy around the globe. Literacy, broadly defined as the ability to communicate effectively in writing, is a key to economic development. The lowest literacy rates (50-60%) exist in developing regions such as Sub-Saharan Africa and Southern Asia, but illiteracy is a challenge in industrialized countries too.

Among the numerous implications of literacy are concerns regarding illiterate workers. For example, one study found that billions of dollars are lost annually by U.S. firms due to low worker productivity, on-the-job mistakes and job-related accidents attributed to illiteracy of workers. So, about 75 percent of *Fortune 500* firms provide some degree of remedial training for workers.

Marketers too are concerned about literacy. For example, when targeting and serving illiterate buyers, marketers may rely more heavily on broadcast media than print media. In print media and on packaging, easily recognizable pictures that show what the product is and what it is used for can be a critical part of the communication. Similarly, logos, color schemes, spokespeople or spokescharacters, and other symbols that represent the brand may assume a more central role than written words. When written words are used, care must be taken to ensure that messages are easily understood by buyers who are only marginally literate. And, additional customer service support may be needed – such as telephone help lines.

Society's literacy challenge

"[L]iteracy can be a major tool for eradicating poverty, enlarging employment opportunities, advancing gender equality, improving family health, protecting the environment and promoting democratic participation... As the foundation of learning throughout life, literacy is at the heart of sustainable development. Yet… there are an estimated 800 million illiterate adults [at least 15 years of age], two thirds of whom are women. More than 100 million children are not in school." – Kofi Annan, former U.N. Secretary-General

September 9, 2017
Saturday

Objectives & reminders

____

____

____

Appointments

Early morning

8 a.m.

9 a.m.

10 a.m.

11 a.m.

Noon

1 p.m.

2 p.m.

3 p.m.

4 p.m.

5 p.m.

6 p.m.

Later evening

Service orientation

"Life is a place of service, and in that service one has to suffer a great deal that is hard to bear, but more often to experience a great deal of joy. But that joy can be real only if people look upon their life as a service, and have a definite object in life outside themselves and their personal happiness." -- Leo Tolstoy, Russian writer, born on September 9, 1828

The Colonel's finger-lickin career advice

"You got to like your work. You have got to like what you are doing, you have got to be doing something worth-while so you can like it -- because it is worthwhile, that it makes a difference, don't you see?" -- Colonel Harland Sanders, founder of Kentucky Fried Chicken (KFC), born on September 9, 1890

Change ➔ understanding

"If you want to truly understand something, try to change it." -- Kurt Lewin, pioneer in social psychology and organizational development, born on September 9, 1890

Advertising for "you"

"Talk to people. That's all it is... [T]he great communicators talk to one person. That's what advertising does... -- this is the right car for you, or beer, or insurance company, or whatever... it is. Only for you. Luckily, there are millions of people like you and they will all buy it, but you don't say that in the ad. There's no 'you' plural in advertising, it's 'you' singular." -- Neil French, British advertising executive, born on September 9, 1944

Brand jokes facilitate publicity and word-of-"mouth": Agree or disagree?

"A duck walks into the pharmacy and says, 'Gimme some Chapstick -- and put it on my bill.'" -- The Amazing Jonathan, American comic, born on September 9, 1958

September 10, 2017
Sunday

Objectives & reminders

____

____

Appointments

Early morning

8 a.m.

9 a.m.

10 a.m.

11 a.m.

Noon

1 p.m.

2 p.m.

3 p.m.

4 p.m.

5 p.m.

6 p.m.

Later evening

Grandparents Day

Grandparents Day is one of the newest U.S. holidays -- first recognized in 1978 when President Jimmy Carter declared that the first Sunday after Labor Day should be designated for the occasion. The day commemorates the unique bonds between grandparents and their families.

The grandparent market

- There are more than 69 million grandparents in the U.S. -- about 23 percent of the population. The number of grandparents grows by about 75,000 each month.
- 57 percent of grandparents have at least one grandchild between the ages of four and seven; 59 percent have grandchildren between eight and twelve.
- Eight percent of children in the U.S. live with a grandparent.
- Hallmark Cards' research has found that terms such as "younger," "more active," and "economically powerful," are used to describe today's grandparents. According to the findings of a survey by the National Council on Aging, about one-third of Americans in their 70s consider themselves to be "middle aged."

Grandparents as a grandchildren market

Marketers don't target only *users* of products, such as toys directed to children. Rather, marketers also target *buyers* who make purchases for others, such as grandparents who spend $30 billion annually on their grandchildren (about $435 per grand-parent). Accordingly, grandparents buy almost 17 percent of the toys in the U.S. and more than a third of the toys for children under the age of five.

September 11, 2017
Monday

Objectives & reminders

___

___

___

Appointments

Early morning

8 a.m.

9 a.m.

10 a.m.

11 a.m.

Noon

1 p.m.

2 p.m.

3 p.m.

4 p.m.

5 p.m.

6 p.m.

Later evening

Patriot Day

September 11, 2001, also known simply as "9-11," is one of the saddest and most horrific days in U.S. history. That's the day when Islamic terrorists turned commercial airplanes into flying bombs to attack the World Trade Center Towers in New York City and the Pentagon in Washington, D.C.. It was also the day terrorists caused the crash of United Airlines Flight 93 near Shanksville, Pennsylvania. Nearly 3,000 people lost their lives that day and almost 10,000 more were injured. Needless to say, America's -- including American businesses' -- concern for safety and security has climbed sharply as a result of the 9-11 attacks.

Marketing after 9-11:
Agree or disagree?
"[I]n the aftermath of September 11, consumers are slowing down and considering their options a little more carefully before making purchasing decisions. They now place more value on stable, reputable, familiar, proven brands. The most important thing to remember about the effects of September 11 is that it's not a passing thing. This event has changed the fundamentals of how we market and merchandise."
-- Sergio Zyman, former marketing director for The Coca-Cola Company

Remembering 9-11 and Tom Landry

Born on September 11, 1924, legendary football coach Tom Landry led the Dallas Cowboys from 1960 until 1988. Although he passed away 19 months before 9-11, his observation that, "something constructive comes from every defeat," was taken to heart by the Points of Light Foundation and the Youth Service America and Citizen Corps. -- sponsors of "One Day's Pay."

To honor the victims of 9-11, the purpose of One Day's Pay is to encourage people to devote each September 11 to help others in need. By donating to a worthy cause an amount equivalent to that earned during one work day, or by setting aside September 11 to work as a volunteer for a nonprofit organization, people everywhere can help turn the tragedy of September 11, 2001, into something positive, something constructive.

September 12, 2017
Tuesday

Objectives & reminders

____

____

Appointments

Early morning

8 a.m.

9 a.m.

10 a.m.

11 a.m.

Noon

1 p.m.

2 p.m.

3 p.m.

4 p.m.

5 p.m.

6 p.m.

Later evening

Subliminal seduction?

During the mid-1950s there was quite a stir in the marketplace over a controversial technique called subliminal advertising. Among other applications, the technique involved flashing brand names or commands (e.g., "buy Coca-Cola" or "eat popcorn") during movies so fast that the ads would register in movie-goers' subconscious minds without their conscious minds realizing it.

Proponents claimed that because subliminal advertising broke through consumers' conscious decision-making barriers, the approach was more effective than traditional forms of advertising. Not surprisingly, consumers viewed subliminal advertising as a form of manipulation, but it intrigued market researcher James M. Vicary who announced the formation of the Subliminal Projection Company on September 12, 1957. Subsequent studies, however, found the promises of subliminal advertising to be without merit. Within a year of Vicary's announcement the American Psychological Association proclaimed subliminal advertising techniques to be totally ineffective. Consumers remained king.

A more effective promotional Bonanza

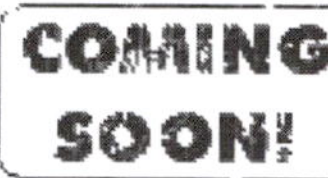

On September 12, 1959, two years after James Vicary's announcement of a bonanza awaiting subliminal advertisers, a much more popular one premiered on NBC television -- the Western melodrama series called *Bonanza*. The weekly show aired for more than 13 years and produced very high Nielsen ratings -- a bonanza for advertisers.

Bonanza's producers were among the first in television to employ the "next week" marketing tactic. That is, at the end of each episode, a few glimpses of the following week's exciting episode would be shown to encourage viewers to tune in again. The tactic worked and the show built a loyal following of repeat viewers. Today, similar tactics in multiple industries provide a glimpse of what's new or coming soon -- to entice customers back to the store, to encourage them to revisit the company's website, or otherwise prompt them to look forward to the next exciting episode in the customer-business relationship.

September 13, 2017
Wednesday

Objectives & reminders

____

____

____

Appointments

Early morning

8 a.m.

9 a.m.

10 a.m.

11 a.m.

Noon

1 p.m.

2 p.m.

3 p.m.

4 p.m.

5 p.m.

6 p.m.

Later evening

Happy birthday: Milton Snavely Hershey

Born in rural Dauphin County, Pennsylvania on September 13, 1857, Hershey left school at the age of 13. He gained some business experience working at an ice cream parlor before opening his own candy store in Philadelphia at the age of 19. For the next several years he opened and closed or sold several candy-related businesses -- finally venturing into the chocolate business in 1895. Chocolate proved to be Hershey's forte when he developed his own chocolate recipe and introduced the Hershey's Chocolate Bar in 1900. Other successful chocolate products followed during Mr. Hershey's life, including Hershey's Kisses (1921), Mr. Goodbar (1925), Hershey's Syrup (1926), and the Krackel bar (1938).

Advertising not necessary: Agree or disagree?
Traditional forms of advertising are not necessary for a company to succeed, according to Milton S. Hershey who often said, "Give them quality. That's the best kind of advertising in the world." Indeed, the company Mr. Hershey founded, Hershey Chocolate Company (now The Hershey Company), prospered. However, as competition intensified the company did begin to advertise in 1967 – several years after Mr. Hershey's death.

Today, The Hershey Company enjoys annual sales in excess of $7.4 billion, employs 14,800 people, and manages 84 brands. That's sweet success!

Memorable

Promises

Quality
Value

Brand-obsessed

"I want us to be (and I want us to be recognized to be) the very best brand-marketing company in the world. I want my company to be brand-obsessed -- from the board to the factory floor." – Niall FitzGerald, former chairman and CEO (1996-2004) of Unilever PLC consumer goods conglomerate with 900 brands, born on September 13, 1945

September 14, 2017
Thursday

Objectives & reminders

___

___

___

Appointments

Early morning

8 a.m.

9 a.m.

10 a.m.

11 a.m.

Noon

1 p.m.

2 p.m.

3 p.m.

4 p.m.

5 p.m.

6 p.m.

Later evening

Happy birthday: Ivan Petrovich Pavlov

Born in Ryazan, Russia on September 14, 1849, Pavlov studied medicine with the intent of pursuing a career in physiology. The first half of his career was spent studying indigestion, winning a Nobel Prize in 1904 for that work.

After reaching the age of 50, Pavlov's research evolved into thirty years of study involving conditioned responses. He discovered that the sight of food was not required for dogs to begin to salivate. Rather the dogs used in his experiments *learned* to associate certain sounds (such as the attendant's footsteps or the ringing of a bell) with food because of their routine association with food; hence the dogs would begin to salivate upon hearing these associated sounds, regardless of the presence or absence of food.

The key point, Pavlov realized, was that dogs' salivation through association was not innate; rather it was a conditioned or learned response -- a phenomenon that became known as a "conditioned reflex" or "conditioned response." Today, social scientists also talk about "classical conditioning" when referring to this phenomenon.

Salivation may not be the objective of modern day applications of classical conditioning and people cannot be conditioned as easily as animals, but the routine association of some forms of environmental stimuli can evoke predictable reactions if the stimuli is associated often enough with the response. For example, workers may become anxious when they see the supervisor walking toward their work area if a supervisor has a reputation for always making derogatory remarks when encountering employees. In the marketplace, some research suggests that because people associate slow-tempo music with a leisurely pace of movement, retail shoppers are more likely to stroll through stores at a slower pace when slow-tempo music is played throughout the store. The slower movement leads to more time spent in the store and greater exposure to merchandise, which leads to larger purchase volumes.

September 15, 2017
Friday

Objectives & reminders

____

____

____

Appointments

Early morning

8 a.m.

9 a.m.

10 a.m.

11 a.m.

Noon

1 p.m.

2 p.m.

3 p.m.

4 p.m.

5 p.m.

6 p.m.

Later evening

Hispanic Heritage Month

September 15 marks the beginning of Hispanic Heritage Month. On this date, five Hispanic countries celebrate the anniversary of their independence in 1821 -- Costa Rica, El Salvador, Guatemala, Honduras, and Nicaragua. Other Hispanic countries also celebrate their independence about this time, including Mexico (September 16) and Chile (September 18).

Today, about 54 million Hispanics live in the United States, representing about 17 percent of the U.S. population. Although Hispanics are scattered throughout the entire country, 2012 data suggest that their numbers tend to be more concentrated in some areas than in others. For example, 47 percent of New Mexico residents are Hispanic, while 38 percent of Californians and Texans are Hispanic. A larger-than-average percentage of consumers in Arizona (30%), Nevada (27%) and Florida (23%) are also Hispanic.

Invitation to debate
For a new firm to effectively reach, appeal to, and serve Hispanic consumers, would it likely be more effective to hire someone who's very familiar with the Hispanic community/culture and then teach them marketing? **OR**, would it be better to hire someone who is very familiar with marketing and then teach them about the Hispanic community and culture?

Understanding consumer choices

"Consumers make choices to accomplish goals. Therefore, motivation is an important component of the choice process. Given some set of goals, the consumer devotes attention to that information available which is relevant to attaining those goals. The consumer then interprets this information in light of previous knowledge and the context in which the information is obtained; that is, the consumer must decide what a particular piece of information means." -- James R. Bettman, consumer research scholar and Burlington Industries Professor of Business Administration, Fuqua School of Business, Duke University. Dr. Bettman was born on September 15, 1943.

September 16, 2017
Saturday

Objectives & reminders

____

____

____

Appointments

Early morning

8 a.m.

9 a.m.

10 a.m.

11 a.m.

Noon

1 p.m.

2 p.m.

3 p.m.

4 p.m.

5 p.m.

6 p.m.

Later evening

Happy birthday: Allen Funt

Born in Brooklyn, New York on September 16, 1914, Funt was an American celebrity best known for the hit television series he created known as *Candid Camera*. The long-running 1950s and 1960s show used hidden cameras to record people's reactions to pranks played on them. Numerous copy-cat shows have been produced since the original *Candid Camera* concept first aired on television.

In one episode a customer pulled into a full-service gasoline station and asked the attendant for a fill-up. The attendant unwittingly pumped gasoline into the normal-looking automobile that was specially equipped with a 200-gallon gasoline tank. As the gasoline meter ran well beyond the expected 24-gallon limit, hidden cameras captured the baffled attendant checking to see if the pump was malfunctioning; he looked underneath the car for leaks and even asked the customer for an explanation. The attendant's reaction was recorded when the customer complained about the impossibility of the enormous bill.

Survey research caveat
Survey respondents didn't always do what they said they did, won't always do what they say they will do, and don't always know what they claim to know.

While humorous, the *Candid Camera* concept reveals some highly marketing-relevant insights about human nature and while doing so, reinforces the potential value of unobtrusive observation techniques in marketing research. That is, in contrast to more frequently used survey research that might involve asking customers about their behaviors, the observation and filming of consumers in real business or consumption settings is much more likely to reflect their behaviors accurately. Attempts to capture comparable data through surveys could be biased by faulty consumer memories, socially-desirable responses, interviewer errors, and other problems.

Observation research not perfect either
While observation may reveal *what* consumers do, it may reveal nothing about *why* they do it.

September 17, 2017
Sunday

Objectives & reminders

____

____

____

Appointments

Early morning

8 a.m.

9 a.m.

10 a.m.

11 a.m.

Noon

1 p.m.

2 p.m.

3 p.m.

4 p.m.

5 p.m.

6 p.m.

Later evening

Bad day for RCA: Who's on first?

On September 17, 1931, Radio Corporation of America (RCA) demonstrated early versions of 33 rpm long-playing records ("L.P.s"). Unfortunately, the innovation proved to be a flop for RCA because L.P.s were prohibitively expensive for the mass-market. Seventeen years later, in 1948, RCA's competitor, Columbia, introduced an economically viable L.P. which became a hit. Sometimes a company can go around and around with an innovation, only to conclude that it still doesn't pay to be first to the market.

Skip forward a few more years, to September 17, 1971, and we find RCA withdrawing from the computer market after trying unsuccessfully to clone IBM's success. Sometimes a company's "me too" efforts simply don't compute, and management learns that it doesn't pay *not* to be first to the market.

Happy birthday: Joel R. Evans

Born in New York City on September 17, 1948, Dr. Evans is Professor of Marketing and International Business at Hofstra University. His best-selling retailing textbook, *Retail Management*, co-authored with Barry Berman, is now in its 12th edition. The book has touched the lives of thousands of business students since the first edition was published in 1979.

Why retail sales are lost

Evans and Berman point out several reasons to explain why retail sales clerks often lose sales. Some of these include:

1. Failure to demonstrate the product
2. Inadequate product knowledge
3. Arguing with customers
4. No attempts made at suggestion selling
5. Failure to understand individual customer needs and identify alternative solutions
6. Failure to customize the sales message for individual customers
7. Inadequate follow-up to ensure customer satisfaction

September 18, 2017
Monday

Objectives & reminders

___

___

Appointments

Early morning
8 a.m.
9 a.m.
10 a.m.
11 a.m.
Noon
1 p.m.
2 p.m.
3 p.m.
4 p.m.
5 p.m.
6 p.m.
Later evening

Marketing regardless of whether "marketing" is in your job title

"There is no man who is not in some degree a merchant; who has not something to buy or something to sell." – Samuel Johnson, British writer & philosopher, born on September 18, 1709

Another marketing "P": Presentation

"People eat with their eyes before they eat with their hands." – Al Lapin, Jr., born on September 18, 1927. Lapin was the American entrepreneur who co-founded the International House of Pancakes (IHOP) in 1958. Today, the chain consists of more than 1,650 restaurants in 50 U.S. states and eight countries.

Retailing success factors determined by shoppers

"[T]he customer determines at the end of the day who is successful and for what reason." – Gerry Harvey, Australian entrepreneur who co-founded (with Ian Norman) the Harvey Norman chain of retail stores, born on September 18, 1939

Customer service

"When you're taking care of the customer, you can never do too much. And there is no wrong way... if it comes from the heart." – Debra Fields, American entrepreneur who founded the $500-million company, Mrs. Fields' Cookies, born on September 18, 1956

Insight for design of higher-involvement products

"People project meaning onto objects. If an object allows you to interact with it, then it becomes part of your being, and over time you see things in it that first you might not have seen." – Karim Rashid, world renowned industrial designer who has designed more than 2,000 objects (including designer wastebaskets for Target stores), born in Cairo, Egypt on September 18, 1960

September 19, 2017
Tuesday

Objectives & reminders

____

____

____

Appointments

Early morning

8 a.m.

9 a.m.

10 a.m.

11 a.m.

Noon

1 p.m.

2 p.m.

3 p.m.

4 p.m.

5 p.m.

6 p.m.

Later evening

Good day for a dance promotion?

Chubby Checker's dance song, "The Twist," first topped the charts on September 19, 1960. After the song's initial climb to the top in 1960, the song went to the number one spot *again* in 1962. The song stayed on the charts for a total of 39 weeks while all across America, people were taking Checker's advice: "Hey, hey everybody, let's dooo-ooo The Twist..."

> **Don't know how to do The Twist?**
> "Try stubbing out cigarettes with both feet while rubbing your back with a towel." -- Chubby Checker

Advertising waste

"Half the money I spend on advertising is wasted, and the trouble is I don't know which half."
-- William Hesketh Lever, co-founder of Lever Brothers Co. (soap producer), now the multi-national conglomerate known as Unilever.

Lever was born on September 19, 1851, and launched Lever Brothers in the U.K. in 1885. For the next 20 years, Lever Brothers spent an estimated £2 million on advertising – far more than any of his competitors. At about the same time, in America, Philadelphia retailer John Wanamaker also invested heavily in advertising for his Wanamaker's department store and is noted for making essentially the same comment about advertising waste. Both businessmen were strong believers in advertising. In the early 1900s, various circulation auditing measures to evaluate the effectiveness of advertising expenditures began to emerge to help reduce advertising waste.

The wealthy are lucky: Agree or disagree?

On September 19, 1927, *Time* magazine reported an interview with Julius Rosenwald shortly after Rosenwald's 65th birthday. Rosenwald was then chairman of Sears, Roebuck & Co. and worth about $115 million (equal to about $1.6 billion today), but he attributed his wealth to mere luck: "I was lucky, not a genius. With rare exceptions, the man who accumulates wealth displays no more genius than the prize-winner in any lottery. It is by luck that a man gets hold of a good thing at the right time and more by luck that he holds on to it."

September 20, 2017
Wednesday

Objectives & reminders

____

____

____

Appointments

Early morning

8 a.m.

9 a.m.

10 a.m.

11 a.m.

Noon

1 p.m.

2 p.m.

3 p.m.

4 p.m.

5 p.m.

6 p.m.

Later evening

Happy birthday: J. Troplong "Jay" Ward

Born in San Francisco on September 20, 1920, Ward became a television animator in 1948 when he formed Television Arts Production with Alexander Anderson, Jr. The two created one of the first animated television stars, Crusader Rabbit, who premiered in 1950. The next year, Bullwinkle the moose and Rocky the flying squirrel were born.

Ward later formed Jay Ward Productions and in 1962 began working with the Quaker Oats Company for whom he created the animated Cap'n Crunch character and accompanying plot-filled television commercials for the children-targeted breakfast cereal also called Cap'n Crunch. The appeal of the Cap'n Crunch character and commercials led Quaker Oats to develop the cereal *after* the creation of the character. The cereal was an immediate success and is still available today.

Appealing to young children
Young children may not be able to read, but they can recognize animated characters they've seen on TV -- more easily than they can recognize spokes-people, brand names or verbal messages. That's why brands targeting children, such as many breakfast cereals, frequently feature animated cartoon characters on their packages and in TV commercials. Not surprisingly, such packages often are placed on lower shelves in stores -- within easy reach of children.

When innovators bypass market research: Hair today, gone tomorrow

The Milwaukee, Wisconsin market proved to be unique in the early 1970s when a new wig design sold well there. When it hit the market on September 20, 1972, the wig was like no other; it contained built-in hair curlers. Presumably women could wear the wig casually -- possibly to curtail rumors that they wore wigs, or possibly for other reasons that are not clear. Still, when the wig-maker attempted to go national with the "innovation," consumers outside of Milwaukee rejected it. The company declared bankruptcy.

September 21, 2017
Thursday

Objectives & reminders

Appointments

Early morning

8 a.m.

9 a.m.

10 a.m.

11 a.m.

Noon

1 p.m.

2 p.m.

3 p.m.

4 p.m.

5 p.m.

6 p.m.

Later evening

The U.N. International Day of Peace

First established by a United Nations resolution in 1981, Peace Day is now observed annually on September 21. According to the U.N.'s resolution, Peace Day "should be devoted to commemorating and strengthening the ideals of peace both within and among all nations and peoples... [and] will serve as a reminder to all peoples that our Organization, with all its limitations, is a living instrument in the service of peace."

Marketing redefined

Definitions of "marketing" are almost as plentiful as the people who try to define it. Clearly the concept means different things to different people and marketing definitions have evolved over many decades. For several years prior to September 21, 2007, the Chartered Institute of Marketing (CIM) defined marketing as "*the management process responsible for identifying, anticipating and satisfying customer requirements profitably*." However, believing that definition was too management-focused, rather than customer-focused, CIM proposed the following definition of marketing on that date:

Important definition

> "*The strategic business function that creates value by stimulating, facilitating and fulfilling customer demand.* It does this by building brands, nurturing innovation, developing relationships, creating good customer service and communicating benefits. By operating customer-centrically, marketing brings positive returns on investment, satisfies shareholders and stakeholders from business and the community, and contributes to positive behavioral change and a sustainable business future."

The CIM challenge
"What we would really like is for marketers to start thinking about who they are, where they think the profession should go and how it should be seen."
– David Thorp, director of research and information, Chartered Institute of Marketing, September 21, 2007

September 22, 2017
Friday

Objectives & reminders

____

____

____

Appointments

Early morning

8 a.m.

9 a.m.

10 a.m.

11 a.m.

Noon

1 p.m.

2 p.m.

3 p.m.

4 p.m. — 4:02 p.m., EDT - Autumn arrives in Northern Hemisphere

5 p.m.

6 p.m.

Later evening

Native American Day

Native American Day (NAD) salutes the original inhabitants of North America who thrived on the continent for thousands of years before it was "discovered" (invaded?) by European explorers (such as Christopher Columbus in 1492). Generally, NAD is observed annually on the fourth Friday in September, although the dates of local observances vary. For example, in South Dakota, NAD is celebrated on (replaces?) Columbus Day, the second Monday in October.

Competitive intelligence

American patriot Nathan Hale was hanged on September 22, 1776. His offense? Spying on British troops while disguised as a Dutch schoolmaster. His last words? "I only regret that I have but one life to lose for my country."

In business, as in war, knowledge of the competition's activities and plans can provide a winning edge. That's why firms pay careful attention to competitor information and often actively search for it. The approaches used to learn about competitors vary, and as the accompanying box implies, some are more ethical than others.

Invitation to discuss: Hanging offenses?
Which of the following competitive intelligence practices are (un)ethical?

- Searching the Internet for information posted by the competitor.
- Asking a stock broker to investigate the financial condition of a publicly-traded competitor.
- Hiring a competitor's employees with the intent of asking them to detail the competitor's plans.
- Asking a competitor's suppliers what the competitor buys, when it is purchased, and in what quantities.
- Visiting a competitor's retail store posing as a customer and taking pictures while "shopping."
- Asking a competitor's executives pointed questions about the business while *pretending* to be a student writing a term paper about the company.

September 23, 2017
Saturday

First *full* day of autumn in the Northern Hemisphere

Objectives & reminders

____

____

Appointments

Early morning

8 a.m.

9 a.m.

10 a.m.

11 a.m.

Noon

1 p.m.

2 p.m.

3 p.m.

4 p.m.

5 p.m.

6 p.m.

Later evening

Writers recognize autumn's beauty!

"Autumn is a second spring when every leaf's a flower." -- Albert Camus

"No spring nor summer beauty hath such grace,
As I have seen in one Autumnal face."
– John Donne

Perhaps bypassing Los Angeles?
"Delicious autumn! My very soul is wedded to it, and if I were a bird I would fly about the earth seeking the successive autumns." – George Eliot

"Fall is my favorite season in Los Angeles -- watching the birds change color and fall from the trees." -- David Letterman, American comedian

National Hunting & Fishing Day

Observed since 1972, National Hunting & Fishing Day (NH&FD) was formally established by Presidential Proclamation #4682 in 1979 to salute two of Americans' favorite pastimes. The occasion is celebrated annually on the fourth Saturday in September, although the specific dates of hunting and fishing seasons vary greatly from state to state.

Statistics for American hunters and fishermen deserve marketers' notice – especially marketers in rural communities where local economies depend heavily on outdoor enthusiasts. According to the U.S. Fish & Wildlife Service, there are 13.7 million hunters and 33.1 million anglers in the country. Annually, hunters spend an average of $2,484 to pursue their interest in hunting, while anglers typically spend about half of that amount.

In addition to obvious opportunities for the sale of hunting and fishing equipment, supplies and apparel, many rural communities capitalize on the seasonal influx of hunting and fishing "tourists" to boost the local economy through lodging, fuel, and food sales.

September 24, 2017
Sunday

Objectives & reminders

____

____

____

Appointments

Early morning

8 a.m.

9 a.m.

10 a.m.

11 a.m.

Noon

1 p.m.

2 p.m.

3 p.m.

4 p.m.

5 p.m.

6 p.m.

Later evening

Planning for cold weather

Seasonal changes in climate are accompanied by changes in buying and consumption patterns. Of course, the demand for weather-related merchandise such as overcoats, cold remedies, and heating oil increases as temperatures drop. Hot food and beverages are substituted for colder alternatives. Consumers' outdoor activities may be moved inside or exchanged for indoor activities. Further, dropping temperatures can play havoc with vehicles and equipment that operate outdoors -- thus auto repair shops see an upturn in business when cold weather arrives.

Shopping behavior also is affected by colder weather. Some frequent shoppers may become infrequent ones as they avoid colder temperatures and the accompanying snow and ice. They may opt for in-home shopping alternatives. Other shoppers may shop only during day-time hours when temperatures are a few degrees warmer.

The seasonal transition affects business operations too. Farmers, nurseries and other agriculture/ horticulture-related businesses are mindful of the effects that colder weather has on plants. For these businesses, the date of the season's first freeze is particularly relevant. Exterior house painters are cognizant of the fact that most paints do not dry properly at lower temperatures. Similarly, construction firms face special materials-related problems when the temperature drops (e.g., concrete doesn't cure properly in freezing temperatures). Transportation companies are challenged too; truck transportation may be delayed by inclement weather and ice may block inland waterway shipping routes altogether.

Who's likely to freeze today?

The U.S. National Climatic Data Center monitors weather conditions for more than 3,100 communities in the U.S. Their data indicate that Yosemite National Park CA, Cambridge City IN, Britt IA, Ainsworth NE, and Rochester MA, among many others, have a 10 percent chance of having experienced a fall freeze of 32 degrees (Fahrenheit) or lower on or before September 24. Colder temperatures tend to arrive earlier in Austin MN, Lovelock NV, Nashua NH, and Madera PA, where there's a 50 percent chance that one or more bouts of freezing temperatures already have occurred by September 24.

September 25, 2017
Monday

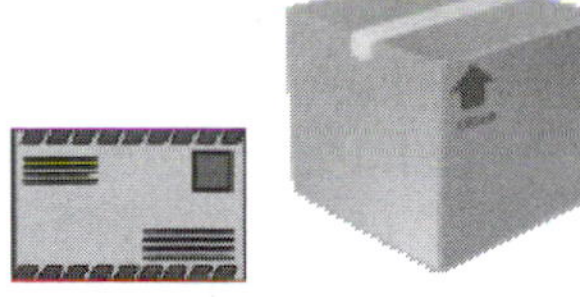

Objectives & reminders

____

____

____

Appointments

Early morning

8 a.m.

9 a.m.

10 a.m.

11 a.m.

Noon

1 p.m.

2 p.m.

3 p.m.

4 p.m.

5 p.m.

6 p.m.

Later evening

Big day for Sears, Roebuck & Co.

The first Sears mail-order catalog was published on September 25, 1887. Initially only a few pages, the catalog soon grew to several hundred pages. At the time, most Americans lived on farms and in small towns where stores or other shopping alternatives were limited, so mail-order catalogs helped to fill a definite need. Still, some consumers felt uneasy about ordering through the mail -- instead preferring to buy from merchants face-to-face. To overcome this hesitancy, Richard Sears offered a money-back guarantee on catalog items. Customers dissatisfied with their purchase for any reason could return merchandise for a full refund.

The extent to which New Yorkers Arthur F. and Agnes Martinez shopped for children in the Sears catalog is not known, but on the catalog's 52nd anniversary -- September 25, 1939 -- they celebrated the stork's delivery of their son -- Arthur C. Martinez. Young Arthur grew up to work for Sears, Roebuck & Co., and in 1992 became the CEO of the company's Merchandise Group, and later served as the firm's chair. Martinez played a key role in restructuring the struggling company and reversing its downturn.

Goodbye catalog ☹
In 1993, financially-challenged Sears announced that it would stop publishing their catalog that had become the "wish book" for millions of consumers. The $3.3 billion catalog operation had lost too much money in recent years. Driving the losses were the changing mix of Sears' competition and the changing demographics of American consumers. Also, the "information super-highway" of the Internet revolution was on the horizon in 1993 -- threatening to make paper catalogues obsolete.

Gender-blind

"I wasn't a woman in a man's world; I was just the person doing the job." -- Olive Beech, co-founder and former chairman, president, and CEO of Beech Aircraft Company, born in Waverly, Kansas on September 25, 1903

September 26, 2017
Tuesday

Objectives & reminders

____

____

Appointments

Early morning

8 a.m.

9 a.m.

10 a.m.

11 a.m.

Noon

1 p.m.

2 p.m.

3 p.m.

4 p.m.

5 p.m.

6 p.m.

Later evening

Happy birthday: Federal Trade Commission (FTC)

With the help of U.S. President Woodrow Wilson, the Federal Trade Commission Act was established on September 26, 1914. The Act created the FTC -- a federal agency charged with the responsibility to enforce antitrust legislation and protect consumers against unfair competition involving interstate commerce. More specifically, four key areas covered by the Act include price fixing, unfair competition, merger prohibition, and deceptive practices such as false advertising.

Ensuring competition: Agree or disagree?

1. ? Companies that grow too large should be broken-up because their size gives them unfair advantages over their competitors (e.g., advantages such as economies of scale, bargaining power with suppliers, and greater access to capital markets).
2. ? The inability of competitors to compete effectively is not in the best interest of consumers. For example, some monopolies may not pass along cost savings to consumers in the form of lower prices.

Job Day: No job is trivial

"We'll give you a chance." -- Isaac L. Hewitt, co-founder of the Cleveland Iron Mining Company, on September 26, 1855, upon hiring a 16-year-old for his first job, as an assistant bookkeeper. The teen was John D. Rockefeller, who began the job on the same day.

Rockefeller grew to become one of the wealthiest businessmen in the world, making his fortune in the oil business. He always celebrated September 26 as "Job Day." Looking back on that pivotal day several years later, Rockefeller commented, "All my future seemed to hinge on that day; and I often tremble when I ask myself the question: 'What if I had not got the job?'"

September 27, 2017 Wednesday

Objectives & reminders

____

____

Appointments

Early morning

8 a.m.

9 a.m.

10 a.m.

11 a.m.

Noon

1 p.m.

2 p.m.

3 p.m.

4 p.m.

5 p.m.

6 p.m.

Later evening

"I think I can, I think I can..."

First published in 1930, the inspirational classic, *The Little Engine That Could*, was republished on September 27, 2005. The children's – but not childish – book is about a locomotive who tries her best to make it up a hill. Despite the discouragement she encounters from others, the little engine clings to the familiar refrain: "I think I can, I think I can, I think I can..." until her positive attitude translates into tangible success.

In his book, *Little Red Book of Selling*, professional sales consultant Jeffrey Gitomer claims *The Little Engine That Could* as his all-time favorite book. In talking about "the little salesman that could," he suggests that salespeople could benefit from adopting the little engine's attitude:

> "The theme of the book is also the theme of your success. Believing that you can achieve whatever you set your mind to. You must believe that you work for the greatest company in the world, that you offer the greatest products and services in the world, and that you are the greatest person in the world, or you are in the wrong job. High self-belief leads to high success. Medium self-belief leads to medium success. Low self-belief... you get the picture." (p. 193)

Nothing as practical as a good theory: Agree or disagree?

"The development of theory is the inevitable outcome of any concerted effort to improve practice. We must become more theoretical in order to become more practical." – Wroe Alderson, leading marketing scholar in the 1950s and 1960s who adopted an interdisciplinary approach to the study of marketing. He also was an early and strong advocate of the development of marketing theory. Alderson was born on September 27, 1898.

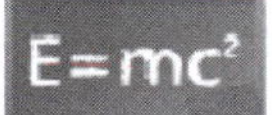

Theory defined
"[A] set of propositions which are consistent among themselves and which are relevant to some aspect of the factual world." – Wroe Alderson

September 28, 2017
Thursday

Objectives & reminders

____

____

____

Appointments

Early morning

8 a.m.

9 a.m.

10 a.m.

11 a.m.

Noon

1 p.m.

2 p.m.

3 p.m.

4 p.m.

5 p.m.

6 p.m.

Later evening

Happy birthday: Confucius

The ancient Chinese philosopher, Confucius, was born on September 28, 551 B.C. Because Confucius was also a teacher, September 28 is celebrated as Teachers' Day in Taiwan.

Confucius business wisdom: Agree or disagree?

1. ? "Desire to have things done quickly prevents their being done thoroughly."
2. ? "The wise man understands equity; the small man understands only profits."
3. ? "Study the past, if you would divine the future."

Economic forces drive automobiles, not life: Agree or disagree?

On September 28, 1966, psychologist B.F. Skinner questioned what he viewed as the misplaced priorities of the marketplace: "The economic forces behind the designers of cars are fantastically powerful. When will the design of a better way of life be as strongly supported?"

Happy birthday: Edwin Harris Colbert

Born in Clarinda, Iowa on September 28, 1905, Colbert pursued a career as a paleontologist and museum curator. He attributed his success to his ability to exercise creativity through his research: "The paramount factor in the development of my scientific career has been a love of original research. Research is creative, and there is true satisfaction in doing creative things."

Copy this idea

COPY

On September 28, 1959, it was announced that Haloid Xerox, Inc. would soon introduce a machine that reproduces documents on ordinary paper. Prior to this development, Xerox machines had required specially treated paper. The rental price of the new machines? $95 per month.

September 29, 2017
Friday

69274956847301841l
38727374850960398
57582 ?2783
94399 ?6778
26402 ?8595
94789478688309348
11137859600281617З

Objectives & reminders

____

____

Appointments

Early morning

8 a.m.

9 a.m.

10 a.m.

11 a.m.

Noon

1 p.m.

2 p.m.

3 p.m.

4 p.m.

5 p.m.

6 p.m.

Later evening

Happy birthday: Harold Hotelling

Born in Fulda, Minnesota on September 29, 1895, Hotelling was a prominent American statistician who did much to advance multivariate analysis. Some of the statistical measures he developed are widely used today, such as the Hotelling t-test.

Why data analysis can be frustrating
Hotelling recognized the quagmire that exists in data analysis. To paraphrase: As the number of variables doubles, the amount of useful information that can be extracted from the data may increase, but the increase is likely to be less (often far less) than a doubling. Yet as the number of variables doubles, the complexity of the analysis required to extract the additional information potentially quadruples.

Happy birthday: Lech Walesa

Born in Popowo, Poland on September 29, 1943, Walesa was a passionate and charismatic labor union leader who had a tremendous impact on the Polish labor movement in the 1980s and 1990s. Speaking for the frustrated working-class that felt oppressed by the Polish and Soviet government, Walesa was instrumental in pressuring the government to grant freedoms to workers -- the freedom to form and join independent trade unions, the freedom to strike, and the freedom of expression. After the government conceded these freedoms in 1980, Walesa was elected as the chairman of Solidarnosc (Solidarity) -- a confederation of multiple unions which soon grew to represent almost ten million workers.

Convenience is the mother of invention
"It's the lazy people who invented the wheel and the bicycle because they didn't like walking or carrying things." -- Lech Walesa

September 30, 2017
Saturday

Objectives & reminders

Appointments

Early morning

8 a.m.

9 a.m.

10 a.m.

11 a.m.

Noon

1 p.m.

2 p.m.

3 p.m.

4 p.m.

5 p.m.

6 p.m.

Later evening

Happy birthday: William Wrigley, Jr.

Born in Philadelphia on September 30, 1861, Wrigley's career as a salesman and manufacturer led him to build the company that would become the largest producer and distributor of chewing gum in the world -- William Wrigley, Jr. Company.

Chew on these stats
Like many consumer products, chewing gum consumption varies greatly around the world. Per capita consumption in the United States is about 175 "servings" per year, in contrast to 125 in the United Kingdom, 95 in Taiwan, 45 in Russia, and 18 in China. A business considering international expansion should not assume that consumption patterns in their domestic markets reflect consumption in other parts of the world.

William Wrigley, Jr. became a big believer in advertising. After introduced Spearmint gum in 1899, sales were sluggish for about eight years until he launched a major advertising campaign in 1907; sales jumped tenfold within one year.

Unlike competitors and most other companies of the day, Wrigley resisted the temptation to curtail his advertising investments during economic downturns. By continuing and often increasing advertising expenditures during recessions, Wrigley was able to build market share during recessions which he then maintained after the economy turned upward.

Taking a long-term perspective
"I have sometimes been asked what single policy has been most profitable in our business, and I have always unhesitatingly answered, 'restraint in regard to immediate profits.' That has not only been our most profitable policy, it has been pretty nearly our only profitable one."
-- William Wrigley, Jr.

Never take a marble for granite! Visit Marketing FAME's official resource support website: www.MarketingMarbles.com

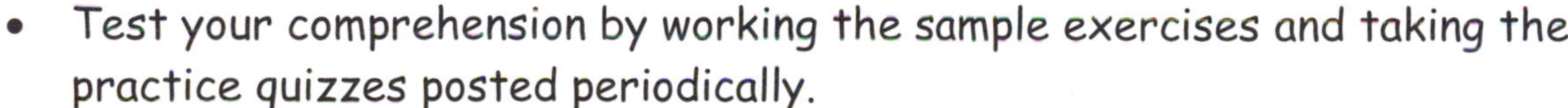

- Test your comprehension by working the sample exercises and taking the practice quizzes posted periodically.
- Read more about the roles that calendars play in marketing and buyer behavior. For example, learn how nature's calendar, different cultures' calendars, and legal calendars affect marketing practices and buyer behavior.
- Learn more about what it means to be "calendar-led." Determine if you are calendar-led.
- Discover how you could contribute to future editions of *Marketing FAME*.
- Find out about the *Marketing FAME* contests that you could enter.
- Communicate with the author and publishing team through the website's "Contact" page.
- Stay tuned for news and updates.

October 1, 2017
Sunday

Objectives & reminders

____

____

____

Appointments

Early morning

8 a.m.

9 a.m.

10 a.m.

11 a.m.

Noon

1 p.m.

2 p.m.

3 p.m.

4 p.m.

5 p.m.

6 p.m.

Later evening

New month and new quarter!

What is October?

"October is the fallen leaf, but it is also a wider horizon more clearly seen. It is the distant hills once more in sight, and the enduring constellations above them once again." -- Hal Borland

Welcome to Q4

Although October is the 10th month of the year, in business circles it's also known as the beginning of the fourth quarter, or "Q4." The transition from

one quarter to the next is not always a seamless one. The implementation of the new quarter's plans may begin. Managers may now be free to spend money budgeted for the quarter. Some sales reps may scramble to make early progress toward meeting their quarterly quotas, while others may relax early in the quarter after sprinting in September to meet Q3 quotas. Personnel at all levels in the organization may find themselves busy early in the quarter as they work overtime to complete their Q3 reports.

Given the sometimes bumpy transition from quarter to quarter, it's useful to consider how the transition affects the organization, competitors, suppliers and customers, and what practices might be revised to increase productivity or otherwise gain an advantage in the marketplace. For example, if salespeople tend to slash prices late in the quarter to meet *sales volume* quotas, perhaps *gross margin* quotas should be introduced to curb the temptation. Or, if past records indicate that suppliers' tend to raise prices at the beginning of a quarter, perhaps inevitable orders could be accelerated into the previous quarter to qualify for the lower prices.

Q1 Q2 Q3 **Q4**

Latent desires: Agree or disagree?

"We read advertisements to discover and enlarge our desires. We are always ready -- even eager -- to discover, from the announcement of a new product, what we have all along wanted without really knowing it." -- Daniel J. Boorstin, American historian and former Librarian of Congress (1975-1987), born on October 1, 1914

October 2, 2017
Monday

"It" Day

Objectives & reminders

____

____

____

Appointments

Early morning

8 a.m.

9 a.m.

10 a.m.

11 a.m.

Noon

1 p.m.

2 p.m.

3 p.m.

4 p.m.

5 p.m.

6 p.m.

Later evening

What is "It"?

A blind advertisement appeared in the *Atlanta Constitution* newspaper on October 2, 1887. The ad was placed by John Pemberton, inventor and founder of Coca-Cola:

> "WANTED: An acceptable party with $2,000 to purchase one-half interest in a very profitable and well established manufacturing business, absolutely no risk, and guaranteed a 50 per cent profit on investment…"

We now know that an investment in The Coca-Cola Company would have been a good one, but consider the creative math of 1887. According to at least one account, the ad led to three partners, each buying a "half" share of the business.

"Coke is It"
This was a promotional slogan once used extensively by The Coca-Coca Company.

Where is "It"?

Fast forward to October 2, 1955, when The Coca-Cola Company stopped marking individual bottles with the name of the location where the drink was bottled. Apparently, some devoted Coke-drinkers had developed loyalties to certain bottlers, while others simply enjoyed collecting bottles from different locations. Apparently the practice became too expensive for the company to continue.

After Coca-Cola customers protested the change, bottling locations reappeared on Coke bottles. However, the names of the locations did not necessarily correspond to where the drink was bottled. When short of bottles, bottlers simply used those marked with another location.

Black is "It"

Meanwhile, women's fashion designer, Donna Karan, was developing her own concept of "it." Possibly inspired by the color of Coke or the flowing lines of its classic bottle, by the time Karan celebrated her 37th birthday on October 2, 1985, she was busy creating her first collection, dubbed The Essentials. The color black was a central element of the collection. According to Karan, black was indeed "it": "*It* goes day-into-evening. *It* packs. *It*'s city friendly."

October 3, 2017
Tuesday

Objectives & reminders

____

____

____

Appointments

Early morning

8 a.m.

9 a.m.

10 a.m.

11 a.m.

Noon

1 p.m.

2 p.m.

3 p.m.

4 p.m.

5 p.m.

6 p.m.

Later evening

Heard comment, herd behavior

On October 3, 1929, three weeks before the stock market crash that propelled the U.S. into the Great Depression, multi-millionaire John D. Rockefeller announced, "Believing that fundamental conditions of the country are sound, my son and I have for some days been purchasing common stocks."

Rockefeller and most other businesspeople of the day were optimistic. The lesson? Business investments can be risky enough by themselves, but their degree of risk can be compounded by the comments of people who are influential enough to affect other people's investment decisions.

First rule of investing
"October. This is one of the peculiarly dangerous months to speculate in stocks in. The others are July, January, September, April, November, May, March, June, December, August, and February." -- Mark Twain, American humorist and author

October 3 in the history of innovation

1899 John S. Thurman received a patent for his "pneumatic carpet renovator" – essentially a motorized vacuum cleaner. Thurman turned his invention into a business by vacuuming homes for four dollars each.

1922 Charles Jenkins used telephone lines to send a facsimile photo from Washington, D.C. to nearby Anacostia, D.C. – a first in the United States.

1941 The first aerosol can for commercial applications was patented by L.D. Goodhue and W.N. Sullivan as a result of their search to find an effective way to apply insecticides in mushroom houses. Aerosol cans were commonly used to apply insecticides for decades after that.

1952 John Mullin used a Video Tape Recorder to make the first quality video recording at Bing Crosby Enterprises in Los Angeles. The tape proved to be less expensive and more convenient to produce than the previously used phonographic method.

October 4, 2017
Wednesday

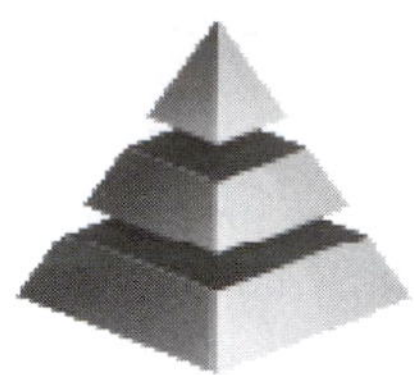

Objectives & reminders

____

____

Appointments

Early morning

8 a.m.

9 a.m.

10 a.m.

11 a.m.

Noon

1 p.m.

2 p.m.

3 p.m.

4 p.m.

5 p.m.

6 p.m.

Later evening

Happy birthday: Rutherford Birchard Hayes

Born in Delaware, Ohio on October 4, 1822, Hayes initially pursued a law career in Cincinnati, followed by military service during the Civil War. Immediately after the war, he entered politics, first serving in Congress and then as governor of Ohio. In 1876 he was elected as the 19th President of the United States.

Keeping loyalties aligned

Sometimes large organizations become faceless and distant to their members, prompting individuals to think in terms of more visible, smaller units within the organization -- such as their work area, department, unit, or function. In other words, rather than thinking in terms of what's best for the organization and focusing on how their job or department meshes with the firm's larger purpose, workers are sometimes guilty of reversing priorities and placing their own jobs or units first.

In his Inaugural Address in 1877, President Hayes seemed to recognize the presence of this phenomenon in government organizations. Encouraging listeners to re-evaluate their allegiances and priorities, Hayes observed, "He serves his party best who serves his country best." Had he been selected as a corporate president instead, he might have said something like this: "He serves his *department* best who serves the *company* best."

Observation from Mr. Change himself

"Successful people stay open to change." – Russell Simmons, "eternal Hip-Hop mogul" who founded Def Jam Recordings and other businesses, born in Queens, New York on October 4, 1957. For more of Simmons' business and career insights, read his book, *Do You!: 12 Laws to Access the Power in You to Achieve Happiness and Success*.

October 5, 2017
Thursday

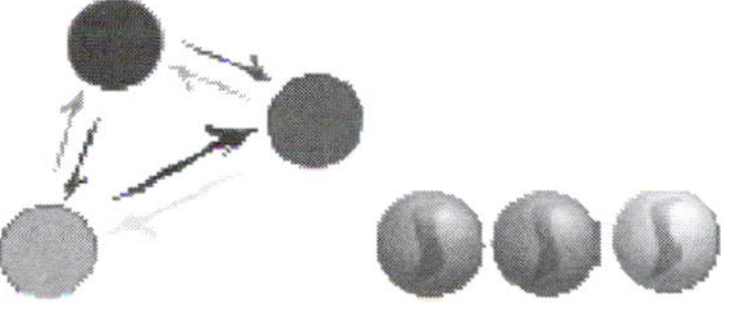

Objectives & reminders

Appointments

Early morning

8 a.m.

9 a.m.

10 a.m.

11 a.m.

Noon

1 p.m.

2 p.m.

3 p.m.

4 p.m.

5 p.m.

6 p.m.

Later evening

McMarbles of business wisdom

Born in Oak Park, Illinois on October 5, 1902, Ray Kroc was the visionary entrepreneur who bought a small drive-in restaurant called McDonald's and parlayed it into the largest fast-food corporation in the world. If you had worked for McDonald's before Ray Kroc passed away in 1984, you might have heard bits and pieces of his business philosophy first-hand. A few of Kroc's McMarbles of business wisdom are noted in the accompanying boxes.

Salesmanship defined: Agree or disagree?
"[T]he gentle art of letting the customer have it your way."

Advice for tomatoes?
"As long as you're green, you're growing. As soon as you're ripe, you start to rot."

Sales pitches
"No self-respecting pitcher throws the same way to every batter, and no self-respecting salesman makes the same pitch to every client."

Customer-focus
"Look after the customer, and the business will take care of itself."

Would you like fries with these McMarbles?

For managers & entrepreneurs
"You're only as good as the people you hire."

Entrepreneurial success-risk relationship
"You're not going to get it free, and you have to take risks. I don't mean daredevil risks. But you have to take risks, and in some case you must go for broke. If you believe in something, you've got to be in it to the end of your toes. Taking reasonable risk is part of the challenge."

Get out of the way!
"I believe if you hire a man to do a job, you ought to get out of the way and let him do it. If you doubt his ability, you shouldn't have hired him in the first place."

October 6, 2017
Friday

Objectives & reminders

Appointments

Early morning

8 a.m.

9 a.m.

10 a.m.

11 a.m.

Noon

1 p.m.

2 p.m.

3 p.m.

4 p.m.

5 p.m.

6 p.m.

Later evening

The 86 Percent Solution

The growing importance played by emerging markets throughout the world is pointed out by Vijay Mahajan and Kamini Banga in their insightful book published on October 6, 2005: *The 86 Percent Solution: How to Succeed in the Biggest Market Opportunity of the Next 50 Years.* The "86%" refers to the percentage of the world's population found in countries that have a per capita annual gross national product of less than $10,000 (less than 25% of that enjoyed in the U.S.). These emerging markets present numerous challenges for marketing managers -- in terms of product design, pricing, communications, packaging, distribution, and branding.

Income in emerging markets

"Although global poverty is being reduced, half the world's workers still make less than $2 per day, and more than 1 billion people make less than $1 per day." -- Mahajan and Banga, p. 213

Product considerations in emerging markets

"Dust and heat, lack of electricity, narrow highways, and low budgets all place strains on products in the developing world. While companies might be tempted to produce second-rate products for the developing world, consumers are very demanding, expecting high value for their scarce cash." -- Mahajan and Banga, p. 19

Emerging markets: Youthful and growing

"While Japan, Europe, and the U.S. are worried about pensions and the rapid aging of their populations, emerging economies are young... While only 21 percent of the U.S. population is under the age of 14, this figure is 33 percent in India, 29 percent in Brazil, and 33 percent in Iran... Most of the world's population growth will take place in developing countries." -- Mahajan and Banga, p. 21

October 7, 2017
Saturday

Objectives & reminders

____

____

____

Appendments

Early morning

8 a.m.

9 a.m.

10 a.m.

11 a.m.

Noon

1 p.m.

2 p.m.

3 p.m.

4 p.m.

5 p.m.

6 p.m.

Later evening

Happy birthday: Thomas "Thom" Edward Yorke

Born in Wellingborough, Northamptonshire, England on October 7, 1968, Thom Yorke is the lead singer and songwriter for the British rock band known as Radiohead.

The band was formed in 1986 and released their first album, *Pablo Honey*, in 1993. Five more albums/CDs followed during the next decade using a traditional record company to produce, promote and distribute their music. The group's worldwide fanbase grew into the millions.

Then Radiohead decided to cut out the middleman, produce their own music and distribute it themselves. So, three days after Yorke's 39th birthday, Radiohead took the do-it-yourself plunge with their *In Rainbows* virtual "CD" – which was made available on the Internet at the creative price of whatever buyers wanted to pay. About three weeks later, early sales data indicated that 1.2 million fans had downloaded the music, with some paying as little as two cents (plus a 90-cent fee for using a debit or credit card) – although the average was a little over two dollars. Some analysts estimated that if Radiohead had used a traditional record label, their royalties would have been about $2.50 to $3.00 per CD, but it is not known how many would have been sold through a record label's traditional channels.

Farewell to you:
Are intermediaries obsolete?
"I like the people at our record company, but the time is at hand when you have to ask why anyone needs one. And, yes, it probably would give us some perverse pleasure to say 'F____ [Farewell to?] you' to this decaying business model."
– Thom Yorke

Leaders are self-selected

"One of my mentors used to say that if you wait for someone to ask you to be a leader, you'll never be one." – Sharon Allen, then chairman of Deloitte & Touche, LLP (2003-2011), born in Kimberly, Idaho on October 7, 1951

October 8, 2017
Sunday

Objectives & reminders

____

____

____

Appointments

Early morning

8 a.m.

9 a.m.

10 a.m.

11 a.m.

Noon

1 p.m.

2 p.m.

3 p.m.

4 p.m.

5 p.m.

6 p.m.

Later evening

Good day for leadership insights

Lofty goals

"Aviation is proof that given the will, we have the capacity to achieve the impossible." -- Edward "Eddie" Vernon Rickenbacker, World War I flying ace and former head of Eastern Air Lines (1935-1960). Rickenbacker was instrumental in Eastern's enviable record of profitability during his years of leadership. He was born on October 8, 1890.

Leadership facts

"If the modern leader doesn't know the facts, he is in grave trouble, but rarely do the facts provide unqualified guidance." -- John W. Gardner, former professor, consultant, author and founder of Common Cause, born on October 8, 1912

Momentum and goals

"One way to keep momentum going is to have constantly greater goals." – Michael Korda, writer and former publishing executive (Editor-in-Chief of Simon & Schuster), born on October 8, 1933

Self-doubt as a leadership asset

"If you're an intelligent leader, then you've got to have self-doubt. Once you start believing you know it all, that becomes self-deception, and that's the start of the end." -- Sam Chisholm, top-level broadcasting executive in New Zealand, Australia and United Kingdom (e.g., Nine Network, Sky TV, Macquarie Radio Network), born in New Zealand on October 8, 1939

Leadership is like cellophane tape

"Leadership has a harder job to do than just choose sides. It must bring sides together." – Reverend Jesse Jackson, civil rights leader, born in Greenville, South Carolina on October 8, 1941

Teams are not for hiding behind

"You need a strong team, because a mediocre team gives mediocre results, no matter how well managed it is." -- Bill Gates, co-founder and at the time of this comment, CEO of Microsoft Corporation, quoted in *The New York Times* on October 8, 1997

October 9, 2017
Monday
Columbus Day (observed)

Objectives & reminders

____

____

Appointments

Early morning

8 a.m.

9 a.m.

10 a.m.

11 a.m.

Noon

1 p.m.

2 p.m.

3 p.m.

4 p.m.

5 p.m.

6 p.m.

Later evening

"Land ho!"

October 12, 1492, was a landmark day in the Americas and the beginning of a new era of exploration by Europeans. That's the day when Christopher Columbus and his crew of 90 first sighted land in the "New World." Today, while the U.S. recognizes October 12 as the original Columbus Day, since 1971 it's the second Monday in October – today! -- that's set aside to celebrate the occasion. However, several other countries in the Americas continue to celebrate Columbus's initial voyage on October 12 – although, as the accompanying box shows, they do not always refer to it as "Columbus Day," per se.

Columbus Day's many aliases
While Mexico, Argentina and Chile celebrate Día de la Raza (Day of the Race) on October 12, Discovery Day is celebrated in the Bahamas. Meanwhile, Costa Rica enjoys Día de las Culturas (Day of the Cultures), Spain observes Día de la Hispanidad (Hispanic Day), and Venezuela commemorates Día de la Resistencia Indígena (Day of Indigenous Resistance).

Despite today's widespread celebration of Columbus's arrival in the New World, it wasn't until October 12, 1792, that the first recorded Columbus Day celebration was held in the United States. One hundred years after that, in 1892, U.S. President Benjamin Harrison issued a proclamation urging the country to recognize and celebrate Columbus Day. Since then, a variety of parades, school programs, festivals, social gatherings, and decorations have become part of Columbus Day celebrations. While banks and federal offices (including post offices) in the U.S. are typically closed on Columbus Day, retailers often celebrate with Columbus Day sales or other events.

Columbus Day intercepted

Although most of the Americas celebrate Christopher Columbus's first visit to the New World in 1492, history suggests that Columbus wasn't the first European explorer to stumble upon the North American continent. That distinction goes to the Norse explorer Leif Eriksson, who arrived in the 11th century. Accordingly, in 1964, U.S. President Johnson proclaimed October 9 to be Leif Eriksson Day.

October 10, 2017
Tuesday

Objectives & reminders

____

____

____

Appointments

Early morning

8 a.m.

9 a.m.

10 a.m.

11 a.m.

Noon

1 p.m.

2 p.m.

3 p.m.

4 p.m.

5 p.m.

6 p.m.

Later evening

Happy birthday: Earle Dickson

Born on October 10, 1892, Dickson was a cotton buyer at Johnson & Johnson when he prepared some ready-made bandages for his accident-prone wife by placing cotton gauze on adhesive strips. In 1924, when Dickson's boss, James Johnson learned of Dickson's innovative solution to minor injuries, he decided to mass produce the adhesive bandages. The Band-Aid brand was born.

Hundreds of millions of Band-Aids were sold and the brand became so dominate in its category that it became somewhat genericized, meaning that many consumers referred to all adhesive bandages in the product category as "Band-Aids."

Over time, the brand acquired an additional meaning as well – referring to quick, easy, and perhaps temporary solutions to problems. However, as Malcolm Gladwell asserts in the accompanying box, Band-Aids should be saluted and the value of "Band-Aid solutions" should not automatically be discounted.

Band-Aid solutions

"The Band-Aid is an inexpensive, convenient, and remarkably versatile solution to an astonishing array of problems. In their history, Band-Aids have probably allowed millions of people to keep working or playing tennis or cooking or walking when they would otherwise have had to stop. The Band-Aid solution is actually the best kind of solution because it involves solving a problem with the minimum amount of effort and time and cost... There are times when we need a convenient shortcut, a way to make a lot out of a little..." – Malcolm Gladwell, *The Tipping Point*, pp. 256-257

Good day to write a "not to do" list?

"Besides the noble art of getting things done, there is the noble art of leaving things undone. The wisdom of life consists in the elimination of non-essentials." – Lin Yutang, Chinese philosopher and writer, born on October 10, 1895

October 11, 2017
Wednesday

Objectives & reminders

Appointments

Early morning

8 a.m.

9 a.m.

10 a.m.

11 a.m.

Noon

1 p.m.

2 p.m.

3 p.m.

4 p.m.

5 p.m.

6 p.m.

Later evening

Benefit bundles

To differentiate themselves from other businesses and increase customers' perceptions of value, firms often think in terms of providing *bundles* of benefits. In 1919, for example, the airline Handley Page Transport viewed air travel as more than simply transportation. Rather, the small airline began to focus on their customers' flying "experience." Accordingly, on October 11, 1919, they became the first airline to provide passengers with in-flight meals. The pre-packed boxed lunches became part of the London-to-Paris experience. Almost two and a half years later, the first "steward" took to the air. About 1925, in-flight *hot* meals started to appear.

Happy birthday: Charles Revson

While London-to-Paris passengers were enjoying the first in-flight boxed lunches, a young man in Manchester, New Hampshire celebrated his 13th birthday -- Charles Revson. Within a few years, Revson had gained some business experience working for a cosmetic firm, but quit his job while still in his mid-20s to team with his brother and a chemist to launch what would become one of the largest cosmetics firms in the world, Revlon.

Cosmetic benefit bundles

Like Handley Page Transport, Revson was interested in the larger bundle of benefits that customers experienced. A big part of the experiential bundle was *hope*: "[C]onsumers approach each jar of skin cream or tube of makeup with the hope that it will make their lives just a little bit better... In the factory we make cosmetics; in the drug store we sell hope."

More than cosmetic changes!

"In the long run, we shape our lives, and we shape ourselves. The process never ends until we die. And the choices we make are ultimately our own responsibility." – Eleanor Roosevelt, social reformer, newspaper columnist, delegate to the United Nations General Assembly, and First Lady (1933-1945), born on October 11, 1884

October 12, 2017
Thursday

Objectives & reminders

Appointments

Early morning

8 a.m.

9 a.m.

10 a.m.

11 a.m.

Noon

1 p.m.

2 p.m.

3 p.m.

4 p.m.

5 p.m.

6 p.m.

Later evening

Business birthdays on October 12

1803 Alexander Turney Stewart – retailing entrepreneur who opened several large stores in the U.S. and Europe, including a women's store called the Marble Palace (New York City) in 1848.

Rolling the innovation marbles
Reinforcing the principle that demonstrated products are more likely to be sold than non-demonstrated products, the Marble Palace was the first store to stage in-store fashion shows for customers.

1897 Samuel Joseph Cohen – co-founder of Canadian-based Army & Navy surplus stores and mail-order catalog, known for avoiding publicity (once told a reporter, "If I want any advertising, I'll pay for it.").

1923 Jean Nidetch – founded Weight Watchers in 1963. Nidetch understood the important role that a strong support system plays in helping people to reach their goals.

1939 Phil Romano – entrepreneur who founded innovative restaurant chains such as Fuddrucker's, Romano's Macaroni Grill, and EatZi's Market and Bakery. Romano is known for his creativity and ability to differentiate his restaurant creations from "ordinary" dining establishments.

More than food for thought
"The restaurant business is show business, but instead of acting for people, you are interacting for people." – Phil Romano

1946 Mary F. Sammons – former president and CEO of Rite Aid Corporation (drug stores), known for encouraging employee involvement in shaping the company's future.

1950 Paul Otellini – former president and CEO of Intel Corporation, known for his "Zen-like" leadership style.

October 13, 2017
Friday

Objectives & reminders

Appointments

Early morning

8 a.m.

9 a.m.

10 a.m.

11 a.m.

Noon

1 p.m.

2 p.m.

3 p.m.

4 p.m.

5 p.m.

6 p.m.

Later evening

Marketing myopia

1893 was a difficult year for railroads in the United States. Several found themselves deep in debt with plummeting stock prices. For some, bankruptcy was eminent. For the Union Pacific, Friday the 13th of October in 1893 proved to be a particularly unfortunate day, as the troubled railroad announced it was in receivership. Even more troubling for the railroads were emerging technologies that would give rise to competing transportation industries – trucking and aviation.

Kicking the competition when down
On October 13, 1894 (the one-year anniversary of the Union Pacific's bankruptcy announcement), the design of the first gasoline-powered truck was completed. The truck was built by the Panhard works in Paris and was almost ten feet long, including an open rear platform (for cargo) which was about half the length of the truck.

Almost seven decades later, in his classic article, "Marketing Myopia," Harvard University business professor Theodore Levitt blamed much of the railroads' woes on their own myopic perception of their business. Levitt claimed that the railroads defined themselves too narrowly -- as in the *railroad* business, rather than in the broader *transportation* business. Had they defined themselves more broadly, the railroads might have been able to capitalize on the soon-to-emerge trucking and airplane technologies which gobbled-up huge portions of what had been the railroads' share of the transportation market. In fairness to the railroads, however, subsequent analysis has found that the railroads did make some attempts to diversify, but their efforts were blocked by government agencies.

Kicking them again
As if trucking wasn't enough competition for railroads, airlines followed a few years later. For example, on October 13, 1926, TWA was founded.

October 14, 2017
Saturday

Lipschitz as a brand?

Objectives & reminders

____

____

Appointments

Early morning

8 a.m.

9 a.m.

10 a.m.

11 a.m.

Noon

1 p.m.

2 p.m.

3 p.m.

4 p.m.

5 p.m.

6 p.m.

Later evening

Good day to be helpful

"You cannot live a perfect day without doing something for someone who will never be able to repay you." – John Wooden, legendary basketball coach of the UCLA Bruins whose teams once won ten NCAA championships in a span of 12 years, born on October 14, 1910

Happy birthday: Ralph Lauren

Born in New York City as Ralph Lipschitz on October 14, 1939, Lauren worked as a salesman for Brooks Brothers early in his career and then started his own tie business in 1968. From there, he went on to become one of the most widely recognized and successful fashion designers in America. His casual ready-to-wear "western-look" clothes were well received when launched in the mid-1970s. In the 1980s, Lauren added more clothing designs and expanded further into home decorations (e.g., rugs, drapes, linens, etc.). Today, the Lauren empire rakes in an estimated $5 billion in annual revenues.

People as brands
When individuals become closely associated with their businesses or products, their names can, in effect, become brands. Ralph Lauren is a great example. But like any brand, the judicious choice of the brand name can play a pivotal role in the brand's success. Do you think his brand would be as successful today had Ralph Lipschitz not changed his name?

Knowledge of customer requirements ➔ Quality ➔ Loyal Customers ➔ Profits ➔ ☺

"Profits come from loyal customers. Loyal customers are created by offering high-quality products. Because only the customer can determine what a high-quality product is, the aim of business should be to find out what the customer wants." – W. Edwards Deming, quality consultant who pioneered processes such as statistical quality control (SQC) and total quality management (TQM). Deming was born in Sioux City, Iowa on October 14, 1900.

October 15, 2017
Sunday

Objectives & reminders

Appointments

Early morning

8 a.m.

9 a.m.

10 a.m.

11 a.m.

Noon

1 p.m.

2 p.m.

3 p.m.

4 p.m.

5 p.m.

6 p.m.

Later evening

Focus on the end, but be flexible on the means

"Many are stubborn in pursuit of the path they have chosen, few in pursuit of the goal." – Friedrich Wilhelm Nietzsche, psychologist who studied the nature of human motivation, born on October 15, 1844

Learning from past decisions

"Everyone needs to establish a system for learning from the results of past decisions... At minimum, managers should sit down for a few hours twice a year with their associates to look back. Have they been collecting enough data to keep track of the lessons of experience? What have they learned in the past six months? How should it change their future work?" – J. Edward Russo and Paul J.H. Schoemaker, in *Decision Traps: Ten Barriers to Brilliant Decision-Making and How to Overcome Them* (p. 3). This thought-provoking and highly-recommended book for decision-makers was published on October 15, 1990.

Top executive learns from examining past decisions

"Invariably, the mistakes you look back on with regret involve situations where you played it too safe. In our case, we decided for a period of time to follow instead of lead. As a consequence, we fell back into mimicking and reacting to what others were doing instead of deciding that leadership was the way we needed to go." – Mike Volkema, president and CEO of Herman Miller, Inc. (multi-billion dollar furniture manufacturer), born on October 15, 1955

Investors too should learn from the past

"Financial memory from one period of sophisticated stupidity to another is about 10 to 15 years... [A]ny new generation getting rich has a vested interest in euphoria." – John Kenneth Galbraith, American economist and diplomat, born on October 15, 1908

October 16, 2017
Monday

Objectives & reminders

____

____

____

Appointments

Early morning

8 a.m.

9 a.m.

10 a.m.

11 a.m.

Noon

1 p.m.

2 p.m.

3 p.m.

4 p.m.

5 p.m.

6 p.m.

Later evening

Watch what you say

Better known by her pen name, Ann Landers, advice columnist Esther Friedman had her first advice column published in the *Chicago Sun-Times* on October 16, 1955. The popularity of her straightforward, no-nonsense advice soon launched her column into syndication.

Friedman's columns frequently advise readers to exercise caution and tact when responding to what others say and do. Sometimes a callous and inconsiderate remark can prove to be one's downfall, so choose your words carefully. The wisdom of this commonsensical advice rang true in 1793 when France's Queen Marie Antoinette was informed of the plight of the poor in Paris, i.e., "they have no bread." Without benefit of Friedman's advice at the time, the Queen retorted, "Then let them eat cake." As a result, her insensitive remark led to her downfall and caused her to lose her head, literally, on October 16, 1793.

Tips to avoid losing your head

People are more prone to losing their composure under some circumstances than during others. Be particularly alert to what you say when:

- You are tired, hungry, uncomfortable, or otherwise not feeling well. Of course, try to avoid these circumstances.
- You are blamed for a mistake you did not commit. Address the situation with accurate information, not with counter-accusations.
- Others are angry or shouting. Resist the temptation to respond in a like manner.
- You are distracted from what you believe to be an important task. Remember that interruptions may be important too, and often are unavoidable.
- You are losing. When performance is sub-par, resist the temptation to lash out at others; focus on what *you* can do.
- The clock is ticking. However, time pressure doesn't alleviate the need for a thoughtful choice of words.
- You are surrounded by fools. Be patient; they may be unaware of their foolishness!

October 17, 2017
Tuesday

Objectives & reminders

____

____

____

Appointments

Early morning

8 a.m.

9 a.m.

10 a.m.

11 a.m.

Noon

1 p.m.

2 p.m.

3 p.m.

4 p.m.

5 p.m.

6 p.m.

Later evening

Happy shopping: Agree or disagree?

"Years ago a person, he was unhappy, didn't know what to do with himself -- he'd go to church, start a revolution -- *something*. Today you're unhappy? Can't figure it out? What is the salvation? Go shopping." -- Arthur Miller, in *The Price* (1968). Miller was a Pulitzer Prize-winning playwright born on October 17, 1915.

Problem-solving insight

"I have yet to see any problem, however complicated, which, when you looked at it in the right way, did not become still more complicated." – Poul Anderson, American writer, born on October 17, 1932

Business-relevant U.S. legislation on October 17

1986 Superfund refunded. President Reagan signed into law legislation that pumped another nine billion dollars into the Environmental Protection Agency's "Superfund" program to clean up toxic waste sites throughout the country.

Originally established in 1980, by fall 1986 the Superfund was within weeks of running out of money, yet hundreds of toxic waste sites were still waiting to be cleaned. In addition to providing the needed funds, the legislation also contained "community-right-to-know" provisions that required chemical producers to notify local communities of potentially harmful chemicals used or manufactured in the community.

2005 The Bankruptcy Abuse Prevention and Consumer Protection Act went into effect. The Act's multiple provisions made it more difficult for consumers to use bankruptcy as an escape vehicle to avoid their debts. Although controversial, by requiring consumers to assume greater responsibility for repaying their debts, the Act reduced business risk associated with consumer credit-granting practices.

October 18, 2017
Wednesday

Objectives & reminders

____

____

____

Appointments

Early morning

8 a.m.

9 a.m.

10 a.m.

11 a.m.

Noon

1 p.m.

2 p.m.

3 p.m.

4 p.m.

5 p.m.

6 p.m.

Later evening

Watch what you say (another reason)

On October 18, 1982, *The New York Times* reported that U.S. President Ronald Reagan failed to watch what he said during a radio sound test when he remarked, "My fellow Americans, the economy is a hell of a mess." He then asked, "We're not connected to the press now yet are we?" Unfortunately for President Reagan, the answer was "yes."

Party matters: Agree or disagree? Critics of *The New York Times* might point out that the newspaper would have not printed Reagan's slip if he were a Democrat instead of a Republican. Do you agree? Does it matter? Coincidentally, journalist Abbott Joseph Liebling was born on October 18, 1904. Consider his comment that, "Freedom of the press belongs to those who own one."

Leadership 101: The courage to make decisions

"In the end you have to have the guts to make a decision. You'll never have all the data you need. You'll never be able to sort through all the alternatives and threats and risks… You get the right information and couple it with the right instincts to enable you [to] make a decision. Then you energize your organization to make that decision work in the marketplace." – Mike Armstrong, chairman and CEO of IBM World Trade Corp. (1992-1993), Hughes Electronics (1993-1997), and AT&T Corporation (1997-2002); and chairman of Comcast Corporation (2002-2003). Armstrong was born in Detroit, Michigan on October 18, 1938.

Co-operation is key

"The three great forces for the improvement of mankind are religion, temperance and co-operation; and, as a commercial force, supported and sustained by the other two, co-operation is the greatest, noblest and most likely to be successful in the redemption of the industrial classes." – John Thomas Whitehead Mitchell, chairman of the Co-operative Wholesale Society in Great Britain from 1869 to 1895, born on October 18, 1828

October 19, 2017
Thursday

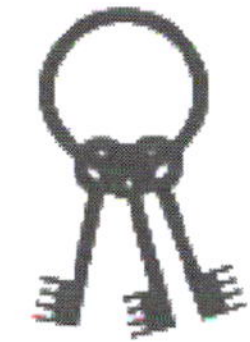

Objectives & reminders

___

___

___

Appointments

Early morning

8 a.m.

9 a.m.

10 a.m.

11 a.m.

Noon

1 p.m.

2 p.m.

3 p.m.

4 p.m.

5 p.m.

6 p.m.

Later evening

Expanding the market

"Bring Wall Street to Main Street" was the philosophy espoused by Charles Merrill, who founded Merrill Lynch & Co. in 1940. Merrill was instrumental in opening the door of investing for ordinary Americans (before Merrill, investing was a world that belonged to insiders and the affluent). Accordingly, Merrill greatly expanded the market for investments by publishing and distributing millions of educational pamphlets (e.g., *How to Invest*), conducting countless seminars, and even setting up exhibits at county fairs to reach the mass-market of consumers. By the time of his death in 1956, the company Merrill founded was serving about 400,000 clients. Today, investment marketers continue to use many of the marketing practices pioneered by Merrill who was born in Green Cove Springs, Florida on October 19, 1885.

The appeal of mass markets: Diversification of the customer mix
"Having thousands of customers scattered throughout the United States is infinitely preferable to being dependent upon the fluctuating buying power of smaller and perhaps on the whole wealthier group of investors in any one section." – Charles Merrill

Another appeal of mass markets: Avoiding the wrath of competition
One way to avoid the retaliation of competitors is to serve "new" or underserved markets that competitors are not interested in serving. That's one reason why many products originally targeted toward affluent consumers are later marketed to mass-markets.

Decision-making: Three more keys

Born in Pennsylvania on October 19, 1909, William H. Newman was a business professor at Columbia University for most of his career. In his 1950 classic, *Administrative Action: The Techniques of Organization and Management*, Dr. Newman encouraged business executives to be mindful of three fundamental decision-making guidelines:

- "Be sure to get the facts.
- Adjust to individual personalities.
- Consider the whole situation." (p. 463)

October 20, 2017
Friday

Objectives & reminders

____

____

____

Appointments

Early morning

8 a.m.

9 a.m.

10 a.m.

11 a.m.

Noon

1 p.m.

2 p.m.

3 p.m.

4 p.m.

5 p.m.

6 p.m.

Later evening

"Bullseye" code patented

On October 20, 1949, Bernard Silver and Norman Joseph Woodland received a patent for their "bullseye code" -- the initial technology we now refer to as bar codes or Universal Product Codes (UPCs). Their original bullseye code consisted of a series of concentric circles that could be scanned with regular light from any angle. Throughout the 1950s Silver and Woodland, among others, improved the original concept and received additional patents, but another quarter of a century passed before UPC technology was used at the check-out aisles in retail stores.

Today, UPCs may be found on products or packages and include a variety of useful information about each item – e.g., price, name, size, description, manufacturer, lot, expiration date, and so on. UPCs and the scanning equipment that read them help retailers track and manage inventory efficiently. The technology also saves labor costs by avoiding the time-consuming chore of price-marking individual items. Scanning UPCs also speeds the check-out process, which further reduces labor costs and slashes waiting time.

UPC alert for budding manufacturing entrepreneurs

UPCs are so central to some retailers' operations that they refuse to carry merchandise that do not include UPCs printed on the merchandise, package or label. Some retailers will affix scanable UPC stickers to merchandise that don't already have them, but they may insist upon a fee for doing so.

*Si*ght, *so*und, *mo*tion

"Television is the greatest selling mechanism ever invented because it combines sight, sound and motion. We call this Sisomo. Sisomo has a guaranteed emotional outcome. Sisomo allows us to feel meaning. Sisomo is the playground of the mind. Sisomo is a medium for the senses. When does anyone ever watch television with their rationality in high gear?!" – Kevin Roberts, current Executive Chairman and former CEO (1997-2014) of Saatchi & Saatchi ad agency, born in Lancaster, England on October 20, 1949

October 21, 2017
Saturday

Objectives & reminders

____

____

____

Appointments

Early morning

8 a.m.

9 a.m.

10 a.m.

11 a.m.

Noon

1 p.m.

2 p.m.

3 p.m.

4 p.m.

5 p.m.

6 p.m.

Later evening

Turn on the lights! 

After thousands of experiments, Thomas A. Edison's efforts to create a lamp using incandescent electric light finally paid off. Edison himself described the captivating breakthrough:

> "The day was -- let me see -- October 21, 1879. We sat and looked and the lamp continued to burn and the longer it burned the more fascinated we were. None of us could go to bed and there was no sleep for over 40 hours; we sat and just watched it with anxiety growing into elation. It lasted about 45 hours and then I said, 'If it will burn 40 hours now I know I can make it burn a hundred.'"

Edison received a patent for his invention in January 1880.

> **A patently productive life**
> Thomas A. Edison holds a record number of *significant* patents. During his life he was granted 1,093 patents.

Turn off the lights ☹

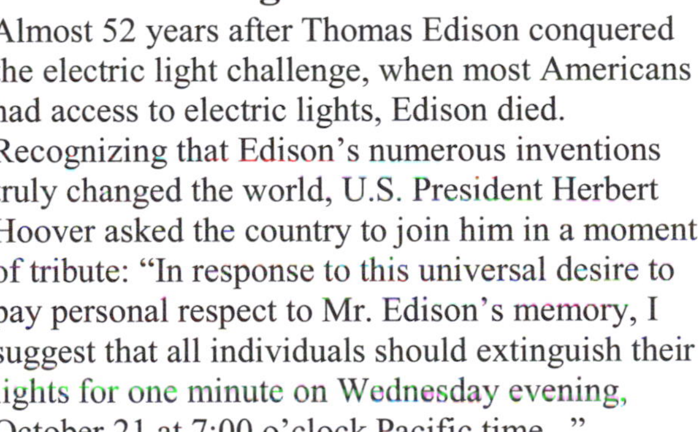

Almost 52 years after Thomas Edison conquered the electric light challenge, when most Americans had access to electric lights, Edison died. Recognizing that Edison's numerous inventions truly changed the world, U.S. President Herbert Hoover asked the country to join him in a moment of tribute: "In response to this universal desire to pay personal respect to Mr. Edison's memory, I suggest that all individuals should extinguish their lights for one minute on Wednesday evening, October 21 at 7:00 o'clock Pacific time..."

Hoover had considered asking power plants across the country to simply cut power for one minute but decided against doing so,

> "because of the many services dependent upon electrical power in protection from fire, the operation of water supply, sanitation, elevators, operations in hospitals and the vast number of activities which, if halted even for an instant, would result in death somewhere in the country... This Demonstration of the dependence of the country upon electrical current for its life and health is in itself a monument to Mr. Edison's genius."

October 22, 2017
Sunday

Objectives & reminders

___

___

___

Appointments

Early morning

8 a.m.

9 a.m.

10 a.m.

11 a.m.

Noon

1 p.m.

2 p.m.

3 p.m.

4 p.m.

5 p.m.

6 p.m.

Later evening

Watch what you say today

☺ Sometimes it's better not to ask

Once the French actress Sarah Bernhardt (born on October 22, 1844) was asked by a male companion, "Do you mind if I smoke?" Bernhardt replied, "I don't care if you burn."

☺ What you say could be held against you in the court of public opinion

When a judge asked Jerome "Curly" Howard (one of "The Three Stooges") if he swore, Curly explained, "No, but I know all da woids." Howard was born on October 22, 1903.

☺ If you can't say something nice about someone, perhaps you should not say anything at all

Apparently actress Constance Bennett was not familiar with this point of verbal etiquette when she took a jab at fellow-actress Marilyn Monroe: "[She's] a broad with a big future behind her." Bennett was born on October 22, 1905.

☺ Just say "don't know"

According to drug abuse advocate Timothy Leary, "there are three side effects of acid [LSD] -- enhanced long-term memory, decreased short-term memory, and I forget the third." Leary thought he was born on October 22, 1920.

> **Counter-culture rallying cry**
> "Turn on, tune in, drop out."
> -- Timothy Leary

It's too bad Leary didn't commit himself to finding an acid healthier to ingest than LSD. Fortunately, American biochemist Charles Glen King did. Born on October 22, 1896, King studied lemon juice, among other things. After five years of research, in 1932 King was the first to isolate ascorbic acid, also known as Vitamin C. Not surprisingly, King lived much longer than Leary.

October 23, 2017
Monday

Objectives & reminders

____

____

____

Appointments

Early morning

8 a.m.

9 a.m.

10 a.m.

11 a.m.

Noon

1 p.m.

2 p.m.

3 p.m.

4 p.m.

5 p.m.

6 p.m.

Later evening

Happy birthday: Anita Roddick

Born in Littlehampton, Sussex, England on October 23, 1942, Roddick had no business training before opening her first bath and cosmetics store in 1976 – The Body Shop. What she did have was a deep concern for the environment and human rights, coupled with a strong belief that businesses should be socially responsible. She believed that how companies operate and *how* they make money is more important than the *amount* of money they make. Accordingly, as Roddick's business grew into an increasingly larger and larger chain of stores, she insisted that her company conduct and publish a social responsibility audit to account for its behavior; moreover, she insisted that other companies do the same.

Although somewhat controversial, Roddick was not afraid of using The Body Shop's global presence and extensive communications to advocate her position on social issues – thus referring to her company as, "a skin and haircare company with attitude."

For more information
To learn more about The Body Shop and Anita Roddick's view of business, read her book, *Business as Unusual*, published on recycled paper by Thorsons (HarperCollins).

In 2004, consumers voted The Body Shop as the second most trusted brand in the United Kingdom. Also in 2004, a survey of British business managers found that 17 percent said that Anita Roddick had most influenced their own management style, second only to Virgin's Richard Branson who garnered 52 percent of the votes. Today, more than 2,500 Body Shop stores serve millions of customers in 60+ countries throughout the world.

Business should be more socially responsible: Agree or disagree?
"We must include in our measures of success enough to sustain communities, cultures and families, and the consequences will be severe unless we do so. The prevailing view of trade could be described as commerce without conscience. And conscience is a key to the way out." – Anita Roddick

October 24, 2017
Tuesday

Objectives & reminders

____

____

____

Appointments

Early morning

8 a.m.

9 a.m.

10 a.m.

11 a.m.

Noon

1 p.m.

2 p.m.

3 p.m.

4 p.m.

5 p.m.

6 p.m.

Later evening

Opening the doors

Gordon Bethune became the CEO of struggling Continental Airlines on October 24, 1994. Almost immediately he began to turn the company around. One of his first decisions on his first day on the job was to establish an open-door policy:

> "I opened the doors... [Before I arrived on the job the] doors to the executive suite were locked, and you needed an ID to get through. Security cameras [were also present]... So the day I began running the company, I opened the doors. I wasn't afraid of my employees, and I wanted everybody to know it."

First comic strip

On October 24, 1897, the first newspaper comic strip was published in the Sunday supplement of the *New York Journal*. Written by Richard Outcault, the initial six-panel episode was titled "The Yellow Kid Takes a Hand at Golf." It illustrated the antics of the strip's key character, "The Yellow Kid" (depicted above), struggling to hit a golf ball but hitting everything else instead.

Today, newspaper comic strips are more than amusing. They help newspapers attract and maintain audiences. For example, data provided by the Newspaper Association of America (NAA) indicates that 39 percent of U.S. daily newspapers' *adult* readers "usually" read the comics section, which as the accompanying box indicates, compares favorably with many other newspaper sections. Knowing which sections of a newspaper are most frequently read gives advertisers a sense of where to place their ads within the newspaper.

Where to place newspaper ads?
Percent of weekly *adult* audience that usually read these sections:

Main news	87
Local news	85
Entertainment	45
Sports	55
Comics	**39**
Business/finance	43
Food/cooking	38
Classified	38

For more detailed information...
See the NAA's website, www.naa.org

October 25, 2017
Wednesday

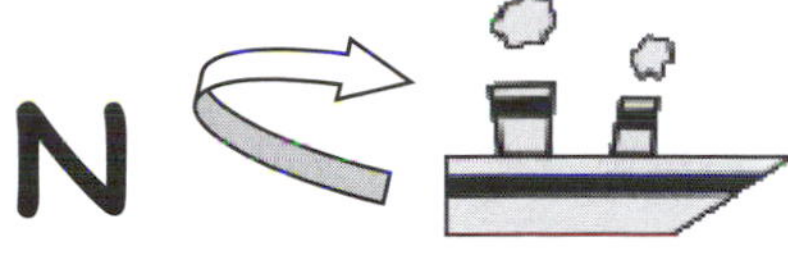

Objectives & reminders

____

____

____

Appointments

Early morning

8 a.m.

9 a.m.

10 a.m.

11 a.m.

Noon

1 p.m.

2 p.m.

3 p.m.

4 p.m.

5 p.m.

6 p.m.

Later evening

Every salesperson's fantasy

What's the Number 1 (printable) fantasy that salespeople share? It's the dream of generating more orders than the company's factories can fill. Such fantasies are rarely realized in today's highly efficient manufacturing environments, but they were realized by one automobile sales rep in 1907 -- John North Willys.

Born in Canandaigua, New York on October 25, 1873, Willys's ability to out-pace his supplier's production capabilities prompted him to take over and reorganize the struggling Overland Company (renamed Willys-Overland) in Indianapolis, Indiana. His efforts were instrumental in increasing the company's production output -- so much so that between 1912 and 1918, Willys-Overland's output was second only to Henry Ford's Ford Motor Company.

Thinking about an internship?

Several business leaders have launched their careers with the help of internships. One example is Steven R. Rogel. In 1964, the 21-year-old college student from the University of Washington in Seattle worked as a summer intern for St. Regis Paper Company. The experience convinced him to continue his life's work in the forest-products industry. By 1995, Rogel had become the president and CEO of Willamette Industries. Two years later, in 1997, Rogel was named President and CEO of Weyerhaeuser Company, then Chairman in 1999.

Rogel on internships
"They bring you into the real world. Even though I was a chemical engineer and had opportunities to enter the chemical and oil industries, I chose forest products." – Steven R. Rogel, born on October 25, 1942

Good day to study, in preparation for internship application

"Most people have the will to win, few have the will to prepare to win." – Bobby Knight, former college basketball coach (West Point, Indiana University, Texas Tech University), born in Massillon, Ohio on October 25, 1940

October 26, 2017
Thursday

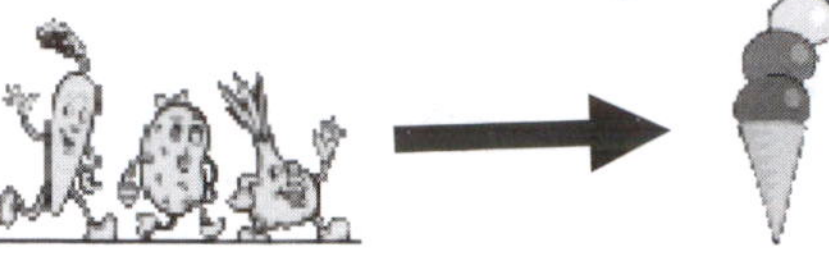

Objectives & reminders

____

____

____

Appointments

Early morning

8 a.m.

9 a.m.

10 a.m.

11 a.m.

Noon

1 p.m.

2 p.m.

3 p.m.

4 p.m.

5 p.m.

6 p.m.

Later evening

Happy birthday: David Premack

Born in Aberdeen, South Dakota on October 26, 1925, Premack enjoyed a successful career as a psychologist and academic. Learning and motivation were among his many interests. Particularly relevant to business managers is his research and articulation of the "Premack principle" which states that the desirability of an undesirable (low-probability) task tends to increase when it is linked to a more desirable (higher-probability) task.

Today, managers routinely employ the Premack principle to motivate workers. Examples: Entry level workers are told that promotions and higher pay await them if they work hard and learn the business from the ground up. A team is promised a pizza party at the end of the week if an important deadline is met. A fatigued employee is promised a "sit-down" job in the afternoon if he or she finishes the physically demanding job of unloading the supply truck in the morning.

What Moms already knew

- "David, if you eat your vegetables you can have a marbleous dessert!"
- "Yes David, you may play a game of marbles *after* you do your homework."
  – promises Sonja Premack may have made to her son in the 1930s

---

Positive thinking matters: Agree or agree?

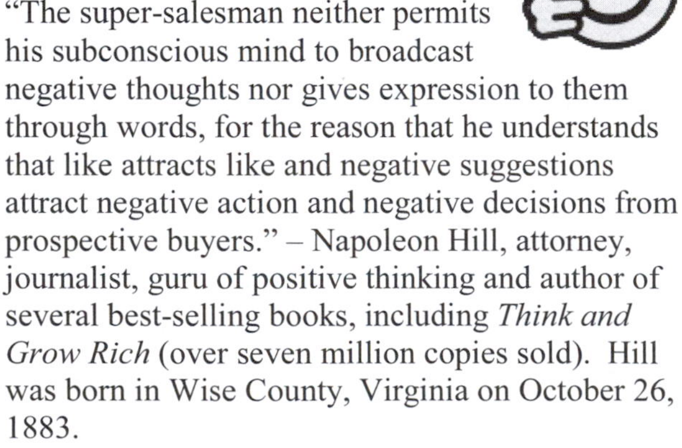

"The super-salesman neither permits his subconscious mind to broadcast negative thoughts nor gives expression to them through words, for the reason that he understands that like attracts like and negative suggestions attract negative action and negative decisions from prospective buyers." – Napoleon Hill, attorney, journalist, guru of positive thinking and author of several best-selling books, including *Think and Grow Rich* (over seven million copies sold). Hill was born in Wise County, Virginia on October 26, 1883.

October 27, 2017
Friday

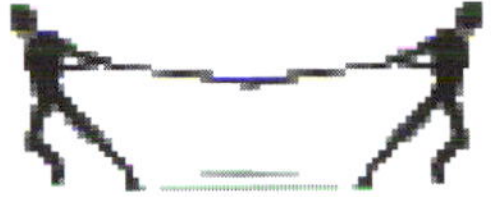

Objectives & reminders

___

___

___

Appointments

Early morning

8 a.m.

9 a.m.

10 a.m.

11 a.m.

Noon

1 p.m.

2 p.m.

3 p.m.

4 p.m.

5 p.m.

6 p.m.

Later evening

"Business cycle" explained with metaphors

Born in Van Hornesville, New York on October 27, 1874, Owen D. Young began his career as a lawyer, then went to work for General Electric in 1913. About nine years later, in 1922, Young was named chairman of the company. Among his many talents, he was able to see the "big picture" of business and was a masterful communicator. For example, in 1924, only five years after the phrase "business cycle" entered the language of business, Young used metaphors to vividly explain the concept:

> "The business cycle is the movement of business over any given period. Like a stream, it finds its way between and around obstacles. It is influenced by many different forces acting and counteracting, but its course is ever onward. The principal influencing forces are political, economic, and psychological. The strength of the respective influences varies. Or take it in another way. The cycle is the rope in a terrific tug of war – now the rope goes this way, now that. It rests when the pulls are exactly equal."

Love is the answer

Years before terms such as "relationship management," "relationship marketing," and "customer intimacy" were routinely batted about by businesses, advertising executive Mary Wells talked about the importance of love in advertising -- love of the audience and love of the advertised item. On October 27, 1967, she was quoted in *Life* magazine explaining her philosophy of advertising:

> "*Love* is the key word. Too many ads are too cold, too filled with jargon. You have to talk person-to-person with people, use *people* words and *people* terms. You have to touch them, show humanness and warmth, charm them with funny vignettes. You have to make them feel good about a product so they'll love you."

October 28, 2017
Saturday

Objectives & reminders

____

____

____

Appointments

Early morning

8 a.m.

9 a.m.

10 a.m.

11 a.m.

Noon

1 p.m.

2 p.m.

3 p.m.

4 p.m.

5 p.m.

6 p.m.

Later evening

Effective sales proposals stress value and inspire buyer confidence

Members of an academic think tank at Portsmouth University conducted research to investigate the criteria that business buyers use to evaluate sales proposals. The study, released on October 28, 2005, found that price, per se, was not the most important purchase criterion. Rather, buyers were interested in knowing the purchases' lifetime costs relative to the long-term value to the business. And they wanted this information "properly quantified."

Further, the research found that buyers' confidence in suppliers was an important consideration. When confidence is absent, the perceived risk of doing business with a particular supplier may be too high. Accordingly, sales proposals that gain buyers' confidence are more likely to be accepted than those that fail the confidence test. Think tank leader Trevor Andrews put it this way:

> "Buyers are looking for confidence in their supplier and we found this took priority over price. In particular, this confidence was generated by suppliers' professionalism in taking time to understand their business – its implicit needs now and in the future. Too often, buyers complained that the salesperson hadn't understood their business or established their needs."
>
> "We found risk was a big factor buying companies took into consideration. 'Can this company do what it says? Can they support us in the long term? Is it too risky to deal with this company?' These were the questions that buyers asked and counted above price. Sellers really do need to take the risk factor into account when making their proposals."

Are we there yet?

"When communication gets inexpensive enough and is combined with other advances in technology, the influence of interactive information will be as real and as far-reaching as the effects of electricity." – Bill Gates, co-founder, and former chairman and CEO of Microsoft Corporation, born on October 28, 1955

October 29, 2017
Sunday

Objectives & reminders

____

____

____

Appointments

Early morning

8 a.m.

9 a.m.

10 a.m.

11 a.m.

Noon

1 p.m.

2 p.m.

3 p.m.

4 p.m.

5 p.m.

6 p.m.

Later evening

"Black Tuesday" in 1929

Optimism is a wonderful thing, except when it turns into blind speculation. That's what happened in 1929 when investors optimistically poured money into the stock market -- often borrowed money. During the late 1920s, "the nation's economy was booming," as one historian put it, "convincing even some of the most cynical souls that America's economy was a powerful machine, capable of spreading wealth and prosperity to the farthest reaches of the land."

The optimism began to falter in early October 1929 when the stock market began to slip and a devastating downward spiral began. Brokers insisted that investors repay the money they had borrowed. In response, investors began selling their stocks to repay their loans, which drove stock prices even lower, prompting more repayment demands, more selling, and so on.

The frenzied spiral hit its bottom on Tuesday, October 29, 1929, when 16.4 million shares were traded on the New York Stock Exchange. When the dust finally settled that day, the value of large industrial stocks had lost almost half of their value in less than three weeks. In the weeks that followed the total losses climbed to $30 billion (an amount equal to almost one-third of the United States' GDP at the time) and directly affected one million investors.

The stock market crash was a major factor leading to the Great Depression that followed. By 1932, stock prices were down about 80 percent from their summer-1929 peak values. By 1933, almost half of American banks had failed and almost 30 percent of the workforce was unemployed. Many investors who had borrowed significant sums of money to invest were financially ruined. Indeed, the decade of the 1930s was a difficult period for the economy and for the people who lived through it.

Today, some consumers and investors remember the Great Depression. Others remember hearing from family elders about the hardships it created. Consequently, a number of seniors today are risk-averse consumers. They live frugally and save for "rainy days." They avoid debt whenever possible and won't let themselves "gamble" in the stock market. So, their buying behaviors and sentiments tend to differ from those of younger consumers who never experienced the Great Depression.

October 30, 2017
Monday

Objectives & reminders

____

____

____

Appointments

Early morning

8 a.m.

9 a.m.

10 a.m.

11 a.m.

Noon

1 p.m.

2 p.m.

3 p.m.

4 p.m.

5 p.m.

6 p.m.

Later evening

Word marketing

Communication is complete when the sender and receiver share the same meaning of a message. Communication fails when the sender intends the message to mean one thing but the receiver interprets ("decodes") it to mean something else. Because communicators' choice of words is likely to affect how audiences interpret messages, people must strive to choose words that convey a shared meaning. That means avoiding words that have ambiguous meanings or unintended connotations.

Recognizing these communication fundamentals, the U.S. Congress passed Public Law 101-476 on October 30, 1990. The law amended the previously passed Education for All Handicapped Children Act by requiring that the word "disability" be used in official communications instead of "handicap."

Salute to salespeople and to their choice of words

"It is the salesman who is the real boss – the real cog in the machine. What he says and does as he faces his prospects and your customers is vitally important to the success of your business. And his success depends, to a great extent, upon the words he uses in the field of selling." – Herbert William Hoover, American industrialist whose family purchased the floundering Electric Suction Sweeper Company in 1908 and began manufacturing vacuum cleaners. Later the company was renamed the Hoover Company and Herbert William Hoover dubbed President. During the early years, the company used some advertising to create buyer awareness and interest, but depended on a large network of salespeople to close sales by demonstrating the vacuum cleaners in consumers' homes. Hoover was born in New Berlin (later renamed North Canton), Ohio on October 30, 1877.

"Recognition" as a key word

"We believe everyone on our team [134,000 employees] is important and deserves our respect... We use, extensively, America's most neglected resource – recognition." – Richard M. Kovacevich, then chairman and CEO of Wells Fargo & Company, born on October 30, 1943

October 31, 2017
Tuesday

Objectives & reminders

____

____

____

Appointments

Early morning

8 a.m.

9 a.m.

10 a.m.

11 a.m.

Noon

1 p.m.

2 p.m.

3 p.m.

4 p.m.

5 p.m.

6 p.m.

Later evening

Boo!

Happy Halloween! Although the history of Halloween has ancient European roots, the holiday as it is now known in America dates back to the 1880s. Today, Halloween celebrations typically center around two separate themes. First, seasonal decorations of food are used to commemorate harvest-time. Food-related contests and activities such as pumpkin-carving and bobbing for apples are popular.

Second, there's a presumably scary dimension to Halloween that stems from the ancient Celtic "day of the dead" during which witches, zombies and ghosts supposedly roamed through communities eating the food and drink left to placate them. This superstition gave rise to the modern-day custom of trick-or-treating involving costumed children roaming from home to home to harvest the neighborhood's candy by asking amused residents "trick or treat?" Haunted houses, costume parties and supernatural decorations play on the "day of the dead" theme.

Halloween is ranked by American children as their second favorite holiday. Christmas is first. However, an increasing number of adults also enjoy Halloween celebrations encouraged or tolerated by employers. For example, Halloween office parties are not uncommon. Promotion-minded businesses involve employees by sponsoring contests to see who can bob for the most apples, or who has the best office decorations, the most effective Halloween-related merchandise display, the scariest costume, the funniest Halloween poem or jingle, or the carved pumpkin that most looks like the boss. Of course, customers can be included in creative Halloween promotions as well.

Trick-or-treat stats

Seventy-eight percent of U.S. households report distributing treats during Halloween, according to the National Retail Federation. The typical U.S. home receives 37 trick-or-treaters on Halloween. Ninety-five percent of the trick-or-treaters say they prefer to receive chocolate.

Make sure you don't lose your marbles in 2018 !

Get a copy of the 2018 edition of *Marketing FAME* from your local bookstore or through our website...
www.MarketingMarbles.com

2018 will be simply marbleous !

"All new stories for 2018 – a calendrical parade of people, events, marketing insights, quotations, ponderable points, tips, career advice, and more."

Remember **PROMOTION CODE RB7229**.
It will be worth something when you reorder through www.MarketingMarbles.com

Bonus marble relations tip

Never roll a marble faster than you would roll your own head.

November 1, 2017
Wednesday

Objectives & reminders

____

____

____

Appointments

Early morning

8 a.m.

9 a.m.

10 a.m.

11 a.m.

Noon

1 p.m.

2 p.m.

3 p.m.

4 p.m.

5 p.m.

6 p.m.

Later evening

Say "yes" to November

"No shade, no shine, no butterflies, no bees,
No fruits, no flowers, no leaves, no birds, --
November!" -- Thomas Hood, 19th century poet and humorist

All Saints Day

This Roman Catholic holiday has been observed on November 1 since 835 when Pope Gregory IV set the day aside to, as historian Mary Hazeltine puts it, "commemorate all the lesser saints who could not have a feast specially set apart for them, as well as all holy men and martyrs whose record had not survived."

McEnvironment Day

On November 1, 1990, McDonald's announced it would begin to phase out its use of polystyrene foam sandwich containers and phase in paper containers in their place. Polystyrene foam is considered environmentally unfriendly because the substance is not particularly biodegradable.

They know, but do you?

November is the month when most farmers have finished their harvests, tallied their yields, and reached their conclusions as to whether the year was a profitable one or not. Not surprisingly, if the year was a good one, farmers are more likely to be in the mood to spend. So, marketers appealing to farmers and rural communities should plan accordingly. Knowing farmers' spending predispositions helps businesses that serve them to plan more effectively. That's why it's a good idea to pay attention to weather reports throughout the year, crop yield data, commodity prices, fuel prices, and other likely indicators of farm profitability.

Trust is a must or the sale is a bust

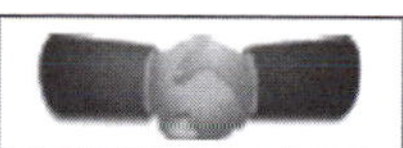

"If a customer trusts me, he will buy from me." – Joe Girard, legendary sales professional who holds the retail record for selling the most automobiles – an average of 18 a week for 14 years. Girard was born on November 1, 1928.

November 2, 2017
Thursday

Objectives & reminders

____

____

____

Appointments

Early morning

8 a.m.

9 a.m.

10 a.m.

11 a.m.

Noon

1 p.m.

2 p.m.

3 p.m.

4 p.m.

5 p.m.

6 p.m.

Later evening

All Souls Day

Immediately following All Saints Day (see November 1), All Souls Day, which is also known as The Day of the Dead, is another Catholic holiday celebrated in many countries throughout the world to commemorate the faithful departed.

All Souls Day is also rooted in ancient Aztec history, so there is some variation in the way the day is interpreted and observed. Generally, however, people who observe the holiday could be expected to attend mass, pray for the souls of their departed loved ones, and visit cemeteries to bless and decorate graves. In many countries, the day is quite a festive occasion; children do not attend school and families enjoy a feast with candy and "Bread of the Dead."

Insights from couponing survey

The findings of a survey of 1,000 American consumers were announced on November 2, 2015. The study, conducted by CreditCards.com, asked consumers about their use of coupons.

One key finding was that 85 percent of the respondents said they use coupons, including 24 percent who reported using them "frequently."

The study also found that despite the fast-growing availability of electronic coupons, 63 percent of those surveyed claimed they most often used paper coupons received in the mail or clipped from newspapers. Typing in discount codes to receive coupons online (17%) or using coupons saved in their smartphones (15%) were less frequently used methods of couponing. Even younger consumers (age 18-24) were about twice more likely to use paper coupons than coupons obtained electronically.

Perhaps lawn and garden retailers should offer discount coupons for tree seedlings?
"Dead trees aren't dead when it comes to coupons." – Matt Schulz, senior analyst of CreditCards.com

November 3, 2017
Friday

Objectives & reminders

______

______

______

Appointments

Early morning

8 a.m.

9 a.m.

10 a.m.

11 a.m.

Noon

1 p.m.

2 p.m.

3 p.m.

4 p.m.

5 p.m.

6 p.m.

Later evening

Cold weather continues

By this time of the season, most – but not all – of the U.S. has experienced one or more freezes. As discussed on September 24, freezes represent both threats and opportunities for many businesses. It follows that cold weather planning can play an important role in offsetting the threats and seizing the opportunities that accompany cold weather.

Generalized planning principle
Knowing when an event is likely to occur potentially enhances an organization's ability to develop plans to respond to the event effectively and efficiently.

However, cold weather planning can be challenging in that freezing temperatures don't necessarily arrive at the same time in some areas as in others, and nature's temperature timetable for one community in one year may not resemble that of the previous year. So, cold weather planning relies heavily on probabilities calculated from historical weather data and provided by the U.S. National Climatic Data Center in Asheville, North Carolina. The list below, provided by the Center, includes a sampling of a few communities that have a 10 percent probability of experiencing one or more instances of autumn freezing temperatures (32 degrees Fahrenheit or lower) on or before November 3. The dates for which the freeze probabilities increase to 50 and 90 percent are noted as well.

Community	*10%*	*50%*	*90%*
Le Grand, CA	Nov 3	Nov 20	Dec 6
Glennville, GA	Nov 3	Nov 18	Dec 4
Huntsville, TX	Nov 3	Nov 27	Dec 20
New Iberia, LA	Nov 3	Nov 23	Dec 14
Uvalde, TX	Nov 3	Nov 17	Dec 1

Did you know?
Short people may be cool
When cold weather arrives it is not uncommon for ground surface temperatures to be four to eight degrees colder (Fahrenheit) than "shelter" temperature readings taken at five feet above the surface. The freeze data reported above generally represent measurements taken at the shelter level.

November 4, 2017
Saturday

Objectives & reminders

____

____

Appointments

Early morning

8 a.m.

9 a.m.

10 a.m.

11 a.m.

Noon

1 p.m.

2 p.m.

3 p.m.

4 p.m.

5 p.m.

6 p.m.

Later evening

Happy birthday: Barbie's Mom

Born in Denver, Colorado on November 4, 1916, Ruth Mosko (later Ruth Handler) was a successful American businesswoman and president of the toy maker, Mattel, Inc. Perhaps she is best known for bringing the Barbie doll into the world in 1959 (before giving birth to Barbie, however, Handler had two life-size children -- not surprisingly named Barbara and Ken).

Conceiving Barbie
"I observed the need, I observed the void in the market. And I defined the characteristics of the product that would fill it." -- Ruth Handler

Since 1959, more than one billion Barbie and Barbie-related dolls have been sold in 150+ countries – making Barbie the world's best-selling doll. Since about 2012, however, Barbie sales have slowed a bit. Part of the decline is attributed to increased competition from Bratz and other dolls, coupled with the core demographic of 3-9 year-old girls constricting to 3-6 year-olds.

The aspiration principle
The success of Barbie dolls may be attributed in part to the dolls' exploitation of what might be called the aspiration principle. That is, people -- including children -- are often less responsive to others who are *like them*, than to those who are *like who they want to become*. As a young girl, for example, Handler's own daughter preferred to play with paper dolls that represented older girls and grown women rather than dolls that represented her own age group.

Today, in advertisements directed toward children, it is common for marketers to use slightly older children as actors or models than to use children that are the same age as those found in the targeted audience. Eight-year-old children aspire to be ten, while ten-year-olds want to be twelve, and so on.

November 5, 2017
Sunday

Objectives & reminders

Appointments

Early morning

8 a.m.

9 a.m.

10 a.m.

11 a.m.

Noon

1 p.m.

2 p.m.

3 p.m.

4 p.m.

5 p.m.

6 p.m.

Later evening

Daylight Saving Time (DST) ends

U.S. time-pieces are moved *back* one hour (at 2:00 a.m.) on the first Sunday in November, today. That is, 2:00 a.m. suddenly becomes 1:00 a.m.

What the end of DST means, in effect, is that sunrise and sunset will occur one hour earlier. The change could have implications for consumers who wish to avoid shopping after sundown or driving in the dark (e.g., for safety and vision reasons). Further, consider how the end of DST might affect the following businesses.

- Retail stores located in *strip shopping centers*?
- Retail stores located in *indoor malls*?
- Quick-service restaurants or banks *with* drive-thru service?
- Quick-service restaurants or banks *without* drive-thru service?

Communication and travel tip
Note that DST is not observed uniformly throughout the U.S. and the rest of the world. Where it is observed, it may begin and end on different dates. Plan accordingly.

Happy birthday: John Berger

Berger was a British author, painter and art critic/historian who was born in London on November 5, 1926. He is probably best known for his book *Ways of Seeing* (1980), which among other topics includes thought-provoking perspectives of the rhetoric of advertising images.

Self-esteem for sale:
Agree or disagree?
"The spectator-buyer is meant to envy herself as she will become if she buys the product. She is meant to imagine herself transformed by the product into an object of envy for others, an envy which will then justify her loving herself. One could put this another way: the publicity image steals her love of herself as she is, and offers it back to her for the price of the product."
-- John Berger, *Ways of Seeing,* p. 134

November 6, 2017
Monday

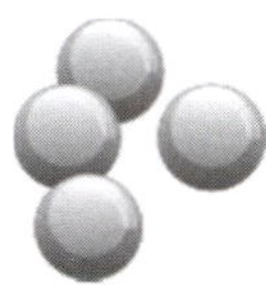

Objectives & reminders

____

____

____

Appointments

Early morning

8 a.m.

9 a.m.

10 a.m.

11 a.m.

Noon

1 p.m.

2 p.m.

3 p.m.

4 p.m.

5 p.m.

6 p.m.

Later evening

Sign of *The Times*

On November 6, 1928, *The New York Times* mounted an animated electric sign atop the Times Building on Times Square in New York. The sign captivated viewers with its electric lights that created the impression that letters and figures on the sign were in motion. As such, the sign was the first of its kind in the United States.

Selected signage principles

P1 Novel signs tend to attract more attention than those that are commonplace.

P2 Signs that incorporate motion tend to be more attention-getting than those that are motionless.

P3 Unless a sign is noticed, the impact of its message is doomed.

According to Gallup

George Gallup, founder of the Gallup polling organization, made significant contributions to the development of market research techniques. Through a number of his company's marketing research studies, he also contributed to the field of advertising in the 1940s and 1950s -- an era when businesses and their ad agencies were too often known for "winging it," i.e., basing advertising decisions on guesses, hunches, whims and personal tastes, rather than on factual, research-based information.

In a 1953 interview with *Printers' Ink* magazine (a key source of information and tips regarding advertising and personal selling at the time), published on November 6, Gallup commented on what makes an effective print or TV advertisement. One of Gallup's recommendations was for advertisers and copywriters to identify and stress "newsy" attributes and issues that relate to the benefits of purchase. Examples include a *new* product, a *new* ingredient, or a *new* price. According to Gallup, newsy information is more credible than empty hype; it helps satisfy buyers' need to know.

November 7, 2017
Tuesday

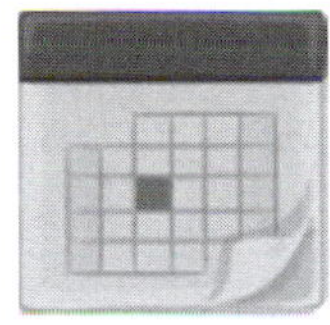

Objectives & reminders

____

____

____

Appointments

Early morning

8 a.m.

9 a.m.

10 a.m.

11 a.m.

Noon

1 p.m.

2 p.m.

3 p.m.

4 p.m.

5 p.m.

6 p.m.

Later evening

Time management is calendar management: Agree or disagree?

"[T]he only for-certain confirmation of the commitment of leaders is the way they spend their time... [T]o signal the need for dramatic change, the calendar must be altered dramatically -- unmistakably enough and visibly enough to overwhelm the growing noise level... [Y]our calendar... is not the calendar of an idiot. It was 'chosen' by you. Perhaps you feel it was foisted on you by superiors, or just grew topsy-turvy... out of maliciousness or mindlessness. And it is true, you are in part a victim -- but never, I contend, decisively so." -- Tom Peters, *Thriving on Chaos*. Peters is a management consultant and prominent business author, born on November 7, 1942.

My way or the highway: Agree or disagree?

"Executive responsibility... requires not merely conformance to a complex code of morals but also the creation of moral codes for others." – Chester I. Barnard, AT&T executive, management thinker, and author of the 1938 business classic, *The Functions of the Executive*. Barnard was born on November 7, 1886.

Leaders as coaches

"The coach's job is not to define every movement or dot every 'i', but to plant the germ of a solution and allow people to discover the answer themselves." – Keith Lockhart, Boston Pops Orchestra conductor, born on November 7, 1959

Small tasks done well lead to bigger ones

"If I set for myself a task, be it so trifling, I shall see it through. How else shall I have confidence in myself to do important things?" – George Samuel Clason, American author and entrepreneur who founded Clason Map Company (publisher of the first U.S. road atlas), born in Louisiana, Missouri on November 7, 1874

November 8, 2017
Wednesday

Objectives & reminders

____

____

____

Appointments

Early morning

8 a.m.

9 a.m.

10 a.m.

11 a.m.

Noon

1 p.m.

2 p.m.

3 p.m.

4 p.m.

5 p.m.

6 p.m.

Later evening

Nutrition Labeling and Education Act (NLEA)

Both American consumers and packaged foods manufacturers should be aware of the NLEA, which was signed into law on November 8, 1990. With some exceptions, the NLEA requires manufacturers to label food packages with the amount of fat, cholesterol, sodium, sugar, fiber, protein and carbohydrates inside.

Among other provisions, the Act also charges the Food and Drug Administration with other labeling-relevant responsibilities, such as establishing standards, definitions, and promotional guidelines for ambiguous and potentially confusing words sometimes used to describe food products, e.g., what it means for a food product to be "low" in fat, have "reduced" cholesterol, or be "lite" or "lean." Follow-up regulations issued by the Food and Drug Administration (FDA) and the U.S. Department of Agriculture (USDA) provide additional guidelines.

Attending to labeling requirements is more than a compliance issue. It's also highly marketing-relevant in that food shoppers often read nutritional information labels and seek out what they believe to be healthy brands. For example, the results of a survey reported by ACNielsen on November 8, 2004, found that 83 percent of shoppers claim they, "regularly look at nutrition labels when buying a product for the first time." About 91 percent say they make their purchase decisions "based on the information they read on the label." What matters most? Sixty-three percent of the respondents wanted low-fat food, 55 percent sought items that were low in saturated fats, 52 percent were interested in low-calorie foods, 48 percent were sodium-sensitive, and 40 percent reported a preference for foods low in carbohydrates.

Happy birthday: Eartha Mary M. White

Born in Jacksonville, Florida on November 8, 1876, White was an African-American educator, administrator, and humanitarian. But she was an entrepreneur too; she owned a dry goods store, a housecleaning bureau, an employment service, a taxi firm, and a laundry with a unique slogan: "Put your duds in our suds; we wash anything but a dirty conscience."

November 9, 2017
Thursday

Objectives & reminders

____

____

____

Appointments

Early morning

8 a.m.

9 a.m.

10 a.m.

11 a.m.

Noon

1 p.m.

2 p.m.

3 p.m.

4 p.m.

5 p.m.

6 p.m.

Later evening

Stepping *into* the limelight

Perhaps the best way to ensure a spot in the limelight is to invent it. Thomas Drummond did just that when he discovered that placing a heated ball of lime in front of a reflector would create a brilliant incandescent form of light. On November 9, 1825, he set his limelight atop a mountain in Scotland. The light was visible more than 66 miles away. Drummond's limelight technology was soon adopted by lighthouses and theaters.

Today, limelights and other forms of direct lighting help retailers draw attention to in-store displays and guide shoppers' eyes toward desired focal points within the displays, such as featured products. Outside, spotlights waving across the night sky also draw attention to the location of businesses staging special events.

Stepping *out* of the limelight

On November 9, 2006, Transversal (www.transversal.com) released the findings of a study of online customer service practices in the United Kingdom. In the gift-popular electronic gadgets category, researchers found that 70 percent of routine customer service and product questions were not answered by the websites of ten "leading" consumer electronics firms. For example, one often ignored question was, "What should I do if my unit requires service or repair?"

When email queries were sent to the electronics firms, an average of 35 hours elapsed before responses were received, and not all of the responses answered the questions asked. Further, 20 percent of *new* customers' specific questions never received a response.

> **Customer responsiveness should be a higher priority: Agree or disagree?**
> "Considering the huge sums of money that... consumers are spending on gadgets, it's a disgrace that they cannot get fast answers to… simple questions."
> – Davin Yap, then CEO of Transversal

Almost a decade later, another study's findings posted on Transversal's website shows that customer service departments fail to resolve 25 percent of the initial customer inquiries received, because 40 percent of the reps lack the necessary knowledge and 22 percent lack technical skills.

November 10, 2017
Friday

Objectives & reminders

____

____

____

Appointments

Early morning

8 a.m.

9 a.m.

10 a.m.

11 a.m.

Noon

1 p.m.

2 p.m.

3 p.m.

4 p.m.

5 p.m.

6 p.m.

Later evening

Happy birthday: United States Marine Corps

In preparation for the Revolutionary War, the Continental Congress passed a resolution in Philadelphia on November 10, 1775, calling for the formation of two battalions of Continental Marines. The battalions were formed and distinguished themselves throughout the War. After the war the Marines were disbanded, but resurrected as a permanent military force in 1798.

Today, U.S. Marine rosters include 200,000 active-duty and reserve personnel, primarily stationed in North Carolina (Camp Lejeune), California (Camp Pendleton), and Okinawa, Japan. In addition to the 200,000 troops, countless other Marine veterans and family members live throughout the United States. November 10 -- the birthday of the Marine Corps -- is a great day for American businesses to say "thank you" to current and past Marines and their families.

Learning from the Marine Corps

In their best-selling book, *The Discipline of Market Leaders* (1995), Michael Treacy and Fred Wiersema suggest that businesses wishing to be operationally excellent can learn a great deal from studying the way the Marine Corps develops personnel and instills organizational values throughout the ranks – values such as teamwork, adherence to standards, dependability and commitment:

> "Operationally excellent companies run themselves like the Marine Corps: The team is what counts, not the individual. Everybody knows the battle plan and the rule book, and when the buzzer sounds, everyone knows exactly what he or she has to do."
>
> "The heroes in this kind of an organization are the people who fit in, who came up through the ranks. They're dependable... For the operationally excellent company, a promise is a promise. For the company's employees, dedication is paramount." (p. 50)

November 11, 2017
Saturday

Objectives & reminders

___

___

Appointments

Early morning

8 a.m.

9 a.m.

10 a.m.

11 a.m.

Noon

1 p.m.

2 p.m.

3 p.m.

4 p.m.

5 p.m.

6 p.m.

Later evening

Veterans Day

Veterans Day -- November 11 -- was originally proclaimed in 1919, but was known as Armistice Day to recognize the end of the "Great War" (World War I), marked by Germany's signing of the armistice agreement on November 11, 1918. Armistice Day was not only recognized in the United States, but in Great Britain, France and Canada as well.

An estimated nine million soldiers died during the Great War and 27 million were wounded. Five million or more civilians also lost their lives from starvation, disease and exposure caused by the war. The war officially ended at 11:00 a.m., i.e., the 11th hour of the 11th day, of the 11th month.

Lest we forget
Today, people still pause for two minutes of remembrance at 11:00 a.m. on November 11. For them, "lest we forget" remains the day's central theme.

Shortly after World War II, the meaning of November 11 was expanded to pay tribute to veterans of *both* World Wars. In 1954, the U.S. further expanded the scope of Veterans Day to recognize and honor veterans of *all* U.S. wars. In Canada and Australia, the day is now observed as Remembrance Day. In the United Kingdom, the Sunday nearest November 11 is set aside as Remembrance Day or Remembrance Sunday.

Happy birthday: William L. McKnight

Born in White, South Dakota on November 11, 1887, McKnight began his career as a teen with Minnesota Mining and Manufacturing Company (3M) in 1907. Be began as an assistant book-keeper for a salary of $11.50 per week. About four years later he found himself in the role of a sales manager. He continued to rise through the company, becoming president in 1929 and chairman of the board in 1949. By the time he retired in 1966, McKnight had invested almost six decades of his life to make 3M one of the most innovative firms in the world. Today, 3M's annual sales are about $30 billion.

November 12, 2017
Sunday

Objectives & reminders

____

____

____

Appointments

Early morning

8 a.m.

9 a.m.

10 a.m.

11 a.m.

Noon

1 p.m.

2 p.m.

3 p.m.

4 p.m.

5 p.m.

6 p.m.

Later evening

Charles M. Manson's birthday

Born in Cincinnati, Ohio on November 12, 1934, Manson led a commune in California in the 1960s. Known as the "Manson Family," members of the commune joined Manson in brutally killing at least six people in August 1969 – including actress Sharon Tate who was eight and a half months pregnant at the time. Manson was sentenced to death (later reduced to life imprisonment) for his role in the gruesome murders.

Not surprisingly, Manson and the murders drew considerable media attention across the United States. It seems that everyone knew of Charles Manson.

In an apparent attempt to capitalize on Manson's bad-boy image, an ad agency in Philadelphia used Manson in a campaign to promote a particular youth-oriented clothing store. Commenting on the campaign in his 2005 book, *Often Wrong, Never in Doubt*, former ad agency head Donny Deutsch made it clear that the campaign had crossed the line, so to speak: "That's just insensitive and moronic. This is a mass murderer, a guy with a swastika on his head; there's no sane way in the world to celebrate him. I guess the concept was edginess, but that's way over the edge" (p. 152).

Salute to Ellis Island

New Jersey's and New York's Ellis Island has a special meaning to the millions of immigrants who flocked to the U.S. between 1892 and 1954. For many of them, Ellis Island was their first stop in America. There, between 12 and 20 million immigrants from numerous Eastern and Southern European countries were processed before being allowed to step foot on the mainland.

Although the island's use as an immigration center ended on November 12, 1954 (after almost 63 years of service), it remains a symbol of hope and opportunity, and a reminder of the nation's richly diverse population. Today, more than half of the U.S. population can claim one or more relatives who entered the country through Ellis Island.

November 13, 2017
Monday

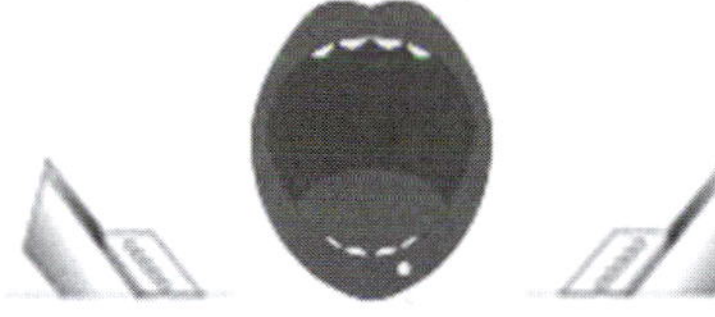

Objectives & reminders

____

____

____

Appointments

Early morning

8 a.m.

9 a.m.

10 a.m.

11 a.m.

Noon

1 p.m.

2 p.m.

3 p.m.

4 p.m.

5 p.m.

6 p.m.

Later evening

Head Start Monday: As usual, calendrical timing is key

Today, the Monday before Thanksgiving week, is a great day for small businesses to send holiday-related emails to customers and prospective customers, according to an analysis of more than a billion emails sent by GoDaddy business clients from November 2014 to January 2015. Email open rates on this Monday were 14 percent higher than average for the holiday period, and click-through rates were 23.5 percent above average.

____

Happy birthday: Ad Council

The Ad Council was formed on November 13, 1941 (then named the War Advertising Council), to harness the collective competencies and resources of America's advertising community in support of the war effort. Early programs were successful, including public service campaigns that

helped to plant 50 million Victory Gardens. The "Rosie the Riveter" campaign helped recruit two million women to enable U.S. factories to expand the workforce.

After the war, the Ad Council continued to develop public service announcements (PSAs) to support American interests -- promoting fire safety, education, preventive health, and discouraging practices such as drug abuse and drunk driving.

Today, more than $1.8 billion of media time and space are donated annually for the Ad Council's campaigns that are disseminated through 33,000 media outlets -- including broadcast, print, outdoor and Internet. And thousands of individuals and organizations contribute their time and talent.

Ad Council creations

Do you recognize these Ad Council slogans?

- "This is your brain on drugs."
- "Only you can prevent forest fires."
- "Keep America beautiful."
- "Take a bite out of crime."
- "Friends don't let friends drive drunk."
- "A mind is a terrible thing to waste."
- "Loose lips sink ships."
- "You could learn a lot from a dummy."

November 14, 2017
Tuesday

Objectives & reminders

Appointments

Early morning

8 a.m.

9 a.m.

10 a.m.

11 a.m.

Noon

1 p.m.

2 p.m.

3 p.m.

4 p.m.

5 p.m.

6 p.m.

Later evening

Happy birthday: Charles Philip Arthur George Mountbatten-Windsor

Better known as the Prince of Wales and heir to the British throne, Prince Charles was born in London on November 14, 1948. Today, in addition to his Royal duties, Prince Charles oversees his own charity work through the Prince's Trust, which he founded. Among other functions, the Prince's Trust helps secure loans for budding entrepreneurs who are not able to secure financing from mainstream institutions. The Trust also trains and finds employment for thousands of inner-city low-income people.

Principle of monarchy marketing
"Something as curious as the monarchy won't survive unless you take account of people's attitudes. After all, if people don't want it, they won't have it." -- Prince Charles

---

Happy birthday: Jawaharlal Nehru

Born into a wealthy family in Allahabad, India on November 14, 1889, Nehru later studied law in England before returning to India in 1912 where he joined the movement for India's independence in 1919. When India finally gained its independence from Britain in 1947, Nehru became independent India's first prime minister.

Quality and timing of ideas
"There are two things that have to happen before an idea catches on. One is that the idea should be good. The other is that it should fit in with the temper of the age. If it does not, even a good idea may well be passed by." -- Jawaharlal Nehru

Today, India is the largest democracy in the world with more than one billion consumers. By 2025, the population of India is expected to surpass that of China, which will make India the most populous country in the world.

Did you know?
November 14 is also Children's Day in India, celebrated throughout the country.

November 15, 2017 Wednesday

Objectives & reminders

______

______

______

Appointments

Early morning

8 a.m.

9 a.m.

10 a.m.

11 a.m.

Noon

1 p.m.

2 p.m.

3 p.m.

4 p.m.

5 p.m.

6 p.m.

Later evening

Cola Wars heat up

The 1930s was a challenging decade for American businesses, as the country suffered through the Great Depression. Pepsi-Cola was particularly challenged. Their 300-plus franchises had shrunk to only two. In 1934, however, Pepsi responded to consumers' price sensitivity by increasing the amount of cola in each bottle without increasing the price. Their accompanying promotional jingle became one of the most recognized and memorable in advertising history. Moreover, the campaign worked; Pepsi sales soared.

Pepsi's 1934 classic jingle
"Pepsi-Cola hits the spot,
Twelve full-ounces, that's a lot.
Twice as much, for a nickel too.
Pepsi-Cola is the thing for you!"

On November 15, 1939, Pepsi-Cola announced the continuation of their marketing offensive with an ad in the *National Bottler's Gazette:* "The BIGGEST national advertising campaign ever! All known promotional resources will be used -- clear across the country." Pepsi's marketing success had encouraged the company to keep investing in the marketing side of the business.

What Pepsi executives might have sung
Marketing, marketing hits the spot,
For twelve full months, that's a lot.
Twice the customers, no fewer will do.
Marketing investment is the thing for you!

♫♬♩♩♩ ♫♬♩♩♩

Pike's Peak discovered

On November 15, 1806, explorer Lieutenant Zebulon Montgomery Pike first discovered a mountain near the present-day town of Colorado Springs, Colorado. Today, the popular tourist attraction is known as Pike's Peak and attracts hundreds of thousands of visitors annually.

Peak demand
"If you think advertising doesn't pay – we understand there are 25 mountains in Colorado higher than Pike's Peak. Can you name one?"
– *The American Salesman*

November 16, 2017
Thursday

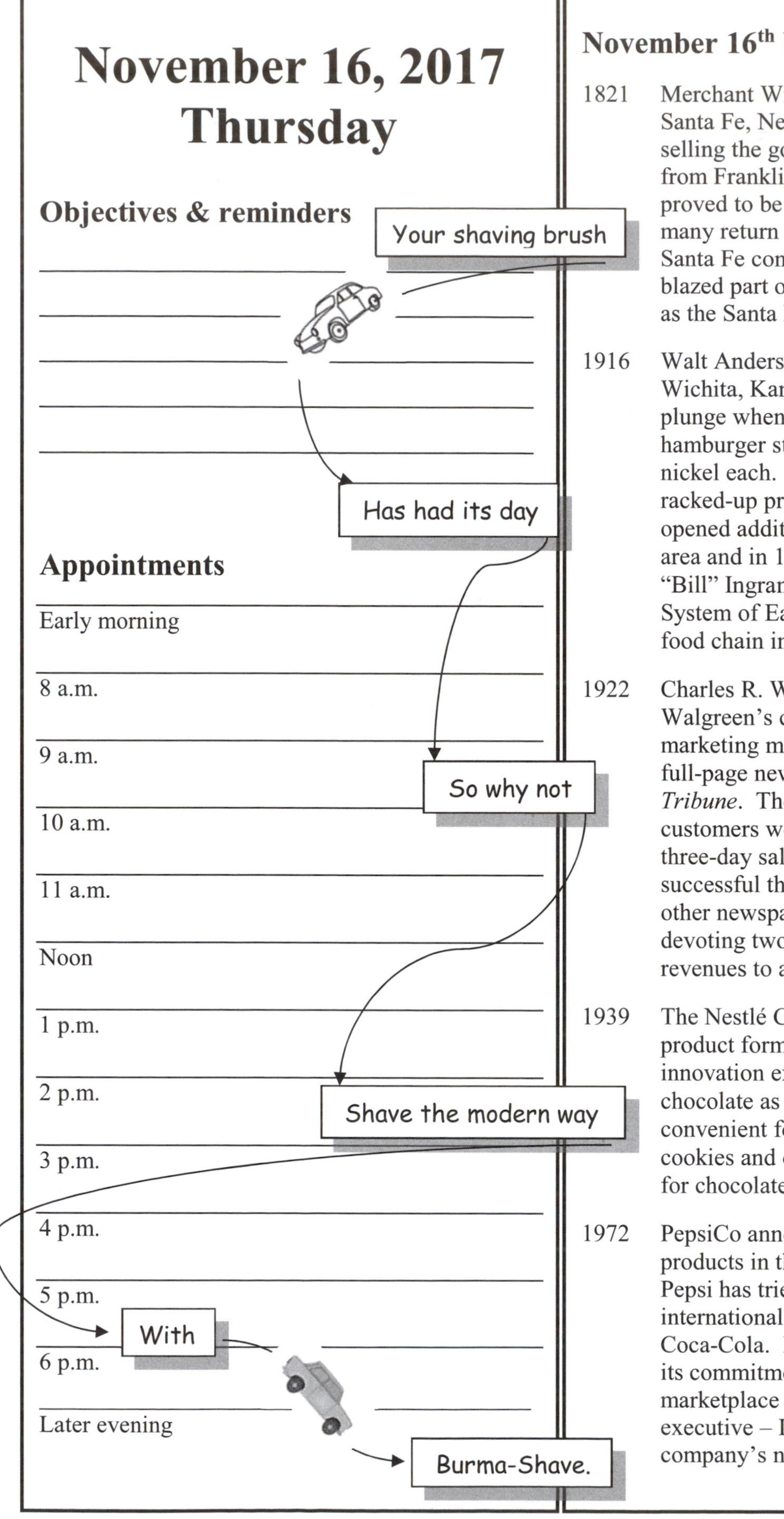

Objectives & reminders

Appointments

Early morning

8 a.m.

9 a.m.

10 a.m.

11 a.m.

Noon

1 p.m.

2 p.m.

3 p.m.

4 p.m.

5 p.m.

6 p.m.

Later evening

November 16th breakthroughs

1821 Merchant William Becknell first arrived in Santa Fe, New Mexico territory and began selling the goods he had brought with him from Franklin, Missouri. The market proved to be so profitable that he made many return visits to serve the needs of Santa Fe consumers. In the process he blazed part of the route that is now known as the Santa Fe Trail.

1916 Walt Anderson, a short-order cook in Wichita, Kansas took the entrepreneurial plunge when he opened his own hamburger stand – selling burgers for a nickel each. By the end of the day, he had racked-up profits of $3.75. Anderson opened additional hamburger stands in the area and in 1921 partnered with Edgar “Bill” Ingram to form White Castle System of Eating Houses – the first fast-food chain in the United States.

1922 Charles R. Walgreen, Sr., founder of the Walgreen’s chain of drugstores, rolled his marketing marbles when he placed his first full-page newspaper ad in the *Chicago Tribune*. The ad touted the bargains customers would find during an upcoming three-day sale. The ad proved to be so successful that Walgreen followed it with other newspaper ads and soon began devoting two to three percent of his store’s revenues to advertising.

1939 The Nestlé Company launched a new product form – chocolate chips. The innovation expanded the market for chocolate as cooks found chocolate chips convenient for baking chocolate chip cookies and other desserts. Recipes calling for chocolate chips proliferated.

1972 PepsiCo announced a deal to sell Pepsi products in the Soviet Union. Since then, Pepsi has tried to catch up with the international presence of its chief rival, Coca-Cola. In 2006, PepsiCo reinforced its commitment to competing in the global marketplace by naming an Indian-born executive – Indra K. Nooyi – as the company’s new CEO.

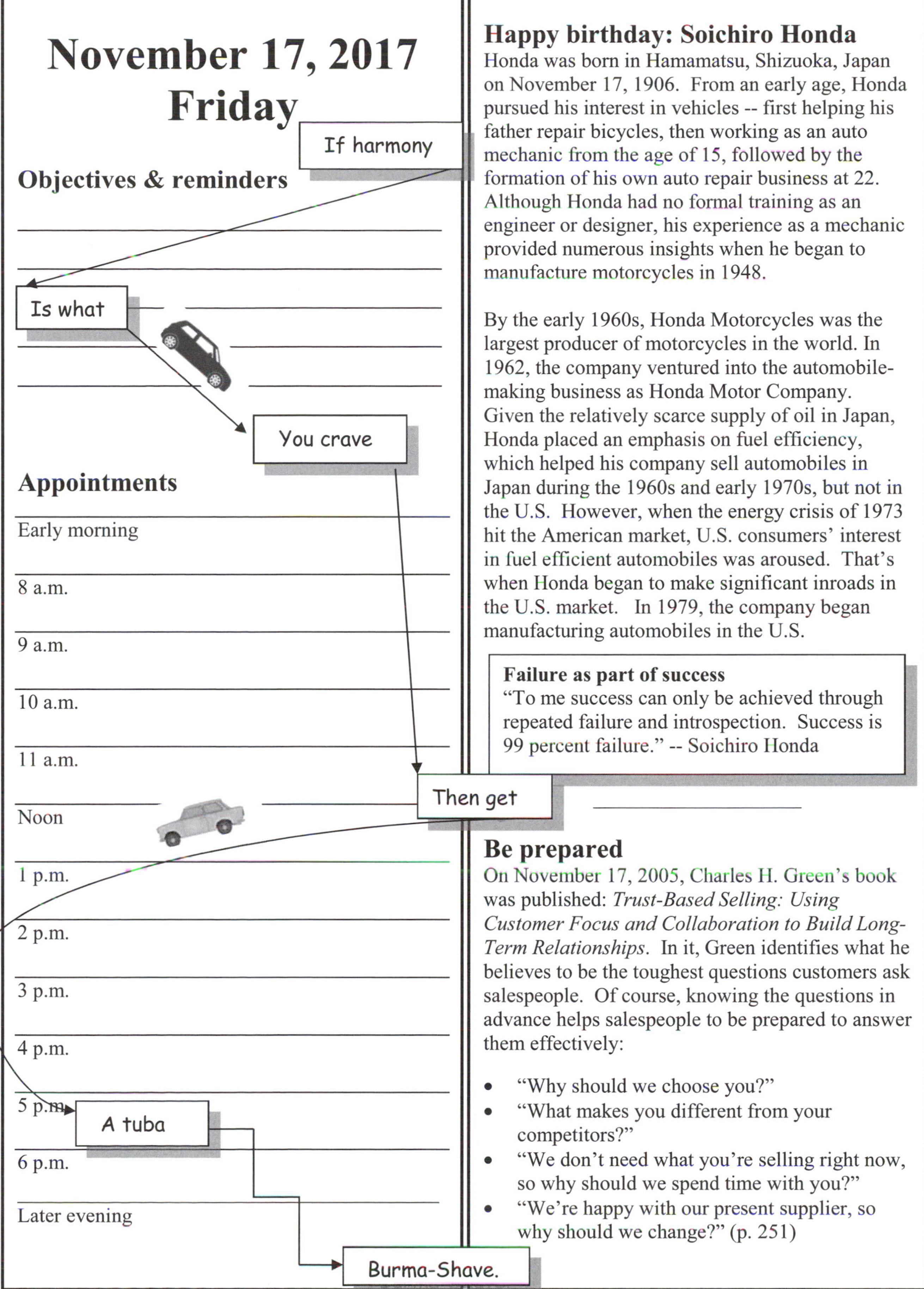

November 17, 2017
Friday

Objectives & reminders

Appointments

Early morning

8 a.m.

9 a.m.

10 a.m.

11 a.m.

Noon

1 p.m.

2 p.m.

3 p.m.

4 p.m.

5 p.m.

6 p.m.

Later evening

Happy birthday: Soichiro Honda

Honda was born in Hamamatsu, Shizuoka, Japan on November 17, 1906. From an early age, Honda pursued his interest in vehicles -- first helping his father repair bicycles, then working as an auto mechanic from the age of 15, followed by the formation of his own auto repair business at 22. Although Honda had no formal training as an engineer or designer, his experience as a mechanic provided numerous insights when he began to manufacture motorcycles in 1948.

By the early 1960s, Honda Motorcycles was the largest producer of motorcycles in the world. In 1962, the company ventured into the automobile-making business as Honda Motor Company. Given the relatively scarce supply of oil in Japan, Honda placed an emphasis on fuel efficiency, which helped his company sell automobiles in Japan during the 1960s and early 1970s, but not in the U.S. However, when the energy crisis of 1973 hit the American market, U.S. consumers' interest in fuel efficient automobiles was aroused. That's when Honda began to make significant inroads in the U.S. market. In 1979, the company began manufacturing automobiles in the U.S.

Failure as part of success
"To me success can only be achieved through repeated failure and introspection. Success is 99 percent failure." -- Soichiro Honda

Be prepared

On November 17, 2005, Charles H. Green's book was published: *Trust-Based Selling: Using Customer Focus and Collaboration to Build Long-Term Relationships*. In it, Green identifies what he believes to be the toughest questions customers ask salespeople. Of course, knowing the questions in advance helps salespeople to be prepared to answer them effectively:

- "Why should we choose you?"
- "What makes you different from your competitors?"
- "We don't need what you're selling right now, so why should we spend time with you?"
- "We're happy with our present supplier, so why should we change?" (p. 251)

November 18, 2017
Saturday

Objectives & reminders

Appointments

Early morning

8 a.m.

9 a.m.

10 a.m.

11 a.m.

Noon

1 p.m.

2 p.m.

3 p.m.

4 p.m.

5 p.m.

6 p.m.

Later evening

He played a sax

Time to sign off

The growing popularity of electric signs in the 1910s met with opposition on November 18, 1917, when U.S. fuel administrators ordered owners to turn off the signs on Sundays and Thursdays. Thus businesses that used electric signs lost the signs' "continuous promotion" advantage. The objective of the restriction was to save fuel.

Had no B.O.

Time to sign on

The struggling Burma-Vita Company founded by Robert Ransom Odell was near collapse after the company's first year's efforts to sell an innovative product for the time -- brushless shaving cream, known as Burma-Shave. The Odell family tried the door-to-door approach to selling Burma-Shave. They even tried selling "on approval," e.g., "Take it home, try it, and if you like it, pay me fifty cents next week." These early marketing efforts failed.

But his whiskers

Scratched

So she let him go

Finally the company decided to advertise with multiple sets of six roadside signs spaced along the side of highways so that motorists would feel compelled to read each sign as they drove by. This novel approach worked. Sales climbed, and retailers began to reorder. With an influx of cash and confidence, the company was incorporated on November 18, 1926, just in time to prevent the company's demise (a close shave ☺).

Burma-Shave.

Soon Burma-Vita turned their series of signs into rhyming jingles and involved the public in contests to write new rhymes "in 20 words or less." Winning entries were initially worth $100 each and later prizes were $1,000. At one point 65,000 entries were submitted annually. Over the next 37 years, the company used several hundred rhymes on their roadside signage throughout the U.S. and around the world.

November 19, 2017
Sunday

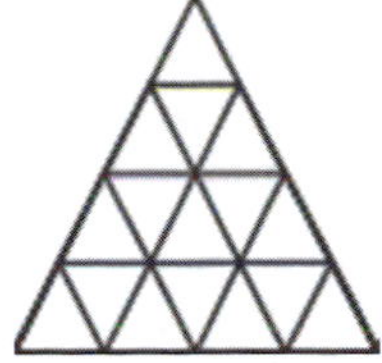

Objectives & reminders

Revisit the <u>triangle</u> introduced on November 12.

____

____

Appointments

Early morning

8 a.m.

9 a.m.

10 a.m.

11 a.m.

Noon

1 p.m.

2 p.m.

3 p.m.

4 p.m.

5 p.m.

6 p.m.

Later evening

Happy birthday: Calvin Klein

Born in the Bronx of New York City on November 19, 1942, Klein developed an interest in fashion from an early age. In college, he studied fashion design and afterward, in 1968, launched his own clothing company and brand, Calvin Klein. His company was an immediate success. Later, he extended the brand to include fragrances, undergarments, swim-wear, eye-wear, cosmetics and other products.

As the company and the brand grew, Klein realized the critical importance of surrounding himself with a capable management team that shares a common vision for the future of the company: "I have a team in place who understands everything that I love, and can do it and can make it happen. My goal has been to set up a company that can run without me."

Paired contrast:
Agree or disagree?

Q: What's the difference between a pair of *jeans* and a pair of *designer jeans*?

A: About $60. ☺

?

No 15-year-old for his birthday

Calvin Klein introduced the world to designer jeans with controversial ads featuring adolescent models such as Brooke Shields. According to many, Brooke Shields' appearance, demeanor and script in the ads were simply too sexually suggestive -- especially considering her young age. On Klein's 38th birthday -- November 19, 1980 -- CBS television banned at least one of the Brooke Shields commercials. Miss Shields was only 15 years old at the time.

Courageous or tasteless?

"Anything we do in advertising is controversial. If it's provocative and sensual and related to what we're selling, I'm willing to take the chance."
– Calvin Klein

November 20, 2017
Monday

Live here?

Objectives & reminders

____

____

Appointments

Early morning

8 a.m.

9 a.m.

10 a.m.

11 a.m.

Noon

1 p.m.

2 p.m.

3 p.m.

4 p.m.

5 p.m.

6 p.m.

Later evening

Community marketing

Marketing activities are not restricted to businesses. That was apparent in 1843 when Blacksnake Hills, Missouri changed its name (brand) to "St. Joseph" on November 20. Seventeen years earlier the town was founded as a trading post by Joseph Robidoux III, but as the area grew it became increasingly apparent that a more impressive-sounding name was needed to attract a higher percentage (market share) of westbound settlers. These settlers represented an important market for food, stock animals, wagons and other supplies they would need for the journey.

Apparently the name-changing strategy worked. In 1849 alone, more than 2,000 wagons made their way through St. Joseph. By 1859, St. Joseph had become one of the largest cities in Missouri – second only to St. Louis.

Hundreds of communities have undergone name changes over the years as part of a rebranding strategy (although they haven't always used the term "rebranding") – in some cases to enhance the communities' appeal to tourists or prospective businesses or residents, or in other cases, to avoid confusion with other cities, to avoid embarrassment, or to reflect new political realities. Occasionally, a city or town will change its name as part of a corporate sponsorship agreement.

St. Joseph is not alone

- Atlanta, Georgia – formerly Marthasville
- Corvallis, Oregon – formerly Marysville
- Derby, Kansas – formerly El Paso
- Dish, Texas – formerly Clark (rebranded in exchange for free satellite TV for ten years)
- Lincoln, Nebraska – formerly Lancaster
- New York, New York – formerly New Amsterdam
- Truth or Consequences, New Mexico – formerly Hot Springs (rebranded in 1950 in exchange for a promise that the popular radio program by the same name would be broadcast from there)
- Sleepy Hollow, New York – formerly North Tarrytown
- St. Paul, Minnesota – formerly Pig's Eye

November 21, 2017
Tuesday

Objectives & reminders

____

____

____

Appointments

Early morning

8 a.m.

9 a.m.

10 a.m.

11 a.m.

Noon

1 p.m.

2 p.m.

3 p.m.

4 p.m.

5 p.m.

6 p.m.

Later evening

Thanksgiving week sales bubble

Holidays frequently serve as retail sales catalysts. ACNielsen data indicate that Thanksgiving week in the United States is no exception. For example, storewide sales in U.S. food, drug and mass merchandising stores (excluding Wal-Mart) during Thanksgiving rivals only the weeks just prior to Christmas. In particular, cookware sales are very strong during Thanksgiving week, accounting for 6.7 percent of total annual cookware sales (note that if sales were evenly distributed throughout the year, one week would account for about 1.9 percent of annual sales).

A few food product categories that account for a disproportionate share of annual category sales during Thanksgiving week include:

- Canned fruit (5.6%),
- Frozen foods (5.2%),
- Baked goods (5.2%),
- Flour (4.1%),
- Spices, seasonings and extracts (4.0%),
- Frozen desserts, fruits and toppings (3.8%),
- Butter and margarine (3.6%),
- Sugar and sugar substitutes (3.3%),
- Canned vegetables (3.3%),
- Packaged milks and modifiers (3.1%), and
- Pickles, olives and relishes (3.0%).

Businesses that know when sales bubbles are likely to occur are better positioned to capitalize on them, e.g., by ensuring adequate inventories and by promoting high-demand products to further stimulate demand.

Riding the demand bubbles
Advertising and promotion efforts tend to be most effective when consumers are already in the mood to buy.

Recipe for making money

"There is no great secret to fortune making. All you have to do is buy cheap and sell dear, act with thrift and shrewdness and be persistent."
– Henrietta "Hetty" Green, American investor and speculator known for her extreme frugality. Born on November 21, 1834, Green also was known by her nickname, "The Witch of Wall Street."

November 22, 2017
Wednesday

Objectives & reminders

____

____

____

Appointments

Early morning

8 a.m.

9 a.m.

10 a.m.

11 a.m.

Noon

1 p.m.

2 p.m.

3 p.m.

4 p.m.

5 p.m.

6 p.m.

Later evening

Kennedy assassination

During the early afternoon of November 22, 1963, 46-year-old U.S. President John F. Kennedy was shot and killed while riding in a motorcade in downtown Dallas, Texas. Later that day Lee Harvey Oswald was arrested and charged with the murder. Vice-President Lyndon B. Johnson was sworn in as the new President.

> **A day to remember**
> "A piece of each of us died at that moment." -- U.S. Senator Michael J. Mansfield, in reference to the Kennedy assassination

The assassination shook the country as only a few other events in recent history have. Most Americans living at that time remember what they were doing and how they felt on that day. That is, Kennedy's assassination wasn't just history; it was experienced on a personal level.

A few other personally-experienced historical events etched in societies' memories include the Japanese attack on Pearl Harbor (1941), Germany and Japan's surrender at the close of World War II (both in 1945), Neil Armstrong's historic walk on the moon (1969), the Challenger Space Shuttle disaster (1986), the Gulf coast devastation caused by hurricane Katrina (2005), and numerous terrorist attacks -- on the U.S. (September 11, 2001), London (July 7, 2007), and Paris (November 13, 2015), to name a few.

"Glocal" (glo̲bal loca̲l̲) businesses interesting in acting *local* as they go *global* are well advised to identify and recognize comparable dates of observance that are particularly relevant in individual markets. When were the area's leaders, heroes, great scientists, and celebrities born? When did they die? When did conflicts end? What are the key dates of political transitions, such as the day independence was gained or a new constitution adopted? When did major natural disasters occur? And so on. While such events, like Kennedy's assassination, may be historically significant, their meaning may be much deeper for those who personally experienced or remember them.

November 23, 2017
Thursday

Thanksgiving Day

Objectives & reminders

___

___

Appointments

Early morning

8 a.m.

9 a.m.

10 a.m.

11 a.m.

Noon

1 p.m.

2 p.m.

3 p.m.

4 p.m.

5 p.m.

6 p.m.

Later evening

A Thanksgiving reminder
"As we express our gratitude, we must never forget that the highest appreciation is not to utter words, but to live by them." -- U.S. President John F. Kennedy

Happy Thanksgiving!

Thanksgiving Day is a major holiday in the United States, now celebrated annually on the fourth Thursday of November. Like many holidays, people vary in their celebration of Thanksgiving, but family get-togethers and feasts are typical. Turkey, ham, sweet potatoes, cranberry sauce and pumpkin pie are likely Thanksgiving menu items. Watching the Macy's parade or football on television also has become part of the Thanksgiving tradition in many American homes.

Self-discipline on Thanksgiving? ☺
"An optimist is a person who starts a new diet on Thanksgiving Day."
-- Irv Kupcinet, newspaper columnist

Another tradition in both religious and non-religious homes is to spend a few moments on Thanksgiving Day to list the family's many blessings, a period of reflection that often leads people to contemplate the plight of those less fortunate. It follows that these sentiments can pave the way for acts of generosity, so the Thanksgiving period is one of opportunity for marketers of non-profit organizations that serve those in need -- especially for marketers who *ask*.

Finally, because the Thanksgiving weekend represents four consecutive days away from the job for most workers, the weekend is also characterized by shopping and travel.

Time away from job means time to shop and travel
Thanksgiving is one of American employers' favorite holidays. A 2015 study found that 94-97 percent of surveyed HR professionals said their organizations observe these holidays with paid time off for employees: New Year's Day, Memorial Day, Labor Day, *Thanksgiving Day*, and Christmas Day.

November 24, 2017
Friday

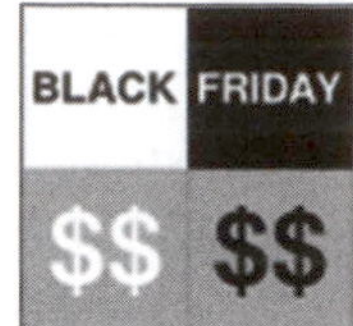

Objectives & reminders

Appointments

Early morning

8 a.m.

9 a.m.

10 a.m.

11 a.m.

Noon

1 p.m.

2 p.m.

3 p.m.

4 p.m.

5 p.m.

6 p.m.

Later evening

Black Friday

As the unofficial start of the Christmas shopping season, the day after Thanksgiving – known as "Black Friday" – is a big day for U.S. retailers. Traditionally, sales receipts on this day suggest that this is *the* biggest single day of the year, although in a few recent years since the 1990s, the Saturday before Christmas has been the sales leader.

Black Friday statistics
Thirty-eight percent of surveyed consumers in 2015 reported plans to shop on Black Friday and/or on Cyber Monday. To possibly explain why Black Friday shopping wasn't appealing to a greater percentage of potential shoppers, about a third of those surveyed said that stores were too busy and lines too long, and a fourth claimed that discounts were too small.

It's not uncommon for retailers to launch the shopping season with sales or other events to lure shoppers. Many stores open early in the morning, some as early as 6:00 a.m. or even earlier. In recent years, the duration of many "Black Friday" sales events has been stretched as some begin on Thanksgiving Day and continue throughout the entire weekend.

More than Rudolph needed to rescue "mis-sled" retailers
Although holiday shopping activity may intensify the day after Thanksgiving for many consumers in the U.S., for most shoppers the holiday shopping season has begun already. That is, a survey conducted by The National Retail Federation suggests that 14 percent of consumers begin their holiday shopping before September, while another 6 percent begin in September, 20 percent in October, 37 percent in November, and 23 percent in December. Misled retailers who wait until the day after Thanksgiving to launch their holiday merchandising programs are likely to miss many sales opportunities.

November 25, 2017
Saturday

Objectives & reminders

____

____

____

Appointments

Early morning

8 a.m.

9 a.m.

10 a.m.

11 a.m.

Noon

1 p.m.

2 p.m.

3 p.m.

4 p.m.

5 p.m.

6 p.m.

Later evening

Small Business Saturday

American Express played a leadership role in 2010 when they coined the phrase "Small Business Saturday" (SBS) and launched the first campaign to encourage American holiday shoppers to patronize small and local businesses on the Saturday following Thanksgiving. To promote SBS, American Express used traditional advertising and public relations campaigns, as well as social media.

Since SBS began, the annual day to recognize small businesses has grown steadily in terms of revenues generated and the number of businesses and shoppers who participate. Thousands of businesses hold sales or other events to lure shoppers and promote SBS. In 2015, 95 million U.S. shoppers responded positively by handing over $16.2 billion to small businesses on the unofficial holiday.

Resurgence of small business
"Americans are returning to Main Street for the things they need and ultimately that's a very healthy economic trend." – Dan Danner, President and CEO of the National Federation of Independent Businesses.

Further, 200 federal officials and agencies chimed in by posting proclamations of support for the occasion on social media or otherwise endorsing the day. Among them was President Obama who shopped at two small businesses on SBS with his two daughters. The growing popularity of SBS and the positive impact that consumer spending has on local economies, coupled with government and Presidential support, has led to considerable positive media coverage of SBS which helps to extend its upward trajectory of success.

Selected small business appeals (explicit or implicit)

- Support us – we're the little guys, the underdogs. We need you.
- We employ your neighbors, keep money in the area to boost the local economy, and we care about the local community.
- Our product mix and practices are customized to fit the needs and tastes of the local community. We're responsive, and we know your name too.

November 26, 2017
Sunday

Objectives & reminders

____

____

____

Appointments

Early morning

8 a.m.

9 a.m.

10 a.m.

11 a.m.

Noon

1 p.m.

2 p.m.

3 p.m.

4 p.m.

5 p.m.

6 p.m.

Later evening

Happy birthday: Willis Haviland Carrier

Born in Angola, New York on November 26, 1876, Carrier is the man who invented practical, successful air conditioning systems that paved the way for the entire industry. In doing so, he also built the world's largest manufacturer of air conditioning, heating and ventilation products -- Carrier Engineering Corporation, founded in 1915.

About a year after earning a Masters degree in Engineering from Cornell University in 1901, Carrier began installing systems to control humidity and temperature. In those early years, the primary purpose of "air conditioners" (the term we use today) was to cool machines, not people. For example, in 1902 Carrier helped stabilize the air in a printing shop to prevent paper from expanding and contracting and thus enabled the printer to print sharper images. In a 1906 assignment, Carrier helped a cotton mill keep its spindles cool so they could remain running for longer periods of time.

It wasn't until 1924 that the potential marketing advantages of air conditioning were realized when Carrier installed an air conditioning system in Detroit's J.L. Hudson Department Store. Air conditioning provided the store with a competitive advantage and shoppers flocked to the store during the hot summer months. It wasn't long before movie theaters and upscale hotels also realized competitive advantages by installing air conditioning systems.

Cool statistics: Agree or disagree?
According to some estimates, without air conditioning, worldwide business productivity would drop by about 40 percent, while the rates of drunkenness, divorce, and violence would be higher.

By 1928, air conditioning units were available for home use, although sales were sluggish through the Great Depression of the1930s and during World War II in the early 1940s. After World War II, however, air conditioning sales for both businesses and homes picked up. As more and more retail stores and service businesses adopted air conditioning in the 1950s and 1960s, what had been an *extra* appeal to attract customers increasingly became an *expected* feature.

November 27, 2017
Monday

Objectives & reminders

____

____

Appointments

Early morning

8 a.m.

9 a.m.

10 a.m.

11 a.m.

Noon

1 p.m.

2 p.m.

3 p.m.

4 p.m.

5 p.m.

6 p.m.

Later evening

Cyber Monday: Monday after Thanksgiving

Whereas the Friday after Thanksgiving is always a big day for retail stores in the U.S., the *Monday* after Thanksgiving (today!) is a big day for online retailers. That's the day when many consumers return to their jobs and shop online at work. In fact, the biggest online shopping days of the year tend to be the Mondays between Thanksgiving and Christmas.

A generational phenomenon
Among American consumers surveyed in 2015, millenials were twice as likely as older consumers (age 55+) to shop online on Cyber Monday.

A milestone was reached on Cyber Monday in 2015 when, for the first time, online retail gift-shopping sales in the U.S. exceeded those of traditional brick and mortar stores. Also in 2015, Kohl's used a calendrical stretch strategy to attract online shoppers. That is, the chain of U.S.-based department stores promoted "Cyber *Week*."

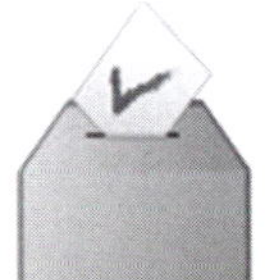

New Zealand leads the world!

Elections were held in New Zealand on November 27, 1893, but unlike any national election ever held anywhere in the world, women voted legally. Largely due to the efforts of political leader Richard John Seddon, New Zealand's parliament had recently passed a female suffrage bill that paved the way for women to vote. Not surprisingly, Seddon was one of the winners in the election.

Profit as a corporate responsibility

"If we cannot make a good profit, we are committing a sort of crime against society. We take society's capital, people and materials, yet without a good profit, we are using precious resources that could be better used elsewhere."
– Konosuke Matsushita, founder of Matsushita Electric (Panasonic, Quasar and other major brands) in Osaka, Japan. Mr. Matsushita was born on November 27, 1894.

November 28, 2017
Tuesday

Objectives & reminders

___

___

___

Appointments

Early morning

8 a.m.

9 a.m.

10 a.m.

11 a.m.

Noon

1 p.m.

2 p.m.

3 p.m.

4 p.m.

5 p.m.

6 p.m.

Later evening

One reason change takes time

On November 28, 1934, German physicist Max Planck commented on the evolution of science, in particular how paradigms are gradually adopted. According to Planck, "A new scientific truth does not triumph by convincing its opponents and making them see the light, but rather because its opponents eventually die out, and a new generation grows up that is familiar with it."

Although Planck was talking about scientific ideas, his observation also applies to a variety of ideas, perspectives, and innovative practices in business. When new managers join a company and introduce new ideas, new directions or new ways of doing things, workers comfortable with the old may resist the new. Over time, the resistance may fade as opponents leave the company or assume new roles.

Embracing the future
Today, few people advocate horse-drawn carriages over "horseless carriages," but that wasn't the case in 1895 as the battle between competing technologies began to emerge. According to an 1895 article in *The Chicago Times-Herald*, "Persons who are inclined... to decry the development of the horseless carriage... will be forced... to recognize it as an admitted mechanical achievement, highly adapted to some of the most urgent needs of our civilization."

Different evaluative criteria for Internet users: Agree or disagree?

"[O]ne of the big problems [with the Internet] is that people… pay very little attention to [the existence of a company Web site or how they got to it, whereas] they might pay a good deal of attention to Michelin versus Firestone tires. Michelin might have a certain reputation and Firestone will have another reputation. In the Internet, it's much more a question of functionality than reputation. This Web site works really well and [is quick]. In the non-Internet culture, what you think of me is the most important thing. In the Internet culture, what you think of me is not as important as whether you enjoyed using me."
– Dick Morris, American political analyst and campaign consultant, born on November 28, 1948

November 29, 2017
Wednesday

Objectives & reminders

____

____

Appointments

Early morning

8 a.m.

9 a.m.

10 a.m.

11 a.m.

Noon

1 p.m.

2 p.m.

3 p.m.

4 p.m.

5 p.m.

6 p.m.

Later evening

Goals are for living, not solely for getting things done

"Far away there in the sunshine are my highest aspirations. I may not reach them, but I can look up and see their beauty, believe in them and try to follow where they lead." – Louisa May Alcott, American novelist (*Little Women*), born on November 29, 1832

The Voice of Firestone Televues

The Firestone Tire & Rubber Company sponsored a radio show, *The Voice of Firestone*, in the early days of the medium, from 1928 until 1956. The show broadcasted classical music over the NBC radio network.

The radio show's popularity prompted Firestone to extend its sponsorship to a televised version which began airing on November 29, 1943. The television version became one of the first television series and enjoyed a relatively small but loyal audience. The show stayed on the airways until 1959, and then again in 1962 and 1963. Harvey Firestone's wife, Idabelle, was personally involved and often played the role of hostess, offering comments at the beginning and end of the show.

"Sponsorship" vs. "ad placement"
Today, there is generally little or no distinction between sponsoring a television program and buying advertising time during a particular program. That is, today a television program is likely to be "brought to you by" many sponsors whose ads appear throughout the program. But this wasn't always the case. In the early days of television, often specific programs were associated with specific, single sponsors without which the program might not exist. Consequently, audiences who appreciated a program were likely to think favorably of its sponsor. Today, audiences may be more likely to view the ads of multiple "sponsors" as interruptions.

November 30, 2017
Thursday

Objectives & reminders

____

____

Appointments

Early morning

8 a.m.

9 a.m.

10 a.m.

11 a.m.

Noon

1 p.m.

2 p.m.

3 p.m.

4 p.m.

5 p.m.

6 p.m.

Later evening

Happy birthday: Samuel Clemens

Born in Florida, Missouri on November 30, 1835, Clemens began his career working as a printer's apprentice at the age of 13. He later worked for his brother's newspaper and as a steamboat pilot.

By 1861, Clemens settled into a career as a writer known as "Mark Twain" -- a pseudonym he would use for almost 50 years until his death in 1910. He wrote travel letters for several newspapers, short stories, and eventually novels. Some of Twain's well-known works include *The Celebrated Jumping Frog of Calaveras County* (1864), *The Adventures of Tom Sawyer* (1876), and *The Adventures of Huckleberry Finn* (1884). As excerpted in the accompanying boxes, Twain's insights of commonsensical wit and wisdom on a variety of business- and marketing-relevant topics are found throughout his writings.

Ethical behavior
"Always do right. This will gratify some people and astonish the rest."

Product demonstrations
"Don't say the old lady screamed. Bring her on and let her scream."

Investments
"The one thing that's more important than the return *on* the principal is the return *of* the principal."

Forecasting
"Climate is what we expect. Weather is what we get."

Creativity
"A person with a new idea is a crank until the idea succeeds."

Honesty
"If you tell the truth you don't have to remember anything."

Recognition
"It is better to deserve honors and not have them than to have them and not to deserve them."

Humor
"The best way to cheer up yourself is to try to cheer up someone else."

December 1, 2017
Friday

Objectives & reminders

____

____

Appointments

Early morning

8 a.m.

9 a.m.

10 a.m.

11 a.m.

Noon

1 p.m.

2 p.m.

3 p.m.

4 p.m.

5 p.m.

6 p.m.

Later evening

Welcome to December

Did you know this about December? Historically the month of December had only 29 days, but Julius Caesar added two more days in 46 b.c. Today, harried consumers would be likely to support a movement to add a few more days to the month.

Birthstones this month December's birthstones are turquoise and zircon, but if you own a jewelry store, the temptation is to add diamonds to the list. ☺

Saving for Christmas

On December 1, 1909, the Pennsylvania Trust Company based in Carlisle, Pennsylvania became the first bank to offer "Christmas Club" savings accounts. The Christmas club concept was fairly straightforward: Early in the year consumers decided how much money they expected to need for gifts, travel and other purposes for the next Christmas season (e.g., $200). Then they opened a Christmas club account into which they made periodic deposits throughout the year to reach their goal (e.g., $4 weekly). When December arrived, club members withdrew the money and used it as they wished. Members of some Christmas clubs received a small gift from the bank when they reached their annual savings goal.

The Christmas club concept spread to other parts of the country and remained popular well into the 1960s. Even as their popularity faded for many consumers (coinciding with the rise in the popularity of credit cards), some financial institutions continued to offer the service in the 1980s for their loyal Christmas club fans.

Christmas clubs benefitted both consumers and financial institutions. The clubs helped consumers plan and discipline themselves to save. Institutions found the clubs profitable because many did not pay depositors any interest. Further, club members' frequent deposits usually meant frequent contact with employees and thus multiple cross-selling and relationship-building opportunities.

December 2, 2017
Saturday

Objectives & reminders

____

____

Appointments

Early morning

8 a.m.

9 a.m.

10 a.m.

11 a.m.

Noon

1 p.m.

2 p.m.

3 p.m.

4 p.m.

5 p.m.

6 p.m.

Later evening

Happy birthday: Anna S. Bissell

Born as Anna Sutherland in River John, Nova Scotia (Canada) on December 2, 1846, Anna began her career as a schoolteacher at the age of 16. After marrying Melville R. Bissell three years later, the couple moved to Michigan and eventually settled in Grand Rapids, Michigan where they owned and operated a crockery shop.

While working in the shop, Anna grew tired of fighting the dirt, dust and bits of straw (used in packing crates) that could not be removed from the carpet easily. Moreover, the dust aggravated Melville's allergies. So, Melville designed and built a patented carpet sweeper in 1876. The device became an instant success and the couple sold several units through their shop.

Anna, Melville and Plato
"Necessity is the mother of invention." – Plato

Anna Bissell was a proactive, marketing-minded entrepreneur, so rather than waiting for customers to visit the shop, she loaded her buggy with carpet sweepers and began selling them door-to-door for $1.50 each. Her ability to demonstrate the sweepers on prospective buyers' floors proved to be a tremendous marketing advantage. She also demonstrated the sweepers at county fairs, and even the World's Fair. Further, she traveled to Philadelphia and convinced John Wanamaker (founder of one of the first U.S. department stores – Wanamaker's) to carry the sweepers in his store.

When her husband died of pneumonia in 1889, Anna Bissell took the reins of the Bissell Sweeper Company – becoming one of the first female CEOs in U.S. corporate history. Reflecting on the company's history, Jim Krzeminski, Bissell's current President (and former Executive Vice-President of Sales, Marketing and Product Development), attributes much of the company's success to the role Anna Bissell played as CEO. Because she was a female, Ms. Bissell was able to empathize with women and understand their perspective regarding household cleaning chores and sweeper requirements. Still today, as Krzeminski points out, "about 75-80 percent of all cleaning product and chemical purchases are either decided by the female head of the household or it's a shared decision."

December 3, 2017
Sunday

Objectives & reminders

____

____

____

Appointments

Early morning

8 a.m.

9 a.m.

10 a.m.

11 a.m.

Noon

1 p.m.

2 p.m.

3 p.m.

4 p.m.

5 p.m.

6 p.m.

Later evening

Congratulations: Morris Hite

Morris Hite, advertising pioneer and 32-year chairman of the Dallas-based ad agency Tracy-Locke (later known as DDB Needham) was inducted posthumously into the American Advertising Federation's Advertising Hall of Fame on December 3, 1996. Hite began his advertising career with Tracy-Locke in 1937 while still in his 20s. By 1950, he was named chairman of the agency and served in that capacity until the 1980s.

History of the metroplex
Morris Hite's advertising and communication campaigns were instrumental in winning passage of a $175 million bond issue to build DFW International Airport, which is now one of the busiest airports in the United States. To build a sense of community -- and thus community support -- throughout the north Texas area, which included the major cities of Dallas and Fort Worth as well as dozens of suburbs, Hite coined the term "metroplex" to describe the area.

What is advertising? "Advertising is salesmanship mass produced. No one would bother to use advertising if he could talk to all his prospects face-to-face. But he can't."

Is adverting moral?
"It is part and parcel of the American free enterprise system... I challenge anybody to show any economic system that has done as much for so many in so short a time."

What makes an ad campaign fail?
"If an ad campaign is built around a weak idea -- or as is so often the case, no idea at all -- I don't give a damn how good the execution is, it's going to fail."

December 4, 2017
Monday

Objectives & reminders

____

____

Appointments

Early morning

8 a.m.

9 a.m.

10 a.m.

11 a.m.

Noon

1 p.m.

2 p.m.

3 p.m.

4 p.m.

5 p.m.

6 p.m.

Later evening

Planning for the holiday season

Here come the shoppers!

Most surveyed consumers (57.2%) report that they begin their holiday shopping in November or during the first two weeks of December.

How prevalent is gift-giving?

83.6 percent of surveyed consumers intend to purchase gifts or cards during the holiday shopping season.

It's in the mail

Almost 70 percent of U.S. adults surveyed said they sent holiday cards. Of those, 40 percent reported sending fewer than 20 cards, while 38 percent claimed to have sent between 20 and 49. Another 18 percent reported sending 50-100 cards, while the remaining 5 percent claimed to have sent more than 100.

Christmas or Xmas?

Long before the political correctness police stirred debate by recommending "Happy Holidays" as a comprehensive and inclusive substitute for the more traditional "Merry Christmas," a debate was waged between the proponents and opponents of substituting "Xmas" for "Christmas." Some opponents find the use of "Xmas" to be offensive, pointing out that it is sacrilegious to take "Christ" out of Christmas. Proponents insist that the X in Xmas actually represents the cross and thus includes Christ symbolically. Today, the use of "Xmas" in marketing communications, greetings and other messages continues to be an issue for a significant number of consumers.

Career management insight

"In the best people I see a commitment to continual learning. I don't mean education, necessarily, in a formal way, but they are people who are constantly in search of new information and new ways they can integrate it into a framework that they carry around in their head." – Paul O'Neill, then chairman and CEO of Alcoa, Inc. (world's largest producer of aluminum), born in St. Louis, Missouri on December 4, 1935

December 5, 2017
Tuesday

Objectives & reminders

Appointments

Early morning

8 a.m.

9 a.m.

10 a.m.

11 a.m.

Noon

1 p.m.

2 p.m.

3 p.m.

4 p.m.

5 p.m.

6 p.m.

Later evening

Happy birthday: Walter Elias Disney

Born in Chicago on December 5, 1901, Walt Disney's career is an inspirational one. He lost one of his first jobs because he wasn't considered creative enough. Later, creativity or "Disney magic" became the cornerstone of his accomplishments. While still in his 20s, he gave life to one of the first animated cartoon characters, Mickey Mouse. Soon after that, he began to produce feature-length animated motion pictures, including *Snow White and the Seven Dwarfs* (1937). In his mid-fifties, Disney's creativity became three-dimensional when he opened his first amusement park, DisneyLand, in California.

Marketing opportunities
DisneyLand receives two million telephone calls each year. More callers ask to speak to Mickey Mouse than to anyone else.

Learning from Disney
Disney amusement parks are noted for their cleanliness. Over the years, the company has learned that the best way to keep the properties clean is to swoop in and pick up any bits of litter as soon as they hit the ground.

Apparently, when some "guests" see trash on the ground they somehow get the idea that it's okay for them to add to the debris. But when litter is not visible, park guests are more likely to toss trash in the trash cans located throughout the park. The same phenomenon seems to hold true for graffiti and other forms of vandalism.

The magnetic trash principle
Litter attracts more litter.
Graffiti attracts more graffiti.

Excellence & customer retention
"Do what you do so well that they will want to see it again and bring their friends."
– Walt Disney

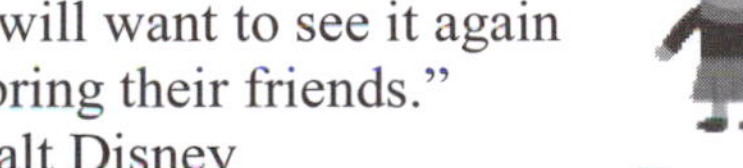

December 6, 2017
Wednesday

Objectives & reminders

____

____

Appointments

Early morning

8 a.m.

9 a.m.

10 a.m.

11 a.m.

Noon

1 p.m.

2 p.m.

3 p.m.

4 p.m.

5 p.m.

6 p.m.

Later evening

Too low, too high?

December 6, 1974, was not a day for stock traders to shout about. The Dow Jones Industrial Average (DJIA) – the major index of 30 large U.S. firms – reached its lowest point of the year and its lowest point since October 1962 -- closing at 578.

Twenty-two years later, on December 6, 1996, then chairman of the U.S. Federal Reserve Board, Alan Greenspan, coined a new phrase to express his concern that the stock market was too high. He suggested that the New York stock market was "irrationally exuberant." The phrase suggested that investors don't always behave in rational, objective ways. Rather, like all consumers, investors sometimes (often?) base their purchase decisions on emotional factors, which may be influenced by their own excitement or by the enthusiasm or behavior of others.

At the time of Greenspan's remark, the DJIA was hovering around 6,400, but subsequently climbed to 11,722 before losing exuberance and falling well below 11,000 again where it languished for several years. It wasn't until 2006 that the DJIA climbed above the 11,000 mark again.

Is it time to turn "up" the marketing dial?: Principle of perceived wealth
As the stock market climbs sharply, middle-income investors are more likely to feel affluent, or that they've received a financial windfall. Accordingly, they are more inclined to purchase big-ticket and luxury items during upswings in the market than during downturns. So, it is to consumer marketers' advantage to follow fluctuations in the stock market and be prepared to turn-up the marketing dial, so to speak, when consumers are in the mood to buy.

Creativity declines with age: Agree or disagree?

In a letter to Heinrich Zangger on December 6, 1917, physicist Albert Einstein wrote: "Truly novel ideas emerge only in one's youth. Later on one becomes more experienced, famous -- and foolish."

December 7, 2017 Thursday

Objectives & reminders

____

____

Appointments

Early morning

8 a.m.

9 a.m.

10 a.m.

11 a.m.

Noon

1 p.m.

2 p.m.

3 p.m.

4 p.m.

5 p.m.

6 p.m.

Later evening

Day of infamy

"December 7, 1941-- a date which will live on in infamy -- the United States of America was suddenly and deliberately attacked by naval and air forces of the Empire of Japan." -- U.S. President Franklin D. Roosevelt

Indeed, Sunday December 7, 1941, was a day of infamy that propelled the U.S. into World War II. On that day 2,403 Americans were killed and 1,178 wounded by the Japanese attack on the U.S. naval base in Pearl Harbor, Hawaii. Nineteen ships and 150 to 200 planes were destroyed.

Today, December 7 is set aside as Pearl Harbor Remembrance Day to commemorate the event and pay tribute to those who died and survived on that day in 1941.

More than history
"I relive Pearl Harbor every day of my life." -- Roland Nee, Pearl Harbor survivor from Rush Springs, Oklahoma, quoted in 2005

Holiday spending

As if consumer marketers did not already know that the holiday shopping season is critical to their success, findings of the National Retail Federation 2015 survey of U.S. holiday shoppers' spending provides plenty of evidence:

- Average spending per person: $806
- Average spending for family members' gifts: $463
- 46 percent of the typical shopper's browsing and buying activity was expected to be done online.

Why holiday shoppers choose a store

Consumer Reports found that 24 percent of surveyed consumers say that merchandise quality is the most important consideration prompting them to shop in particular stores during the holiday season. Pricing factors (i.e., sale events and discounted items) were reported as most important for 19 percent of those surveyed, closely following by merchandise selection (17%) and location convenience (17%). Whereas price tends to be relatively more important to female shoppers, merchandise selection is generally more important to male shoppers.

December 8, 2017
Friday

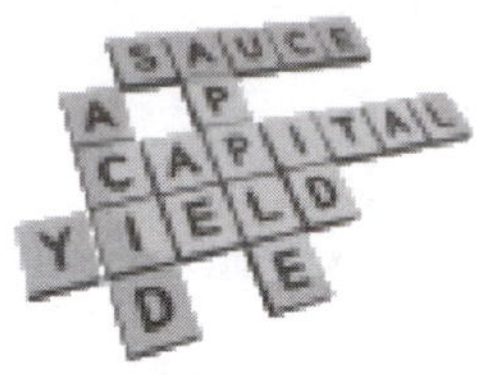

Objectives & reminders

___

___

___

Appointments

Early morning

8 a.m.

9 a.m.

10 a.m.

11 a.m.

Noon

1 p.m.

2 p.m.

3 p.m.

4 p.m.

5 p.m.

6 p.m.

Later evening

How many words is a picture worth?

The advertising trade journal, *Printers' Ink*, published a classic ad on page 96 in its December 8, 1921 issue. The ad, written by copywriter and publicist Frederick R. Barnard, touted the benefits of using advertising pictures on street cars. Its headline asserted, "One Look is Worth A Thousand Words." In ads published in *Printers' Ink* later in the decade, Barnard revised the headline to, "One Picture Is Worth Ten Thousand Words." Over the years, the now familiar cliché evolved: "One picture is worth a thousand words."

Picture this

"'Buttersweet is Good to Eat' is a very short phrase but it will sell more goods if presented, with an appetizing picture of the product, to many people morning, noon and night, every day in the year than a thousand word advertisement placed before the same number of people only a limited number of times during the year." – Frederick R. Barnard, December 8, 1921

Today, marketers generally agree with the upshot of Barnard's assertion. Ads with relevant pictures tend to be more effective than ads without pictures. Food items posted on fast-food restaurants' menu boards with accompanying pictures of the items outsell pictureless menu items by up to 40 percent. And products offered on eBay with accompanying pictures tend to sell at premium prices relative to comparable products without pictures.

Despite the generally accepted wisdom of using pictures, it may be that not all marketing communications lend themselves to picture-perfect presentations. For example, a 2008 study by Veronica Wong and Stephanie Feiereisen at the Aston Business School in Birmingham, England, found that words sometimes are more effective than pictures in terms of educating buyers. According to Wong, "We found that the use of words in marketing communications for utilitarian products will have the most favorable impact on the learning outcome, whereas for products that are concerned with pleasure, pictures are better."

December 9, 2017
Saturday

Objectives & reminders

___

___

___

Appointments

Early morning

8 a.m.

9 a.m.

10 a.m.

11 a.m.

Noon

1 p.m.

2 p.m.

3 p.m.

4 p.m.

5 p.m.

6 p.m.

Later evening

Happy birthday: Esther Peterson

Born in Provo, Utah on December 9, 1906, Peterson went on to graduate from Brigham Young University (Bachelor's degree) in 1927 and then earned a Masters degree in 1930. She supported the consumerism movement in various capacities throughout her career -- first working for unions and then as president of the National Consumers League and as Special Assistant for Consumer Affairs in the Johnson and Carter administrations. She worked in corporate America too, as VP for Consumer Affairs at Giant Food. In 1981, she was awarded the Presidential Medal of Freedom.

Thank you Esther!
Here are a few examples of the many consumer causes Esther Peterson fought for during her distinguished career:

1. Unit pricing on grocery products.
2. Laundry-instruction labels on clothing.
3. Access to accurate consumer information for seniors.
4. Publication of lists of products banned in some countries, but still available in others.

Consumerism movement as the "shame of marketing": Agree or disagree?
Sometimes vilified as a consumer rights advocate and considered by some as an enemy of business, Ester Peterson was once described by the Advertising Federation of America as "the most dangerous thing since Ghengis Khan."

However, business guru Peter Drucker argues that businesspeople have only themselves to blame for the rise of the consumerism movement. In his book, *Management*, he dubs the consumer movement as the "shame of marketing" and asserts that it would not have emerged if firms were truly marketing oriented, i.e., "that business start out with the needs, the realities, the values of the customer [and]… define its goal as the satisfaction of customer needs [and]…base its reward on its contribution to the customer" (p. 64).

December 10, 2017
Sunday

Objectives & reminders

____

____

____

Appointments

Early morning

8 a.m.

9 a.m.

10 a.m.

11 a.m.

Noon

1 p.m.

2 p.m.

3 p.m.

4 p.m.

5 p.m.

6 p.m.

Later evening

Happy bicentennial: Mississippi

It was 200 years ago today -- December 10, 1817 -- when Mississippi traded-in its "territory" status to become the 20th U.S. state. Over the 142 years that followed, 30 more states joined the Union.

Statehood was celebrated in 1817 and is an opportunity today to commemorate the occasion and celebrate the state's achievements since then. Indeed, numerous 2017 events are planned throughout the state to celebrate "…a reflection on Mississippi's history and culture… honoring our people and places, music and food, achievements in agriculture, science, and industry, sports legends, literary and artistic genius, and more" (http://mstourism.com/mississippi-bicentennial/). Many of the events are "co-branded," i.e., they involve businesses with a local presence that celebrate the bicentennial while building awareness of their brands and demonstrating their firms' commitment to the state and its citizens.

By definition, anniversaries are recognized annually, but some command more attention than others. Thanks to the *principle of round numbers*, anniversaries ending in zeros (e.g., 10th, 20th, 30th, etc.) are more likely to be accompanied by bigger celebrations than those that immediately precede or follow, and anniversaries ending in two zeros (e.g., 100th or 200th) are even bigger occasions. So, expect more grandiose parties for Mississippi's 200th birthday this year than for its 199th birthday last year or its 201st anniversary next year. It follows that marketers at work in Illinois, Alabama, Maine and Missouri should anticipate something special and plan accordingly for upcoming bicentennial celebrations in those states in 2018, 2019, 2020 and 2021, respectively.

Further, the principle of round numbers prompts calendar-led marketers to identify other round anniversaries on the planning horizon that could serve as bases for brand-building promotions or other celebrations. Examples: When was the company founded, or local branch, store or plant first opened? When were key patents granted? What is the birth date of the firm's founder, oldest employee or oldest customer? What's the birth date of the town where the firm is located or for the person for whom the town is named? And so on. There's always a reason to celebrate and there's always a "round" anniversary date coming soon.

December 11, 2017
Monday

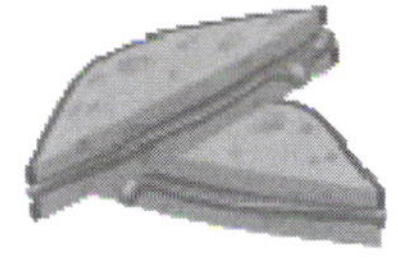

Objectives & reminders

___

___

___

Appointments

Early morning

8 a.m.

9 a.m.

10 a.m.

11 a.m.

Noon

1 p.m.

2 p.m.

3 p.m.

4 p.m.

5 p.m.

6 p.m.

Later evening

Happy birthday: James Lewis Kraft

Born near Stevensville, Ontario (Canada) on December 11, 1874, Kraft started his own business at the age of 28, the Kraft Company – a wholesale cheese business in Chicago. But soon Kraft was more than a middleman. His experiments converting milk solids into a low-cost, nutritious cheese product that would not spoil came to fruition in 1916 when he was granted a patent for a cheese pasteurization process. He called his innovation "American Cheese."

Despite the mass-market appeal of the name, the general public generally was not receptive to Kraft's American Cheese. Fortunately for Kraft, however, the U.S. Army did like the concept and bought six million pounds. During the Great Depression (1930s), an increasing number of consumers did acquire a taste for American Cheese as real cheese was both scarce and expensive.

Substitution opportunities
Although downturns in the economy generally are perceived negatively by businesses, they often present opportunities for companies whose products are positioned as "value" substitutes for more expensive alternatives. That is, when financially-strapped consumers re-evaluate their purchase priorities, they may choose to eat chicken and tuna instead of beef, or they may decide to shop at discount stores instead of department stores, dine at fast-foods instead of full-service restaurants, go to the theater on Saturday night instead of taking the family on a weekend skiing trip, and so on. As was the case with American Cheese, when the period of economic hardship ends, many consumers who made the switch to value substitutes may remain loyal.

Emotions intercept reason

"It is not because the truth is too difficult to see that we make mistakes... we make mistakes because the easiest and most comfortable course for us is to seek insight where it accords with our emotions – especially selfish ones." – Aleksandr Solzhenitsyn, Russian novelist and historian, born on December 11, 1918

December 12, 2017
Tuesday

Objectives & reminders

Appointments

Early morning

8 a.m.

9 a.m.

10 a.m.

11 a.m.

Noon

1 p.m.

2 p.m.

3 p.m.

4 p.m.

5 p.m.

6 p.m.

Later evening

Happy Hanukkah

Hanukkah begins at sundown today. It is an eight-day Jewish festival that begins on the 25th day of Kislev, the ninth month on the Jewish calendar. The specific dates vary from year to year on the Gregorian calendar, but Hanukkah typically occurs near the time of the Northern Hemisphere's winter solstice.

The Festival of Hanukkah (or the Feast of Dedication) is observed in memory of the purification and rededication of the Temple of Jerusalem in the year 164 B.C. after the Temple had been desecrated by the Syrians and used for "heathen ceremonies."

Hanukkah is also known as the Feast of Lights to signify the relighting of the perpetual lamp in the Temple. Accordingly, the lighting of the eight-branched candlestick -- the Hanukkah Menorah -- remains a custom in synagogues and Jewish homes.

Hanukkah is one of the most joyous periods on the Jewish calendar -- celebrated by exchanging gifts or donating gifts to charity.

The Jewish calendar
The 12 months in the Jewish calendar are based largely on *lunar* months, consisting of 29 or 30 days each. Most years include 353-355 days, but several include an extra 30-day month called "First Adar" (analogous to the leap year concept on the Gregorian calendar). Consequently, the lengths of Jewish years vary considerably – ranging from 353 to 385 days – which is why the dates of Jewish holidays can vary greatly from year to year when recorded on the Gregorian calendar.

Jewish markets
Estimates vary, but worldwide there are about 15 million Jews (i.e., adherents of Judaism). An estimated 6.3 million live in North America, 5.6 million in Israel, and 2.5 million in Europe.

December 13, 2017
Wednesday

Objectives & reminders

____

____

____

Appointments

Early morning

8 a.m.

9 a.m.

10 a.m.

11 a.m.

Noon

1 p.m.

2 p.m.

3 p.m.

4 p.m.

5 p.m.

6 p.m.

Later evening

St. Lucia Day

Legend has it that St. Lucia brought food, drink and encouragement to persecuted Christians hiding in caves in Sicily, Italy during the third century. Later, the Swedish adopted the story of St. Lucia and believe St. Lucia visited their country in the 13th century to aid the poor during a famine. According to the Swedish version of the story, St. Lucia appeared one night -- dressed in white, wearing a crown of candles, and accompanying a ship loaded with food.

Today, households in Sweden, Denmark and Finland honor St. Lucia and celebrate the season by waking family, friends or neighbors with trays of rolls and Swedish coffee while wearing crowns of candles. Several Swedish hotels hire their own Lucias on December 13; the young women dress in long, flowing white gowns and serve guests coffee and saffron buns ("lussekatter") in the morning.

Recipe for marketing success

Eighty-eight year old veteran of St. Lucia Day, Emma Sundberg offers her recipe for Swedish coffee: "You put a raw egg in with the grounds and let the water come to boil and let it simmer for four or five minutes. The egg clears the coffee and it will keep for more than a day... It's a joyful time."

Advertising career launch: Birth of the Pepsi generation

On December 13, 1950, a little known teen actor by the name of James Dean danced around a jukebox with a group of other teens in a television commercial for Pepsi Cola. Within the next five years Dean would come to symbolize the restless and rebellious youth culture in movies such as *Rebel Without a Cause* (1955) and *East of Eden* (1955). Pepsi Cola had begun targeting younger consumers and positioning itself accordingly.

Corny holiday riddle ☺

Q: If Jack Frost was a retail clerk, what would he say to customers?

A: Have an ice day!

December 14, 2017
Thursday

Objectives & reminders

____

____

____

Appointments

Early morning

8 a.m.

9 a.m.

10 a.m.

11 a.m.

Noon

1 p.m.

2 p.m.

3 p.m.

4 p.m.

5 p.m.

6 p.m.

Later evening

Happy birthday: Joel Dean

Born in Midland, Ohio on December 14, 1930, Joel Dean pursued a career as a business manager for Simon & Schuster (publishing firm) before teaming with New York cheese shop owner Giorgio DeLuca to form a unique gourmet and specialty food store in 1977 – Dean & DeLuca. By the time of Dean's death in 2004, the food shop had grown into a chain of 19 stores in the U.S. and Japan.

At least two sets of elements have meaningfully differentiated Dean & DeLuca from would-be competitors. First, atmospherics. The stores' customer experience officers accentuate the shopping experience in several ways – by broadcasting Bach and Mozart arrangements throughout the stores, by placing interesting decor throughout the "food museums," by displaying food products in novel arrangements, and by attending to the details of colors and textures throughout the store environments. Much of the atmospheric emphasis may be traced to Dean himself; as one employee noted, Dean had "such an eye for marble, wood, textures, details. For Joel, form always won over function."

Just say "no"
"[We reject] the sterile, pre-wrapped environment that has characterized the sale of food in America."
– Joel Dean and Giorgio DeLuca

Second, Dean & DeLuca strives to maintain a unique product mix, featuring merchandise typically not available at traditional mass-market grocery outlets. Leah Rosenthal, corporate buyer for the chain, summarizes what she looks for when evaluating prospective items to carry in the stores: "The first and foremost thing... is quality and taste. Really clean ingredients and an outstanding product. We generally look at smaller production companies, more or less artisan-produced. Behind that we look at how a product is presented and packaged, but we're not a gift store. The product should speak for itself."

December 15, 2017
Friday

Objectives & reminders

____

____

____

Appointments

Early morning

8 a.m.

9 a.m.

10 a.m.

11 a.m.

Noon

1 p.m.

2 p.m.

3 p.m.

4 p.m.

5 p.m.

6 p.m.

Later evening

In celebration of the 150th anniversary, don't place this ad again

Eight years after the 1867 invention of the typewriter, the demand for typists emerged. The New York newspaper, *The Nation*, ran the following ad for Remington (typewriter) agents on December 15, 1875. It is the earliest known ad to recruit female office workers:

> "Mere girls are now earning from $10 to $20 a week with the 'Type-Writer' and we can secure good situations for one hundred expert writers on it in counting-rooms in this City."

Five years later (1880), an estimated 60,000 "mere girls" were hammering away on typewriters throughout the United States. Their average age was 22. Some female typists earned as little as 50 cents per day.

Happy birthday: John Paul Getty

Born in Minneapolis, Minnesota on December 15, 1892, Getty entered the oil business in Tulsa, Oklahoma shortly after earning a degree from Oxford University (England) in 1913. For several decades, Getty acquired a number of independent oil companies and built an empire of almost 200 affiliated and subsidiary firms. In 1957, Getty was thought to be the wealthiest person in the United States. By the time of his death in 1976, Getty Oil Company was worth an estimated $1 billion.

Penny-pincher?
Despite Getty's wealth, many people believed he was far from generous with his money. Critics point out that Getty once had a *pay* telephone installed on his estate near London. Getty probably helped perpetuate his miserly reputation when he observed, "The man who tips a shilling every time he stops for petrol is giving away annually the cost of lubricating his car."

What astute marketers already know

"The universe is made of stories, not atoms."
-- Muriel Rukeyser, American writer, born on December 15, 1913

December 16, 2017
Saturday

Objectives & reminders

____

____

____

Appointments

Early morning

8 a.m.

9 a.m.

10 a.m.

11 a.m.

Noon

1 p.m.

2 p.m.

3 p.m.

4 p.m.

5 p.m.

6 p.m.

Later evening

Boston Tea Party: Early sentiments regarding consumer sovereignty

On December 16, 1773, in protest over the British Tea Act of 1773 that restricted free trade of tea, 60 colonists dressed as Mohawk Indians boarded three British cargo ships in Boston Harbor and dumped 90,000 pounds of tea (worth about £18,000) into the sea. The incident, and the British retaliation that followed, were pivotal in the Colonies' movement toward independence.

Tea parties not restricted to Boston
The "Boston Tea Party" has been studied by generations of American school children so the event is well recognized. Businesses may capitalize on this awareness level with promotions featuring tea party celebrations of their own.

There's always a reason to celebrate!

Packaging's multiple roles

Most product packages serve more than one purpose. For starters, they protect the contents, facilitate distribution, and provide useful and persuasive information for buyers. Some packages also provide buyers with additional value after the contents have been consumed, such as reusable containers used to package food items. One of the first packages reusable as something other than a container or dispenser was introduced by the National Biscuit Company on December 16, 1902, when the company began selling Barnum's Animal Crackers. The small, colorful boxes of cookies included string straps so that children could hang them on Christmas trees as ornaments.

Seasonal lessons from three teachers

"I will honour Christmas in my heart, and try to keep it all the year. I will live in the Past, the Present, and the Future. The Spirits of all Three shall strive within me. I will not shut out the lessons that they teach." -- Charles Dickens, *A Christmas Carol*

December 17, 2017
Sunday

Objectives & reminders

____

____

Appointments

Early morning

8 a.m.

9 a.m.

10 a.m.

11 a.m.

Noon

1 p.m.

2 p.m.

3 p.m.

4 p.m.

5 p.m.

6 p.m.

Later evening

Happy birthday: Aviation

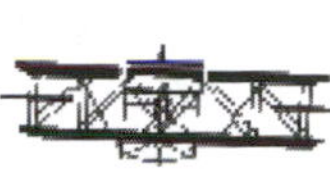

Brothers Orville and Wilbur Wright made their first sustained manned flight at Kitty Hawk, North Carolina at 10:35 a.m. on December 17, 1903 -- thus giving birth to the aviation industry. Today, the wingspan of some aircraft is longer than the entire distance of the Wright brothers' first flight.

Happy birthday: Francis Wolle

Born in Jacobsburg, Pennsylvania on December 17, 1817, Wolle began his career as a clerk in the store his father owned. It was that experience which led him to make a significant marketing contribution in 1852 when he invented and patented a unique machine to manufacture paper bags. Seventeen years later Wolle teamed with his brother and other bag makers to form the Union Paper Bag Machine Company.

The introduction of paper bags was marketing-relevant because retailers soon learned that customers would buy more goods and in larger quantities if they had a convenient means to carry their purchases -- like paper bags. Also note that several decades later retailers learned that shoppers would buy even more if the weight of the purchases could be made less burdensome; hence the shopping cart was introduced.

Bag these facts

1. Today, Americans consume 40 billion paper bags annually -- an average of more than 130 bags for every man, woman and child.
2. The largest paper bag plant in the U.S. is located near Savannah, Georgia. It produces 35 million bags per day.
3. "Paper or plastic?" The plastic grocery bag was introduced in 1977 as an alternative to paper. However, many consumers still prefer paper.
4. The challenge regarding "punching your way out of a wet paper bag" is not recommended. ☺

December 18, 2017
Monday

Objectives & reminders

____

____

____

Appointments

Early morning

8 a.m.

9 a.m.

10 a.m.

11 a.m.

Noon

1 p.m.

2 p.m.

3 p.m.

4 p.m.

5 p.m.

6 p.m.

Later evening

Chocolate word-of-mouth tactic

On December 18, 2007, AT&T offered $25 gift cards to customers who referred friends and family members to AT&T. To sweeten the offer, AT&T gave customers four recipe cards for "Heavenly Hot Chocolate." Below the recipe was an invitation to call AT&T's toll-free telephone number "for another sweet deal." Because all four recipe cards were the same, presumably the recipients would keep one for their own recipe file and share the others.

Anatomy of successful word-of-mouth promotions

1. Referrals from friends, family members and other consumers are generally perceived more positively than recommendations from salespeople or advertisements.
2. Consumers are more likely to spread positive word-of-mouth if they are rewarded for doing so (e.g., $25 gift cards).
3. Consumers are more likely to spread positive word-of-mouth if they are equipped with literature or sales devices that will help facilitate the information exchange (e.g., recipe cards with company phone number).
4. Recipients of promotion-related items are more likely to keep them, refer to them, and respond to them if they are perceived to be valuable (e.g., recipe cards may be perceived as being more valuable than ordinary sales brochures).

____

Breaking the glass ceiling

The December 18, 1950, issue of *Time* magazine reported the recent appointment of 52-year-old

Beatrice Rosenberg as R.H. Macy & Co.'s first female vice-president in the company's 92-year history. Rosenberg began working for the department store 32 years earlier. As Vice-President, 400 millinery and shoe salespeople would report to her. According to Rosenberg, "picking a woman for such a high position... [is] an inspiration to all the little girls who work here."

December 19, 2017
Tuesday

Objectives & reminders

____

____

____

Appointments

Early morning

8 a.m.

9 a.m.

10 a.m.

11 a.m.

Noon

1 p.m.

2 p.m.

3 p.m.

4 p.m.

5 p.m.

6 p.m.

Later evening

Shopping procrastination heating up

Although the holiday shopping season unofficially begins the day after Thanksgiving, many consumers -- especially males -- tend to postpone much of their gift shopping until Christmas draws nearer. One study conducted by BIGresearch, for example, found that typical consumers had completed only 82 percent of their holiday spending as of December 19. For a many shoppers, the percentage was much smaller.

When shoppers procrastinate, the time pressure to find gifts for everyone on the gift list is likely to push shoppers toward time-efficient rules-of-thumb for shopping. Here are seven examples:

First, stick with well-known name brands. Name brands suggest quality and imply good taste.

Second, avoid store-to-store price comparisons. There's no time for that.

> **Warning!**
> These are *not* shopping recommendations. Rather they are examples of self-imposed rules-of-thumb that shoppers may use when facing time constraints. Retailers who understand these shopping heuristics can be better positioned to serve procrastinating shoppers during the final shopping days before Christmas.

Third, consider the gift items placed on tables at the front of the store. In effect, let the store do the shopping.

Fourth, forget the budget. Buy appropriate gifts and sort out the finances later. Finding the right gifts is tough enough without having to find the right gifts at the right price points.

Fifth, shop at larger department stores or discount stores likely to have suitable gifts for the most people on the gift list. There's no time to bounce from one specialty boutique to another.

Sixth, buying one joint gift (e.g., for a married couple) may be faster than buying multiple individual gifts. Items for the home usually create this efficiency.

Finally, buy gift cards. They're easy to find, buy, budget, carry, and wrap.

December 20, 2017
Wednesday

Objectives & reminders

____

____

Appointments

Early morning

8 a.m.

9 a.m.

10 a.m.

11 a.m.

Noon

1 p.m.

2 p.m.

3 p.m.

4 p.m.

5 p.m.

6 p.m.

Later evening

Happy birthday: Joseph Marion Hagger

Born as Maroun Hajjar on December 20, 1892, in Jazzin, Lebanon, Hagger immigrated to the United States at the age of 16 without the benefit of any formal education. During his first few years in the U.S., Hagger worked in various jobs in Texas, Louisiana, and Missouri. He worked for the railroad for a short time, and for a cotton farmer. He also washed dishes for one hotel and washed windows for another, among several other jobs.

> **Losing a job isn't necessarily a bad thing**
> When one door closes, another one opens.

Perhaps the longest job tenure for Hagger was the period from 1921-1926 when he worked as a traveling salesman for the King Brand Overall Company. Fortunately, as it turned out, Hagger lost his job when the company dropped Hagger's territory. In response, Hagger went into business for himself. He formed the Dallas (Texas) Pant Manufacturing Company, which later evolved into the Hagger Company, then Hagger Apparel Company. Today, the company Mr. Hagger built is a multi-million dollar enterprise employing thousands of workers in Texas and elsewhere.

As noted in the accompanying boxes, Hagger's marketing practices positively influenced the success of the company.

> **Branding and positioning**: To position his apparel as casual and convenient, Hagger popularized the word "slacks" and coined the term "wash and wear."

> **Distribution**: Hagger maintained positive relations with suppliers, but insisted on high-quality materials.

> **Advertising**: Hagger recognized and seized the opportunity to advertise his brand nationally, beginning in the 1940s -- a first in the apparel industry.

> **Pricing**: Hagger introduced a "one price policy" to prevent haggling from cutting into profit margins.

> **Promotion**: Hagger enrolled the help of superstar athletes such as Mickey Mantle (baseball), Roger Staubach (football), and Arnold Palmer (golf) to serve as brand endorsers.

December 21, 2017 Thursday

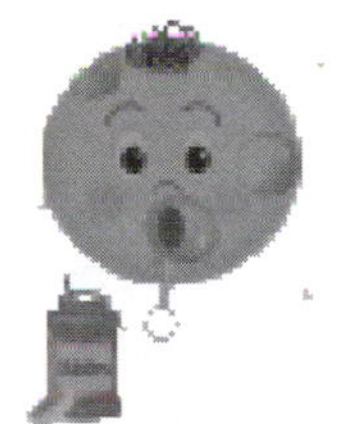

Objectives & reminders

Appointments

Early morning

8 a.m.

9 a.m.

10 a.m.

11 a.m.

11:28 a.m. EDT: Winter arrives in the Northern Hemisphere, while summer begins in the Southern Hemisphere.

Noon

1 p.m.

2 p.m.

3 p.m.

4 p.m.

5 p.m.

6 p.m.

Later evening

A Winter Walk

"Now commences the long winter evening around the farmer's hearth, when the thoughts of the indwellers travel far abroad, and men are by nature and necessity charitable and liberal to all creatures. Now is the happy resistance to cold, when the farmer reaps his reward, and thinks of his preparedness for winter..." -- Henry David Thoreau

Happy birthday: Paul Winchell

Born in New York City as Pinkus Wilchinski on December 21, 1922, Winchell was an American ventriloquist and actor who is most remembered for lending his voice to a number of animated characters for Disney, Hanna-Barbera, and other film-makers – characters such as Tigger (in several *Winnie the Pooh* films), Boomer (*The Fox and the Hound*), a Siamese cat (*Aristocats*), and Sam-I-Am (*Dr. Seuss on the Loose*), among others.

Winchell also lent his voice to the world of advertising to pitch fast-food, candy and other consumer products. In perhaps his most effective advertising role, Winchell gave voice to the chief bubble of Dow Bathroom Cleaner's mascots – the Scrubbing Bubbles. When the brand was sold to S.C. Johnson in 1997, its name was changed to Scrubbing Bubbles to reflect the brand's strong association with the animated brushy-looking characters known for effortlessly whisking around bathroom surfaces as their bristly undersides generated thousands of grime-fighting bubbles.

In analyzing the marketing effectiveness of the Scrubbing Bubbles, at least two points regarding the brand's mascots are noteworthy. First, their animated nature and perky personalities pleasantly portray an otherwise filthy and disgusting phenomenon – cleaning the bathroom. If, instead, the reality of bathroom cleaning chores was depicted, consumers might turn away from the message rather than being attracted to it.

Second, the animation visually brings to life and magnifies the cleaning power of the brand, thereby making it more tangible. The more tangible a brand's qualities, the easier it is for buyers to identify, understand and remember reasons to purchase the brand.

December 22, 2017
Friday

First *full* day of winter in the Northern Hemisphere

Objectives & reminders

____

____

Appointments

Early morning

8 a.m.

9 a.m.

10 a.m.

11 a.m.

Noon

1 p.m.

2 p.m.

3 p.m.

4 p.m.

5 p.m.

6 p.m.

Later evening

Snow in South America?

When asked to select the month during which it is most likely to snow in South America, almost three of every eight respondents participating in the Calendar Literacy Survey answered incorrectly, saying "December" or "January," rather than "July." A debriefing session indicated that those who answered the question incorrectly simply did not know that the seasons are reversed in the Southern Hemisphere.

So, while today is the first full day of winter in the Northern Hemisphere, it's the beginning of summer in the Southern Hemisphere. It follows that in another six months, summer will begin in the northern half of the world and winter in the southern half. Therefore, while many U.S. consumers may experience snow during the next few months, the snows are not likely to arrive in South America for several more months. And, of course, in some parts of South America, it doesn't snow at all.

Much more than a trivia question: Invitation to discuss
Understanding that seasons are reversed in the Northern and Southern Hemispheres has important marketing implications for many industries and product categories. For example, consider the implications for agriculture, transportation, and tourism.

Christmas gift facts

In 1913, the most popular Christmas gifts for children were Erector sets. A few generations later, in 1981, the Rubik's Cube was the "must have" Christmas toy, followed by Teenage Mutant Ninja Turtle action figures in 1988.

For Christmas 2015, *Stars Wars* action figures and memorabilia topped the list, making it the first movie to generate more revenues from merchandise sales than from box office receipts.

December 23, 2017
Saturday

Objectives & reminders

Appointments

Early morning

8 a.m.

9 a.m.

10 a.m.

11 a.m.

Noon

1 p.m.

2 p.m.

3 p.m.

4 p.m.

5 p.m.

6 p.m.

Later evening

The big day!

Traditionally the Friday after Thanksgiving has been the biggest sales day of the year for American retailers, but the tradition has not been consistently upheld since the year 2000. Now the Saturday before Christmas is frequently the biggest day. Demographically, males are more likely than females to postpone Christmas shopping.

A Visit From St. Dad

Twas the Saturday before Christmas
and all through the store

Late-shopping fathers were traversing
the floor.

The gifts in the cart were for Brandon,
Julie and Honey.

"There goes the budget, I've spent *all*
of the money."

Happy birthday: Sarah Breedlove McWilliams Walker

Born as Sarah Breedlove in Delta, Louisiana on December 23, 1867, she later became known as Madam C.J. Walker -- one of the first successful female African-American entrepreneurs in the United States. Between 1900 and 1905 she began selling hair care products door-to-door. Over the years her product line expanded greatly, as did her sales force and the mail order segment of her business. In 1908, Walker founded Lelia College in Pittsburgh, which offered a correspondence course for "hair culturists." By 1917, her business was the largest black-owned firm in the country.

Self-promotion

"I am a woman who came from the cotton fields of the South. I was promoted from there to the washtub. Then I was promoted to the cook kitchen, and from there I PROMOTED MYSELF into the business of manufacturing hair goods and preparations... I have built my own factory on my own ground."
-- Madam C.J. Walker, 1912

December 24, 2017
Sunday
Christmas Eve

Objectives & reminders

____

____

Appointments

Early morning

8 a.m.

9 a.m.

10 a.m.

11 a.m.

Noon

1 p.m.

2 p.m.

3 p.m.

4 p.m.

5 p.m.

6 p.m.

Later evening

Gift cards: Last-minute opportunities to market to last-minute shoppers

Gift cards may be the most popular category of last-purchased Christmas gifts. On December 24, 2014, Starbucks alone sold 2.5 million gift cards across the United States and Canada.

Further, gift cards tend to be welcomed gifts. According to a 2015 study by the National Retail Federation, 59 percent of surveyed consumers said that they would appreciate receiving one.

Entertainment as a Christmas gift?

On December 24, 1906, Canadian-born inventor Reginald Audrey Fessenden first entertained radio listeners when he played a violin during an initial broadcast from the radio station at Brant Rock, Massachusetts. Later in the broadcast he sang, recited some Bible verses and played a gramophone record.

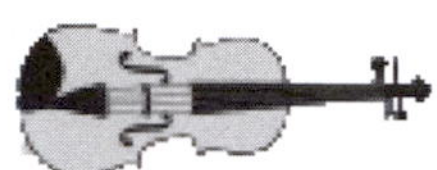

Exactly 20 years later -- on December 24, 1926 -- the Wheaties Quartet further explored radio's entertainment potential while also starting an advertising trend that continues today. That is, they became the first to *sing* an advertisement on radio: "Have you t-r-i-e-d Wheaties?"

Today, advertising jingles are commonplace in a world filled with advertisers vying for audiences' attention. The entertainment value of incorporating music into advertising helps advertisers "break through the clutter," so to speak. As an added bonus, advertising jingles also help to stimulate word-of-mouth which further spreads the advertised message.

Be cautious with this Christmas tradition

Think twice before using candles for Christmas decorations, because more candle-caused house fires occur on Christmas Day than on any other day of the year. Christmas Eve and New Year's Day tie for second place.

December 25, 2017
Monday
Christmas Day

Objectives & reminders

____

____

Appointments

Early morning

8 a.m.

9 a.m.

10 a.m.

11 a.m.

Noon

1 p.m.

2 p.m.

3 p.m.

4 p.m.

5 p.m.

6 p.m.

Later evening

Merry Christmas!

Today commemorates the birth of Christ, Jesus of Nazareth. As such, it is one of the most important and most widely observed Christian holidays. The origin of the holiday is uncertain, as is the exact date of Christ's birth, although Christians in Rome were celebrating the Feast of the Nativity on December 25 by the year 336 A.D. Elsewhere during that era, Christ's birthday was observed in January or May, and some combined Christ's birthday celebration with the Feast of Epiphany on January 6.

Happy holidays!
Despite the political correctness of the generic greeting "happy holidays," Christmas is the happy holiday most Americans have in mind. According to one survey, 96 percent of surveyed American registered voters say they celebrate Christmas, while five percent report celebrating Hanukkah and two percent celebrate Kwanzaa. The survey allowed multiple responses, indicating that a few respondents celebrate two or more of the holidays.

By the year 440 A.D., however, December 25 was chosen to commemorate Christ's birth. In addition to the Feast of the Nativity, other festivals and events also coincided with the winter solstice, so Christmas could be observed as both a religious and a secular holiday. Accordingly, a number of religious and nonreligious symbols and customs have blended together over the centuries to make Christmas what it is today -- a holiday that is observed in a variety of ways because it means different things to different people.

Christmas symbols and customs that could have religious or non-religious meanings, depending on the content and context

- gift-giving
- caroling
- stories
- tree ornaments
- cards
- candles
- lawn and house decorations

December 26, 2017
Tuesday

Objectives & reminders

____

____

____

Appointments

Early morning

8 a.m.

9 a.m.

10 a.m.

11 a.m.

Noon

1 p.m.

2 p.m.

3 p.m.

4 p.m.

5 p.m.

6 p.m.

Later evening

Kwanzaa begins

Held for the first time in Los Angeles on December 26, 1966, Kwanzaa was inspired by African harvest festivals. Today, the seven-day non-religious observance still begins on December 26 and celebrates the African-American family, culture and community.

Kwanzaa celebrations vary across families, but often include a feast, storytelling, poetry readings, songs and dances. During each of the seven nights of the celebration a candle is lit and a Kwanzaa principle is discussed. The principles -- Nguzo Saba -- represent central values in African cultures that build and reinforce a sense of community.

The seven principles of Kwanzaa, according to Maulana Karenga, Kwanzaa founder

Unity: "To strive for and maintain unity in the family, community, nation and race."

Self-Determination: "To define ourselves, name ourselves, create for ourselves and speak for ourselves."

Collective Work and Responsibility: "To build and maintain our community together and make our brothers' and sisters' problems our problems and to solve them together."

Cooperative Economics: "To build and maintain our own stores, shops and other businesses and to profit from them together."

Purpose: "To make our collective vocation the building and developing of our community in order to restore our people to their traditional greatness."

Creativity: "To do always as much as we can, in the way we can, in order to leave our community more beautiful and beneficial than we inherited it."

Faith: "To believe with all our heart in our people, our parents, our teachers, our leaders and the righteousness and victory of our struggle."

December 27, 2017 Wednesday

Objectives & reminders

____

____

____

Appointments

Early morning

8 a.m.

9 a.m.

10 a.m.

11 a.m.

Noon

1 p.m.

2 p.m.

3 p.m.

4 p.m.

5 p.m.

6 p.m.

Later evening

Post-Christmas "season" underway

Now that Santa has returned to the North Pole, the post-Christmas season is underway. Consumers are busy returning or exchanging gifts, redeeming their gift cards, snatching reduced-price Christmas merchandise, and buying complementary products that Santa forgot (e.g., helmets for new bicycles, batteries for everything). According to some estimates, the week after Christmas accounts for 10-15 percent of holiday retail sales. So, while this may be the ideal time for Santa and his elves to take a break, it is not time for retailers to do so.

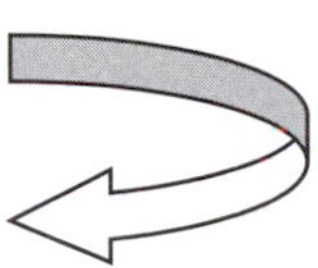

Reverse distribution

Consumer products normally flow "downstream" through the channel, e.g., from manufacturers to wholesalers or distributors, to retailers and then to household consumers. But when products don't quite fit what consumers want, the distribution process may be reversed and goods begin an "upstream" journey. Unfortunately, upstream or reverse distribution is much less efficient -- typically costing about *nine* times as much, per item, as downstream distribution.

Gift-recipients are likely to return gifts to the stores where the merchandise was purchased and the days immediately following Christmas represent the peak period for returns. About 20 percent of all Christmas gifts are returned after Christmas.

Not surprisingly, many retailers have taken steps to curb the post-Christmas returns phenomena. Some limit gift returns to a short period of time, e.g., 30 days or less. Others exchange non-defective merchandise only for other merchandise, i.e., no cash refunds. Some require receipts to prove the gifts were purchased in that store, while others charge a "restocking" fee.

> **Did you know?**
> "Return fraud" costs U.S. retailers an estimated $16 billion annually.

Advances in technology allow stores to track the purchase and return behavior of individuals to limit the number of returns made by "serial returners." Also, many retailers now aggressively promote the sale of gift cards, in part because they know the return phenomenon is less problematic because gift card recipients select their own merchandise.

December 28, 2017
Thursday

Objectives & reminders

____

____

Appointments

Early morning

8 a.m.

9 a.m.

10 a.m.

11 a.m.

Noon

1 p.m.

2 p.m.

3 p.m.

4 p.m.

5 p.m.

6 p.m.

Later evening

National Chocolate Day

Although every day is chocolate day to devoted chocolate-lovers, December 28 has been set aside to recognize the important role that chocolate plays in consumers' lifestyles. Marketers in general, and event planners in particular, should know that virtually any event can be celebrated with chocolate.

For American consumers, chocolate is a clear favorite flavor for desserts and sweet snacks. In one recent survey sponsored by the Chocolate Manufacturers Association, 52 percent of the respondents voted for chocolate as their favorite flavor -- far ahead of vanilla, strawberry and other berry flavors that tied for second place, each tallying only 12 percent of the first-place votes. Cherry followed with only 3 percent. Although both men and women tended to express a preference for chocolate, the preference tends to be stronger among women (57%) than males (46%). The survey also found that milk chocolate tends to be preferred over dark chocolate.

Box of factual chocolate treats

- The first chocolate candy in the world was made in 1828 by Dutch candy-maker Conrad J. Van Houten.
- Seven billion pounds of candy (including chocolate) are made annually in the U.S.
- Americans each eat an average of more than 20 pounds of candy annually.
- Tootsie Rolls were invented in 1896 by Leo Hirshfield. He named the candy after his five-year-old daughter, nicknamed Tootsie.

Breeding rabbits

Children's author Beatrix Potter is known for her *Tales of Peter Rabbit* and other animal stories. On December 28, 1903, she extended her rabbitly growing interests by applying for a patent on a Peter Rabbit doll she had developed. Since then, many other writers' book characters have become dolls or action figures. Sorry, the Miss Ng Marbles doll isn't available... yet.

December 29, 2017
Friday

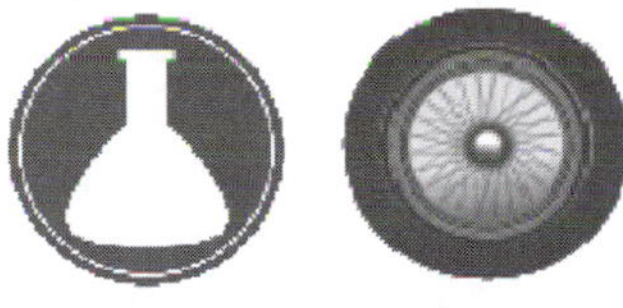

Objectives & reminders

____

____

Appointments: bounce through the day!

Early morning

8 a.m.

9 a.m.

10 a.m.

11 a.m.

Noon

1 p.m.

2 p.m.

3 p.m.

4 p.m.

5 p.m.

6 p.m.

Later evening

Happy birthday: Bouncing rubber baby boys?

Scottish chemist Charles Macintosh was born on December 29, 1766. In 1823, his work in the textile industry led him to invent rubberized waterproof clothing, including raincoats.

On Macintosh's 34th birthday, Charles Goodyear, for whom the Goodyear Tire & Rubber Co. was named, was born on December 29, 1800, in New Haven, Connecticut. By mixing sulphur with rubber and then cooking it, Goodyear was able to vulcanize rubber -- a process that he patented in 1844. Vulcanization enabled rubber to maintain its properties in cold and heat without cracking or melting, thus making it much more practical for commercial purposes.

As Macintosh celebrated his 47th birthday, future competitor Alexander Parkes was born (December 29, 1813). Parkes was a British chemist who patented an alternative process for coating fabrics with rubber to waterproof them. He then developed the process of eletroplating and produced the first plastic known as "Parkesine."

Small rubber businesses bounce back

Bad news for some businesses is often good news for others, or "when one door is slammed shut, others open for those willing to jiggle a few door knobs." Apparently that was the case in late December 1941 when it was announced that new tires would be rationed in the U.S. (rubber was needed to support the war effort). While rationing was interpreted negatively by tire makers, the nation's 4,500 small businesses that retread used tires experienced a sharp bounce in demand. On December 29, 1941, one retreader in Cleveland, Ohio, exclaimed: "The rush is on. It's like the Klondike [gold rush]. No use answering my phone. I can't handle the business."

Was rubber the secret ingredient?
An ad in *The Arkansas Gazette* (Little Rock), December 29, 1894: "**Thin, Pale Cheeks**. Those who use Paine's Celery Compound soon grow plump with solid flesh, and have a clear, rosy complexion. It is the best strength-giver we know of. Bradfield & Dowdy. Bond's Pharmacy Co., John B. Bond, Jr."

December 30, 2017
Saturday

Objectives & reminders

____

____

Appointments

Early morning

8 a.m.

9 a.m.

10 a.m.

11 a.m.

Noon

1 p.m.

2 p.m.

3 p.m.

4 p.m.

5 p.m.

6 p.m.

Later evening

Happy birthday: Eldrick "Tiger" Woods

Born in Cypress, California on December 30, 1975, Woods is one of the greatest golfers of all time. He has won more PGA Tour tournaments than any other active professional.

Not surprisingly, Woods has been one of the most sought after athletes for endorsements. He has or has had agreements with several firms, including American Express, Accenture, General Motors (Buick), General Mills, and Nike. Before Woods' $100-million five-year contract with Nike, the sporting goods company wasn't particularly known for its association with golf.

To Tiger or not to Tiger?

"People... acquire products and services because they associate them with qualities they find attractive and they wish they had... If your brand doesn't already conjure up the images and associations you want consumers to get when they think it, you'll need to *borrow* those qualities from someone or something that already has them. Otherwise, consumers will never make the connections you want them to and they'll keep looking until they find someone who'll do it for them." – Sergio Zyman, former marketing director for The Coca-Cola Company, in *The End of Advertising As We Know It* (2002, pp. 101-102)

Ponderable points to putt around

Beyond his golfing skills, what traits make Woods a (un)desirable product spokesperson?

What characteristics of products and target markets are best suited for association with Tiger Woods? In other words, is Tiger Woods likely to be more effective endorsing some types of products than others, and if so, why?

How much is an athlete's endorsement worth? How is this amount determined?

December 31, 2017
Sunday
New Year's Eve

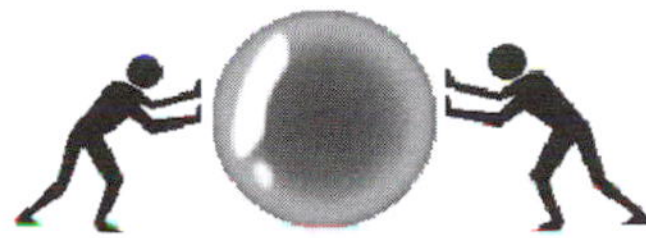

Objectives & reminders

Don't drink and drive, and don't get drunk with anyone who can fire you. "Incidents" from company parties on New Year's Eve are remembered *throughout* the New Year.

Appointments

Early morning

8 a.m.

9 a.m.

10 a.m.

11 a.m.

Noon

1 p.m.

2 p.m.

3 p.m.

4 p.m.

5 p.m.

6 p.m.

Later evening

Year-end *sales* push

Sales reps whose compensation is tied to their performance for the calendar year often find themselves scrambling to close year-end sales. As such, they may be willing to negotiate a lower price or make other concessions for buyers willing to commit to purchase before the year expires. So, buyers who are aware of this year-end phenomenon may pressure salespeople to make year-end concessions.

To keep the sales force from being beaten up near the end of the year, sales managers could consider moving the boundaries of the performance evaluation period. For example, rather than using the 12-month calendar year, why not use the period from December 1 through November 30 instead?

Year-end *buying* push

On the flip side of the salesperson-buyer dyad is the year-end phenomenon that some organizational buyers face. That is, any budgeted money that's not spent during the year may be "swept" from the account and reallocated elsewhere in the company. So, to keep from losing this money (and possibly having the following year's budget cut as well), buyers are sometimes eager to spend their remaining budget as the end of the year approaches. Understanding this phenomenon, salespeople are quite happy to help buyers find year-end ways to spend the leftover money.

B2B sales tip
Find out when buyers' fiscal years end (it may not be December 31) and whether their unspent budgets carry forward to next year.

Party tonight?

Whereas Christmas celebrations often center around religious observances and spending time with family, New Year's Eve celebrations are more often celebrated with spouses or "significant others." Unfortunately or not, alcohol tends to play a role in New Year's Eve celebrations, as do fireworks and music.

Did you know?
About 75 percent of the world's population celebrates New Year's Eve and/or New Year's Day.

Index

Numbers after each entry refer to the corresponding month and day of month on which information about the entry may be found. Examples: 1-23 refers to January 23, while 10-6 refers to October 6.

Speaking of birthdays… 

If you're interested in learning someone's birthday, hand them a copy of *Marketing FAME*. If they're like most people, one of the first two pages they will turn to will be their birthday. What are the marketing implications of this phenomenon?

E

H

Be marbleous in your career, but knuckledown.

Marbleous farewells

Thanks for a great read. Remember *all* of us throughout your career.
As we say in marketing, buy now.
Have a great marketing career. You can do it!
I'll look for you next year.
Even for me

For me

And for me too
Especially for me

For all of us!

XXX-rated? That's not so marbleous.
Wanna get together again for the 2018 edition?

I'm so sad to leave 2017. Please don't shred us.

Who dared to write *Marketing FAME*?

Mini-biography of Charles L. Martin

Dr. Martin spent his youth in the northern suburbs of Atlanta, Georgia where he developed a love of tenpin bowling and began his business career in the bowling business before venturing to college as a collegiate bowler at Vincennes University (community college in Vincennes, Indiana) and then to West Texas State University (now West Texas A&M, Canyon) where he earned a BBA in Marketing (1981) and an MBA (1982). He went on to earn a Ph.D. in Marketing at Texas A&M University (College Station).

In 1985, Dr. Martin joined the faculty at Wichita State University (WSU) in south central Kansas where he's taught a variety of both undergraduate and graduate courses. Today, Dr. Martin is the Full Professor of Marketing in WSU's W. Frank Barton School of Business.

Dr. Martin also has served as the Marketing Editor of the world's leading trade and consumer publication for tenpin bowling, *Bowlers Journal International* (1990-2000), and as the Editor of an academic journal that focuses on the marketing-related challenges faced in the service sector, *The Journal of Services Marketing* (1990-2014). Also, as a consultant, he's worked with numerous organizations such as the National Bowling Council, Bowling Proprietors' Association of America, American Bowling Congress, and several bowling-related companies.

Outside of the U.S., Dr. Martin has gained valuable international experience as a visiting scholar and/or visiting editor at several universities throughout the world, including Comenius University (Bratislava, Slovakia), Sogang University (Seoul, Korea), University of Westminster (U.K.), University of Liverpool (U.K.), Manchester Business School (U.K.), Queensland University of Technology (Brisbane, Australia), and Bond and Griffith Universities (Gold Coast, Australia). Further, he has spoken as a keynote speaker at several international conferences in recent years, e.g., Lahore (Pakistan), Macau (China), Hong Kong (China), Kyrenia (Cyprus), Manchester (U.K.), and Calgary (Canada).

In addition to teaching, consulting, editing journals and visiting faraway lands, Dr. Martin is an active researcher and business writer as well. He's had more than 300 sole- or co-authored manuscripts published including dozens of professional journal articles and several books. His publications address a wide variety of topics pertaining to marketing management, services, consumer behavior, retailing and sports marketing, among others.

Most recently, Professor Martin has pioneered research in the role that calendars play in shaping marketing practices and influencing buyer behavior – what he has dubbed as "calendar-led marketing" and "calendar-led buyer behavior." This research has contributed greatly to the development of the *Marketing FAME* book series and to several published and forthcoming journal articles regarding the interplay of calendars, marketing, and buyer behavior. If you'd like to learn more about these topics – including opportunities for future research – see the discussion and the list of student-friendly articles on the sixth page of the "Welcome Readers!" section, near the beginning of *Marketing FAME*.

Dr. Martin expects to continue the *Marketing FAME* series with new editions published annually. Each year's content will differ greatly from that of the previous year, so you'll never be bored reading *Marketing FAME* from year to year. So, in the spirit of improving future editions, please relay your questions and comments to Professor Martin. For example, use the opportunity to vote for your most or least favorite stories or to suggest new stories for future editions. Dr. Martin may be reached through CIBER Publications' website, www.MarketingMarbles.com or directly at WSU, Charles.Martin@wichita.edu